CW01663511

GERRY ANDERSON
A LIFE IN PICTURES

Foreword by
JAMIE ANDERSON

Published by Anderson Entertainment Media Limited,
Hornbeam House, Bidwell Road, Rackheath, Norwich,
Norfolk, NR13 6PT

First published 2014

Copyright © Anderson Entertainment Media Ltd 2014

All rights reserved. No part of this book may be reproduced in any form by any means without permission in writing from the publisher, except by a reviewer, who may quote brief passages and reproduce a small number of images in a review.

Edited by Stephen La Rivière
Design by Justin T Lee
Foreword by Jamie Anderson

With thanks to The Gerry Anderson Estate, Chris Dale, James Fielding, Andrew T Smith, Ralph Titterton, Penny Hill, Peter Greenwood, Terry Adlam and Rodney Matthews.

Anderson Entertainment Media would like to thank all those who contributed photographs and gave permission to reproduce copyrighted material. While every effort has been made to trace and acknowledge all copyright holders, we would like to apologise should there be any omissions.

Printed by Lightning Source

ISBN 978-0-9928695-0-2

A CIP record for this title is available from the British Library.

A percentage of the profits from sales of this book will go to the Alzheimer's Society's Gerry Anderson Tribute Fund.

www.anderson-entertainment.co.uk
www.gerryanderson.co.uk

TABLE OF CONTENTS

FOREWORD

'The least nostalgic man you could ever meet.' That's how many people described my late father – Gerry Anderson. And for the most part I would have agreed with them.

Despite the huge success of his many productions, including *Fireball XL5*, *Thunderbirds* and *Space: 1999*, he kept almost nothing as a memento to remind him of a creatively prolific period that led to worldwide success. In fact, other than a Parker puppet that hung in my wardrobe (wrapped in a plastic bag) for a few years, growing up I could see very few signs of the fact that Dad was such a prolific creative.

He didn't talk about the previous decades of incredibly successful shows and films that he had produced. In his mind, once a project was completed, that was that. It was done. No point looking back – only in looking forward. This wasn't just the case for his work life, but his private life too. He tended not to keep photographs. He seemed to constantly live for tomorrow – for the future.

When he became ill and was diagnosed with Alzheimer's disease, beyond the shock and distress that came with that diagnosis, the time was tinged with a very particular sadness. Here was a man who was not only my father, but was one of the most successful British television producers of the 20th Century, and he was losing memories that would now never be shared with me – or any of his countless fans around the world.

Although Dad did open up to me in the last few months of his life, speaking (in some cases for the first time) about his thoughts and feelings towards his life and career, the memories slowly became muddier, corrupted and eventually inaccessible to him.

Dad died on 26th December 2012.

After a few days, I decided to start going through his possessions. It was a difficult time, but it felt like a very natural thing to do. As expected, there wasn't much to find: his copy of Winston Churchill's biography, some cufflinks, a few letters about more recent productions... Then suddenly, I made a discovery.

At the bottom of a small pine chest in the spare bedroom at the family home, I came across something I really didn't expect to find. Hundreds of photos. Photos from his childhood – of his parents and brother. Photos from the very early days of his career – well before A.P. Films, Century 21 and the glamour of *Thunderbirds*. In fact, as I looked into it, I found photographs, letters and newspaper cuttings that documented every decade of his life.

In some cases the photographs fitted perfectly with stories Dad had already told me, while others gave me brand new insights into the life and career of the man I called Dad. For me, the photographs provide a unique look back upon an incredible 83 years, and it feels only right that we should now share them, supplemented by carefully chosen pictures from other collections, with those that loved, and were fascinated by, the man and his work.

Jamie Anderson
March 2014

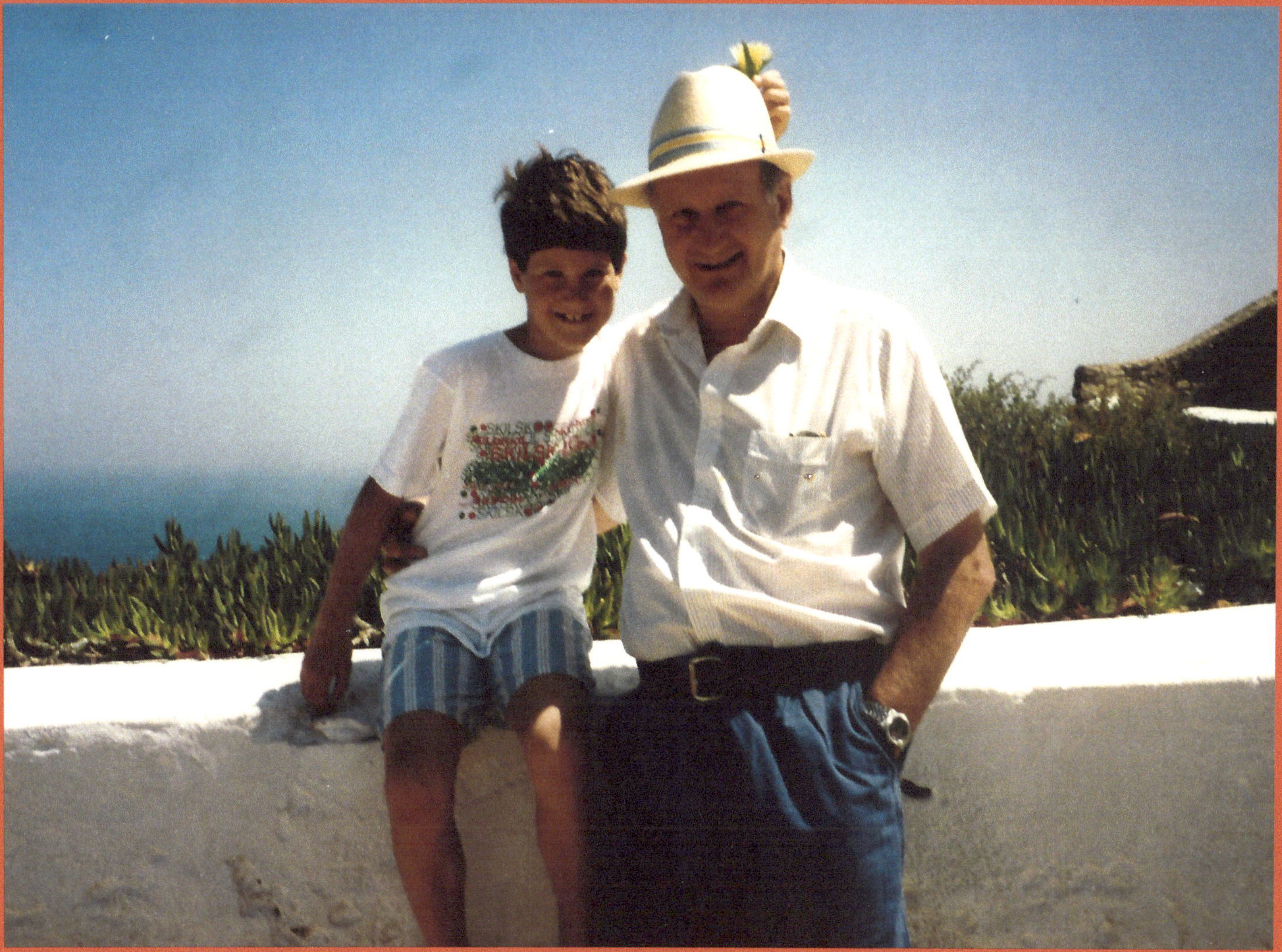

Jamie on holiday in Portugal, one of his father's favourite destinations.

EARLY YEARS

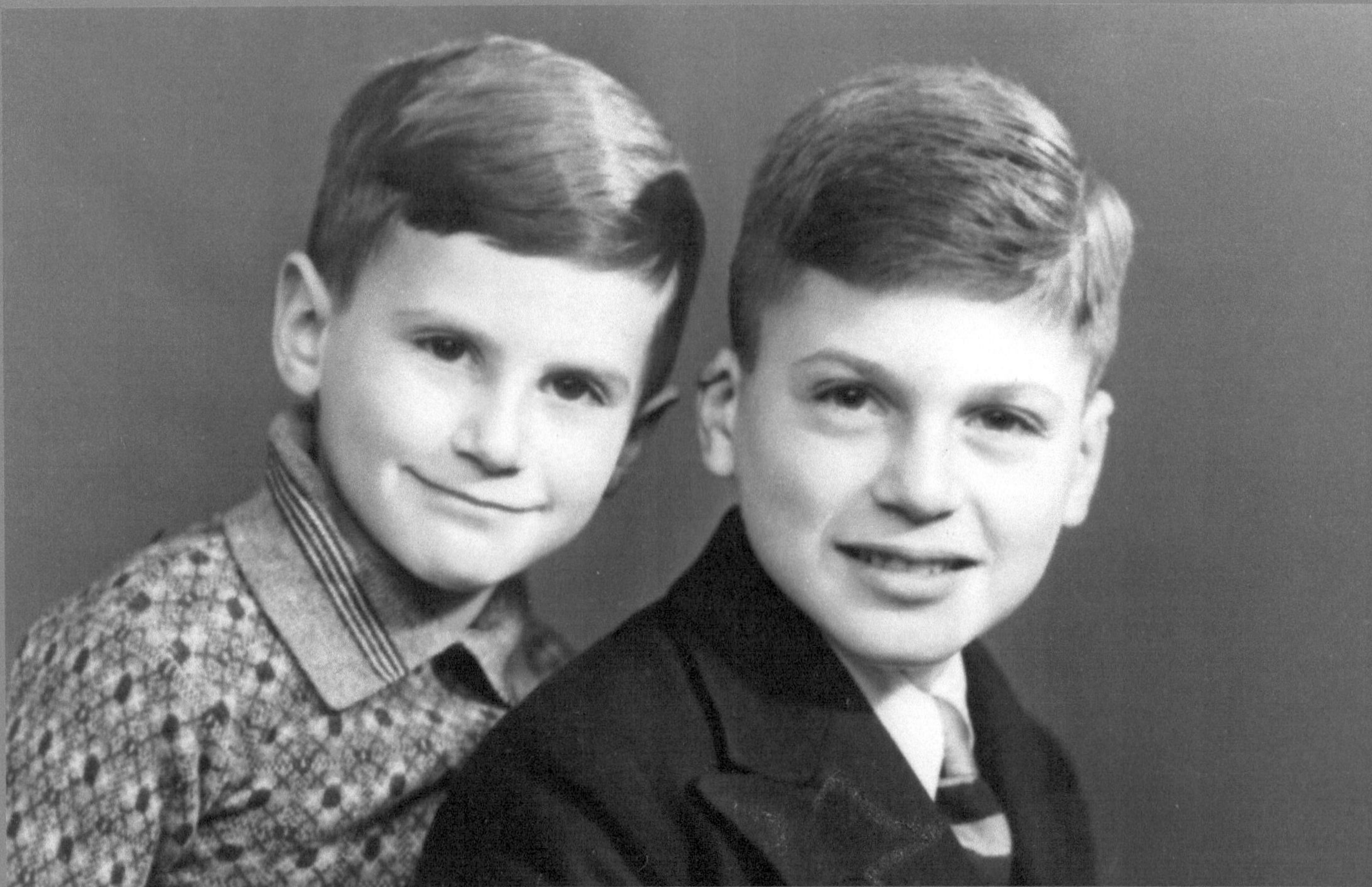

Those who go on to achieve great things often have difficult beginnings. Gerry Anderson was no exception. Born in 1929, Gerry's early years were dominated by his parents' internecine war. His father, Joseph Anderson, ambled his way through a variety of menial jobs in order to keep the family together and rarely failed to attract the open disdain of his wife, Deborah. In those early years it was Lionel, Gerry's brother, that he really looked up to. Seven years older than him, when the Second World War broke out Lionel signed up to become a pilot. In 1944, the Andersons received the message that all families dreaded: Flight Sergeant Anderson had been killed in action. This single event had a devastating effect on Gerry. However, it went on to shape many of his greatest creations.

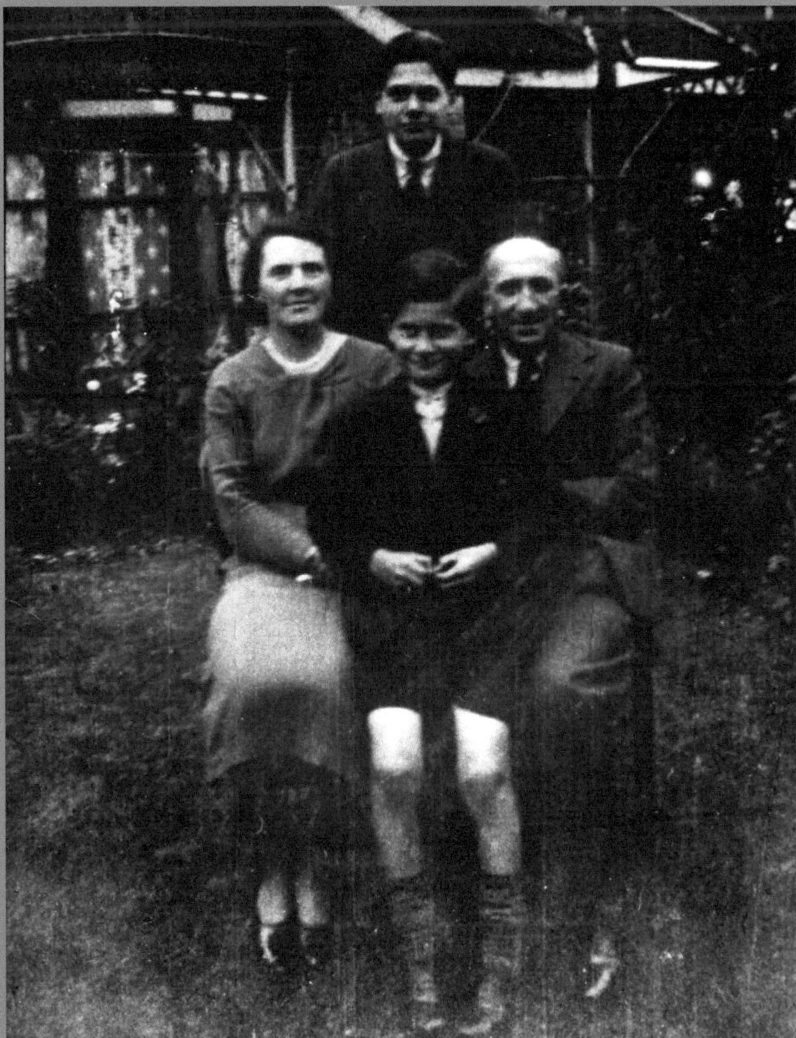

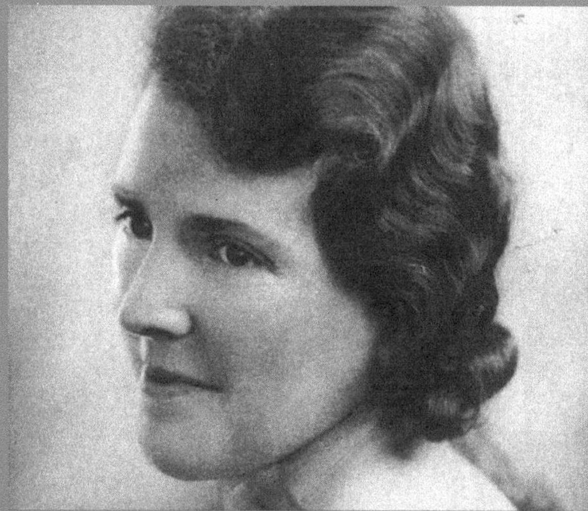

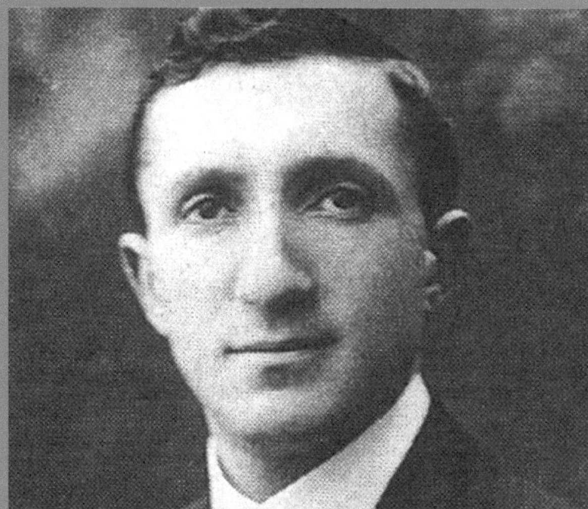

Gerry Anderson's extraordinary journey began on 14th April 1929. **Previous:** Gerry with Lionel, perhaps the biggest single influence on his life. **Left:** The two brothers at home with their parents. The family lived in London in near poverty, and Gerry's early years were tainted by conflict. Gerry's father's family were Jewish refugees from eastern Europe. Upon arriving in London, immigration officials forced the family to change their name from 'Bieloglovski' to 'Abrahams'. In the '30s, anti-semitism pushed Gerry's mother to rename the family once again, this time to 'Anderson'. **Above and below right:** Gerry's parents, Deborah and Joseph.

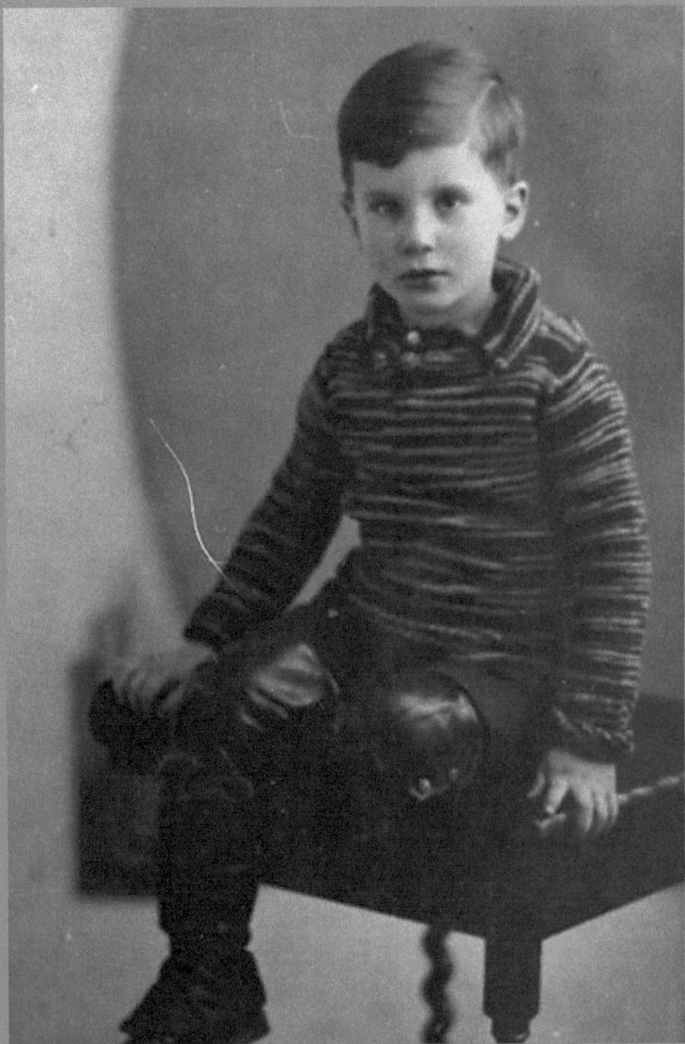

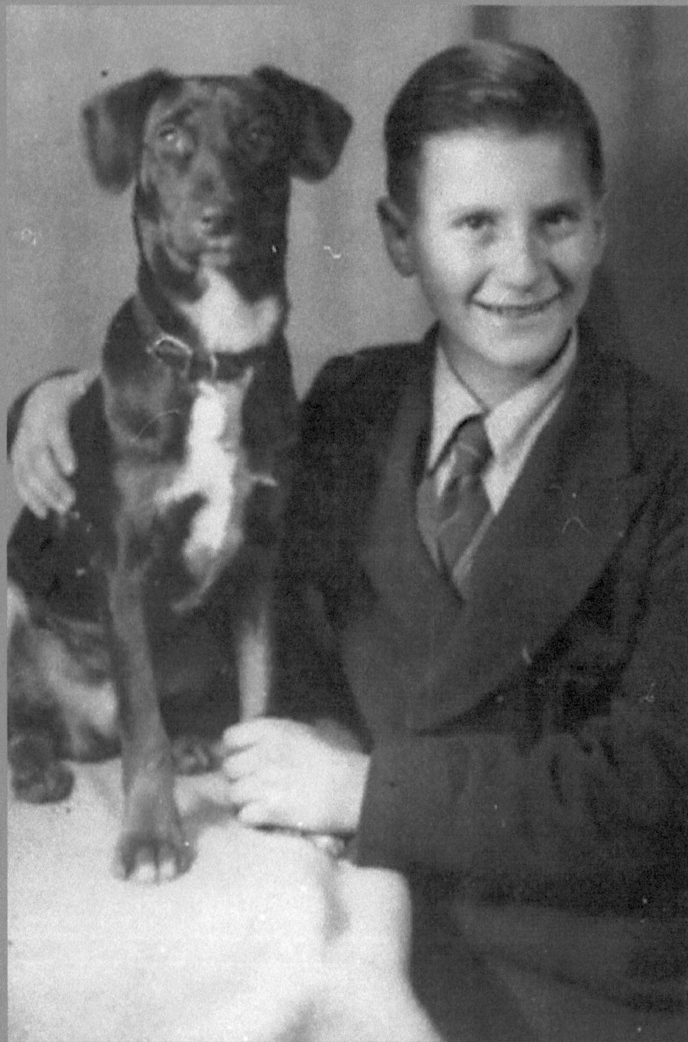

Gerry was a shy and awkward child who found his parents' conflict difficult to deal with. Their war would continue right up until his father's death in the 1960s. **Left:** Gerry as a young child in the 1930s. **Right:** Gerry with his beloved dog, Micky.

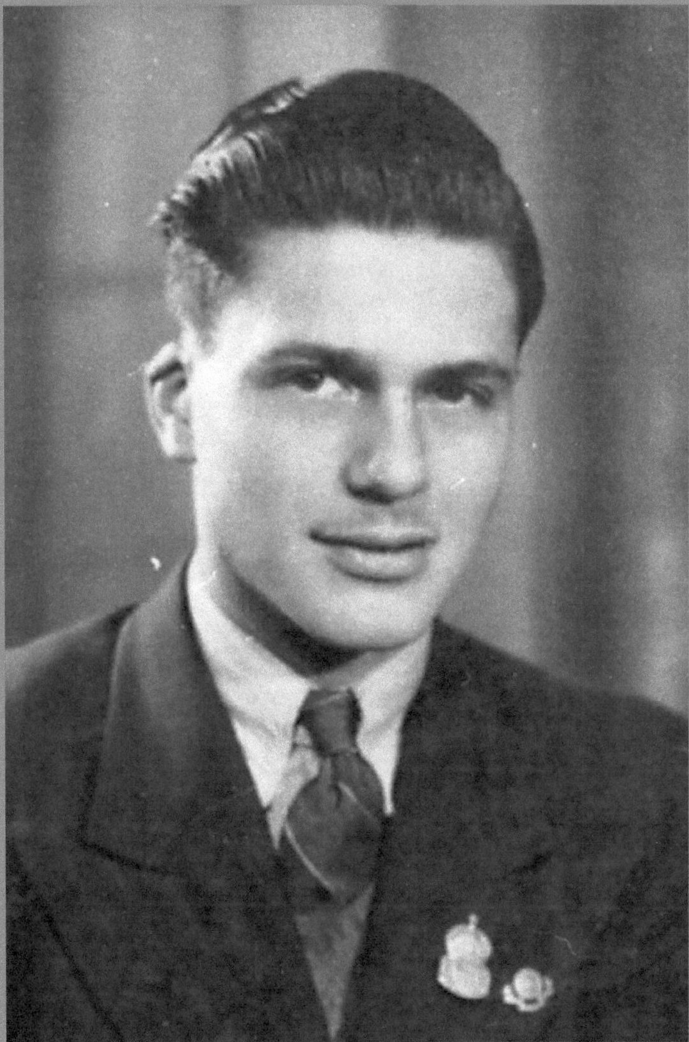

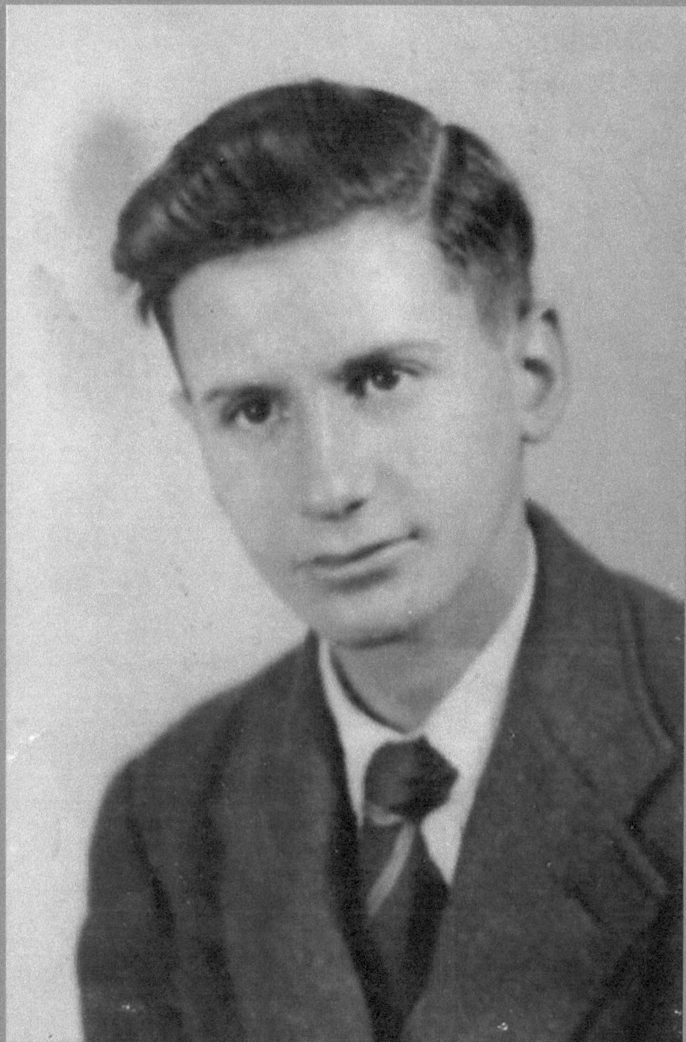

A seven-year age gap between Lionel (**left**) and Gerry (**right**) meant that they were not especially close. However, Gerry idolised his brother, and his admiration for him grew when Lionel became a dashing RAF pilot during the war.

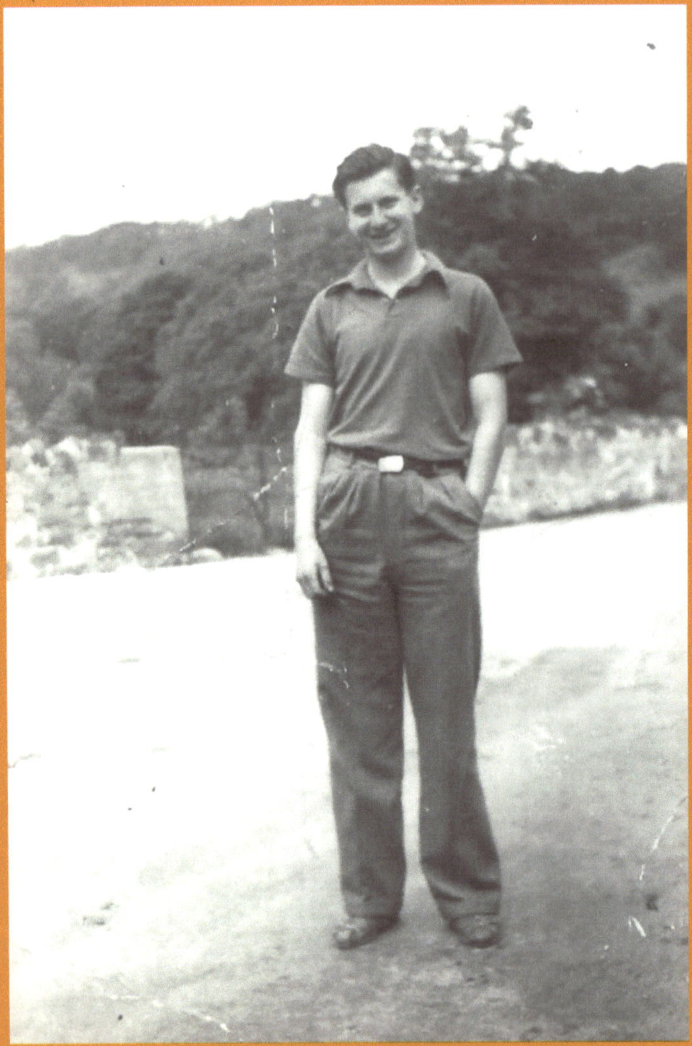

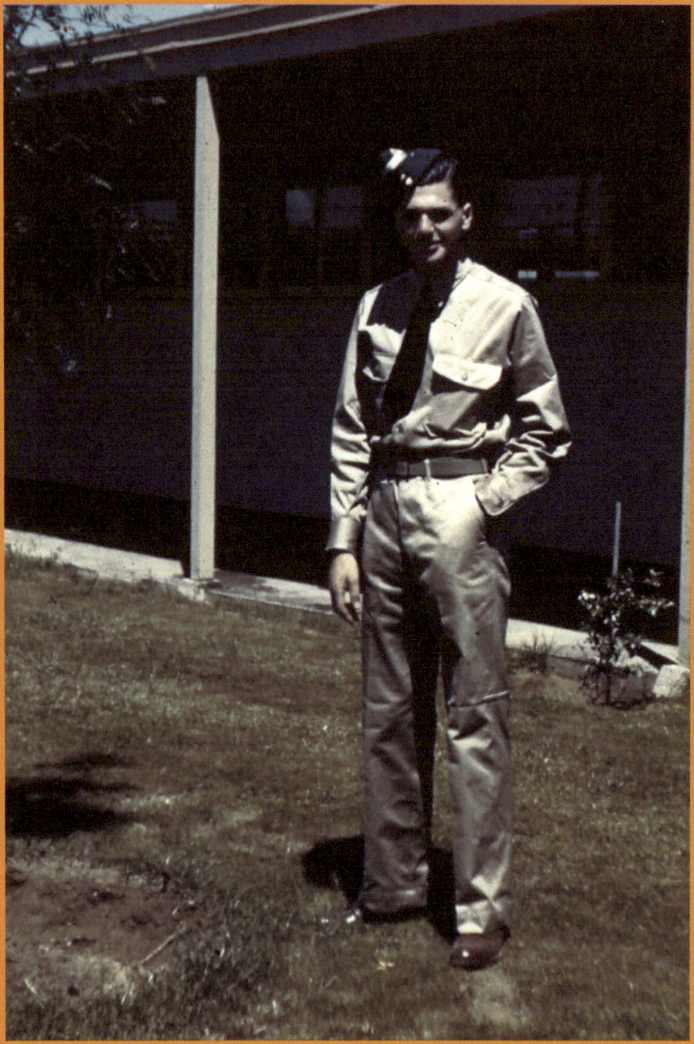

Left: Gerry as a teenager. **Right:** A rare colour shot of Lionel taken when he was stationed in America for a period of the war.

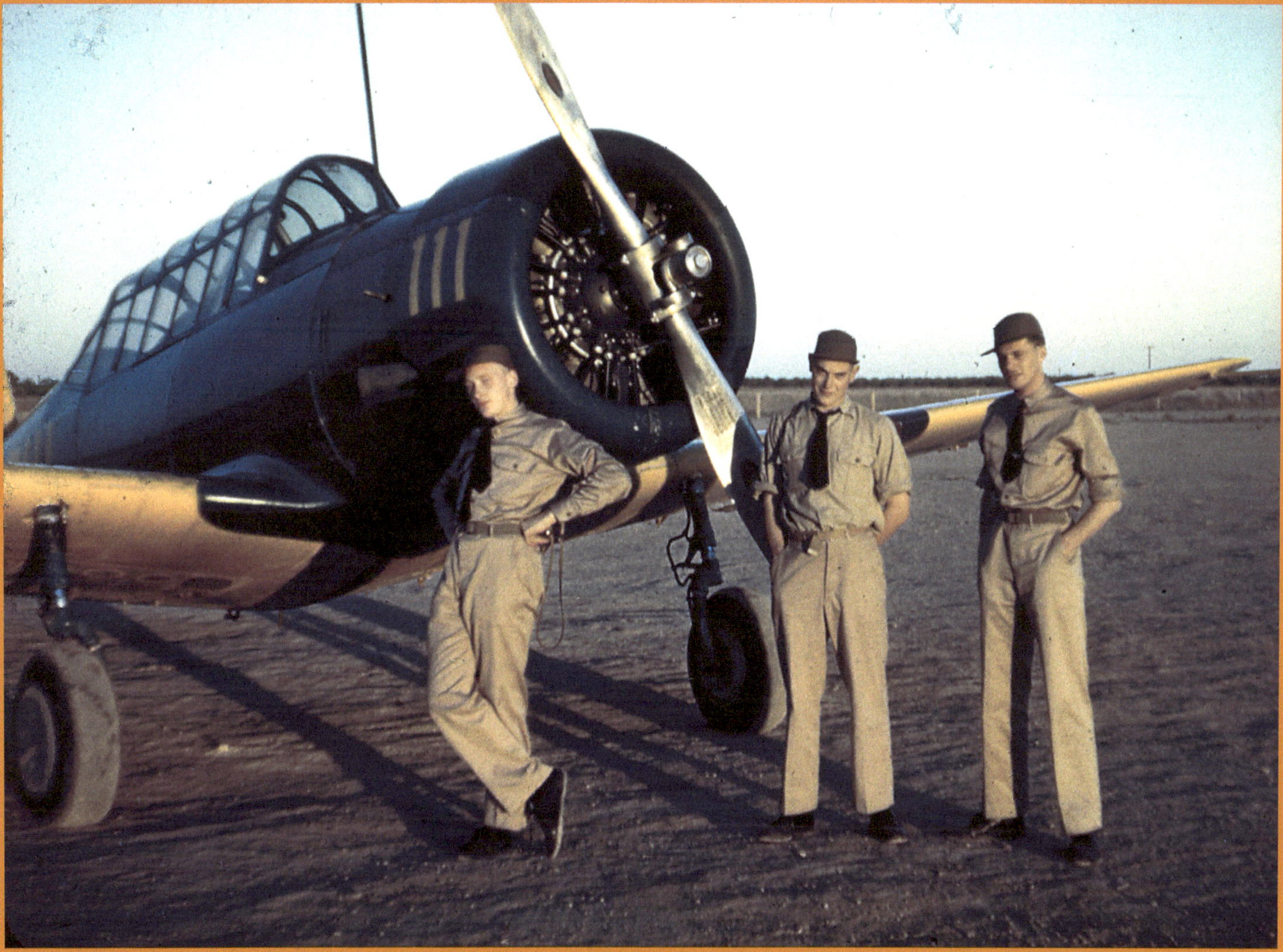

Lionel (far right) with fellow RAF pilots. He sent many letters to the family recounting his adventures, including a trip to Hollywood where he and his friends met Judy Garland. He also spoke of a film in which he had a brief appearance. Its title? *Thunder Birds.*

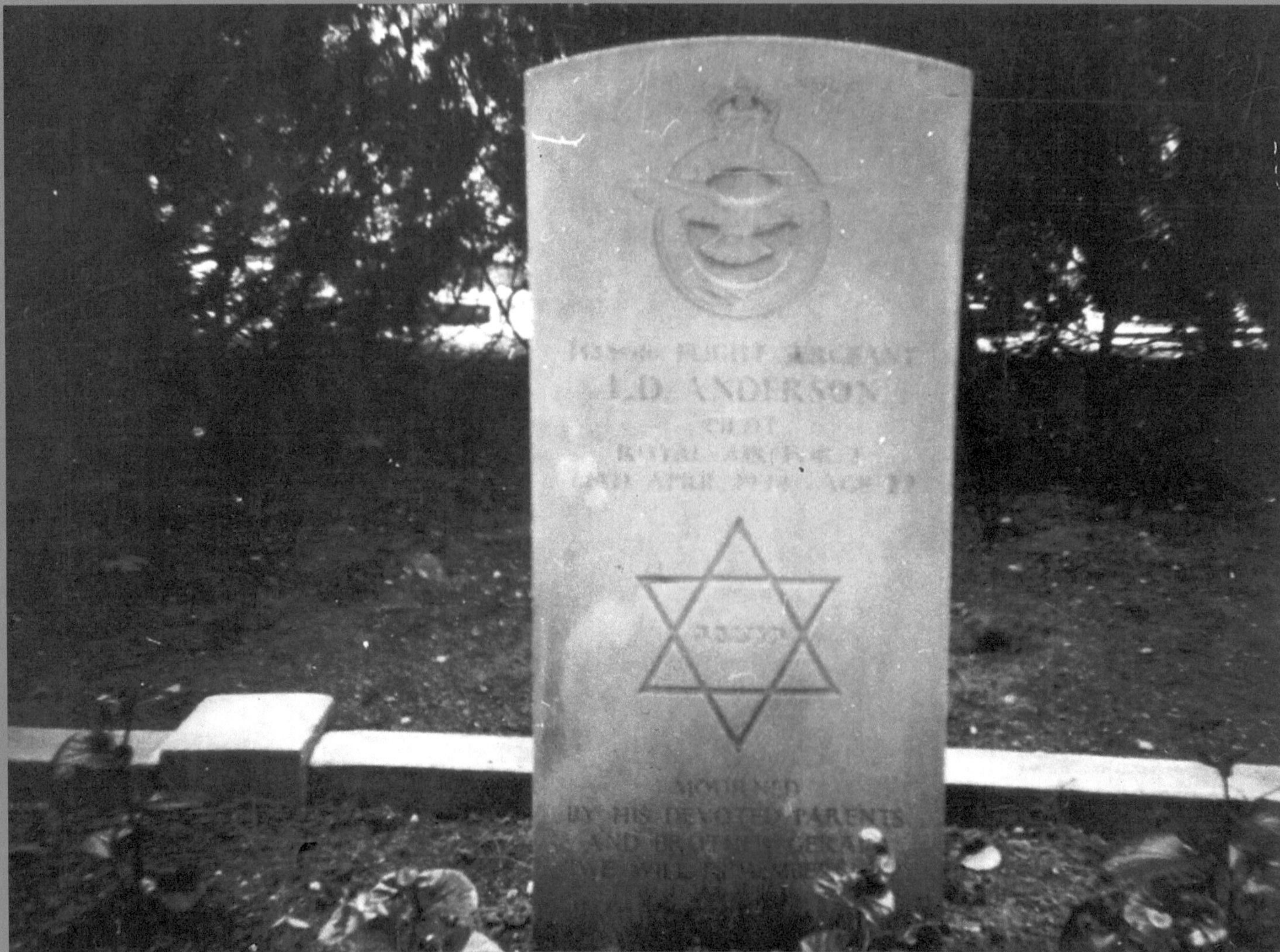

Fate can be cruel, though. In 1944, Lionel, for whom everybody had such high hopes, was killed in action. It shook the family, particularly Gerry's mother; she became ever more distant and unkind to her remaining son. The heroic pilot brother would remain a strong influence through the whole of Gerry's life and work.

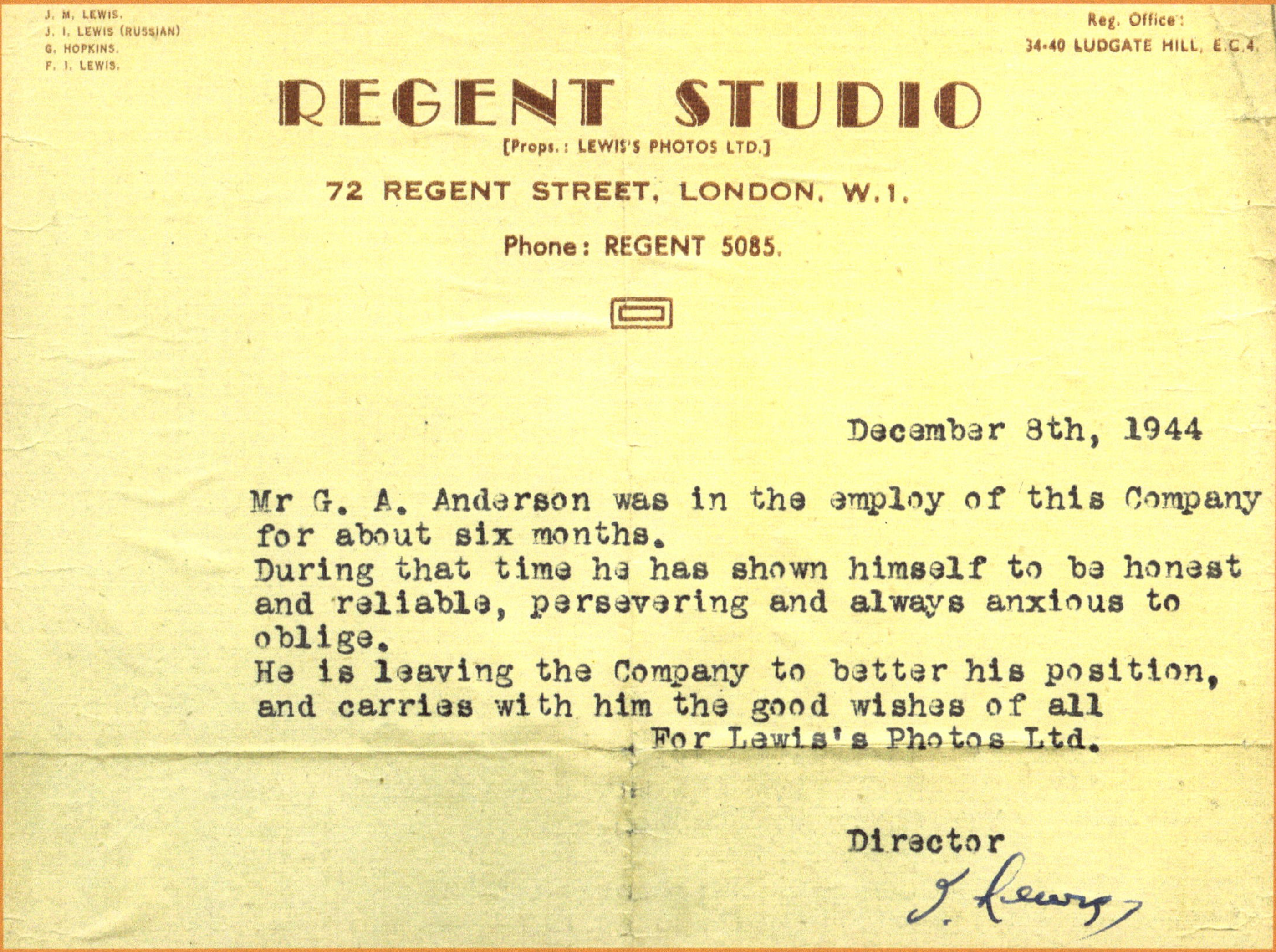

J. M. LEWIS.
J. I. LEWIS (RUSSIAN)
G. HOPKINS.
F. I. LEWIS.

Reg. Office:
34-40 LUDGATE HILL, E.C.4.

REGENT STUDIO

[Props.: LEWIS'S PHOTOS LTD.]

72 REGENT STREET, LONDON, W.1.

Phone: REGENT 5085.

December 8th, 1944

Mr G. A. Anderson was in the employ of this Company for about six months.
During that time he has shown himself to be honest and reliable, persevering and always anxious to oblige.
He is leaving the Company to better his position, and carries with him the good wishes of all

For Lewis's Photos Ltd.

Director

J. Lewis

Later that year, Gerry found his first employment. He had originally harboured aspirations of being a plasterer. However, an allergy to plaster forced him to reconsider his career options, and so he set his sights on the film business. His first stepping stone into this world was when he took a job working at a London photographic studio, aged only 15.

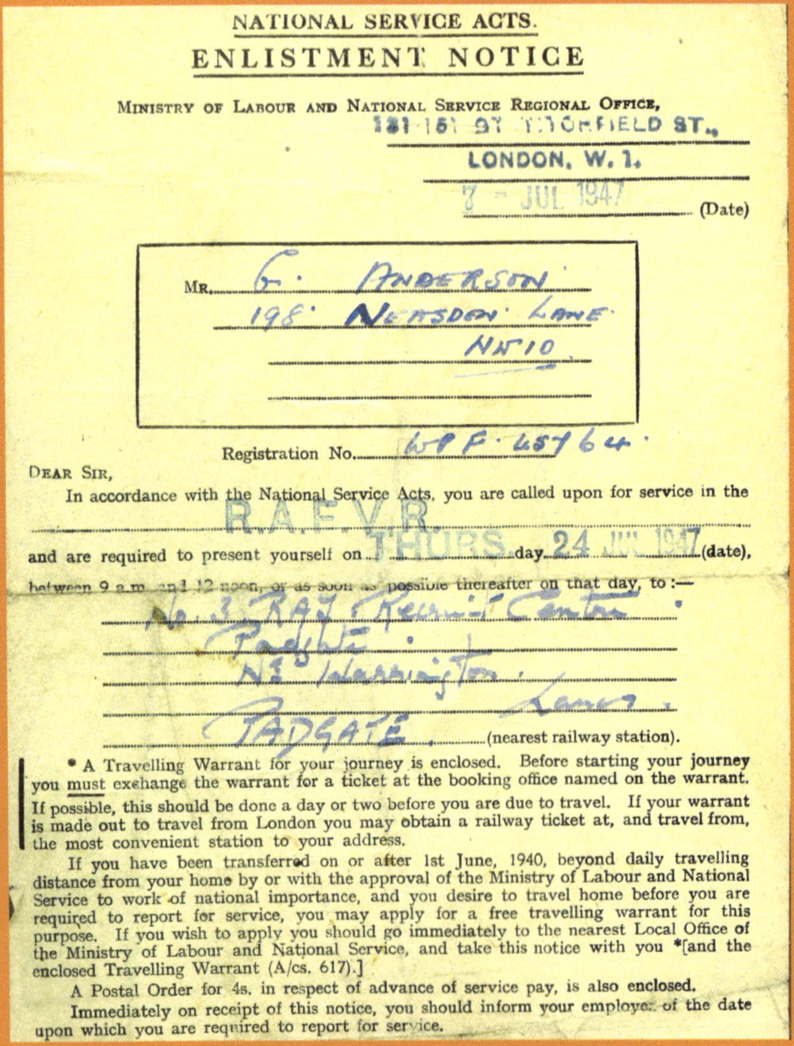

NATIONAL SERVICE ACTS.

ENLISTMENT NOTICE

MINISTRY OF LABOUR AND NATIONAL SERVICE REGIONAL OFFICE,
131-151 GT. TITCHFIELD ST.,
LONDON, W. 1.
7 - JUL 1947 (Date)

MR. G. ANDERSON
198 NEASDEN LANE
NW10

Registration No. WPF 45764

DEAR SIR,

In accordance with the National Service Acts, you are called upon for service in the R.A.F.V.R.

and are required to present yourself on THURS day 24 JUL 1947 (date),

between 9 a.m. and 12 noon, or as soon as possible thereafter on that day, to :—

No. 3 RAF Recruit Centre
Padgate
Nr Warrington
Lancs.

PADGATE (nearest railway station).

* A Travelling Warrant for your journey is enclosed. Before starting your journey you must exchange the warrant for a ticket at the booking office named on the warrant. If possible, this should be done a day or two before you are due to travel. If your warrant is made out to travel from London you may obtain a railway ticket at, and travel from, the most convenient station to your address.

If you have been transferred on or after 1st June, 1940, beyond daily travelling distance from your home by or with the approval of the Ministry of Labour and National Service to work of national importance, and you desire to travel home before you are required to report for service, you may apply for a free travelling warrant for this purpose. If you wish to apply you should go immediately to the nearest Local Office of the Ministry of Labour and National Service, and take this notice with you *[and the enclosed Travelling Warrant (A/cs. 617).]

A Postal Order for 4s. in respect of advance of service pay, is also enclosed.

Immediately on receipt of this notice, you should inform your employer of the date upon which you are required to report for service.

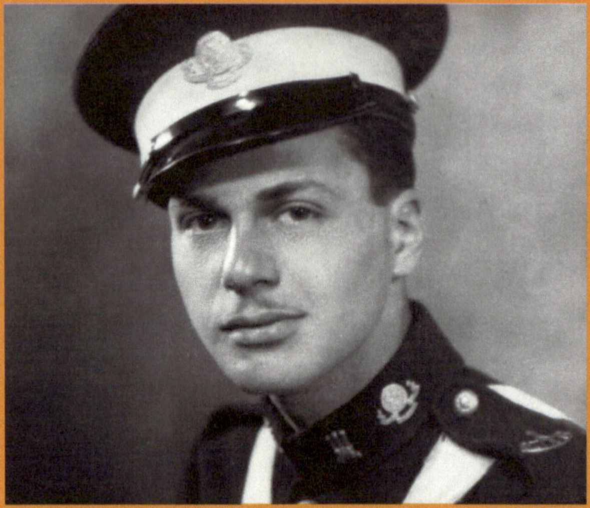

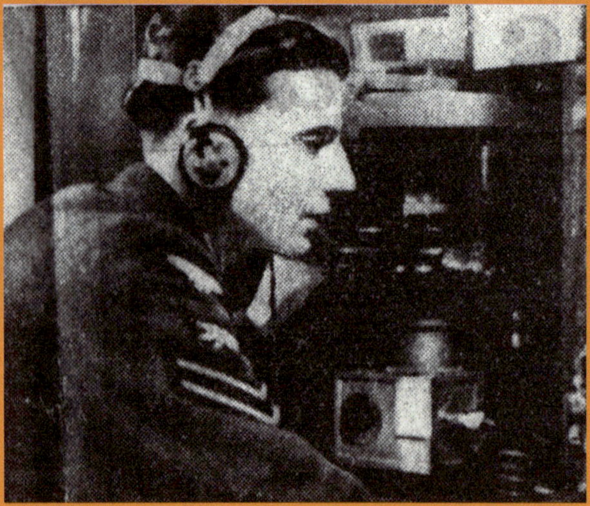

Gerry eventually got a job in the film business and entered the cutting rooms. However, as was common for men of his age at that time, his career was interrupted by National Service. **Left:** Gerry's RAF enlistment notice. **Below right:** Gerry decided to follow in Lionel's (**above right**) footsteps and joined the RAF, where he worked as a radio telephone operator.

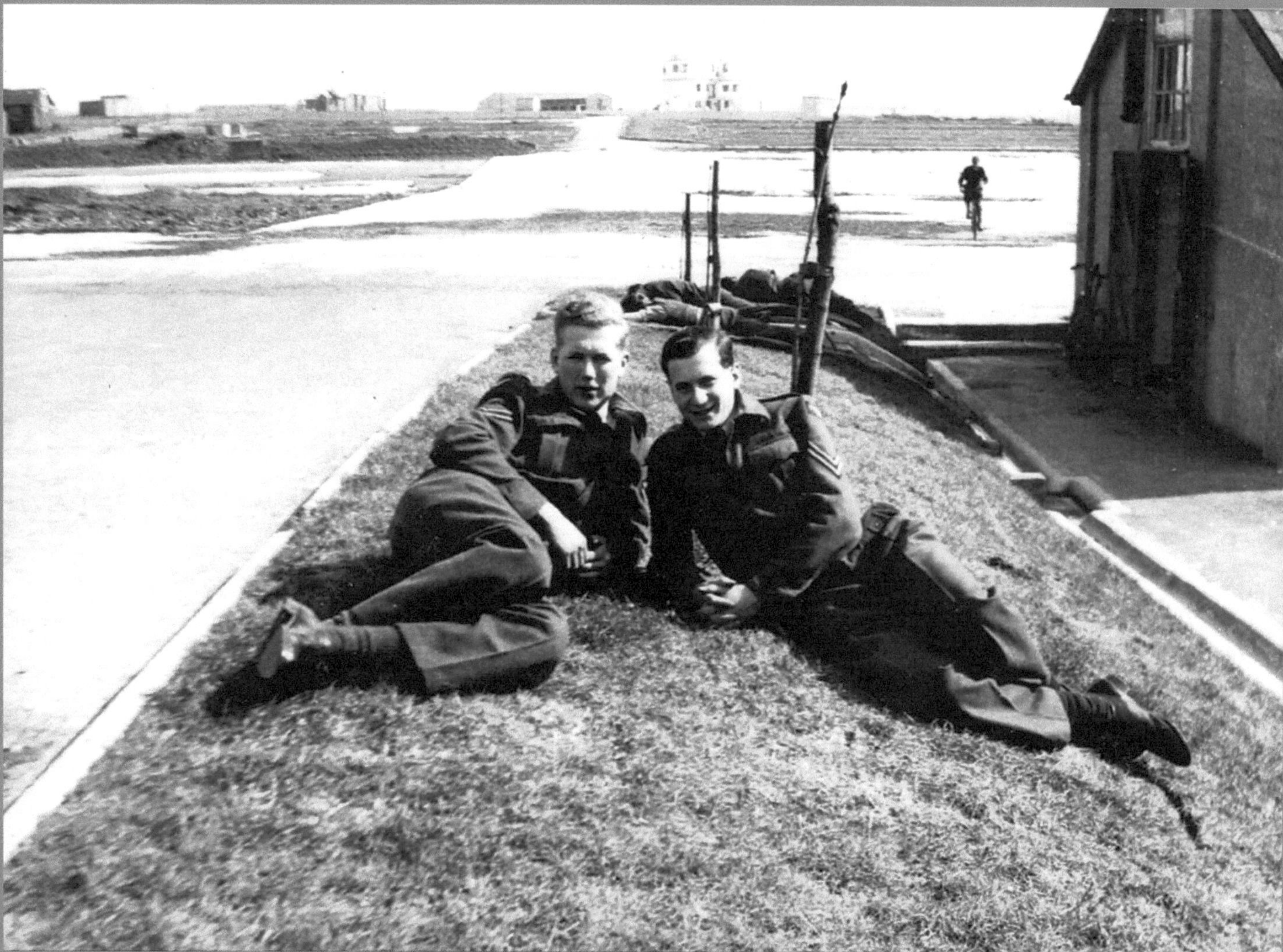

Gerry spent two years in the RAF, rising to the rank of corporal. Despite initially being a scary experience, Gerry soon settled in. He started to overcome some of his childhood shyness, allowing him to make proper friends for the first time.

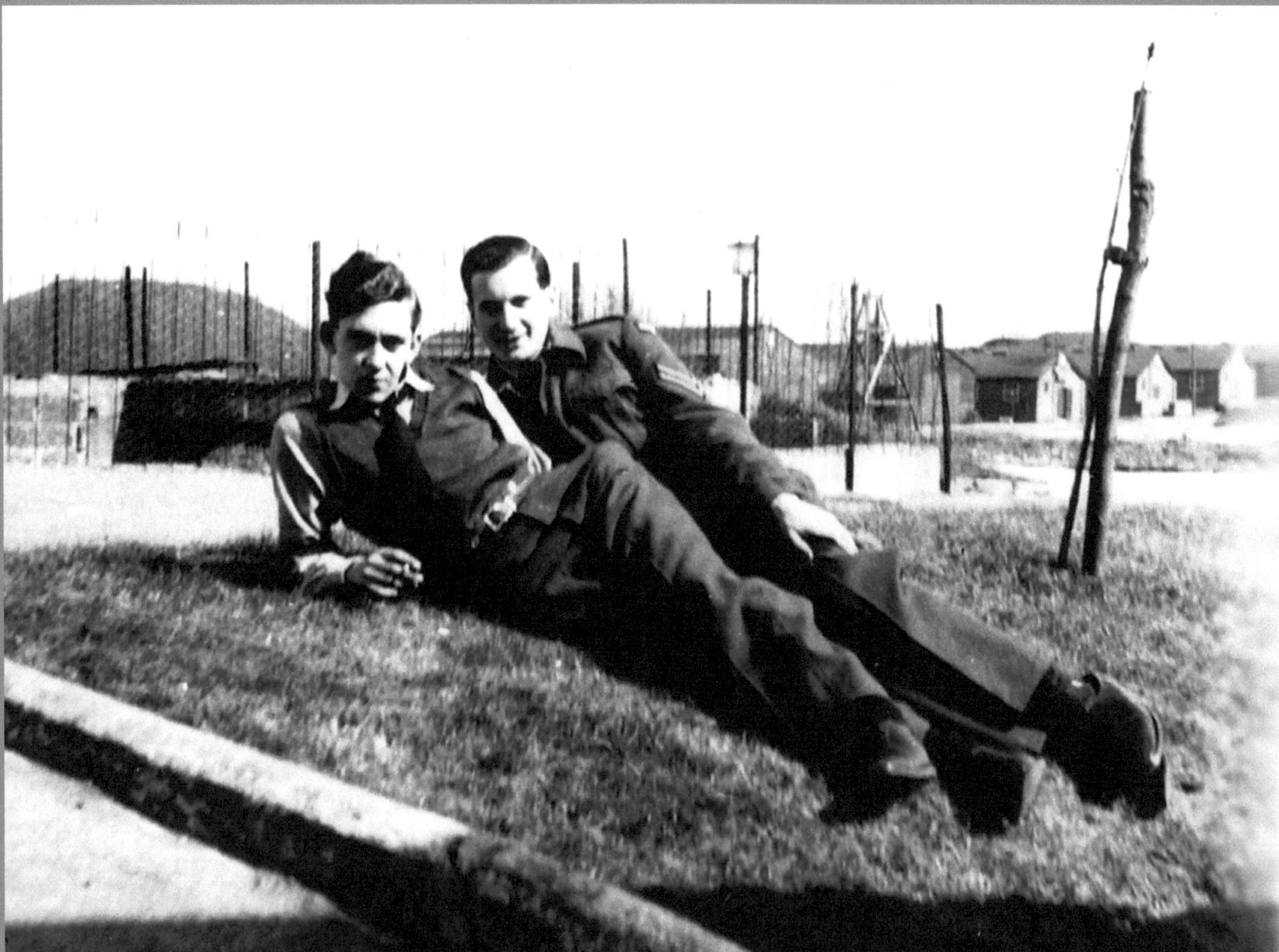

Previous and above: Gerry relaxes with RAF friends and colleagues.

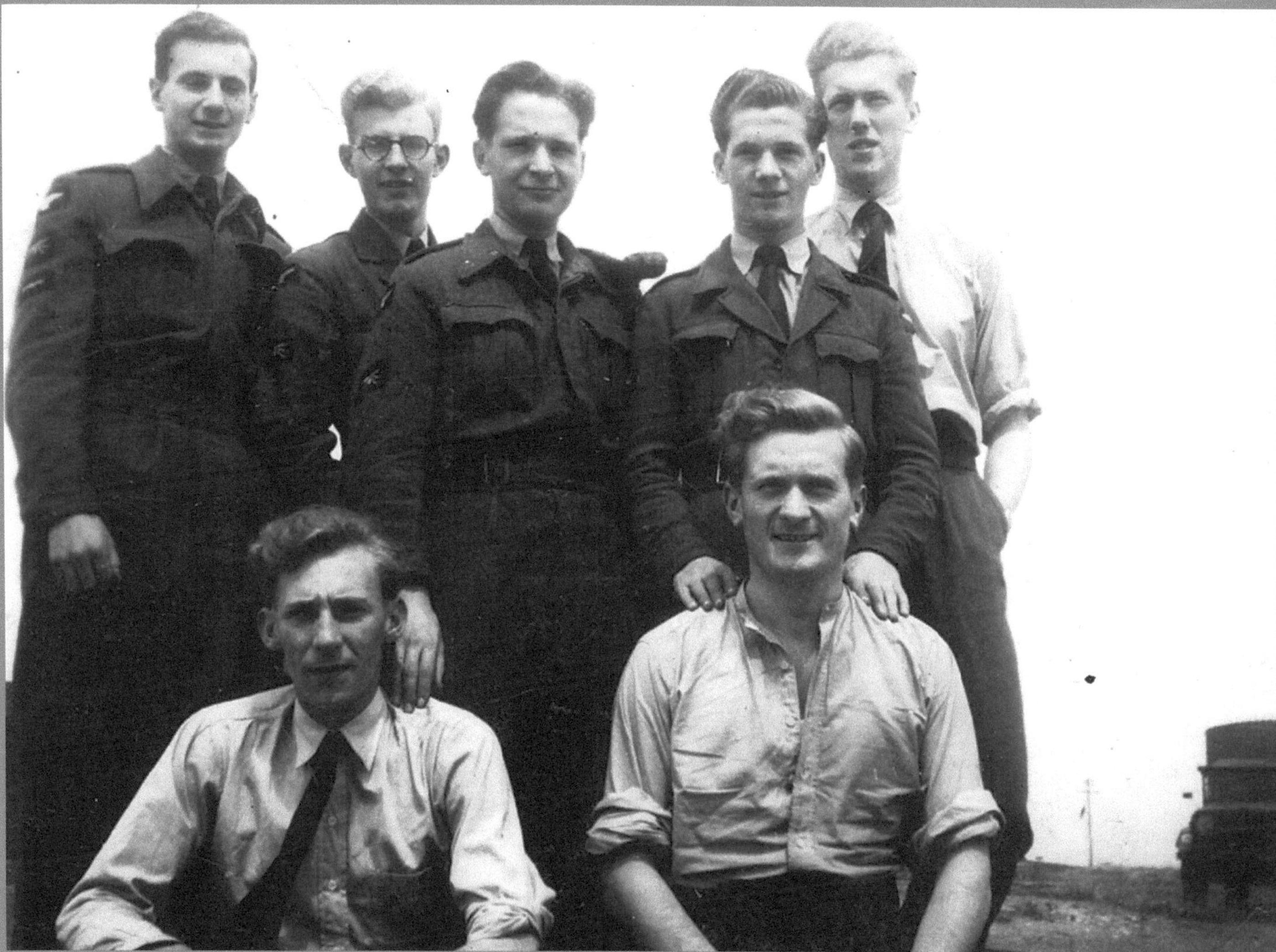

Gerry (far left) with his fellow officers.

1950s

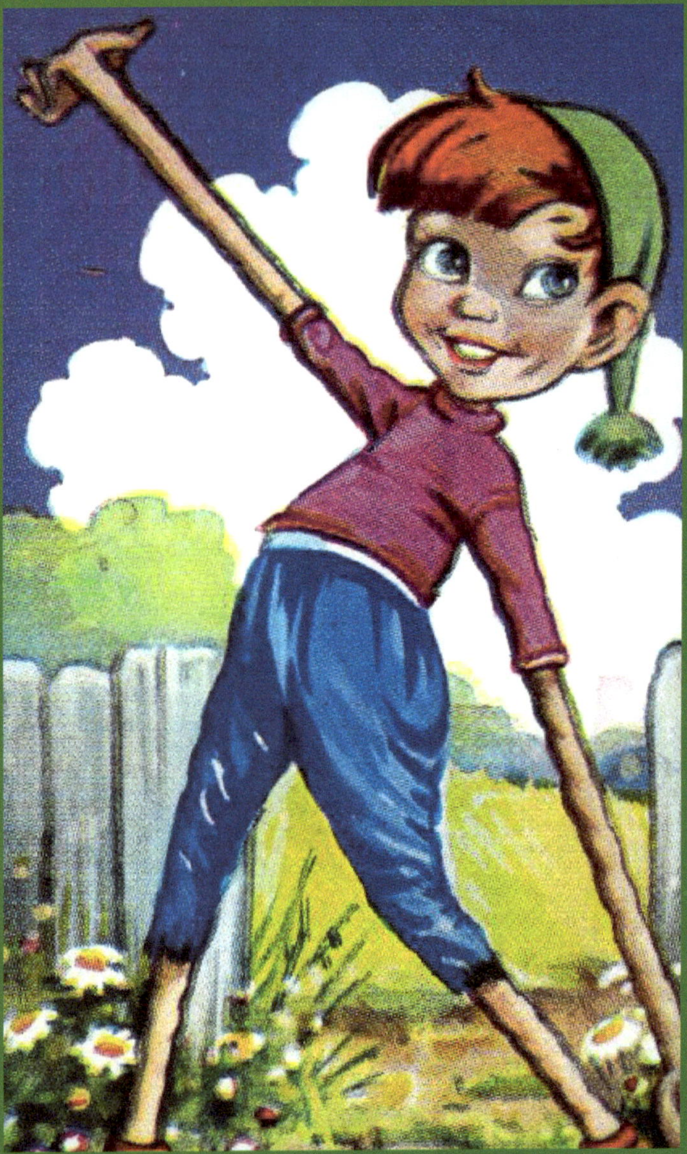

Upon the end of his National Service, Gerry returned to the film business. He went to Pinewood Studios where he gained a reputation for being an excellent dubbing editor.

However, always searching to better himself, Gerry started to look for other opportunities. In 1955, he applied for his first job as a director on a documentary series called *You've Never Seen This*. The series was made by a small company called Polytechnic Films, which was run out of a ramshackle house in Taplow. During this project, which involved time spent in various locations across Europe, Gerry struck up a friendship with his cameraman, Arthur Provis.

Polytechnic's boss, E. Smith Morris, was a brilliant inventor, but a less successful businessman. He invited Gerry and Arthur to join him in a new venture called Pentagon Films with two other colleagues. This company, which operated out of the same dilapidated house, produced all manner of bits and pieces, including a handful of advertisements.

One of these commercials featured a puppet of Noddy promoting Kellogg's Riccicles. "Perhaps we should abandon actors and use puppets," Gerry quipped to the amusement of the others.

This advert brought Pentagon Films to the attention of children's novelist Roberta Leigh, who was looking for someone to turn her idea *The Adventures of Twizzle* into a puppet show. Gerry and Arthur, disillusioned with their Pentagon colleagues, decided to take the commission and go it alone with a new company, A.P. Films.

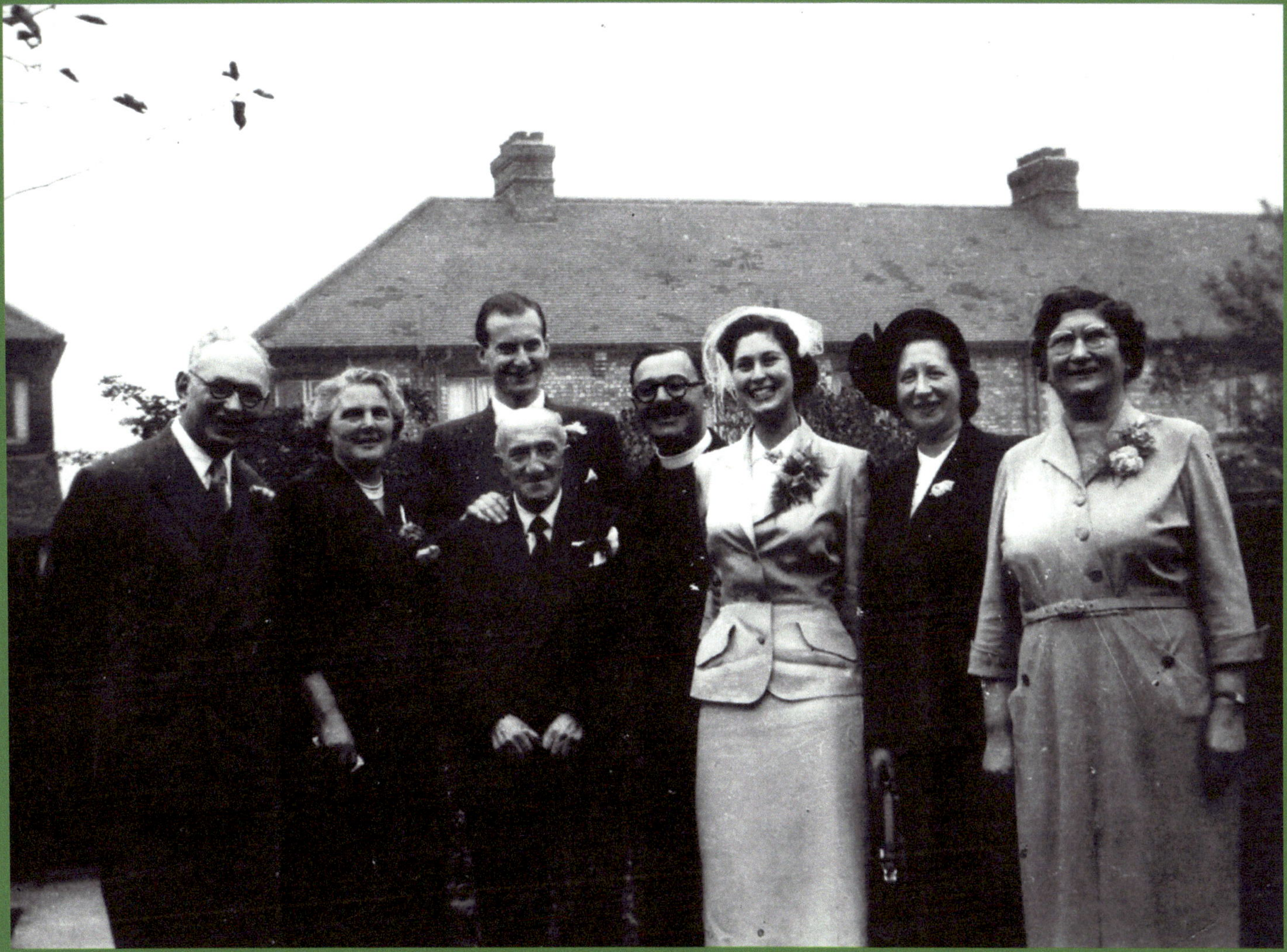

Previous: An illustration of Twizzle, a doll who could extend his arms and legs and got into a series of adventures with friend Footso the Cat. **Above:** In the early 1950s, whilst Gerry was working at Pinewood Studios, friends of his would go out dancing. Though a reluctant dancer, Gerry accompanied them with the hope of meeting girls. During one of these outings, he met Betty Wrightman. After a brief courtship, the couple were married in 1952.

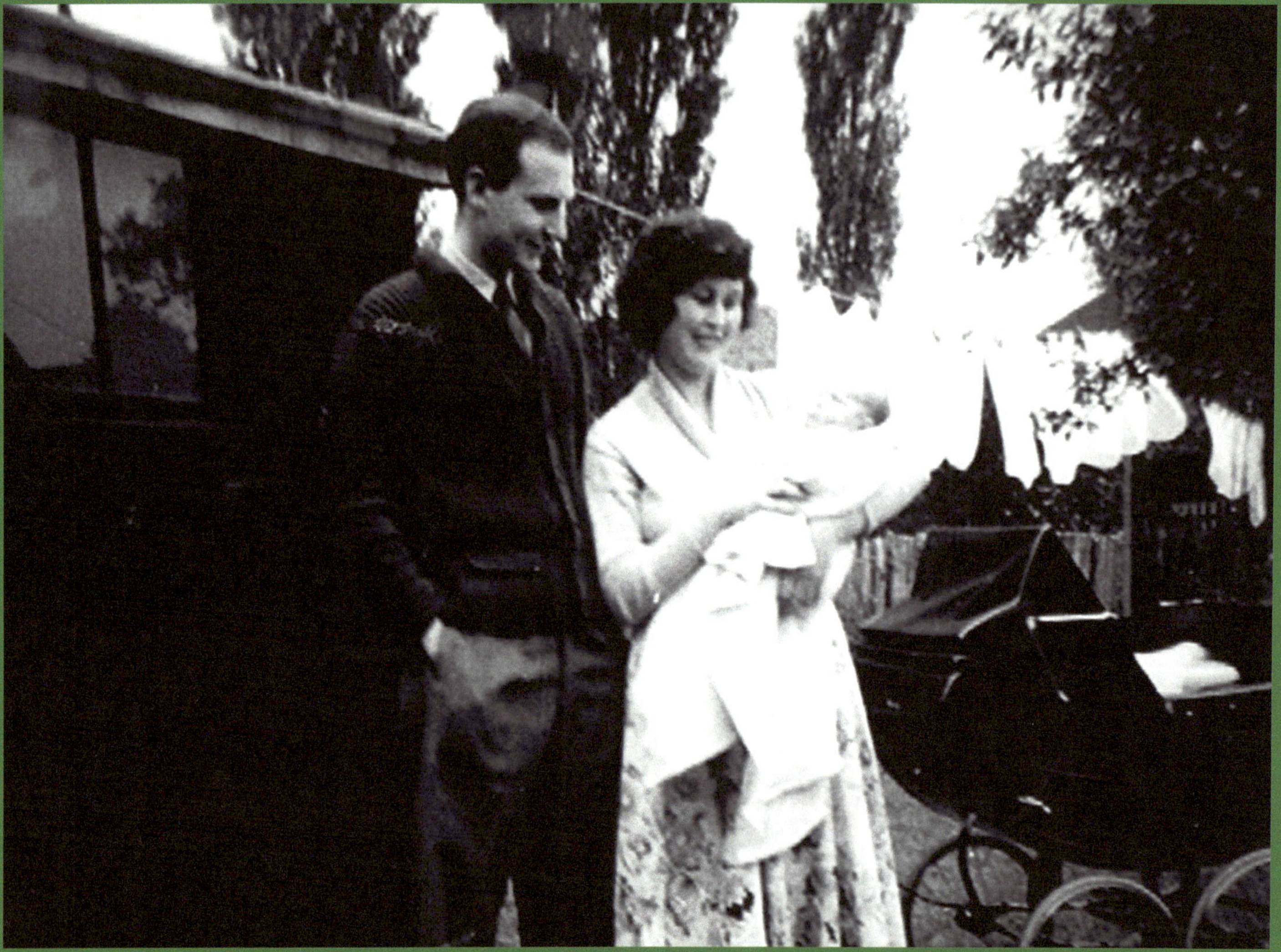

Gerry and Betty's marriage produced two daughters, Linda in 1954 and Joy in 1958. Even at this early point in his career, Gerry's life was dominated by work, and he spent most of his time in the cutting room. Here, the couple pose with baby Linda.

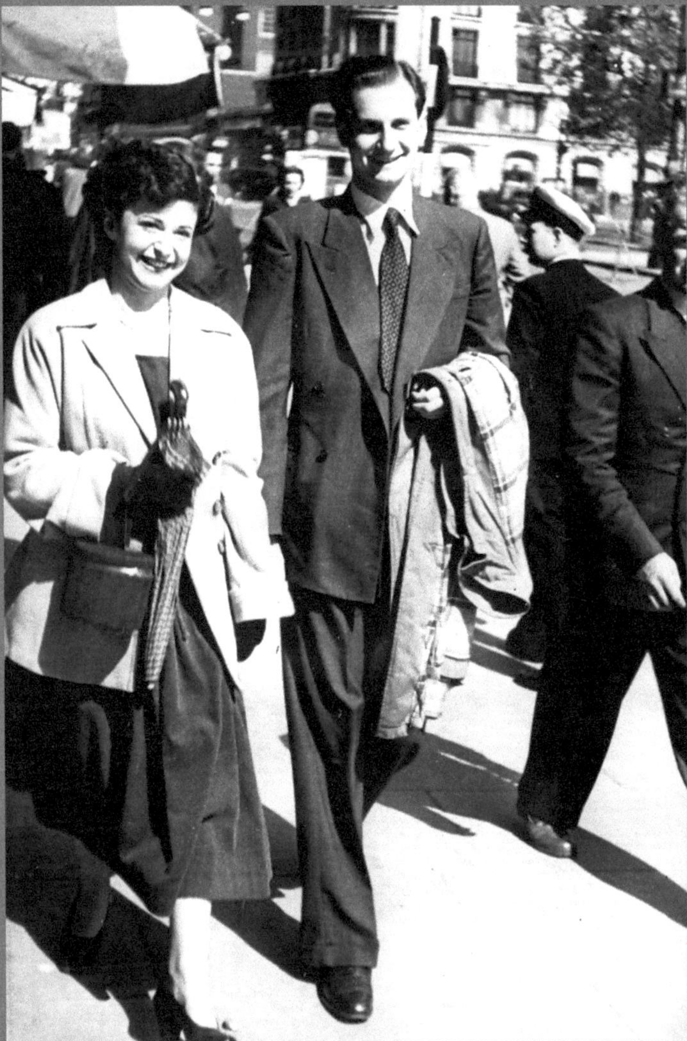

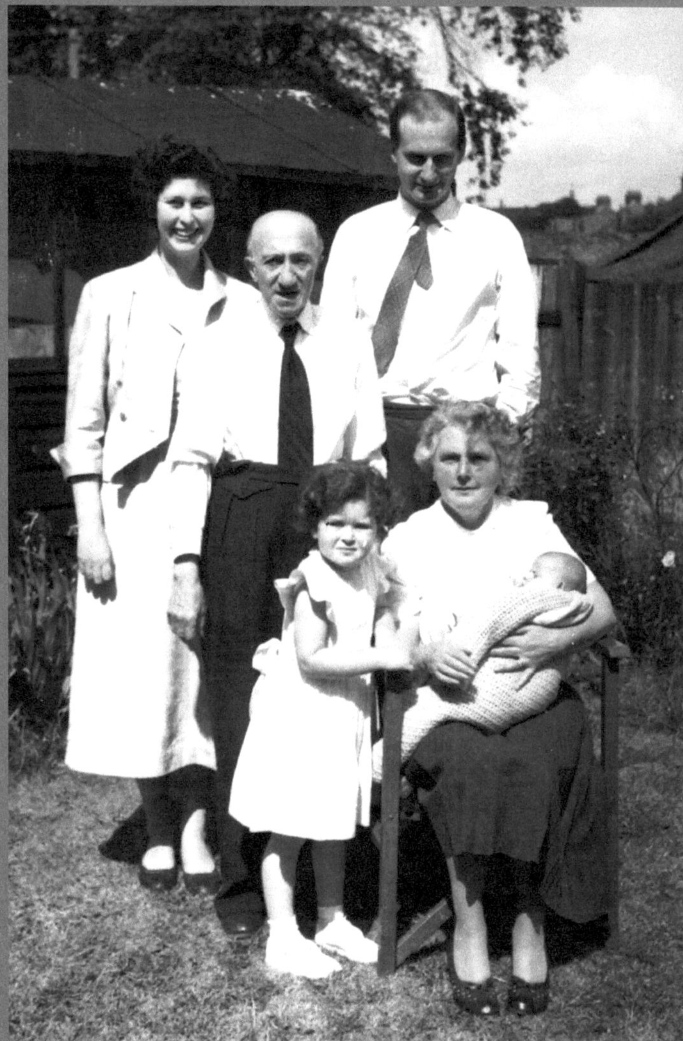

Left: Gerry and Betty take a stroll. **Right:** Gerry and Betty with Deborah, Joseph, Linda and newly born daughter Joy.

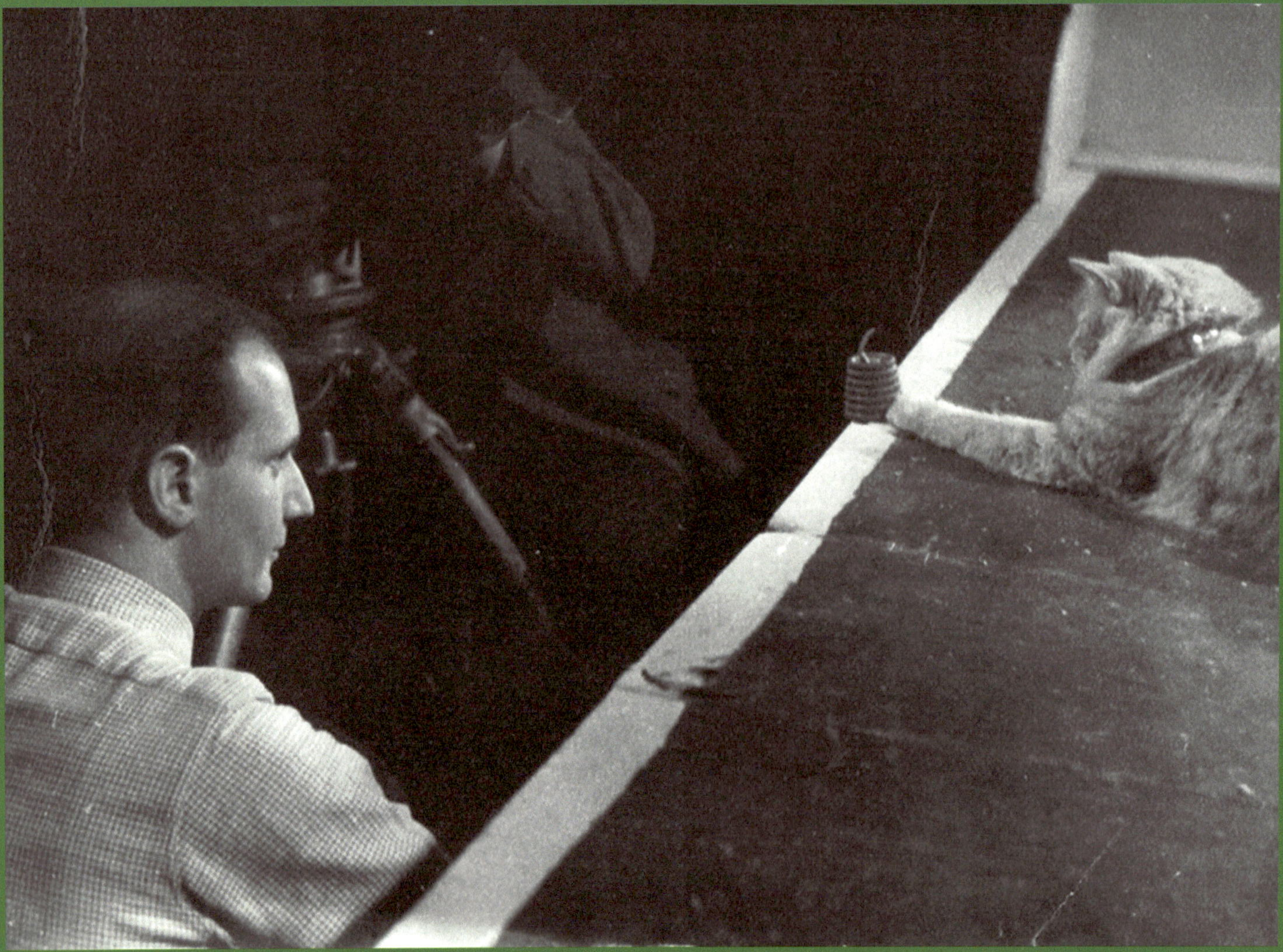

Gerry's career as we know it began in 1955, when he decided to try his hand at directing. *You've Never Seen This* was a show that set out to find people and creatures with rare and unusual talents. The trip across Europe was fraught with difficulties, but it helped lead Gerry to a friendship with his cameraman, Arthur Provis, with whom he decided to go into business.

TELEPHONE:
MAIDENHEAD 140

PENTAGON FILMS
LIMITED

STOCKWELLS
BERRY HILL, TAPLOW
MAIDENHEAD, BERKS

G. A. ANDERSON
DIRECTOR

APF

A. P. FILMS LIMITED. IPSWICH ROAD.
SLOUGH . BUCKINGHAMSHIRE
TEL. SLOUGH 21370 / 23698

PRESENTED BY
G. A. ANDERSON, *Managing Director*

The films are now going to be shot in a wonderful Studio located in the ballroom of a Country Mansion near Maidenhead. I have met the Director, Camera-man and Art Director (a girl) and they are all most likable. They are all most keen and enthusiastic to make these the best puppet films ever made in this country. I too feel that this is a wonderful opportunity, and may well be the beginning of something big!

As we will be working with long strings from an overhead bridge, it will only be feasable for us to rehearse on the actual set. The first (or pilot) film is not too complicated, and there will be adequate opportunities for us to rehearse in the ordinary way as we go along, but as both the puppets and the surroundings will be new, I think it would be a great help if wee three (you, Murray and I) spent Saturday 30th. Sept. down at Maidenhead, feeling our way round, and trying out things generally, if this day is convenient.

Gerry and Arthur initially worked at Pentagon Films with three others. However, when Roberta Leigh approached them about producing a puppet series called *The Adventures of Twizzle*, they decided to go it alone and set up A.P. Films. **Above left and right:** Gerry's business cards for Pentagon Films and A.P. Films. **Below:** Gerry always seemed surprised by his success, but others saw it coming from afar. This excerpt from a letter from puppeteer Joy Laurey to colleague Christine Glanville describes her visit to the unusual team hoping to make puppet films.

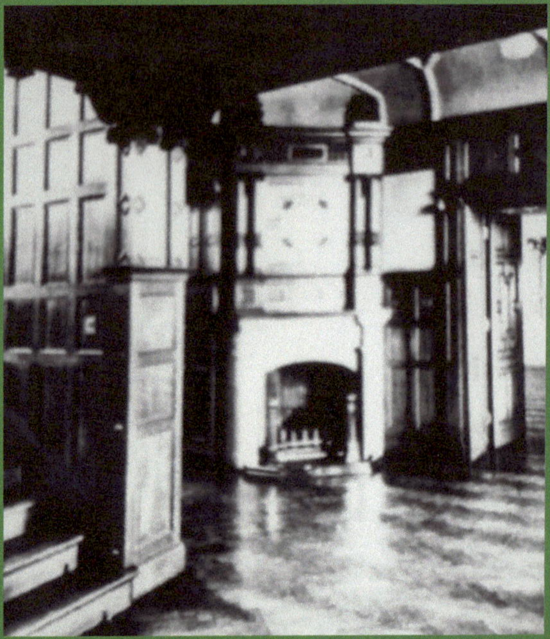

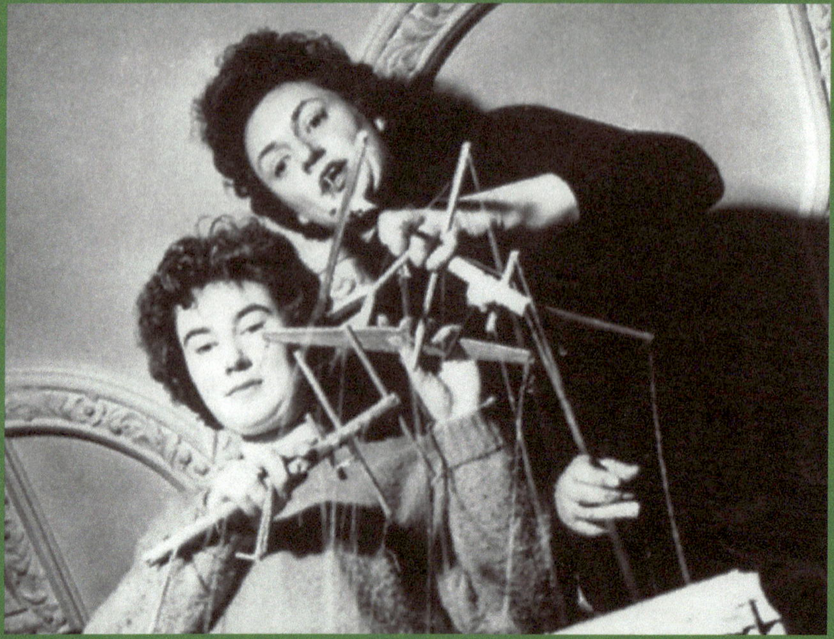

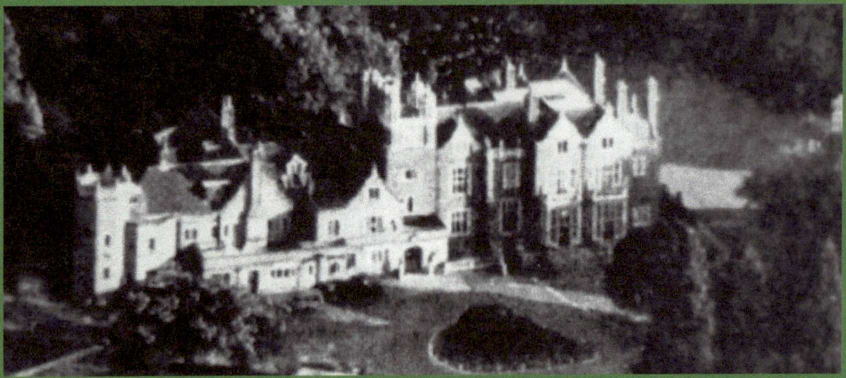

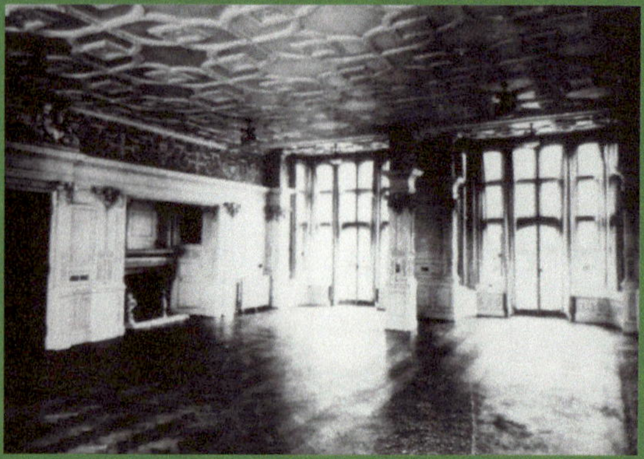

Above and below left: A.P. Films set up shop at Islet Park, a faux-Gothic mansion on the banks of the Thames in Maidenhead. *Twizzle* and their second series, *Torchy the Battery Boy,* were filmed in the ballroom, which was converted into a studio (**below right**). **Above right:** Puppeteers Mary Turner (left) and Christine Glanville operate the puppets from a bridge above the set. The ornate ceiling at Islet Park was very low, making it difficult to operate comfortably.

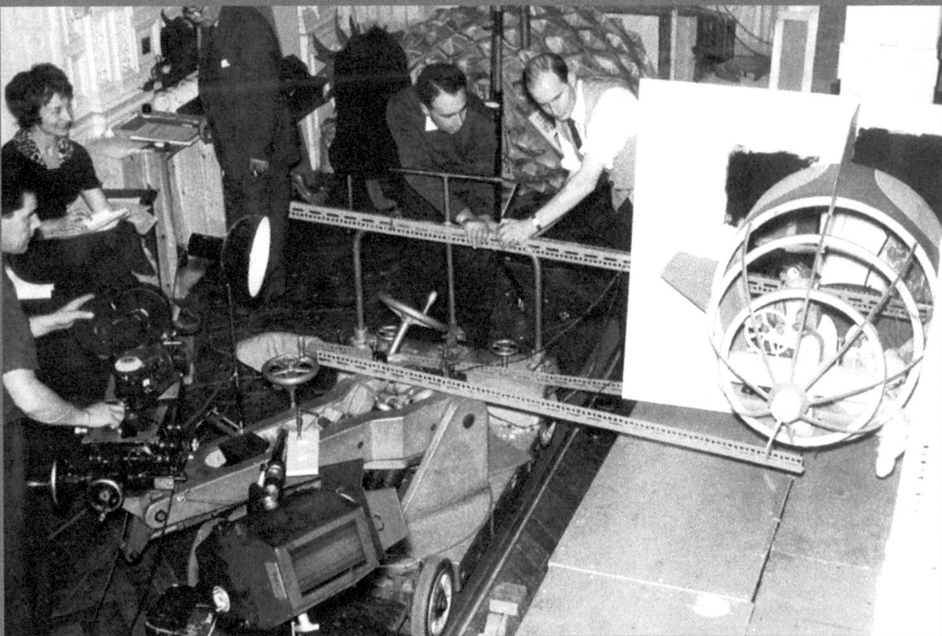

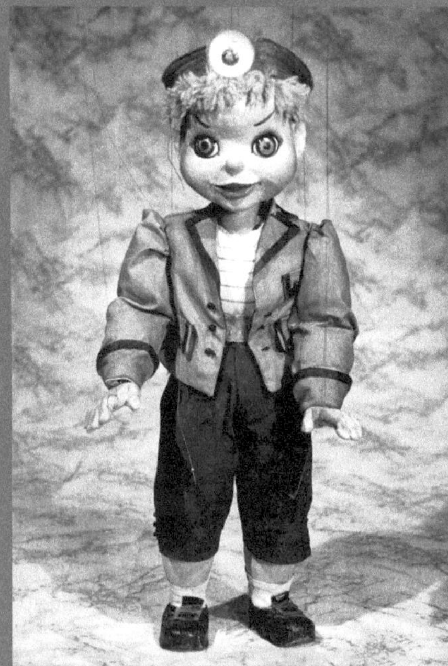

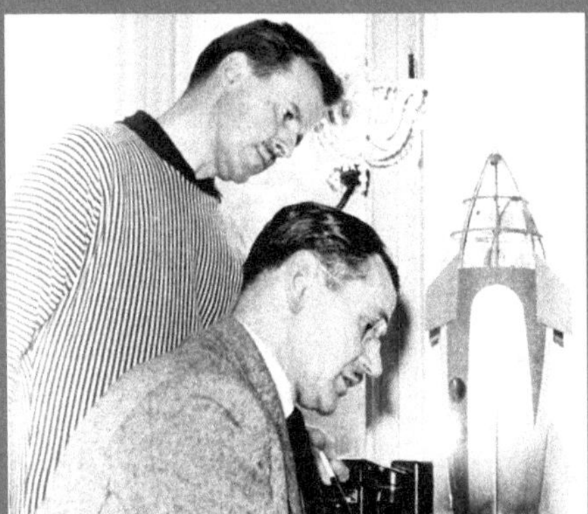

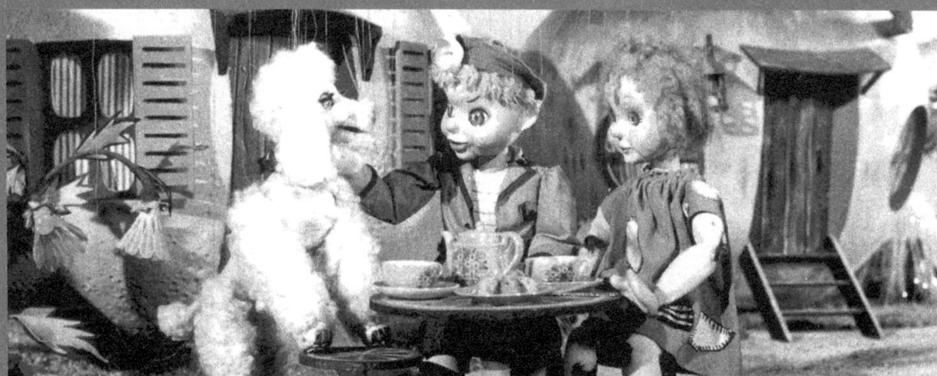

Above left: Filming Torchy in his rocket. Gerry and Arthur ready the vehicle for filming. Business partner and cameraman extraordinaire John Read films, whilst Gerry's future wife Sylvia Thamm takes notes for continuity. **Above right:** A publicity photo of Torchy the Battery Boy. **Below left:** Business partner and designer Reg Hill with his assistant Bob Bell. The miniature of Torchy's rocket sits by the window. In order to simulate the rocket engine's exhaust, sparklers were fitted to the model. **Below right:** Torchy, Pom-Pom the Dog and Flopsy the Ragdoll in Topsy Turvey Land.

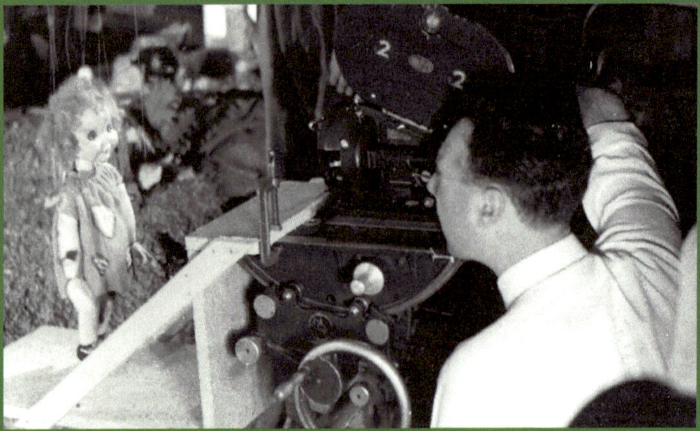

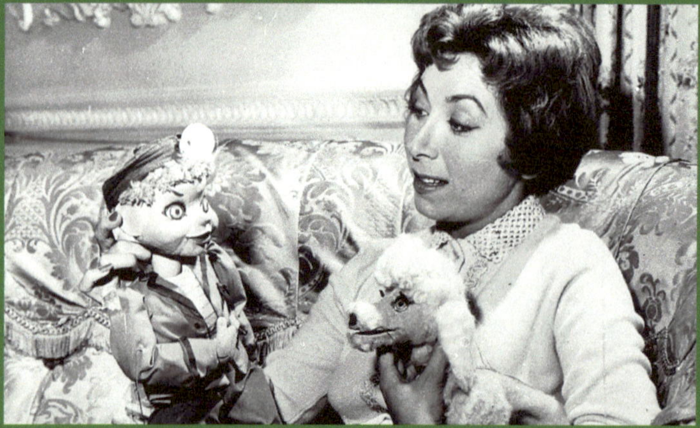

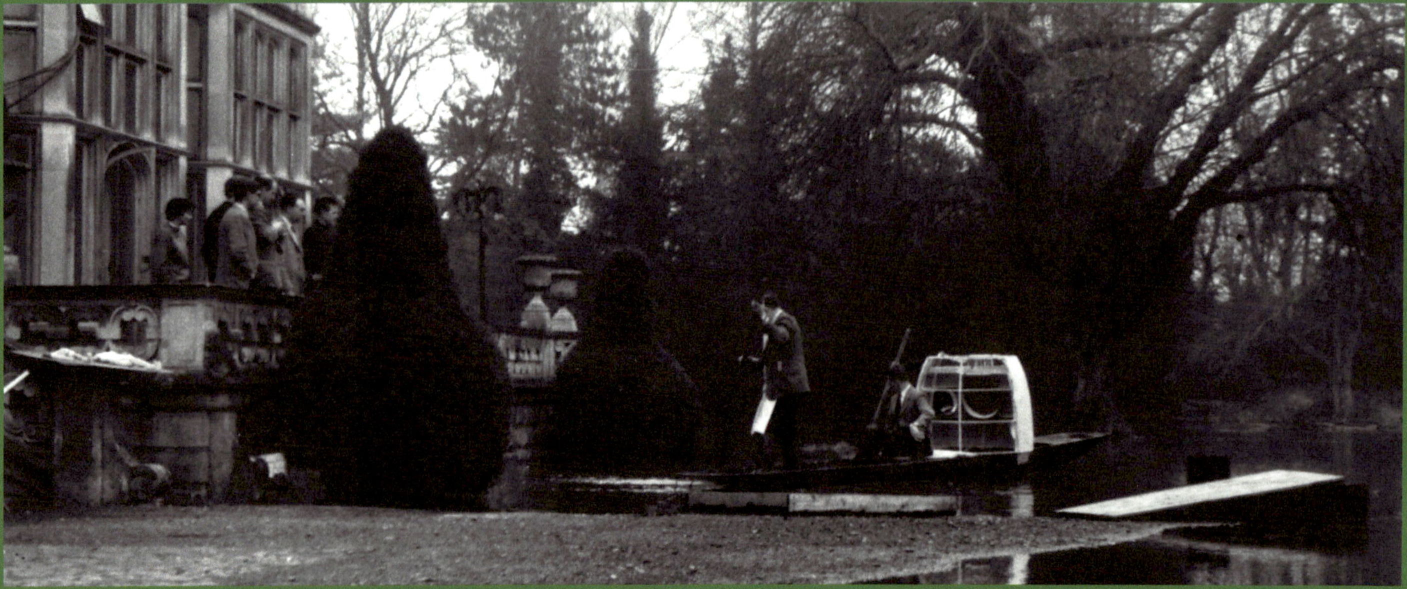

Above left: Arthur Provis films a scene with Flopsy. **Above right:** Author Roberta Leigh poses with Torchy and Pom-Pom. Despite giving them a much-needed commission, Roberta was not popular with the A.P. Films crew due to her stern and unsympathetic temperament. **Below:** During filming of *Torchy*, the banks of the Thames burst and surrounded Islet Park with water. However, the tight schedule meant filming had to continue; crew and sets were punted to and from the ballroom.

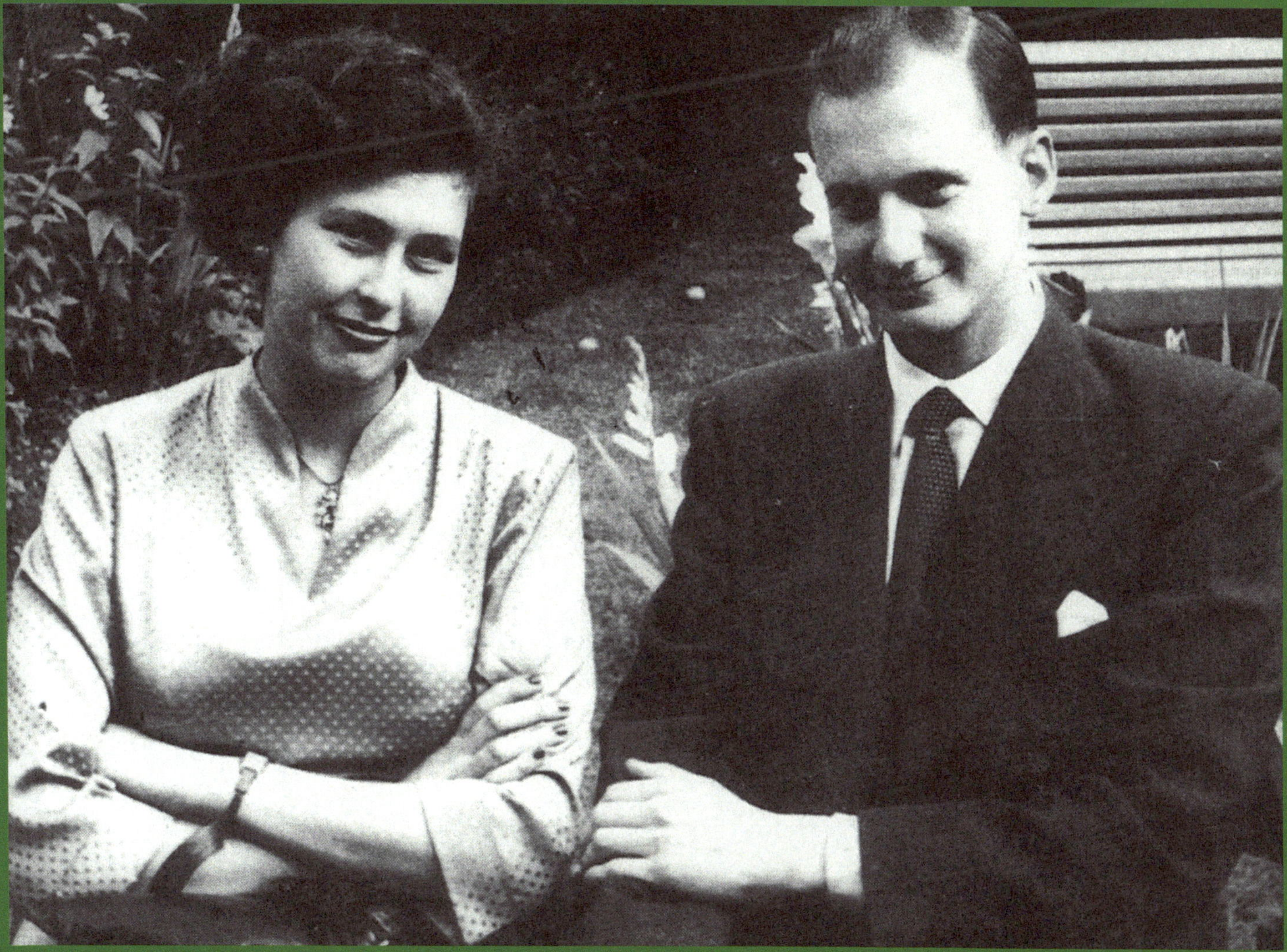

Gerry and Betty's marriage was not an easy one. In the late '50s, Gerry began and an affair with Sylvia Thamm, leading to his eventual divorce from Betty. Perhaps as a result of his turbulent upbringing, family life did not come easily to Gerry. Difficulties at home would dominate a significant portion of his life.

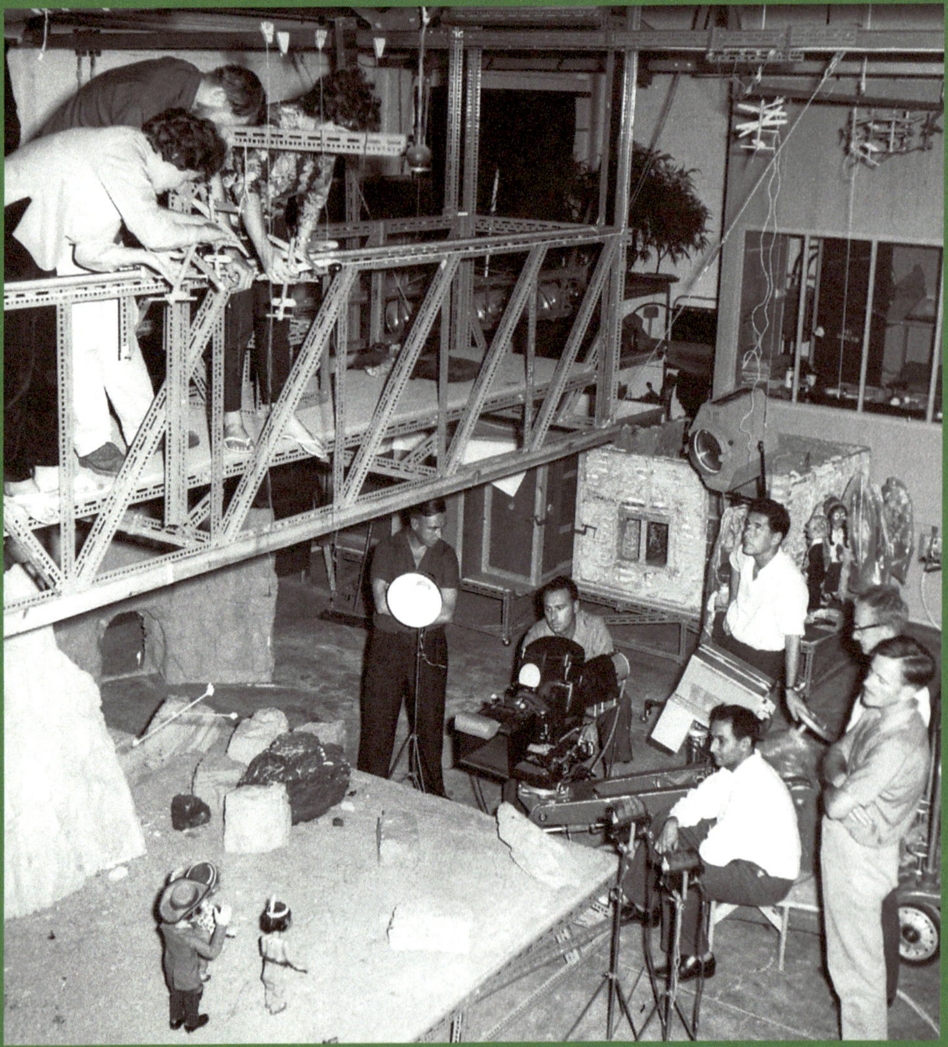

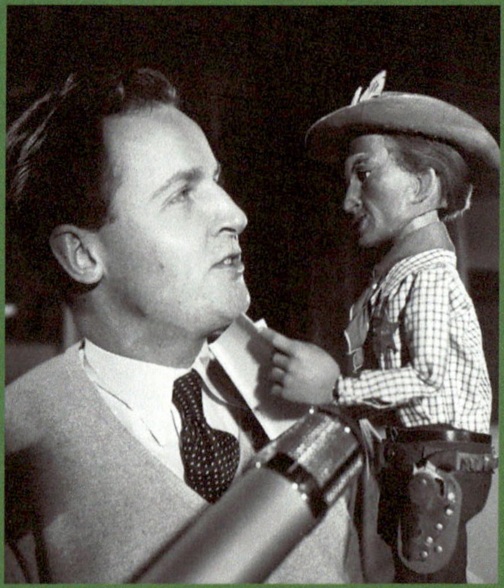

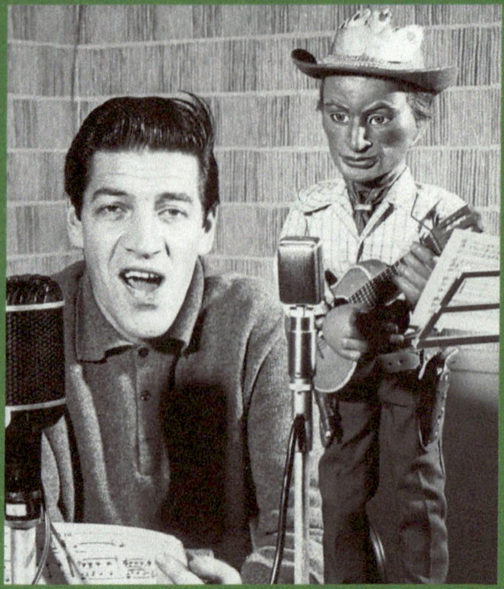

Left: Gerry was keen to become an independent producer, and in 1959 A.P. Films cut ties with Roberta and went on to produce its own series, *Four Feather Falls.* Space was limited at Islet Park, and so the team relocated to a factory unit at Ipswich Road on the Slough Trading Estate. Arthur Provis, seen operating the camera here, left APF later that year and rejoined Roberta. **Above right:** Voice artist Nicholas Parsons poses with Tex Tucker. **Below right:** When it came to Tex's singing voice, a large chunk of the series' budget was spent procuring the Bing Crosby-like tones of '50s star Michael Holiday.

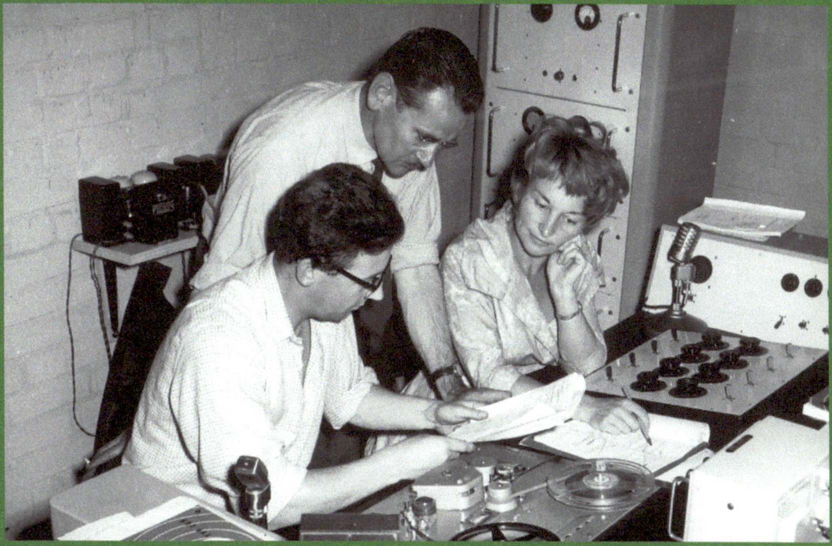

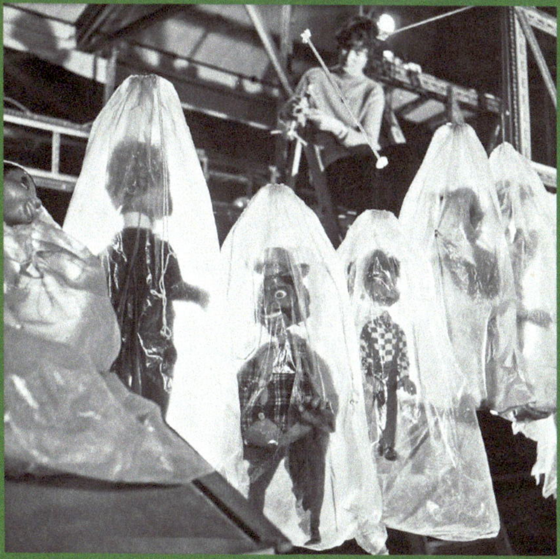

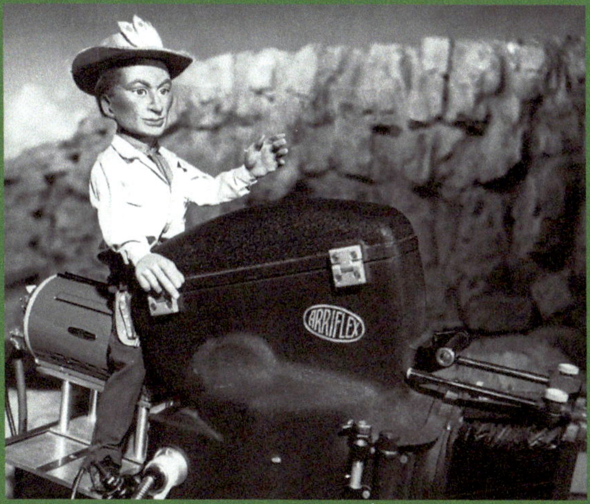

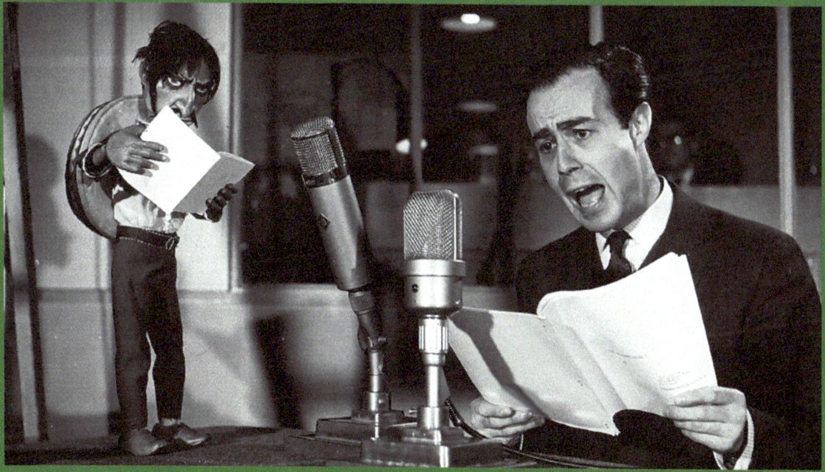

Above left: *Four Feather Falls* marked the arrival of what Gerry would later dub 'Supermarionation': pre-recorded dialogue was converted into electrical impulses that drove a solenoid in the puppet head, allowing the lips to move in sync. Here, David Elliott, Reg Hill (standing) and Sylvia Thamm mark a script at the lip sync console in the control room. **Above right:** The marionette cast hang in protective bags, awaiting their call. **Below left:** Another APF invention: Tex Tucker poses with an Arriflex film camera hooked up to a Pye Lynx video camera, which relayed what was being filmed to studio monitors for all to see. **Below right:** Talented voice actor David Graham poses with Fernando. He'd later voice Parker, Brains and many others.

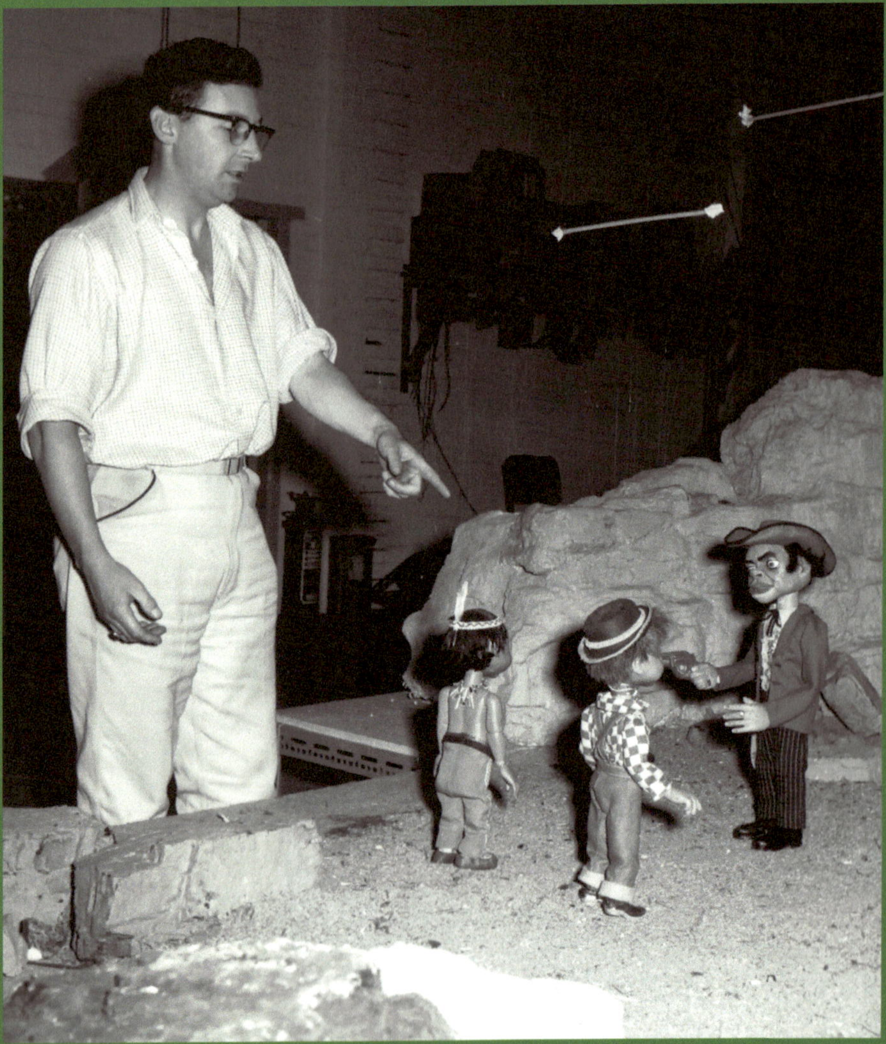

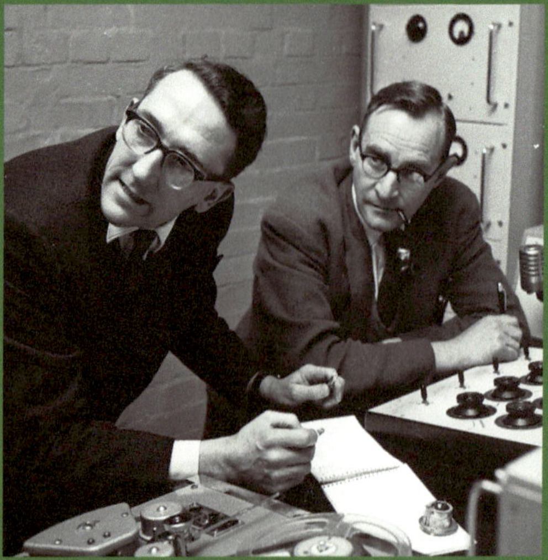

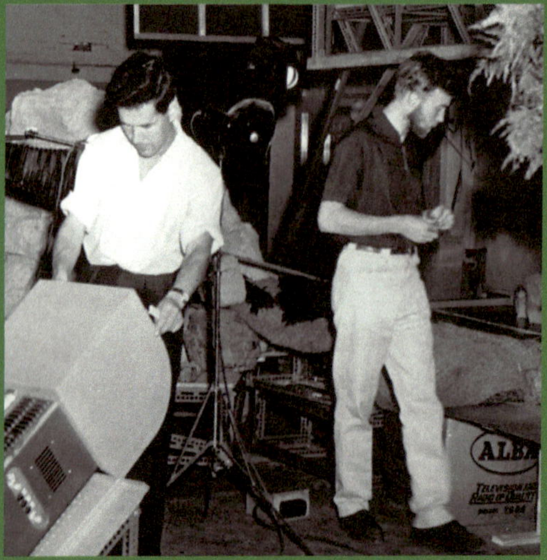

Left: David Elliott directs the action for the episode 'Trapped'. **Above right:** John Taylor (left) and Roland Wright, the designers of the 'Electronic Natterer' lip-sync system, work on the equipment. **Below right:** Cameraman John Read (left) and puppeteer Roger Woodburn prepare for the next shot.

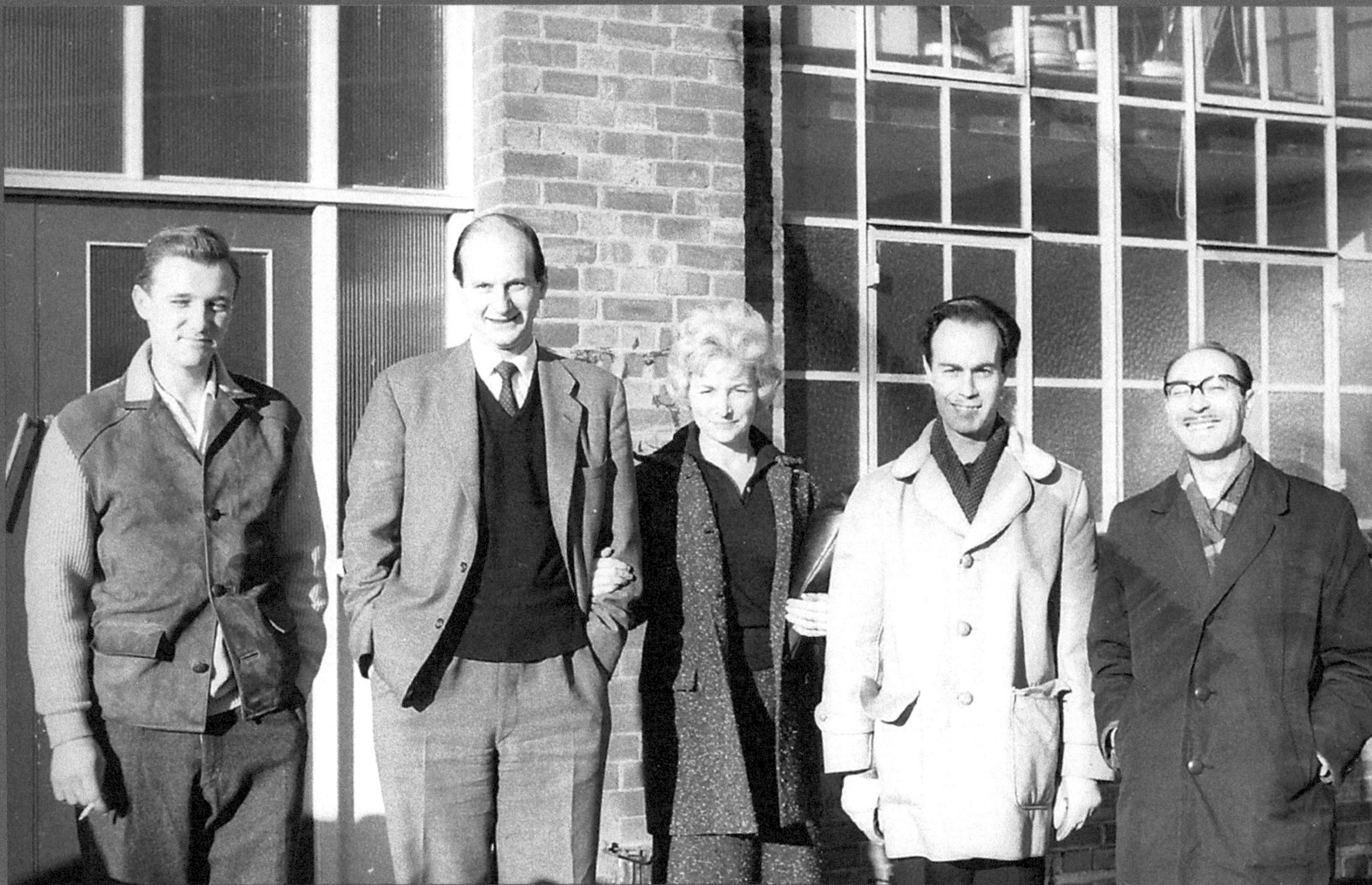

The 1960s, the decade that was to define Gerry's career, started with difficulty. Despite great publicity for *Four Feather Falls* at the beginning of 1960, Granada Television refused to fund any further puppet series from APF. The team scrabbled around to find any work they could, producing a low-budget B-feature called *Crossroads to Crime*, as well as a series of commercials and a travel film for Blue Cars Travel and Nicholas Parsons.

By the summer of 1960, it was becoming clear that the writing was on the wall. At the eleventh hour, a friend of Gerry's, Frank Sherwin Green, helped effect a meeting with ATV mogul Lew Grade. Lew saw potential in this small, unlikely group of filmmakers, and a historic partnership was formed. APF was saved from liquidation, and a golden era of filmmaking began.

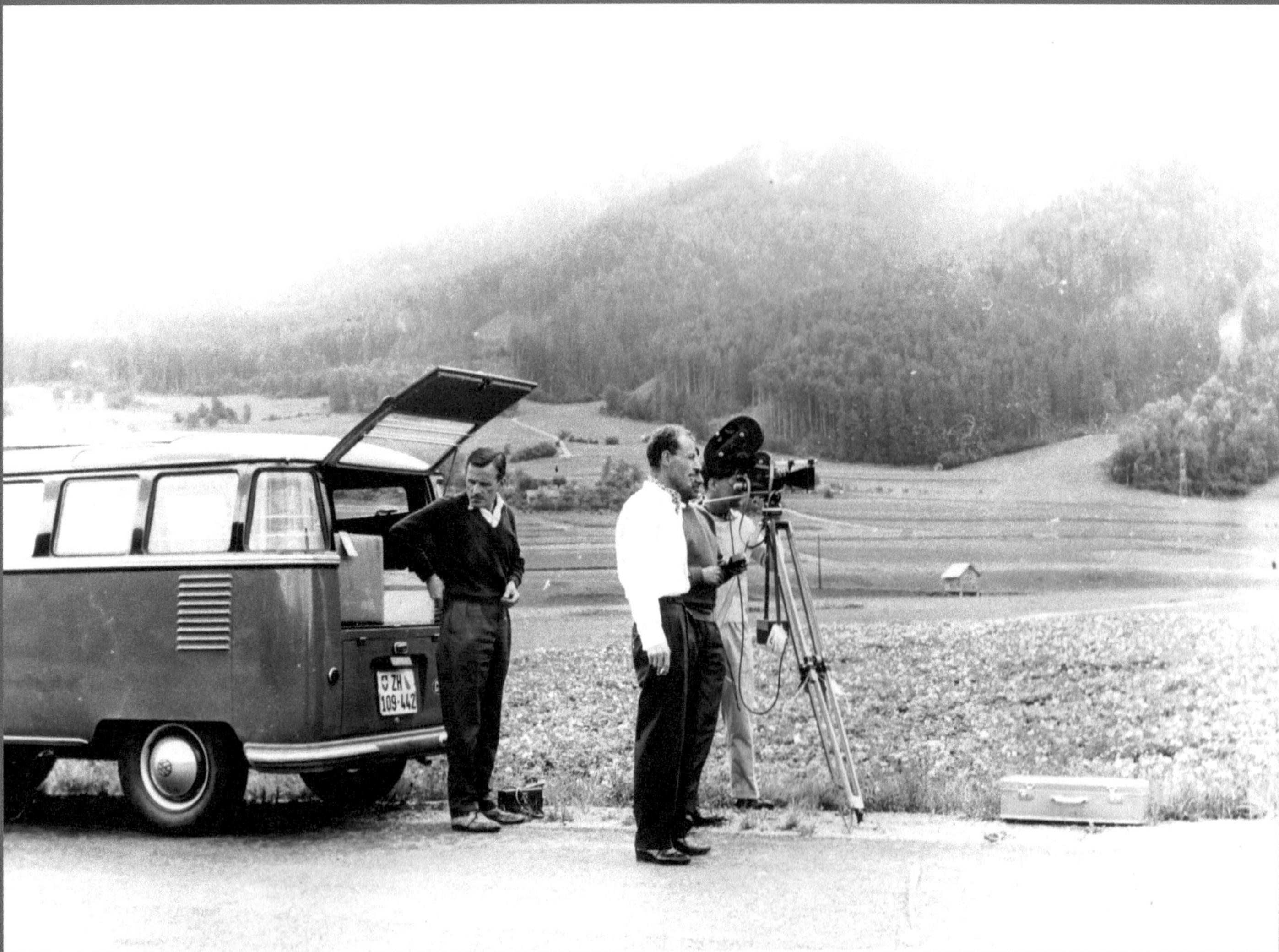

Previous: Gerry and Sylvia outside the Ipswich Road studios with the voice cast from *Supercar*'s second series: Graydon Gould (far left), David Graham and Cyril Shaps. **Above:** The crew films on location in mainland Europe for the Blue Cars travel documentary with Nicholas Parsons.

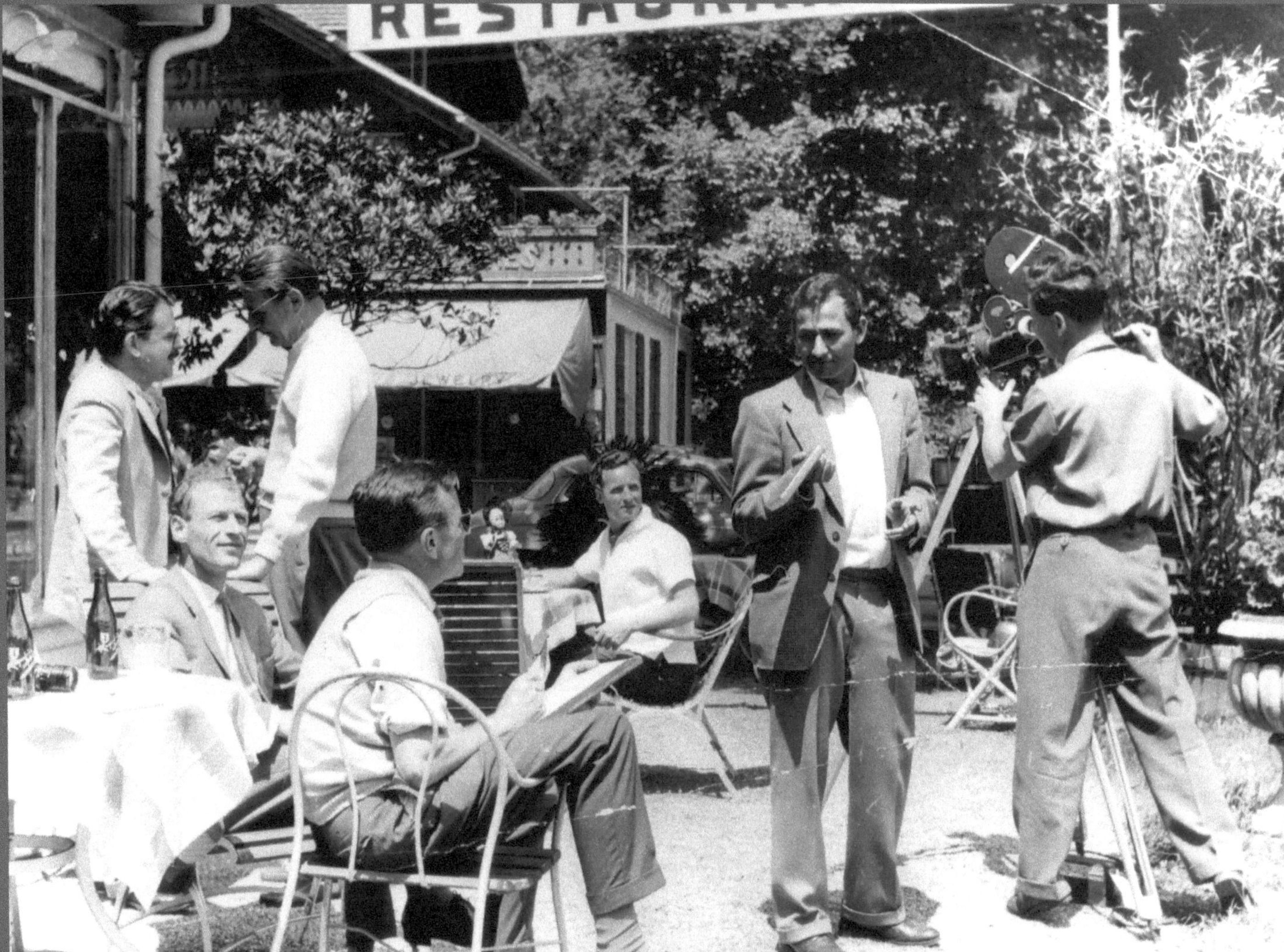

The crew gather whilst John Read sets up the next shot with Nicholas Parsons. In addition to the film, APF also shot an admag and three commercials for Blue Cars. One of these commercials, 'Martians', went on to win the 1961 Television Mail Grand Prix award for best advert and marked the beginning of Gerry's lesser-known career in advertising. A.P. Films set up a subsidiary, Arrow Productions, to produce further commercials.

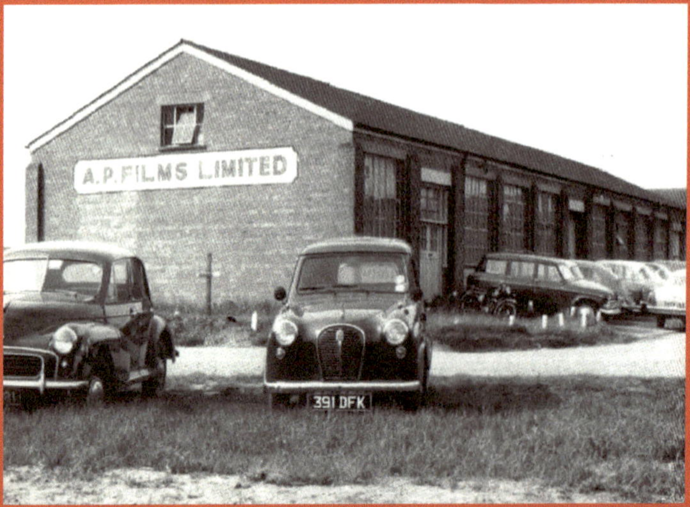

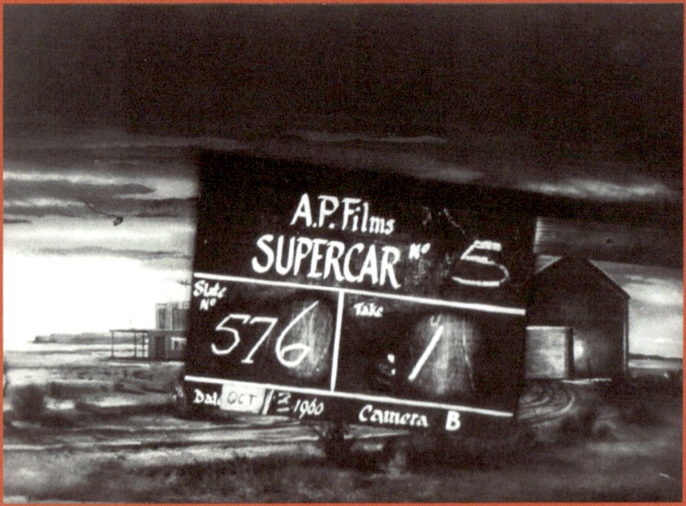

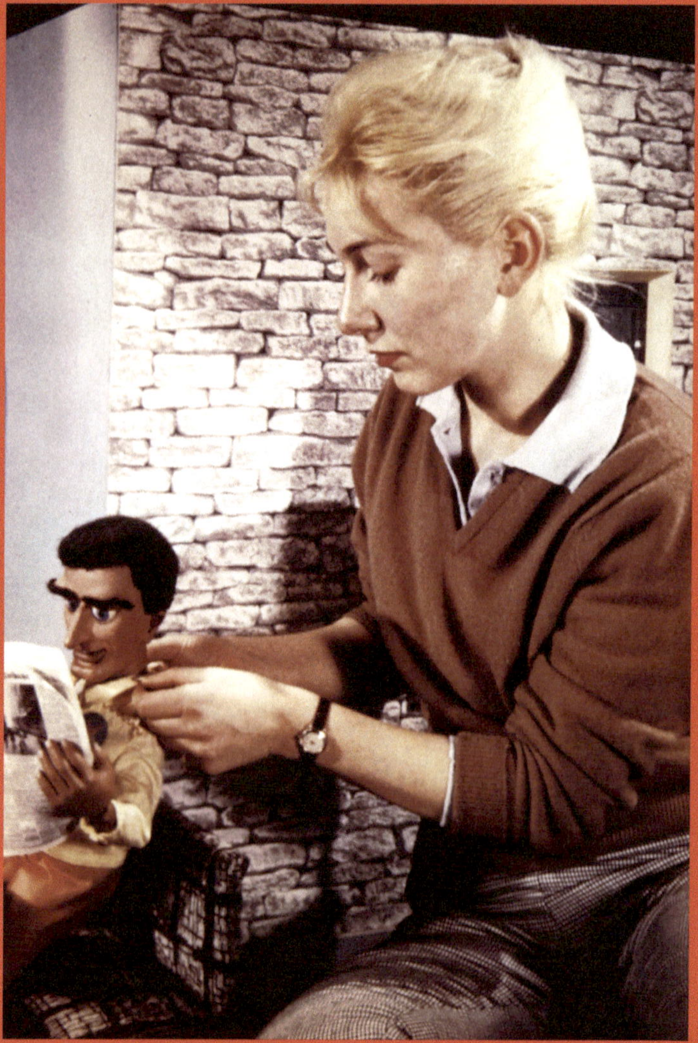

Above left: The factory unit at Ipswich Road, Slough. **Below left:** *Supercar* commenced filming in September 1960. A stipulation of the finance agreement was that the series would be ready to air within six months, leaving APF with a punishing schedule. **Right:** Puppeteer Yvonne Cutler adjusts Mike Mercury's collar for a shot in 'Island Incident'.

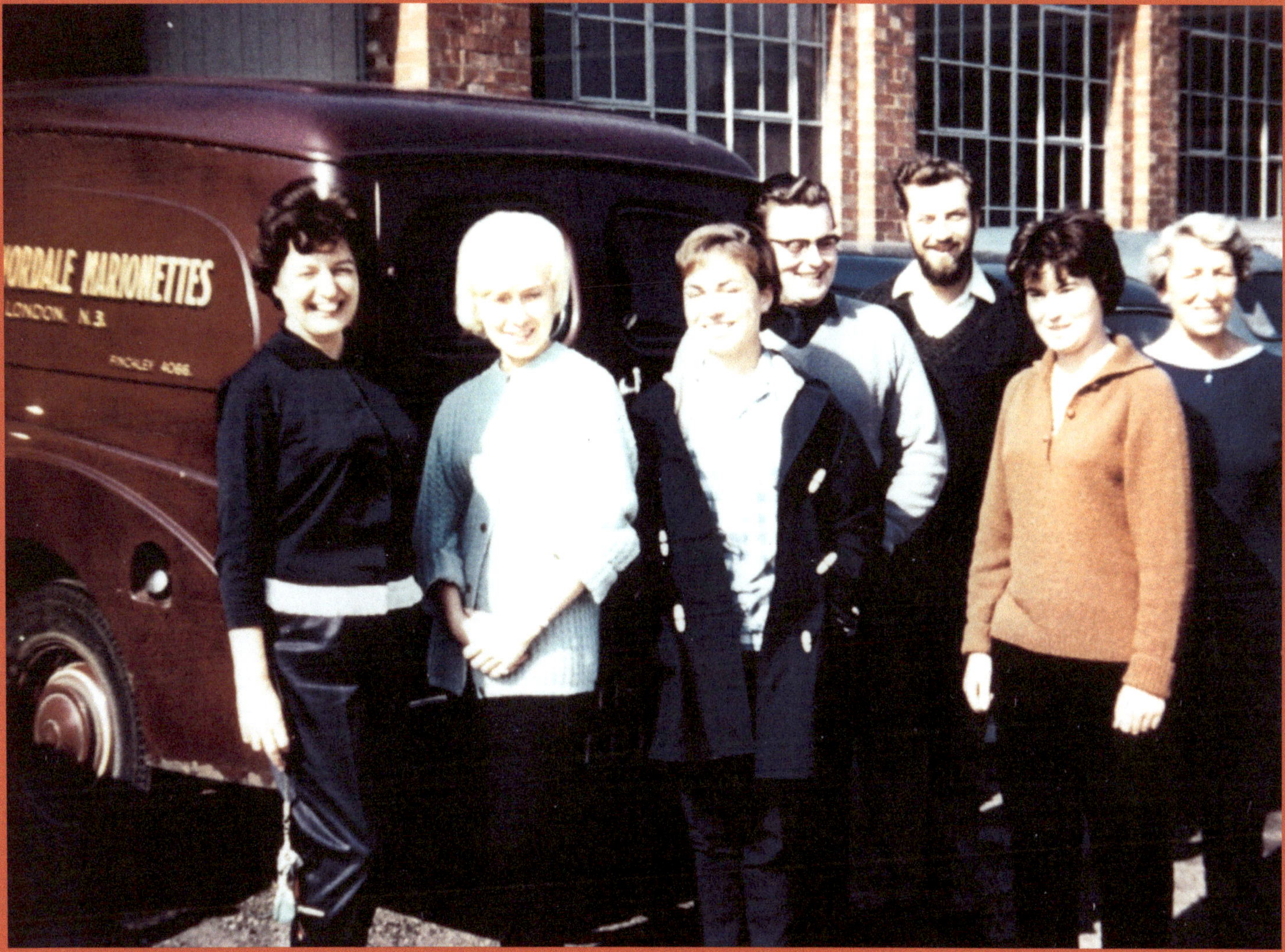

Some of the puppet crew pose for a rare colour shot outside the studios. Among them are puppeteers Christine Glanville, Yvonne Cutler, Eddie Hunter, Mary Turner and Madge Stavordale.

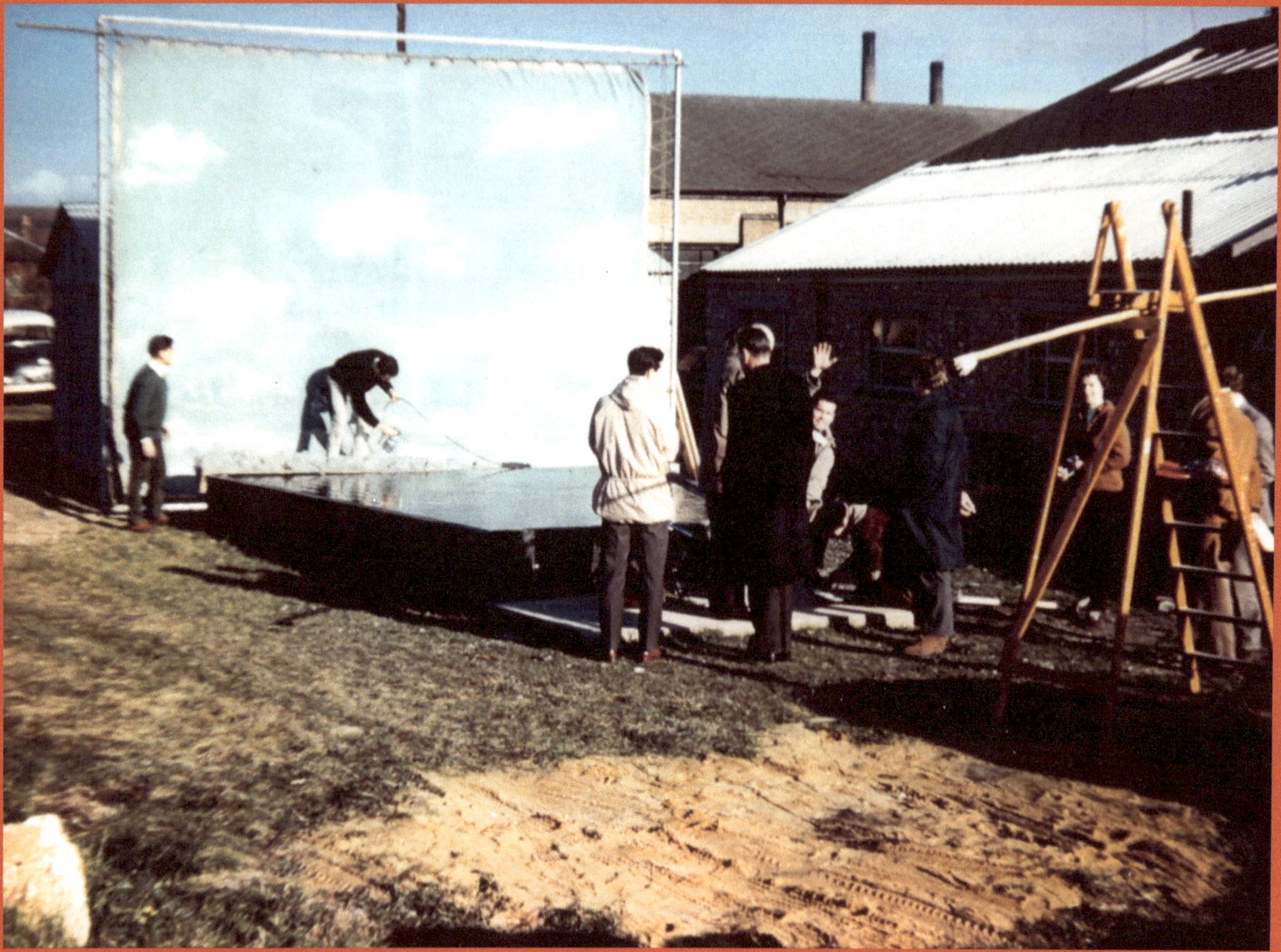

Special effects maestro Derek Meddings joined the team full time on *Supercar*. He'd been popping in to help since the early days of *Twizzle*, but from the second series of *Supercar* onwards he was the master of his own effects department. Thanks to his ingenuity, the quality of the special effects improved rapidly across subsequent series. His contribution proved to be vital to the success of A.P. Films.

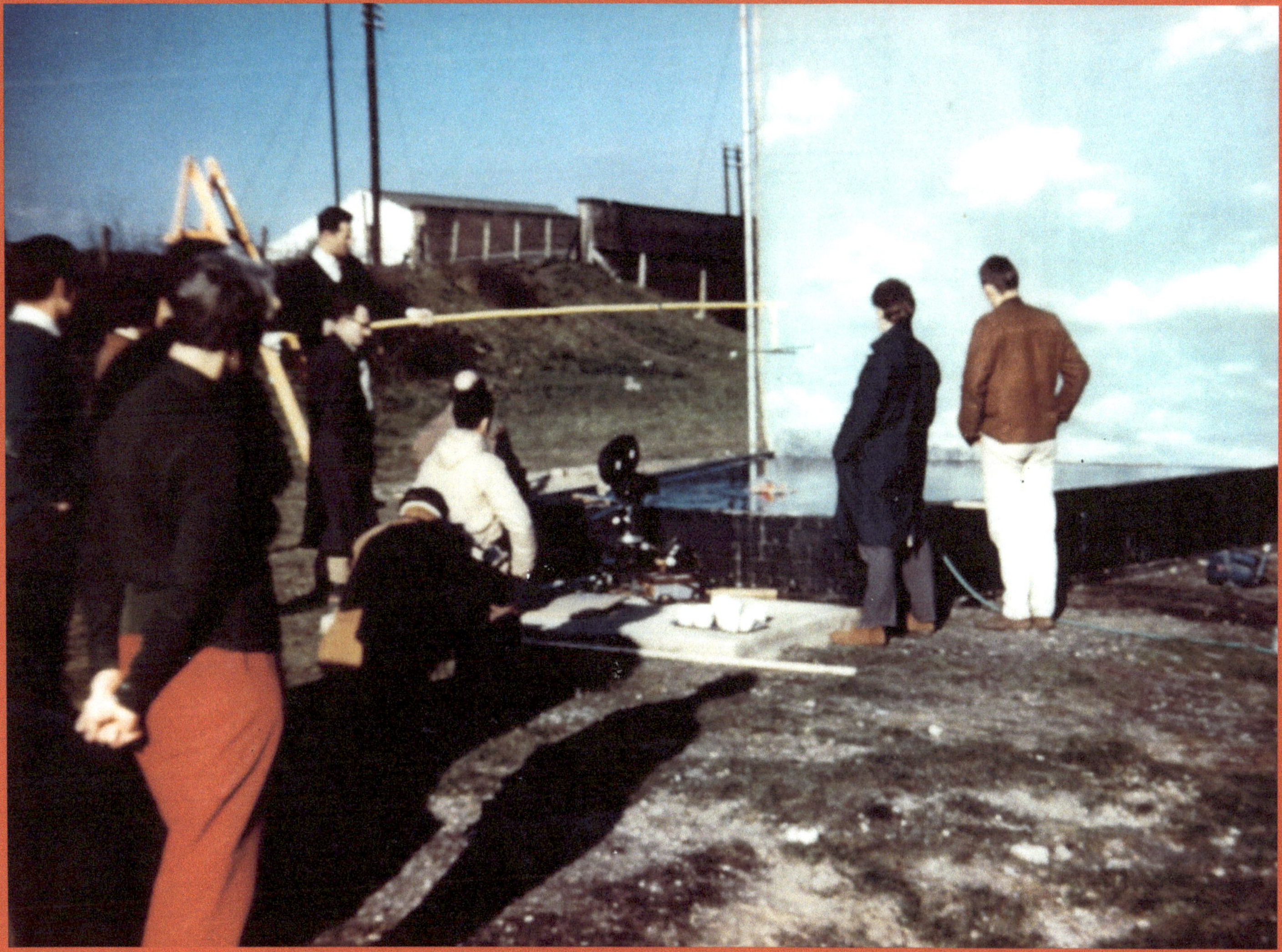

Derek operates the small model of Supercar. The brick water tank was constructed by John Read at the back of the Ipswich Road studios. Whilst filming the title sequence for *Supercar*, the traffic on the bridge came to a halt as people tried to see what was happening!

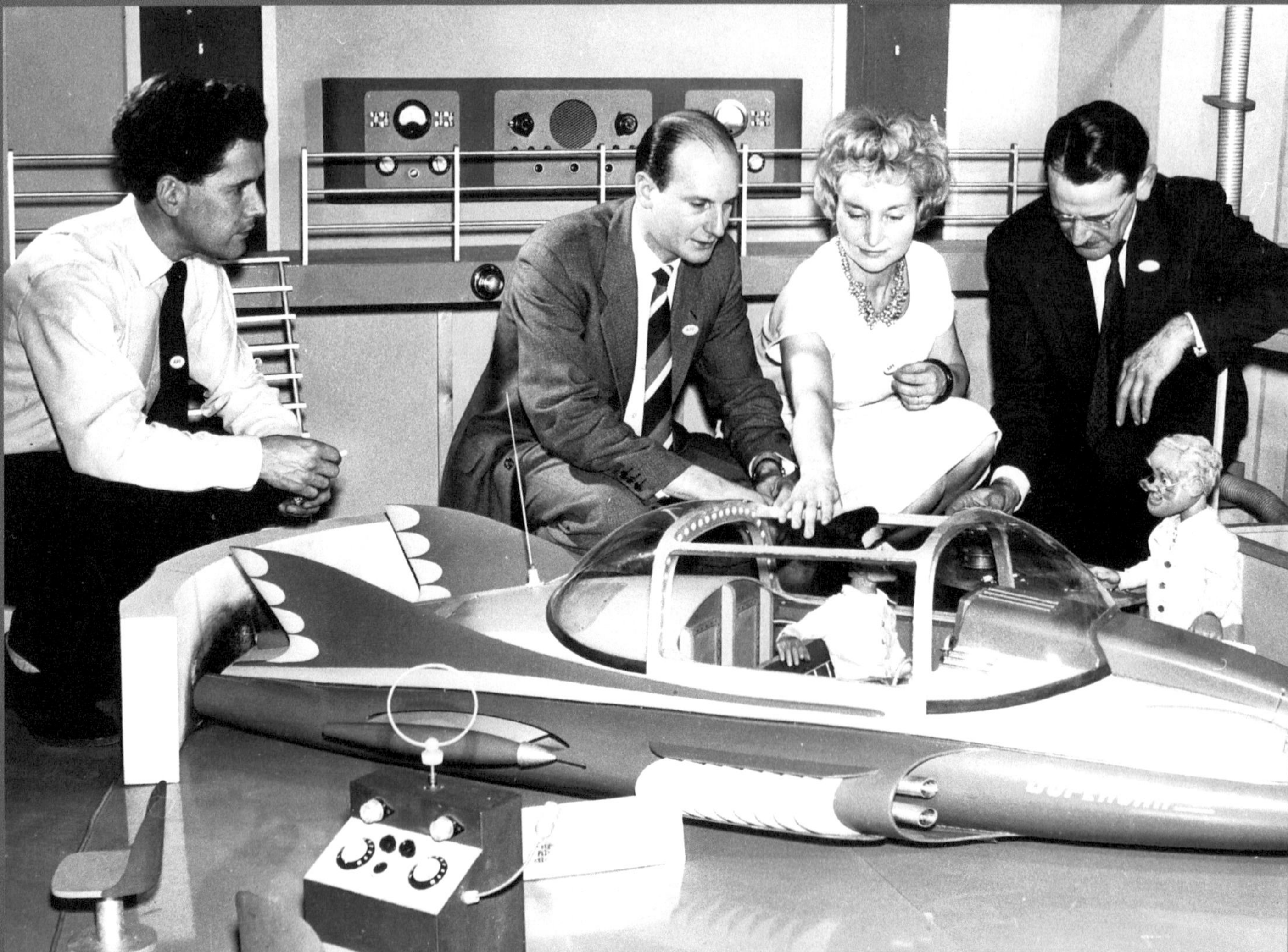

The four A.P. Films directors pose with their heroes on a press day to promote the new series. Gerry and Sylvia (centre), John Read (left) and Reg Hill.

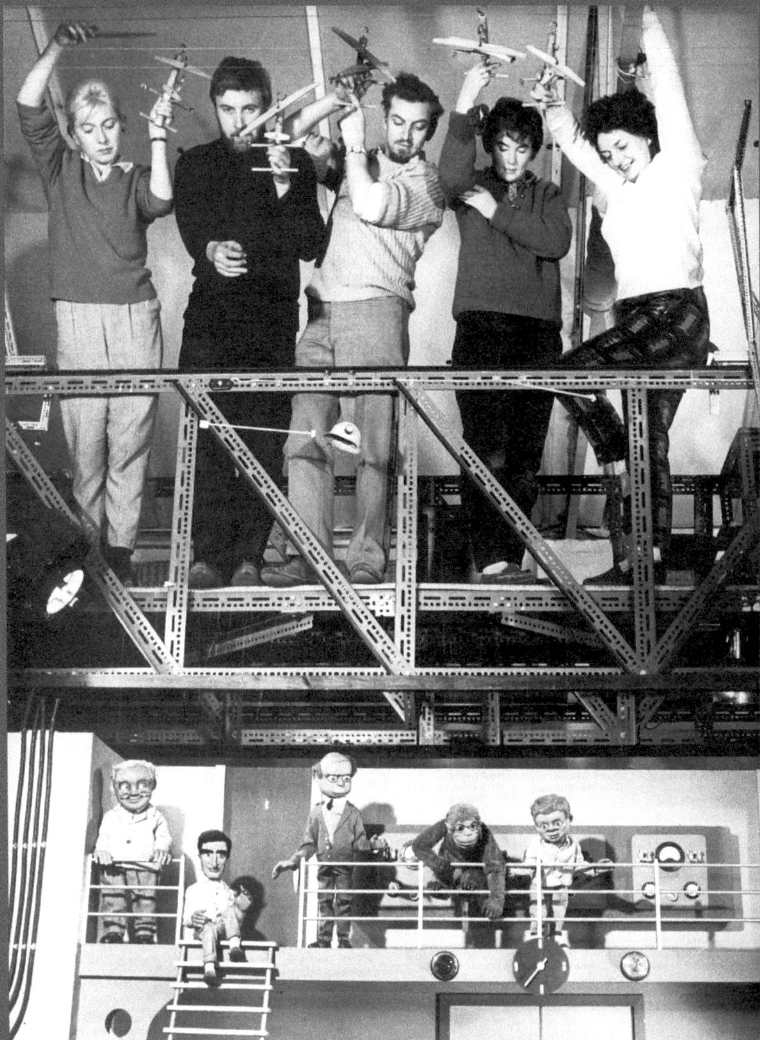

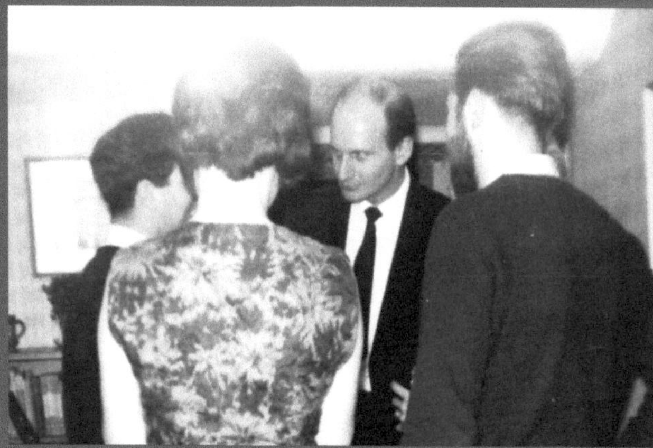

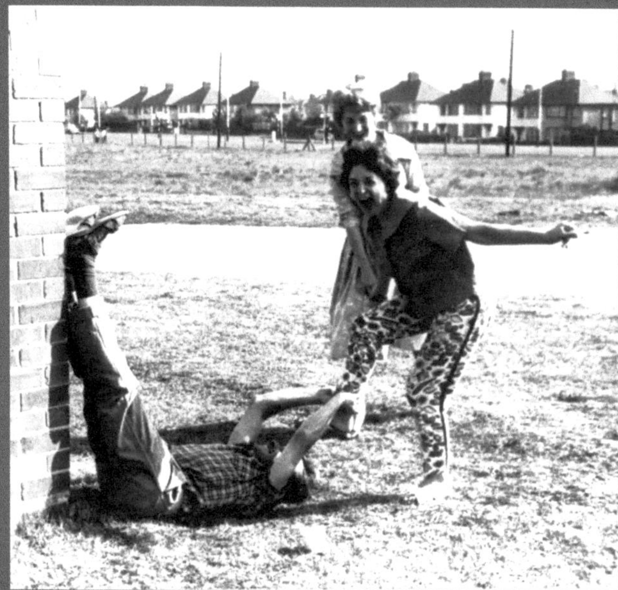

Left: Puppeteers Yvonne Cutler, Roger Woodburn, Eddie Hunter, Mary Turner and Christine Glanville pose with the *Supercar* cast. **Above right:** Gerry, Des Saunders, Roger Woodburn and an unknown woman at an APF party. **Below right:** Sylvia, Christine Glanville and Bob Bell lark about outside the studios.

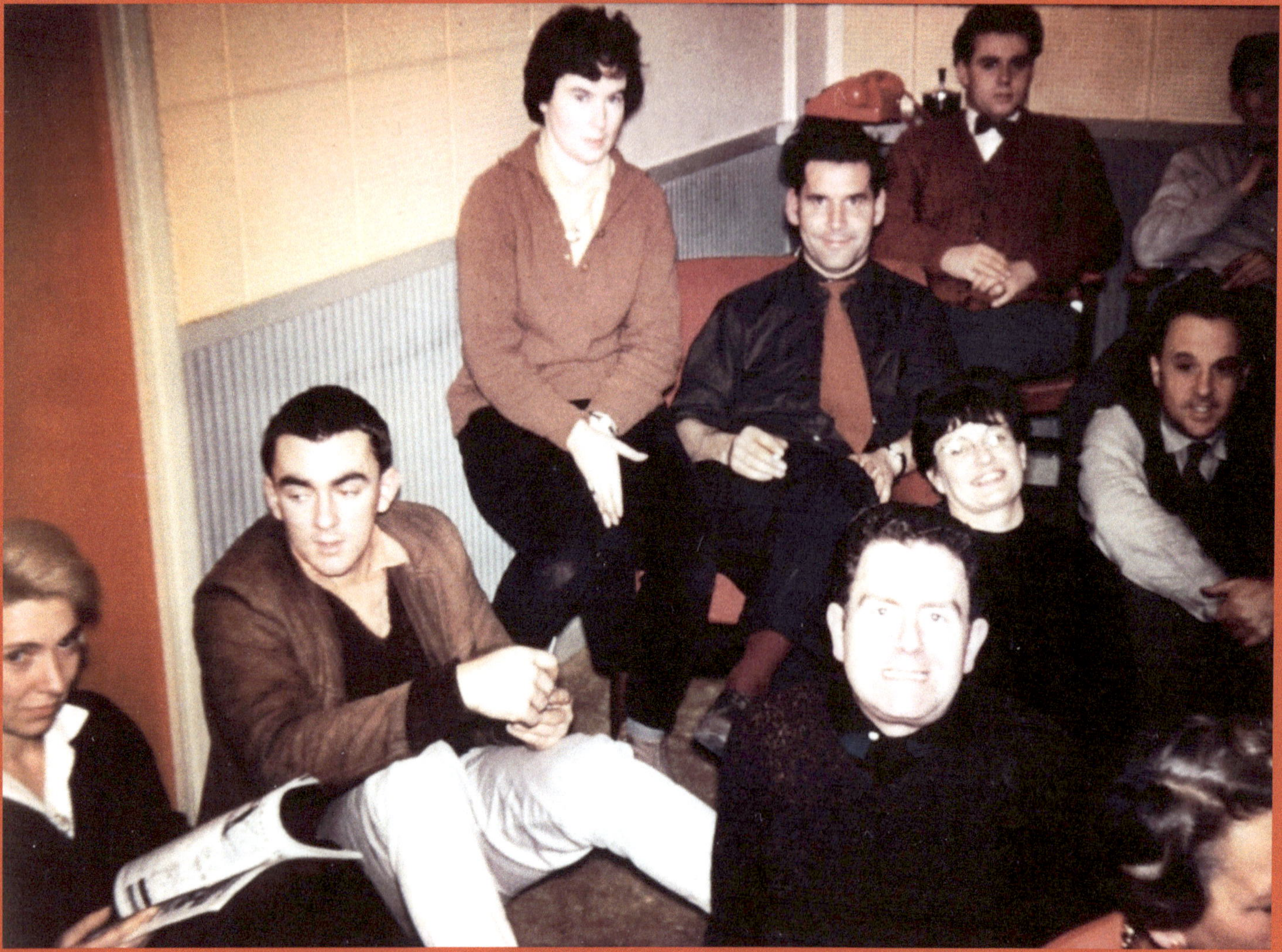

The team sit around in the projection theatre. People in this shot include Yvonne Cutler, Brian Johnson, Mary Turner, John Read, Alan Pattillo, Alan Perry and Christine Glanville.

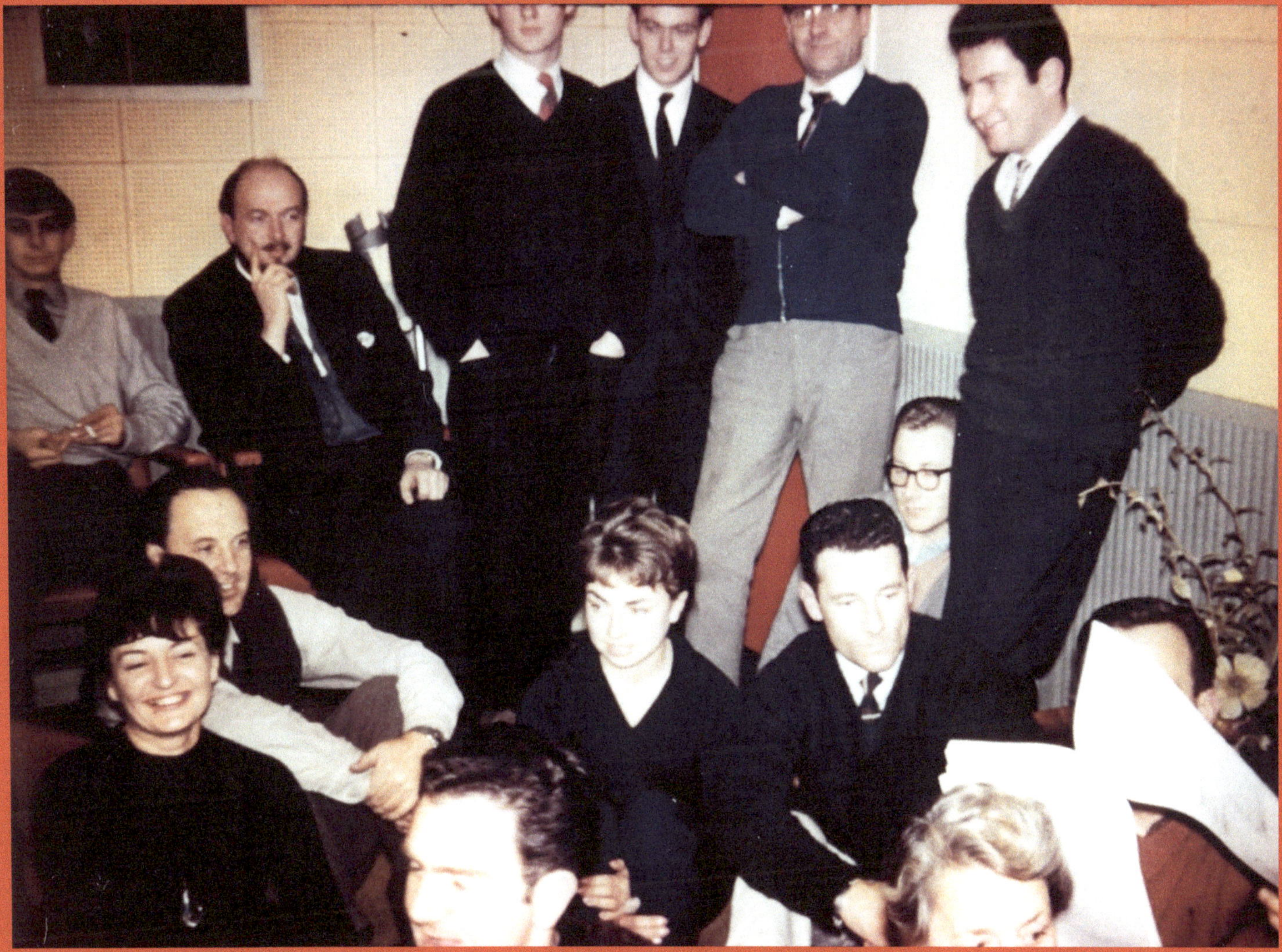

Another shot taken at the same time. Julien Lugrin sits pensively at the back, whilst Derek Meddings, seated on the floor, ponders something. Filmmaking is very rarely easy, but many of the crew remember these days as being the happiest of their lives.

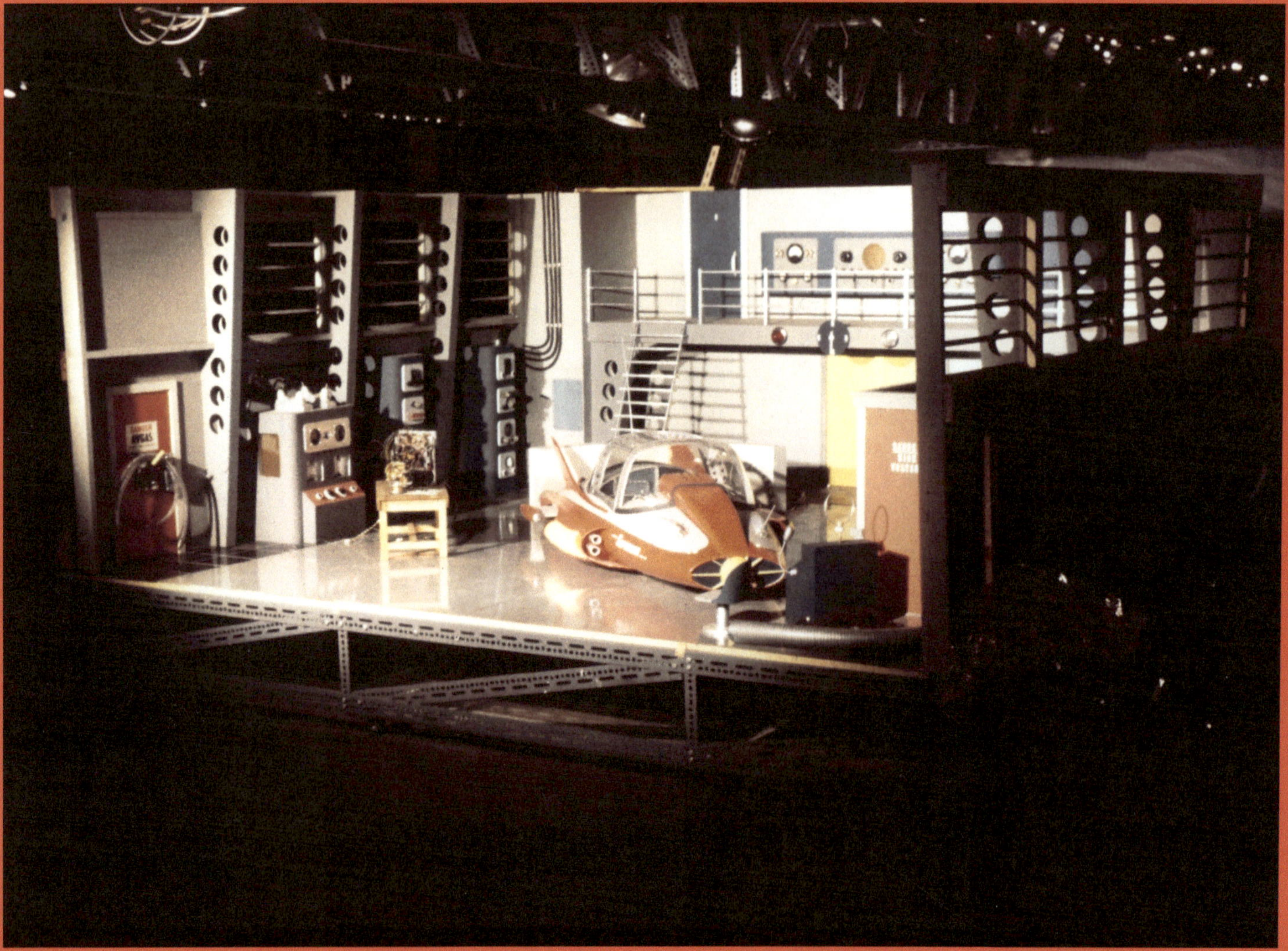

Another rare behind the scenes colour shot. This shows Supercar at home in the Black Rock laboratory. Supercar was designer Reg Hill's pride and joy, and he was notoriously protective over the very fragile puppet-sized model.

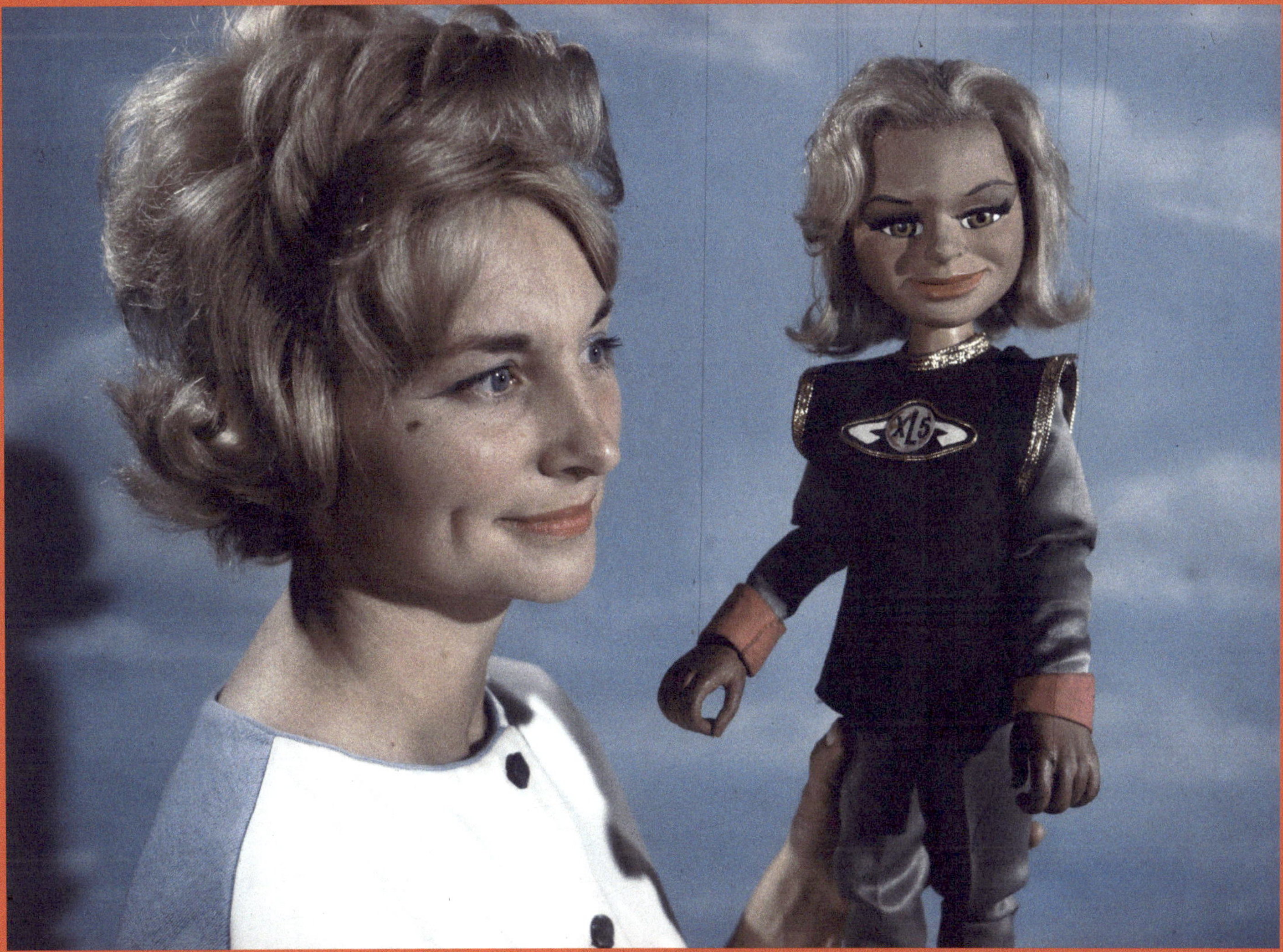

Sylvia Thamm had joined Pentagon Films as a secretary in 1956. When Gerry and Arthur formed A.P. Films, she followed them and undertook secretarial and continuity duties. She and Gerry began an affair in the late '50s and, following his divorce from Betty in 1960, the two tied the knot. Across successive series, Sylvia's role increased, and she co-created some of A.P. Films' most successful formats. Here, she poses with Venus from *Fireball XL5*, the puppet heroine that she voiced.

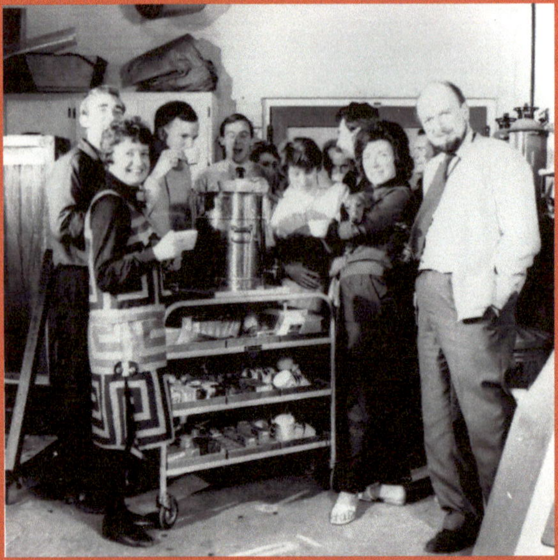

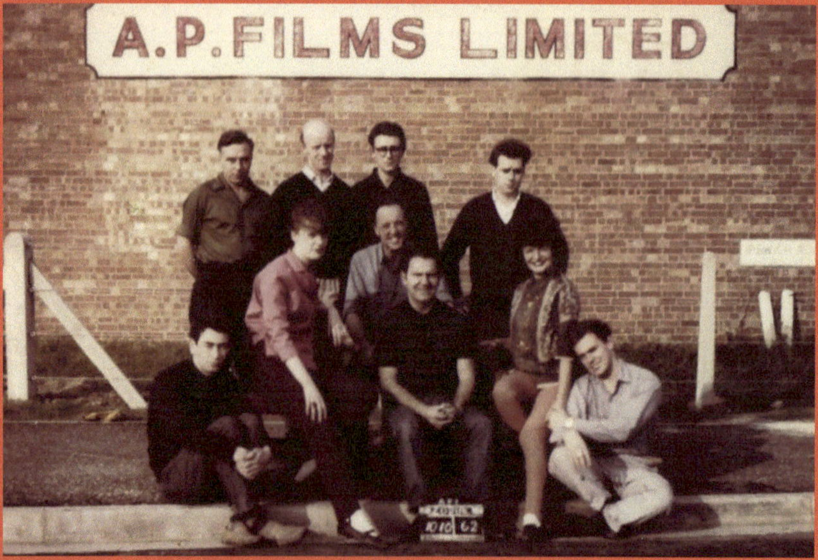

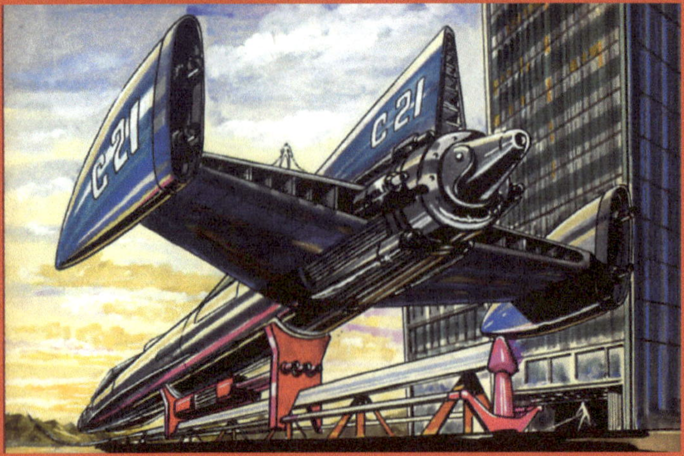

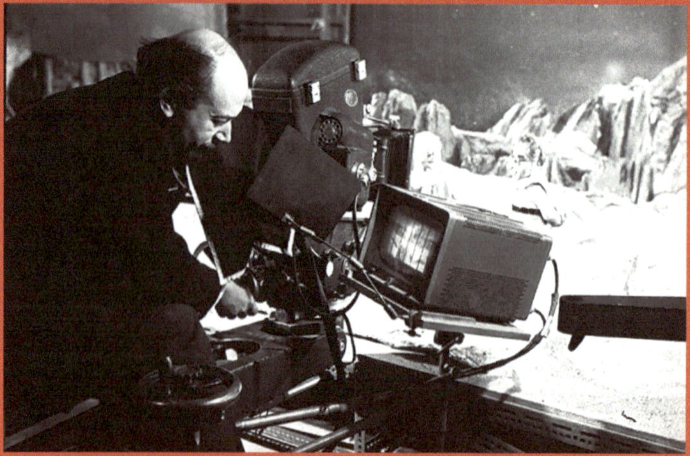

Supercar was a huge success, both at home and overseas, and so Lew Grade wanted an even bigger and better brand new series. The team commenced filming on *Fireball XL5* in 1962. **Above left:** Tea time! A much needed break for the crew. **Above right:** Some of the team pose for a group shot outside the studios. This picture even appeared in a *Fireball* episode! **Below left:** Reg Hill's concept design for Fireball XL5, originally named Century 21. **Below right:** Camera Operator Julien Lugrin lines up the next shot. As a result of polio, Julien was unable to walk unaided. He found working on the puppet series a joy, as the miniature sets were easier for him to light.

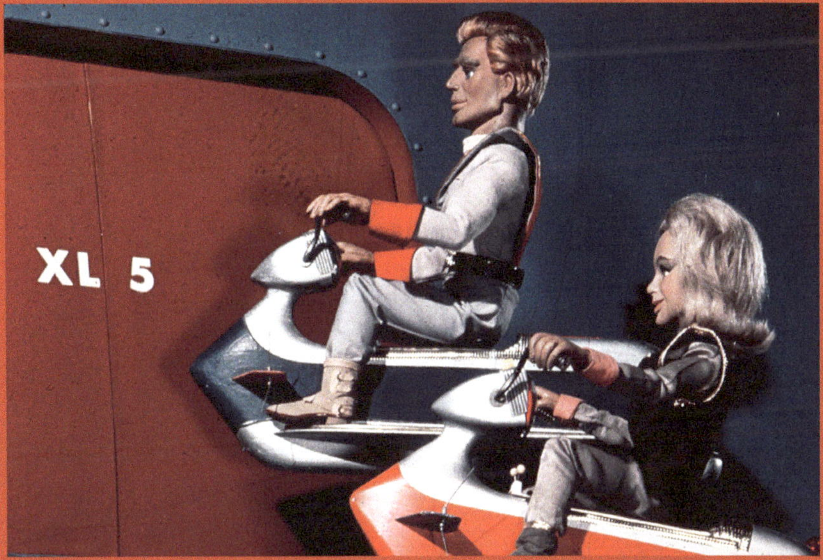

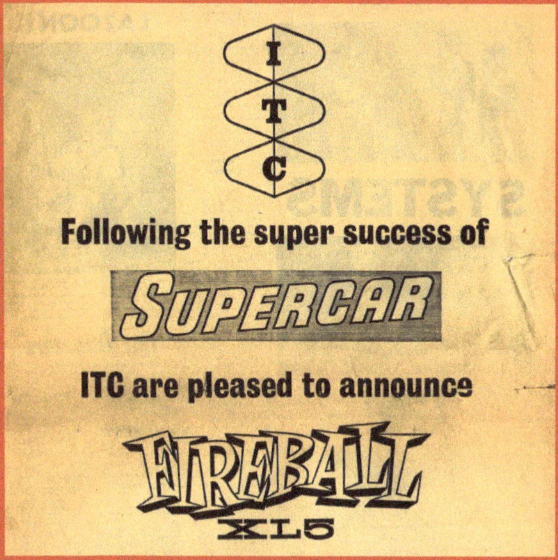

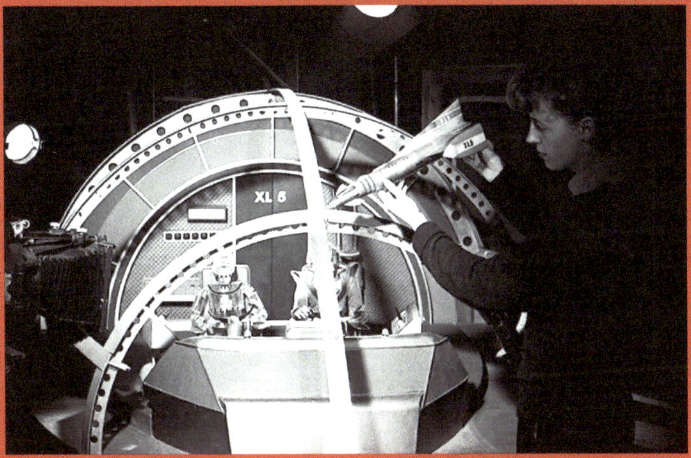

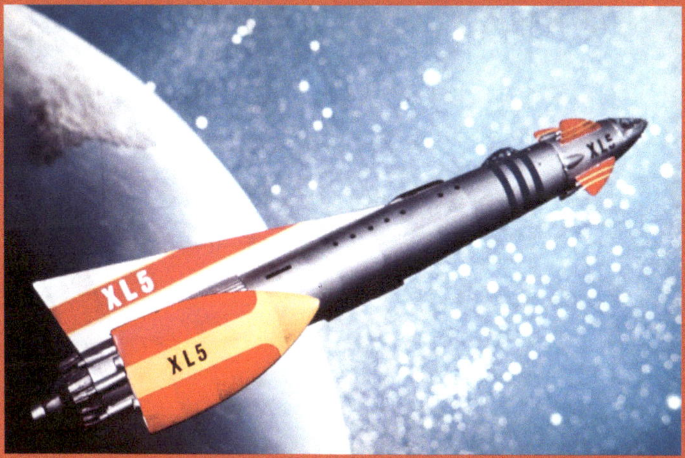

Above left: Gerry was always looking for ingenious ways to avoid the puppets walking. Here, Steve Zodiac and Venus use their Jetmobiles. **Above right:** An advert announcing the new series. **Below left:** Puppeteer Judith Shutt poses with the model Fireball XL5 and the puppet-sized cockpit set. **Below right:** The titular spacecraft.

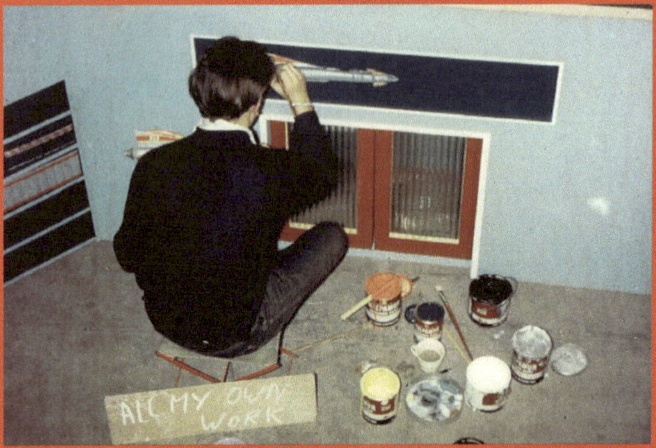

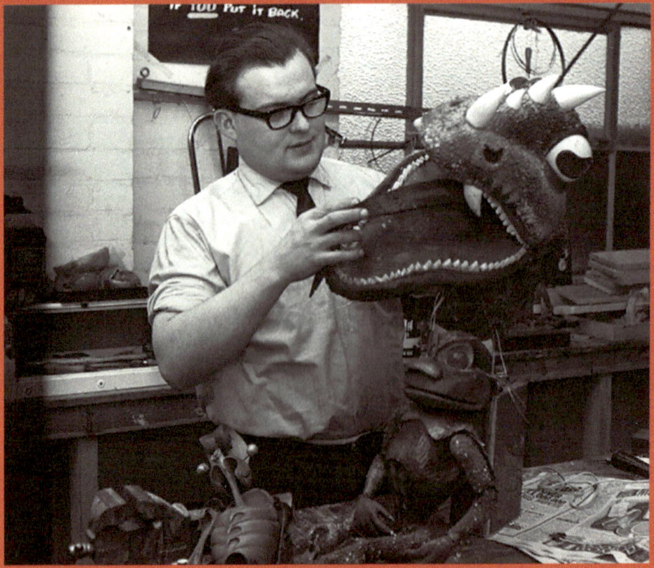

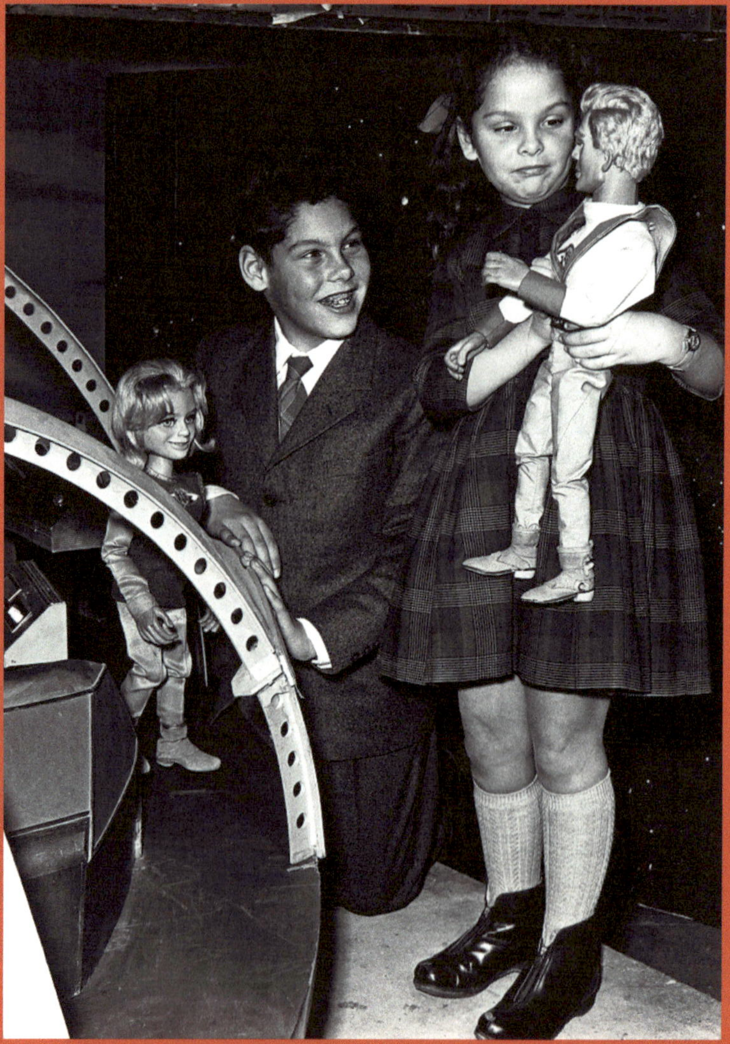

Above left: A set builder toils away. **Below left:** John Blundall examines the head of the Space Monster. Note the Aquaphibian from 'XL5 to H_2O' and the villainous Plant Man from Space on the bench. **Right:** During production of 'Ghosts of Space', band leader Edmundo Ros visited with his children (pictured).

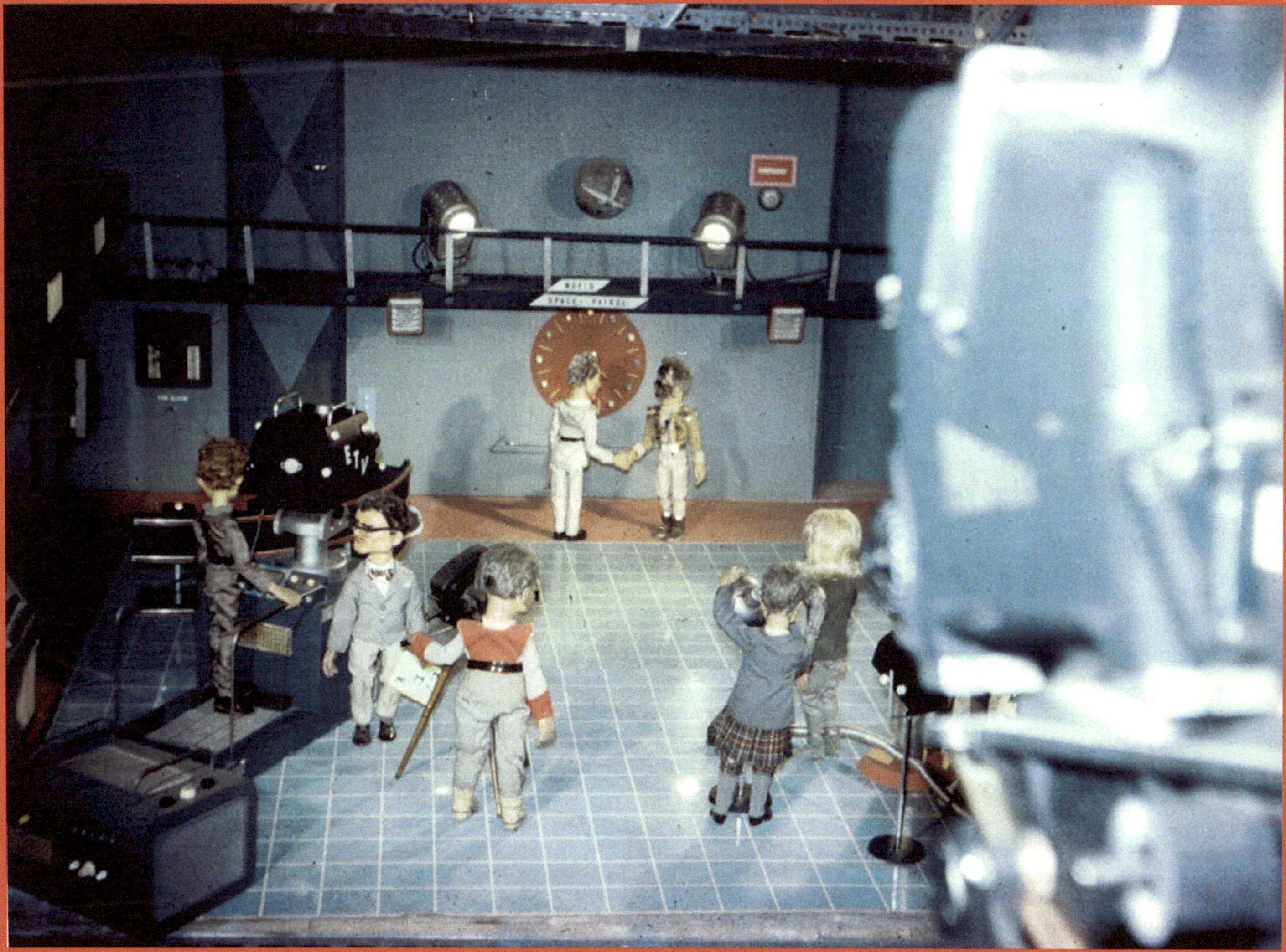

A rare behind the scenes colour shot from 'Space City Special'.

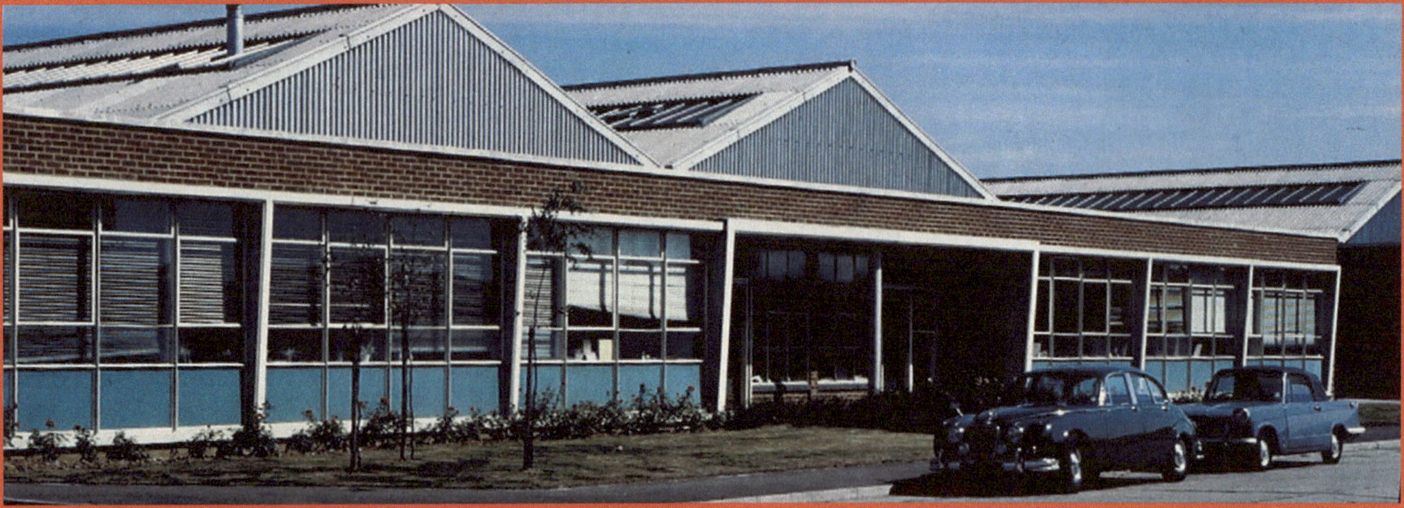

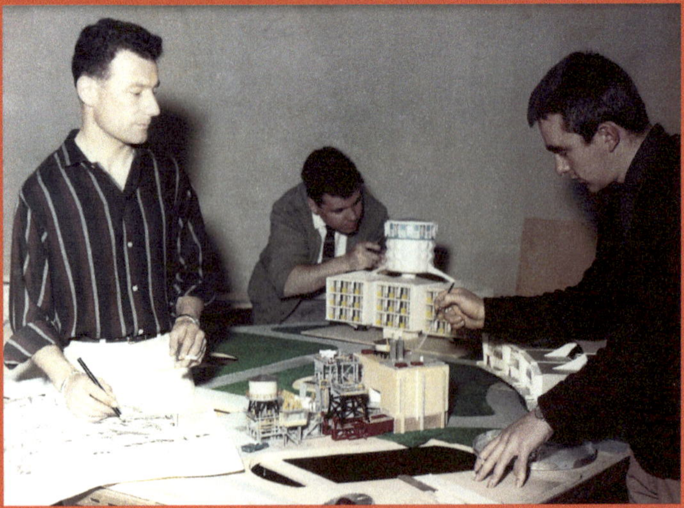

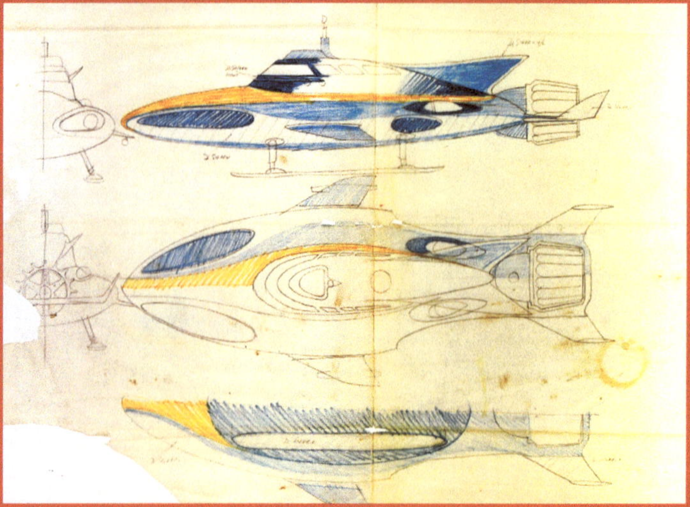

Fireball XL5 was an even bigger success than *Supercar*, securing a network transmission in the USA. Lew Grade bought APF and pumped a huge amount of money into the company for its next series, *Stingray*. **Above:** APF moved to this larger factory unit on Stirling Road in Slough. **Below left:** Building Marineville (left to right): Derek Meddings, Eric Backman and Brian Johnson. **Below right:** Plans of the new hero vehicle, Stingray.

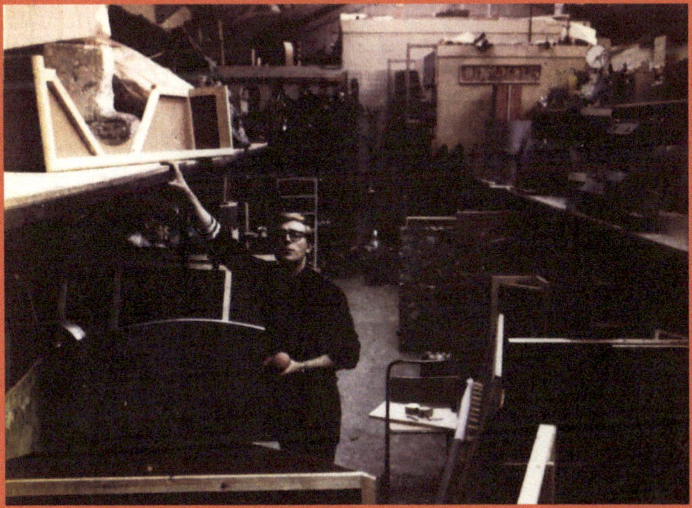

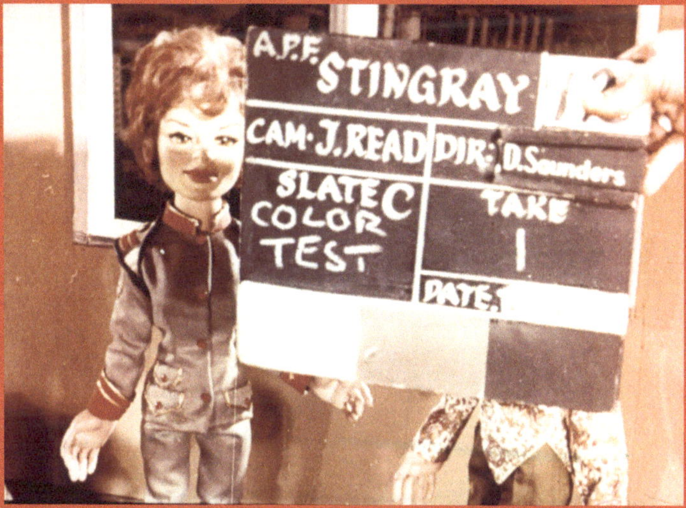

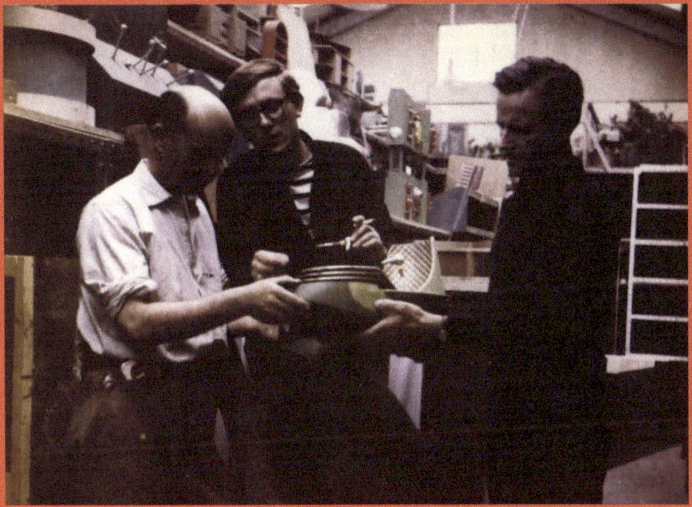

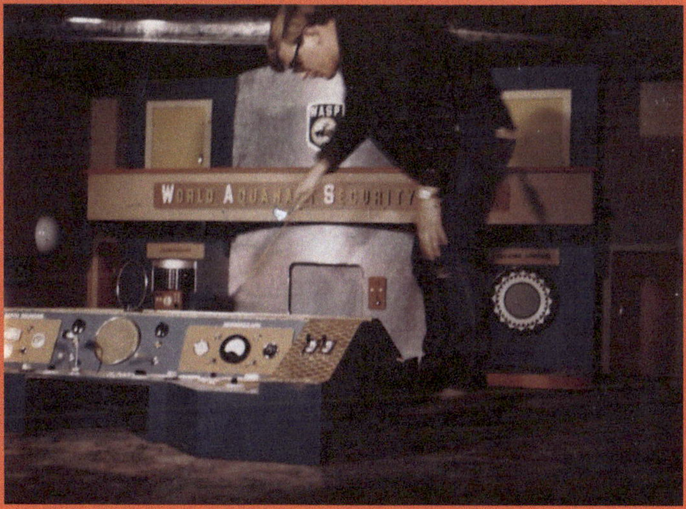

Above left: Art assistant Keith Wilson in the props store. **Above right:** *Stingray* was the first series to be filmed entirely in colour in the UK. Shooting in colour presented many challenges, and so a series of tests were undertaken to ensure optimal results. **Below left:** Art department heroes (left to right): Grenville Nott, Keith Wilson and Art Director Bob Bell in the props store with Commander Shore's hover chair. **Below right:** Keith Wilson on the Marineville Tower set.

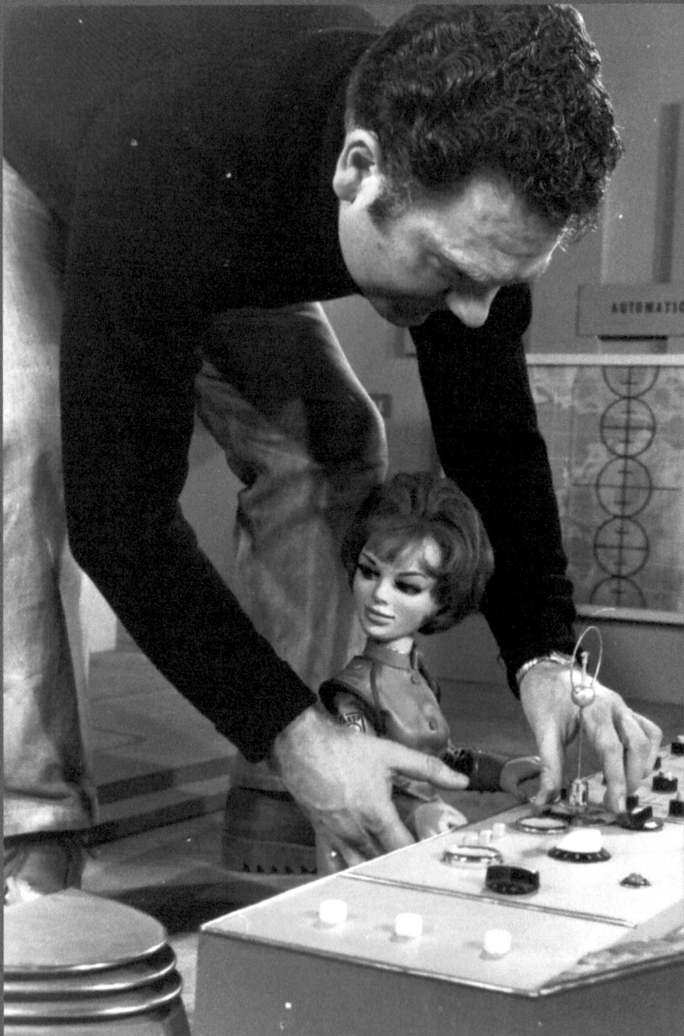

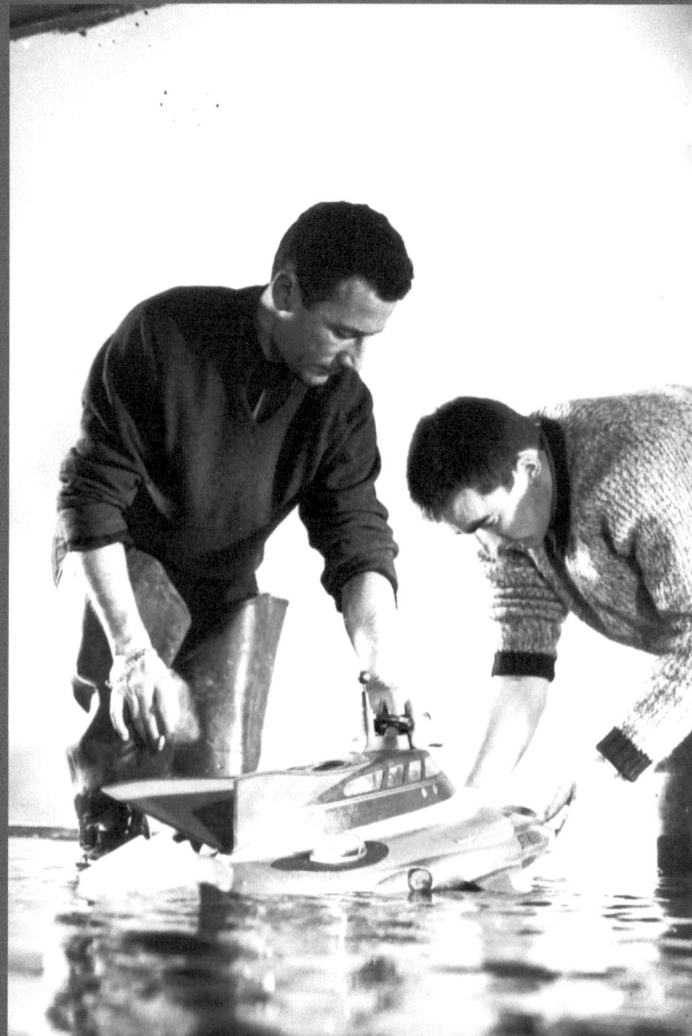

Left: Alan Pattillo helps Atlanta find the correct pose. **Right:** Special effects supremos Derek Meddings (left) and Brian Johnson set up a shot with the large model of Stingray.

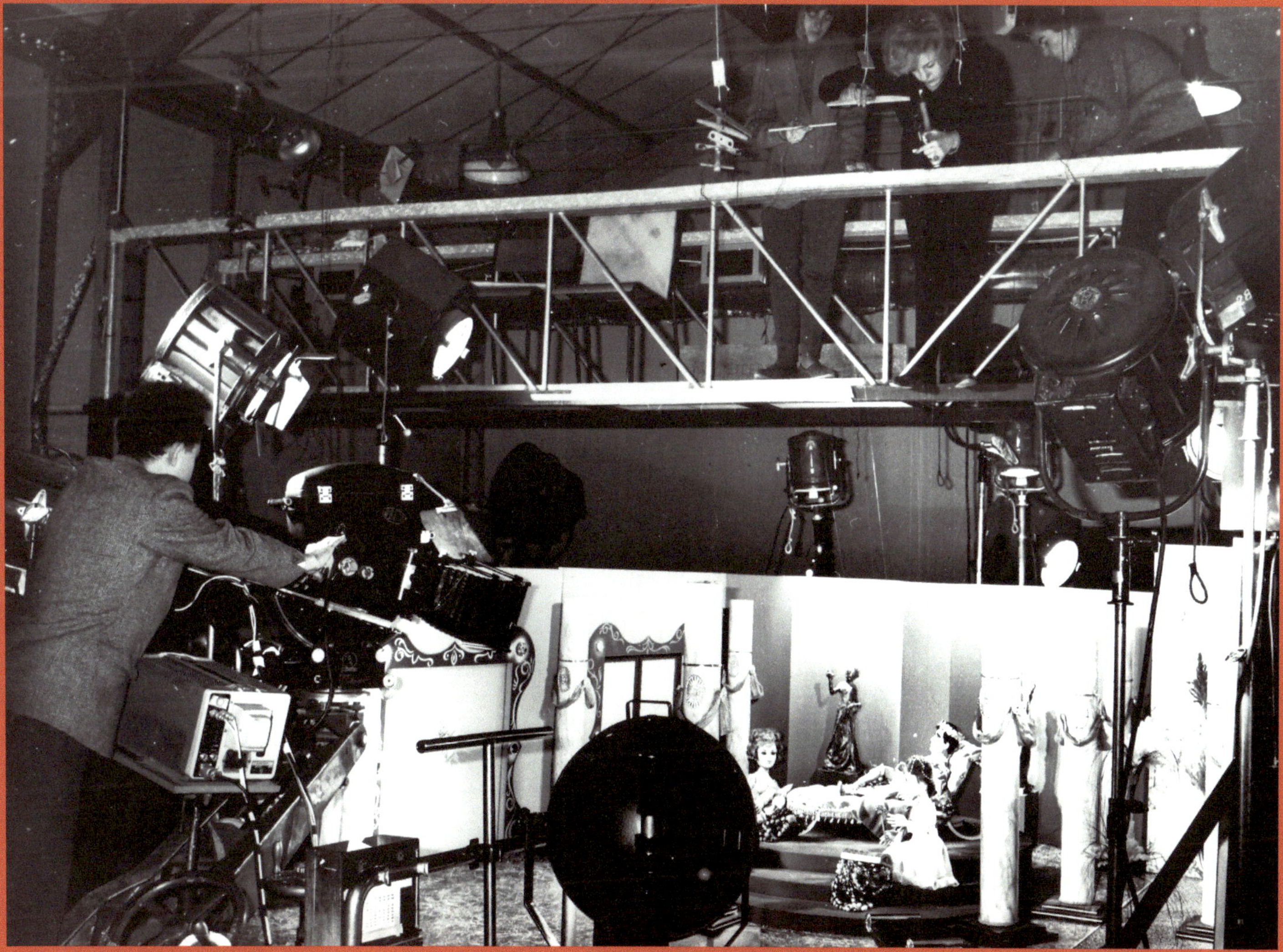

Filming Troy's palace for the episode 'Raptures of the Deep'.

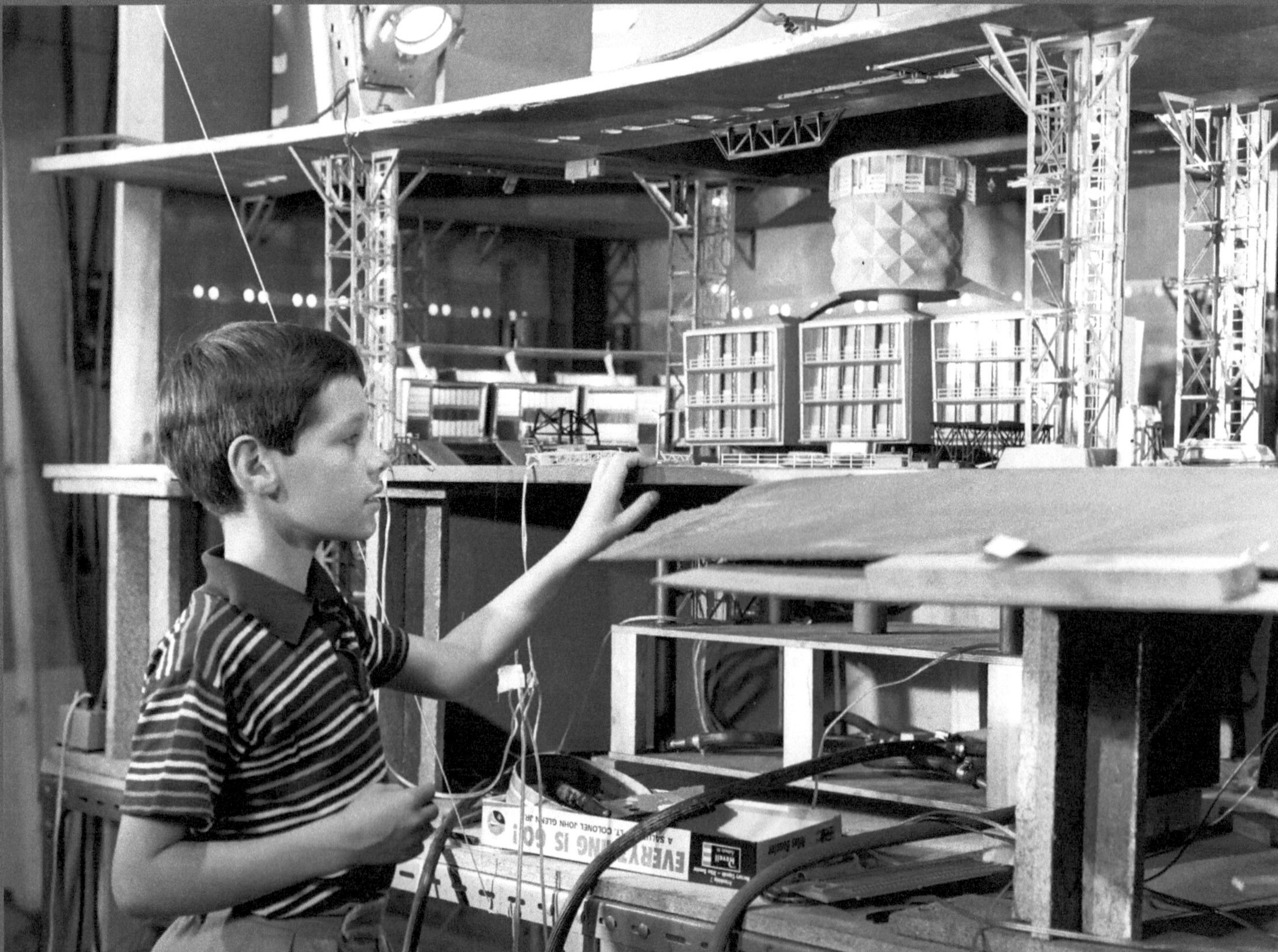

A young visitor takes a trip to Marineville.

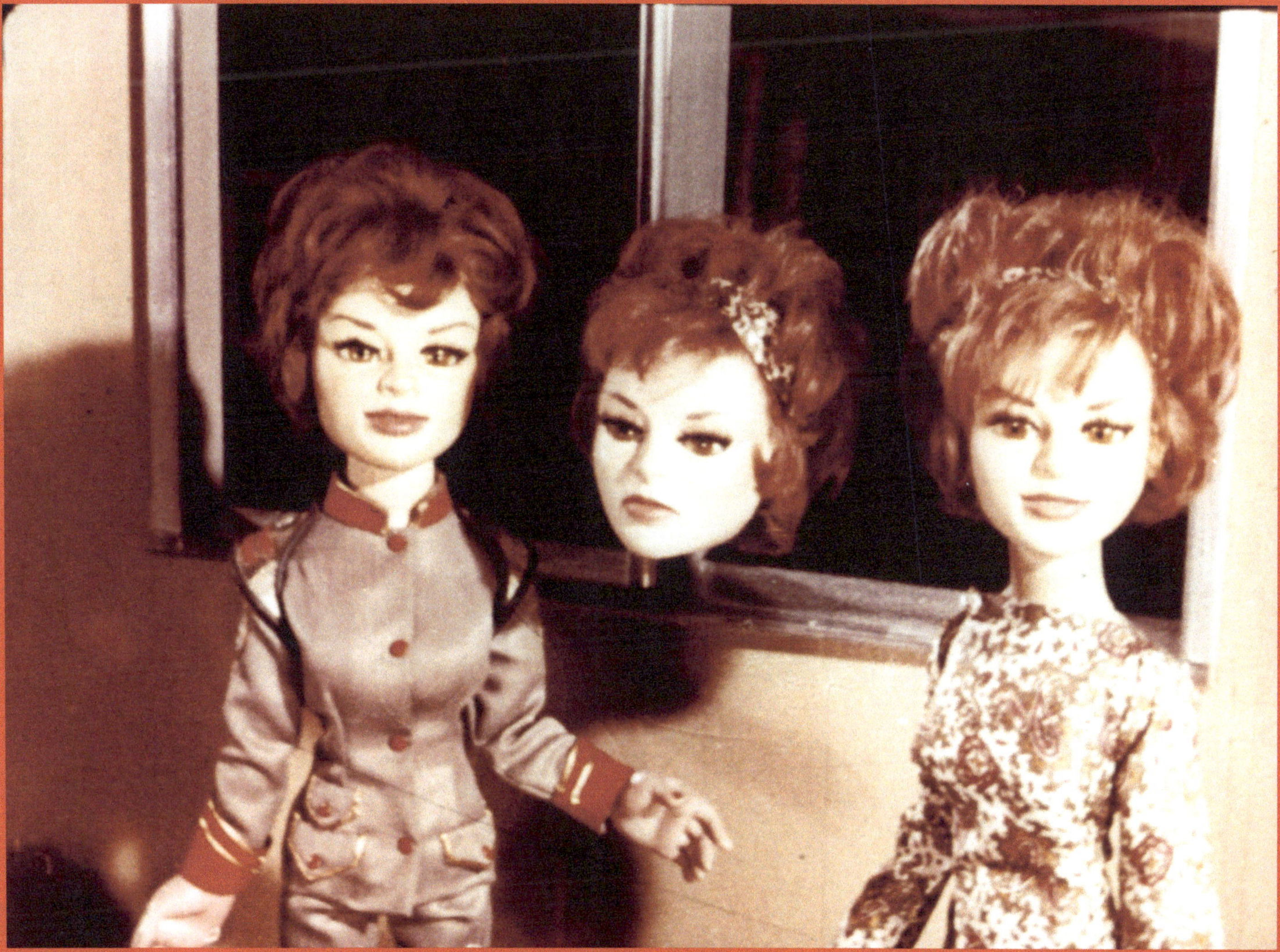

Stingray marked the introduction of using heads with different expressions. Here, two of Atlanta's 'normal' heads can be seen with her 'frowner'.

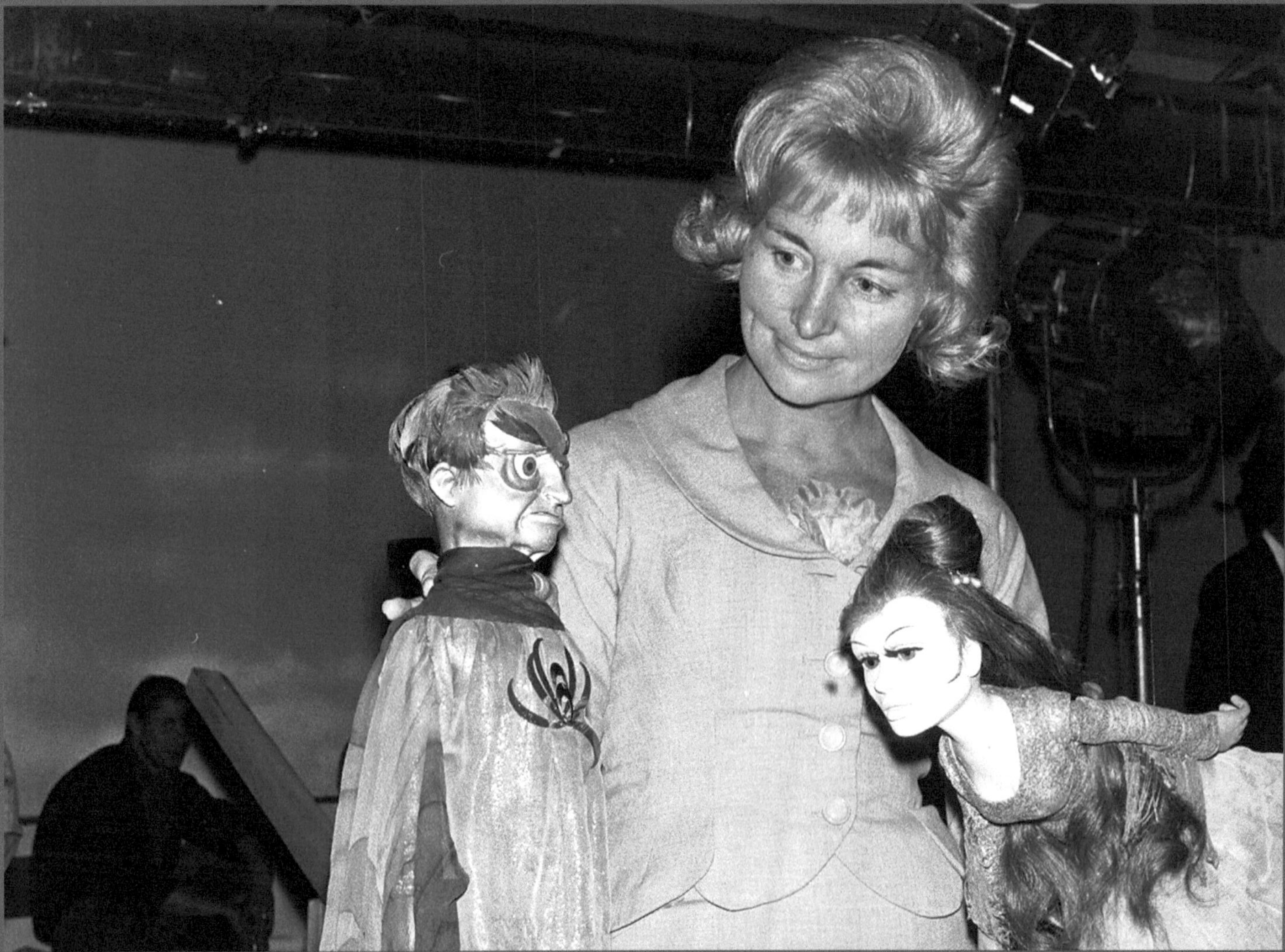

Sylvia poses with the villainous X20 and silent heroine, Marina.

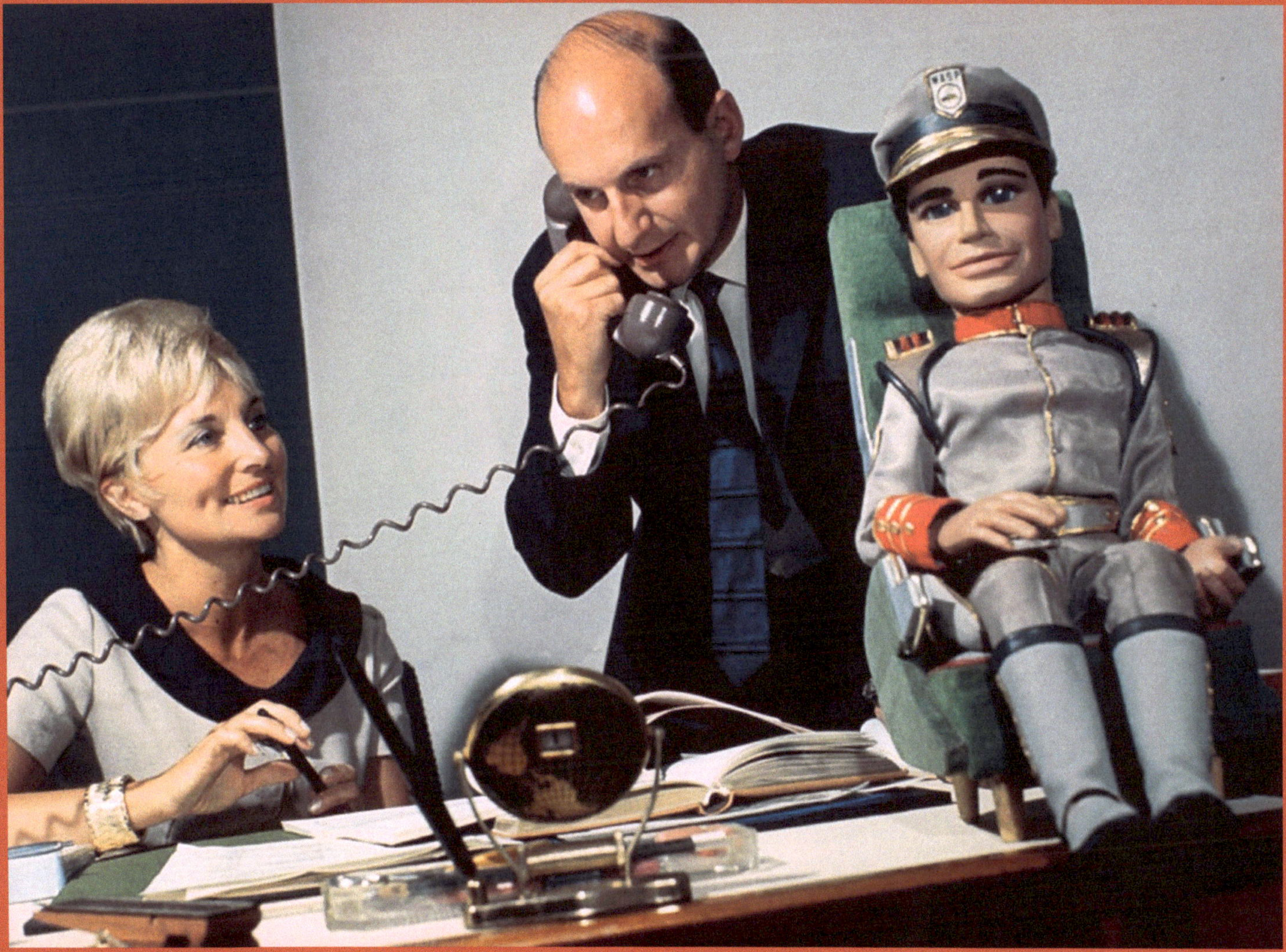

The bosses (Sylvia, Gerry and Troy Tempest) pose for a dynamic action shot.

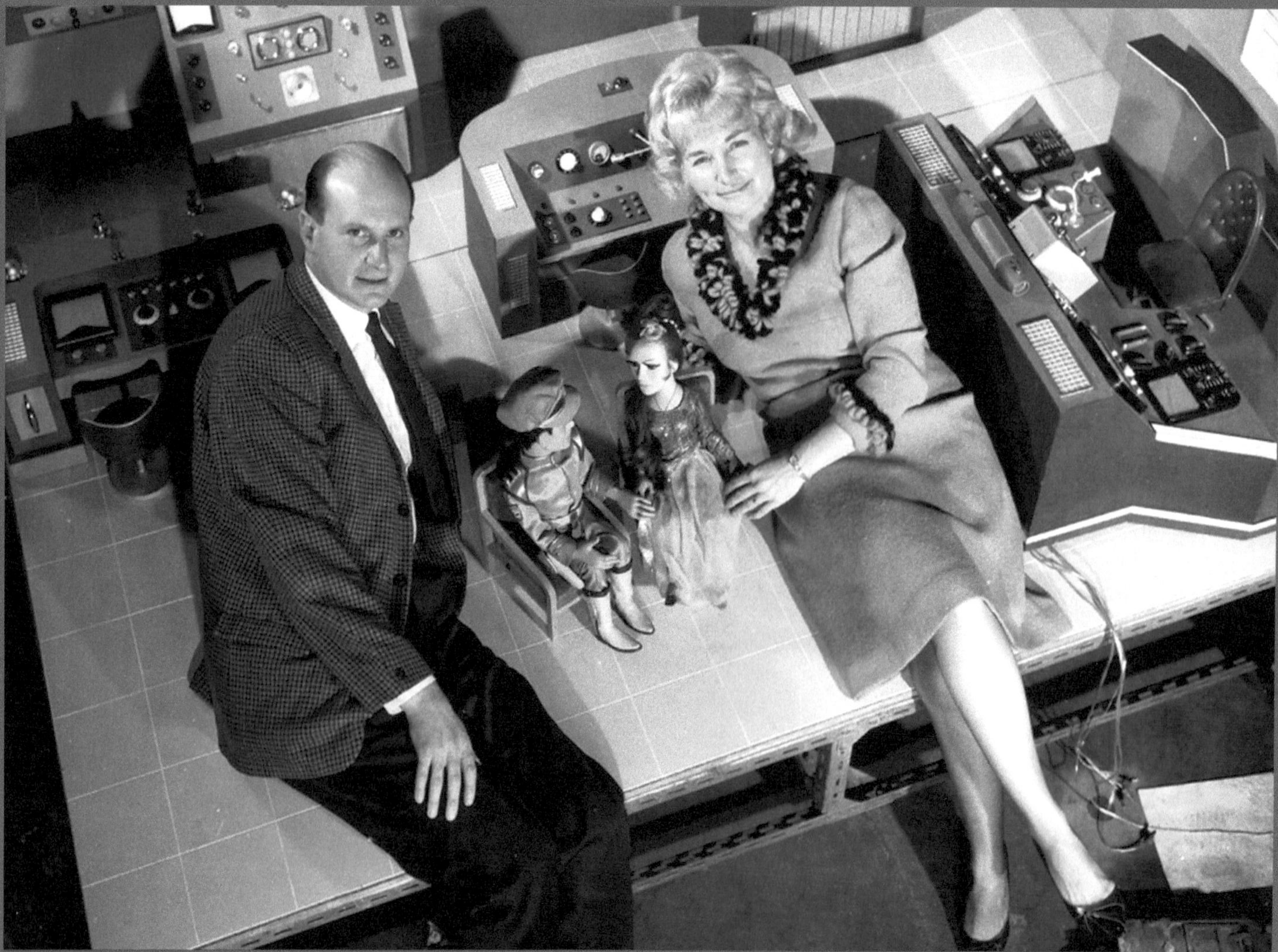

By the time *Stingray* launched on British Television, APF had already left behind the underwater world and was hard at work on what was to be their most successful production. As a result, when it came time to promote *Stingray*, puppets and props from the series were often placed on sets for *Thunderbirds*. Here, Gerry and Sylvia sit with Troy and Marina on the set of the *Thunderbirds* episode 'Sun Probe'.

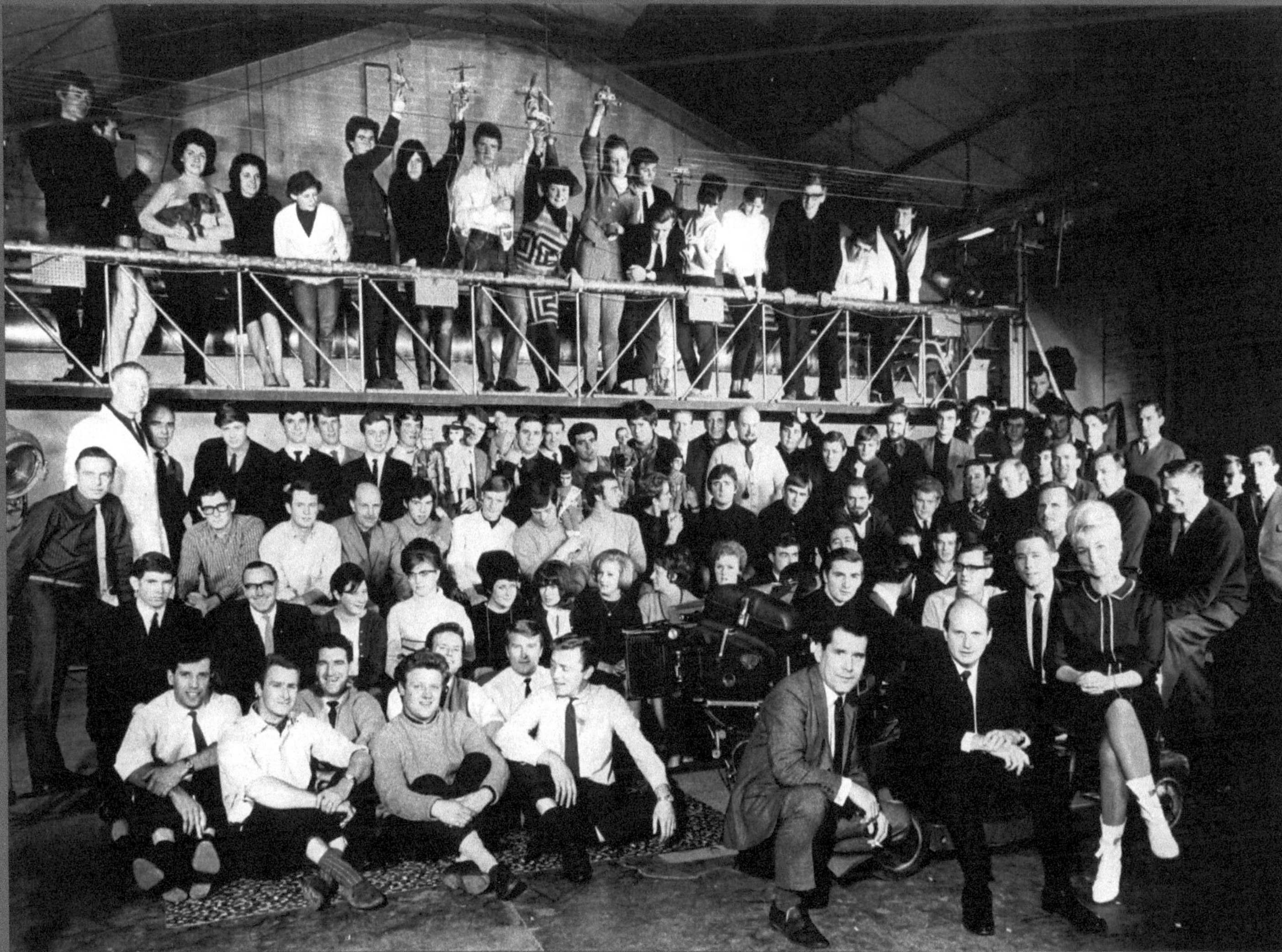

As *Stingray* drew to a close, Lew Grade once again demanded a new idea. After hearing radio reports about miners trapped in a flooded mine in Germany, Gerry and Sylvia developed the idea of an organisation with advanced equipment for rescuing those in peril. Here, the APF team pose for a group shot at the height of their success.

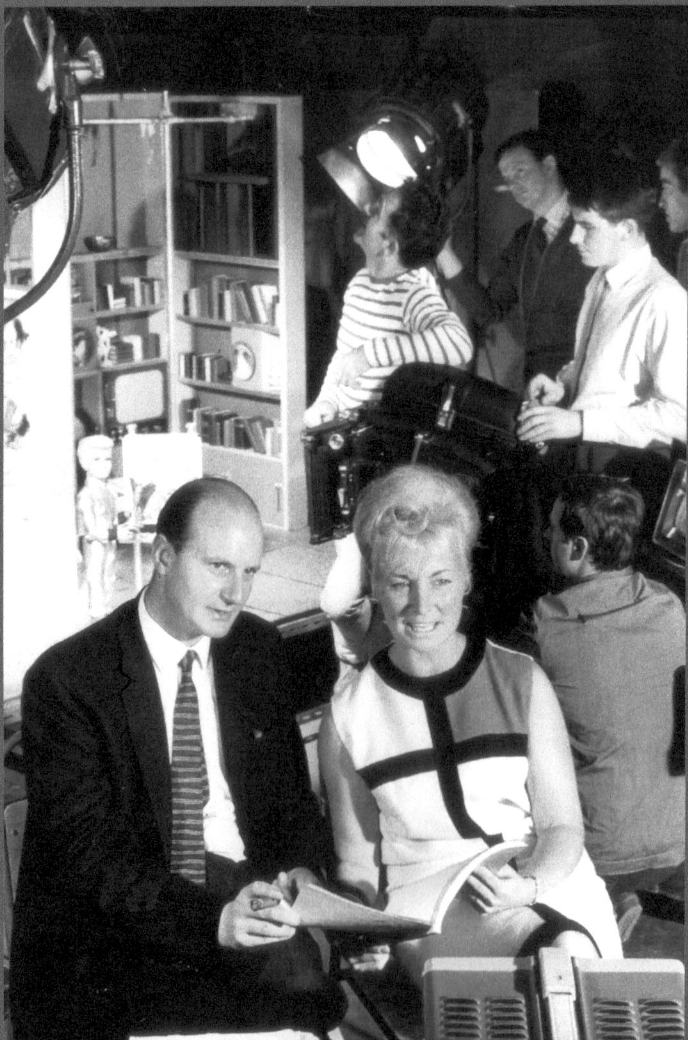

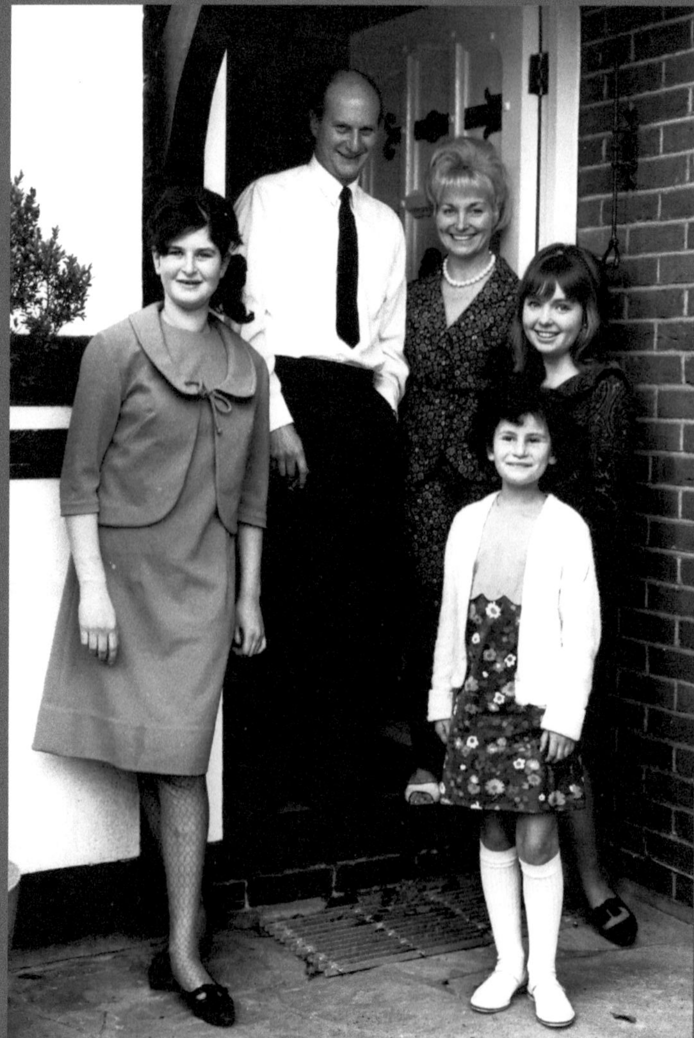

Left: Gerry and Sylvia pose in October '65 whilst additional filming for 'Move – And You're Dead' is carried out. Sylvia took great interest in the fashions, and helped to ensure each series was fresh and modern. Here, she can be seen wearing a life-sized version of Lady Penelope's Mondrian-inspired dress from 'The Duchess Assignment'. **Right:** At home with the family. The Andersons with Gerry's two children, Joy and Linda, and Sylvia's daughter, Dee.

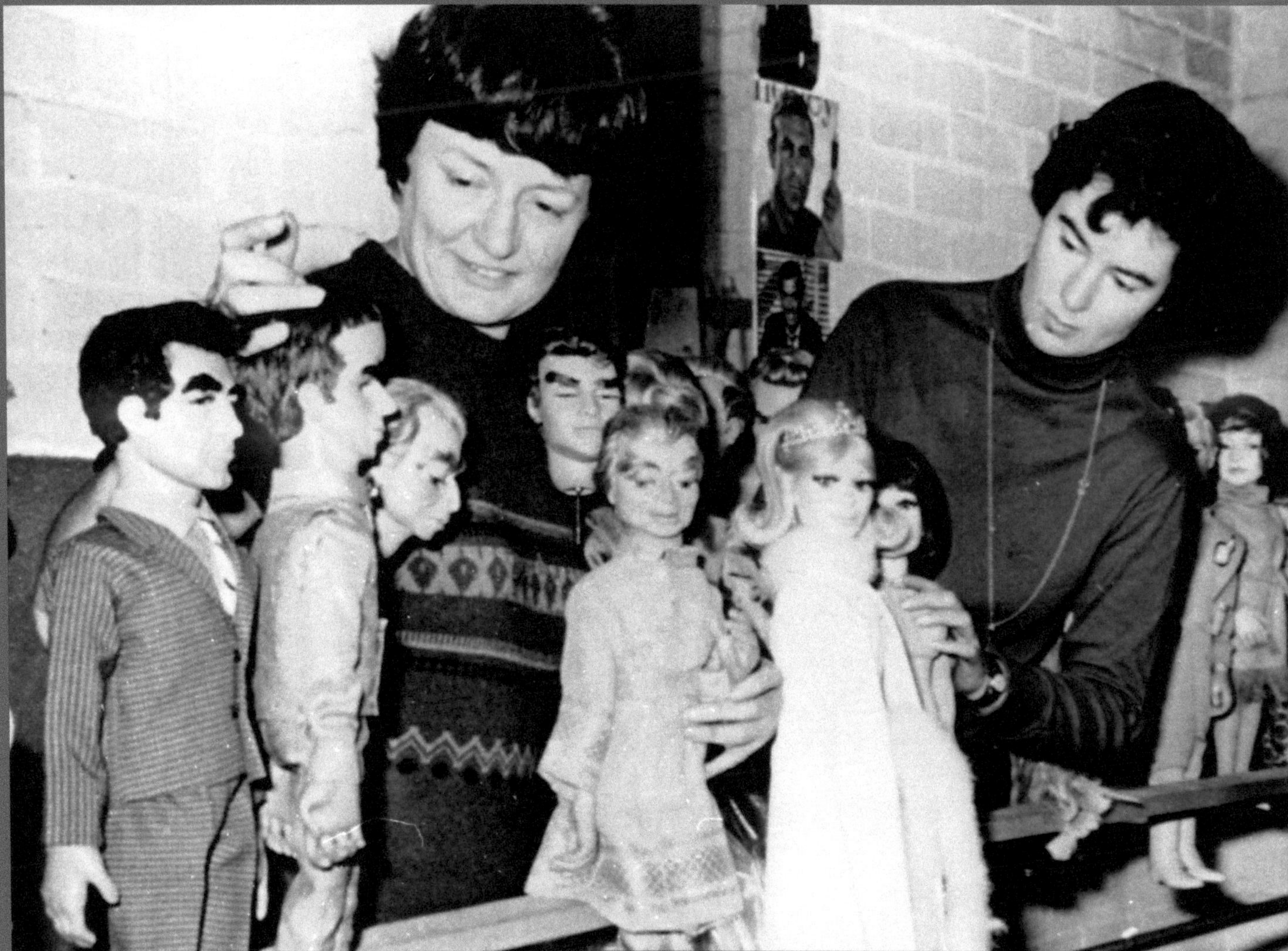

Christine Glanville (left) and Mary Turner were the talented bosses of the puppet department. Between them, they sculpted many of the hero and guest characters, and oversaw separate puppet units.

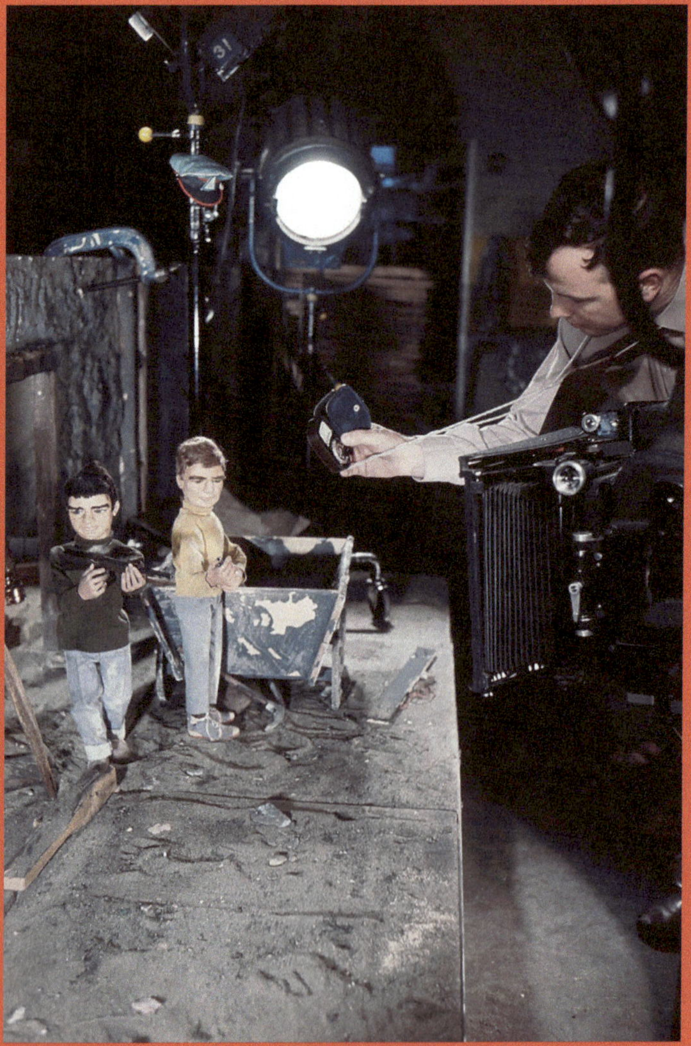

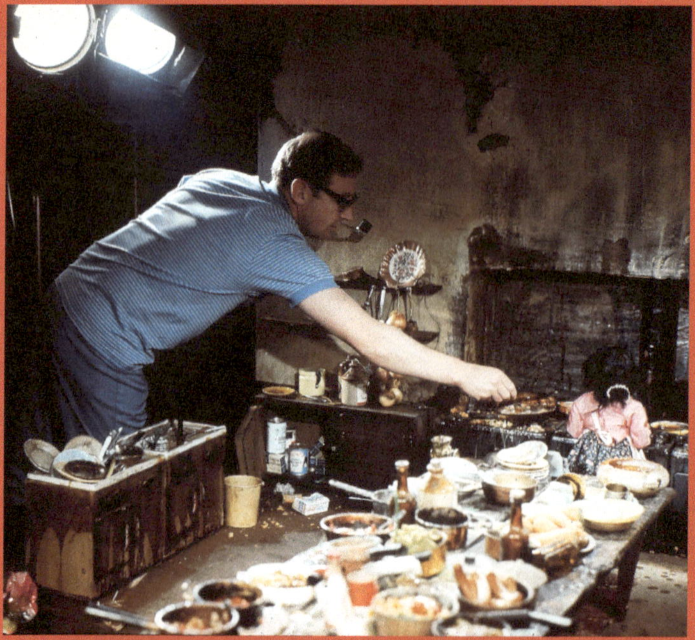

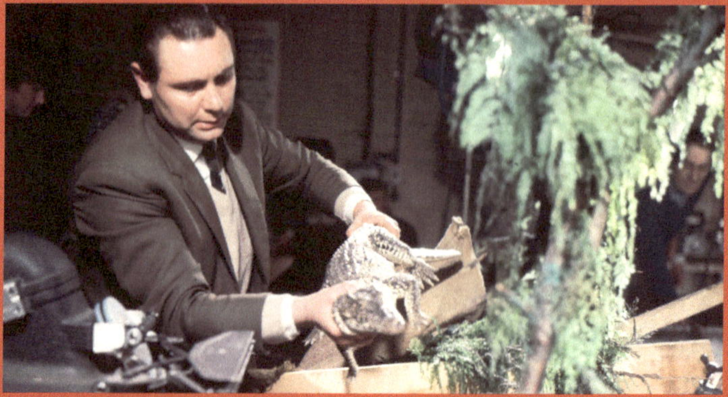

Left: Lighting Cameraman Paddy Seale checks the light meter prior to filming a scene in the villains' hideout for 'The Impostors'. **Above right:** David Elliott, a longtime friend and colleague of Gerry's, sets up a miniature kitchen for 'Path of Destruction'. One of APF's key collaborators since the early days, David decided to leave the company upon completion of the episode. **Below right:** Tentatively placing a dwarf crocodile on set for 'Attack of the Alligators!'

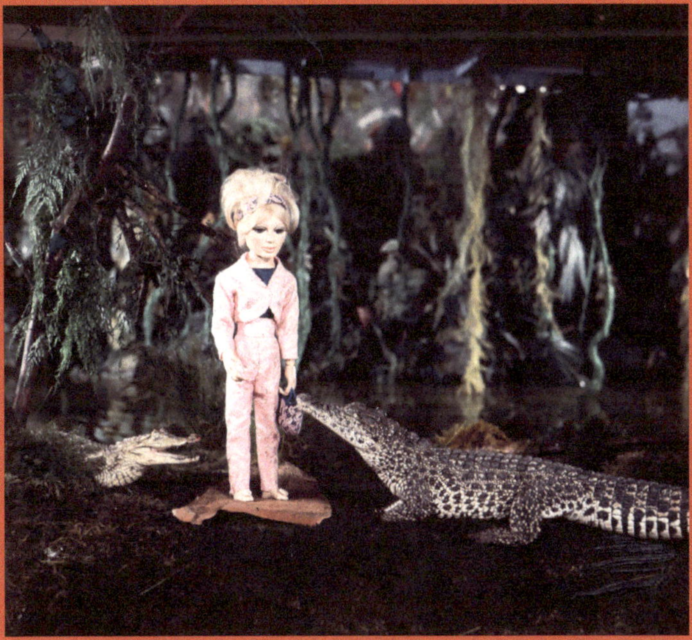

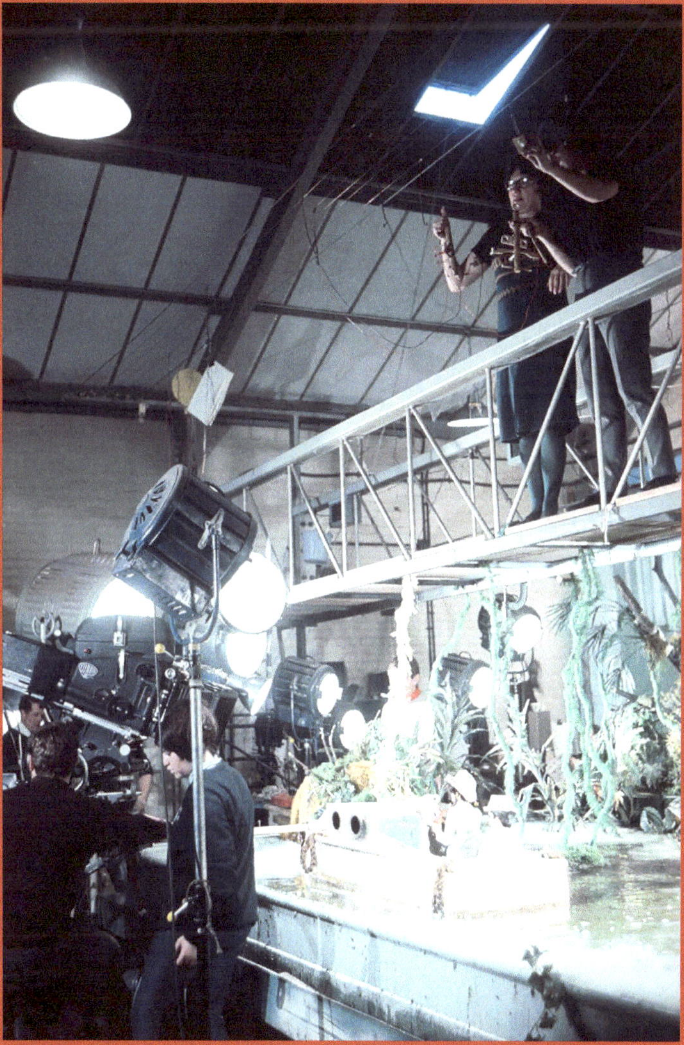

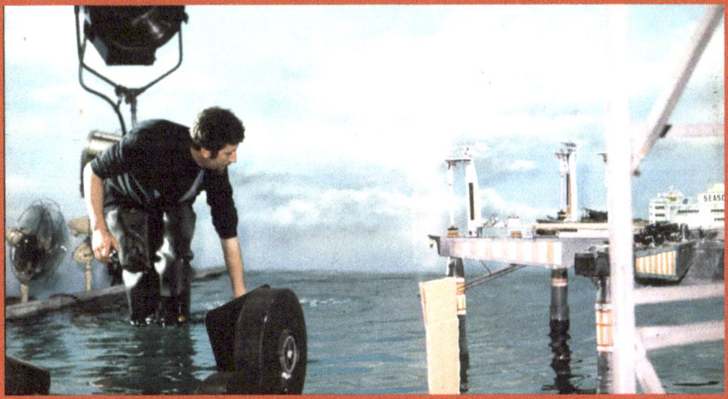

Above left: Although these crocodiles were dwarves, they still had a ferocious nip. Shortly after this shot was taken, one of the crocodiles deprived 'er ladyship of her leg! **Right:** Filming a complicated boat scene for 'Attack of the Alligators!' Bringing puppets and water together was always a risky business, as the puppet wires carried an electrical current for the lip-sync. **Below left:** Jimmy Elliott sets up a scene for 'Atlantic Inferno'. Fire and water are notoriously the most difficult elements with which to film. Here, the team are faced with both in the same shot.

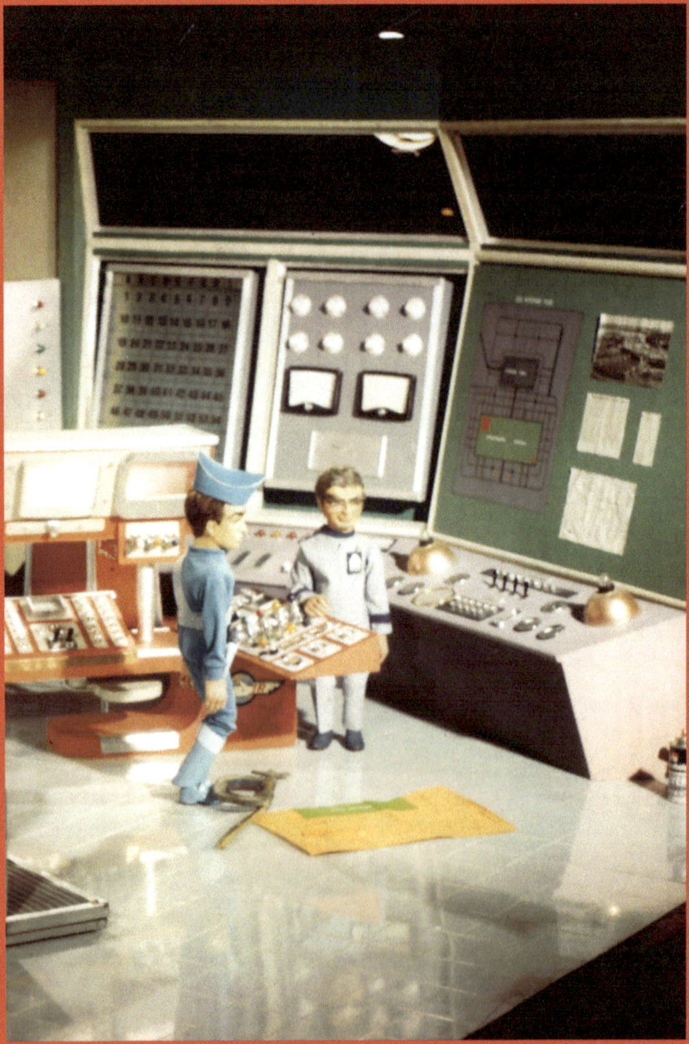

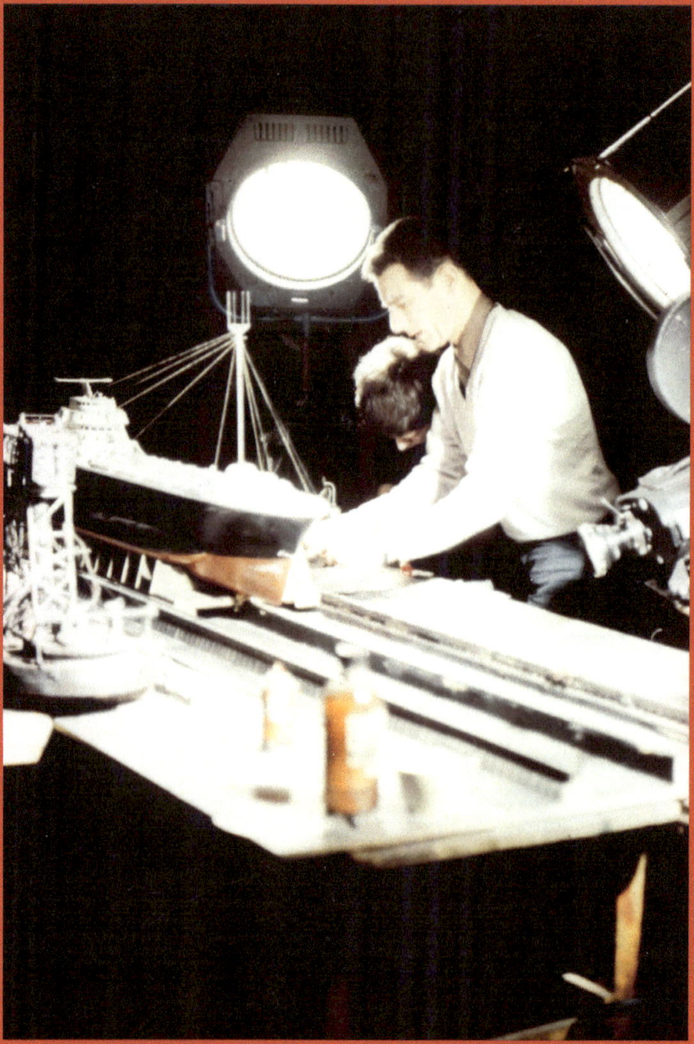

Left: A rare behind the scenes shot from 'City of Fire'. **Right:** Derek Meddings prepares Ocean Pioneer for launch in 'Danger at Ocean Deep'.

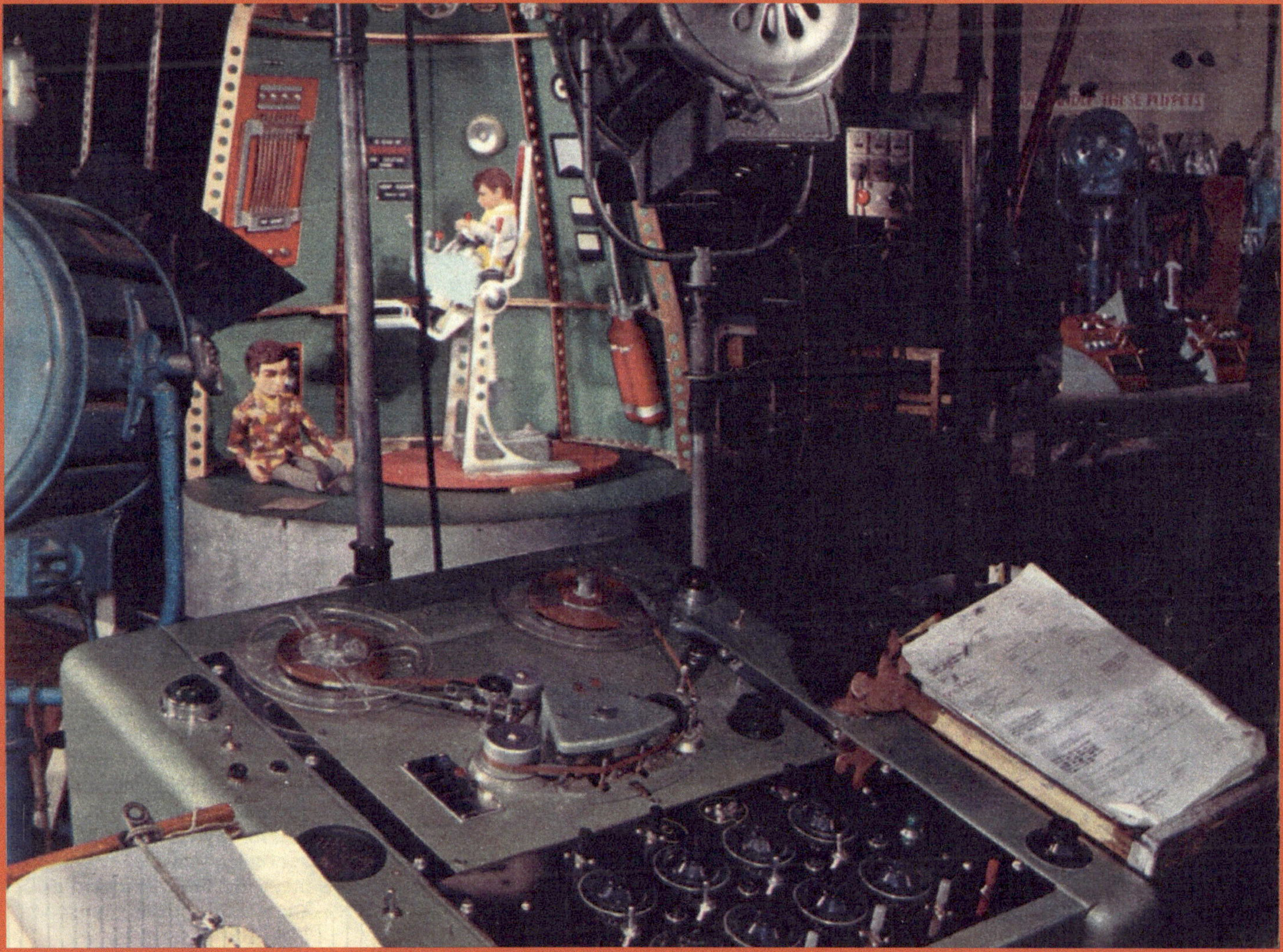

A glimpse into APF during filming of 'Security Hazard'. The lip-sync unit in the foreground is adorned with script, pocket watch, and Troy Tempest's disembodied head for running tests (poor Troy). Thunderbird 4's control console sits in the background.

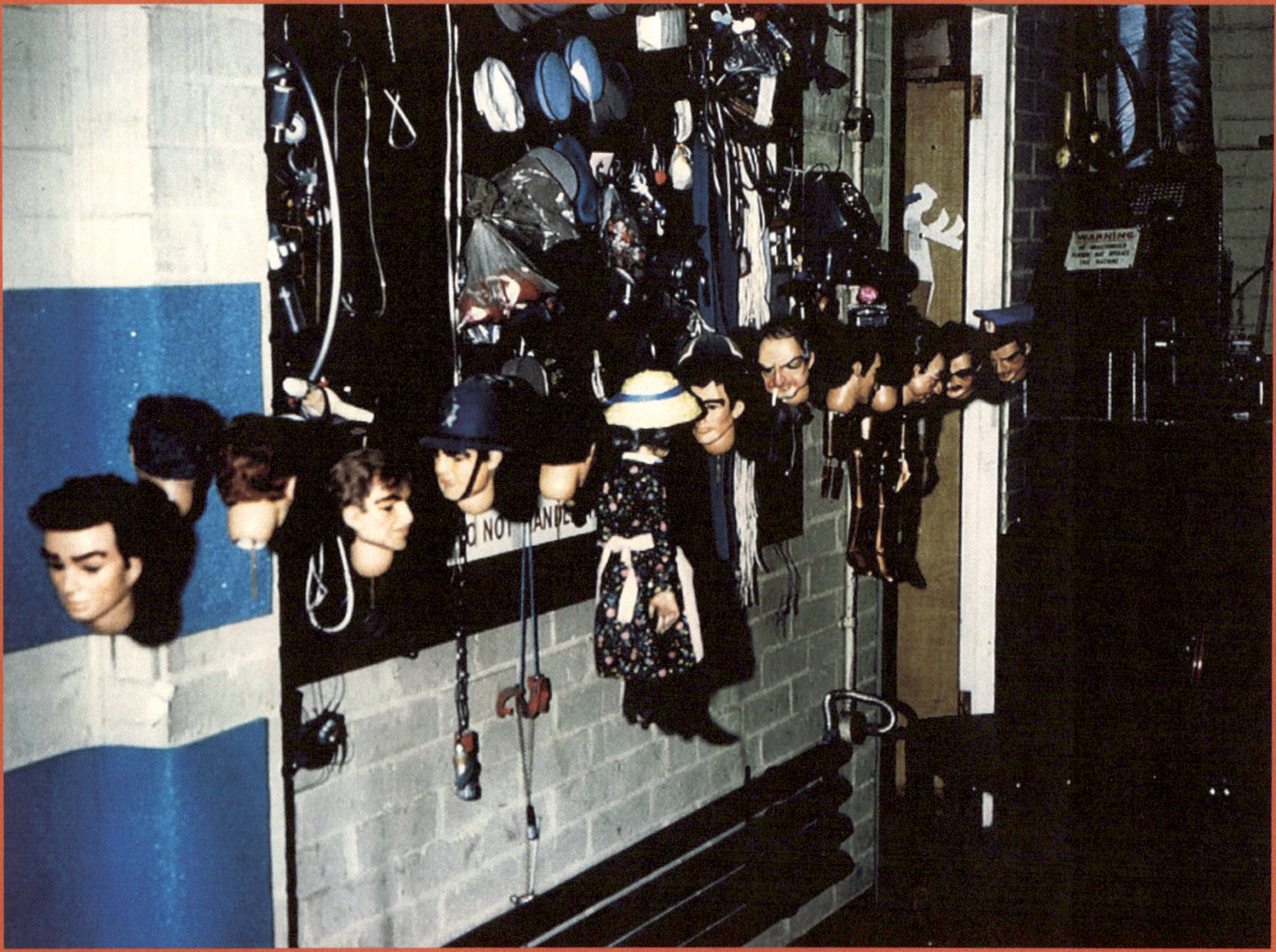

All around the studio, a collection of disembodied heads could be found.

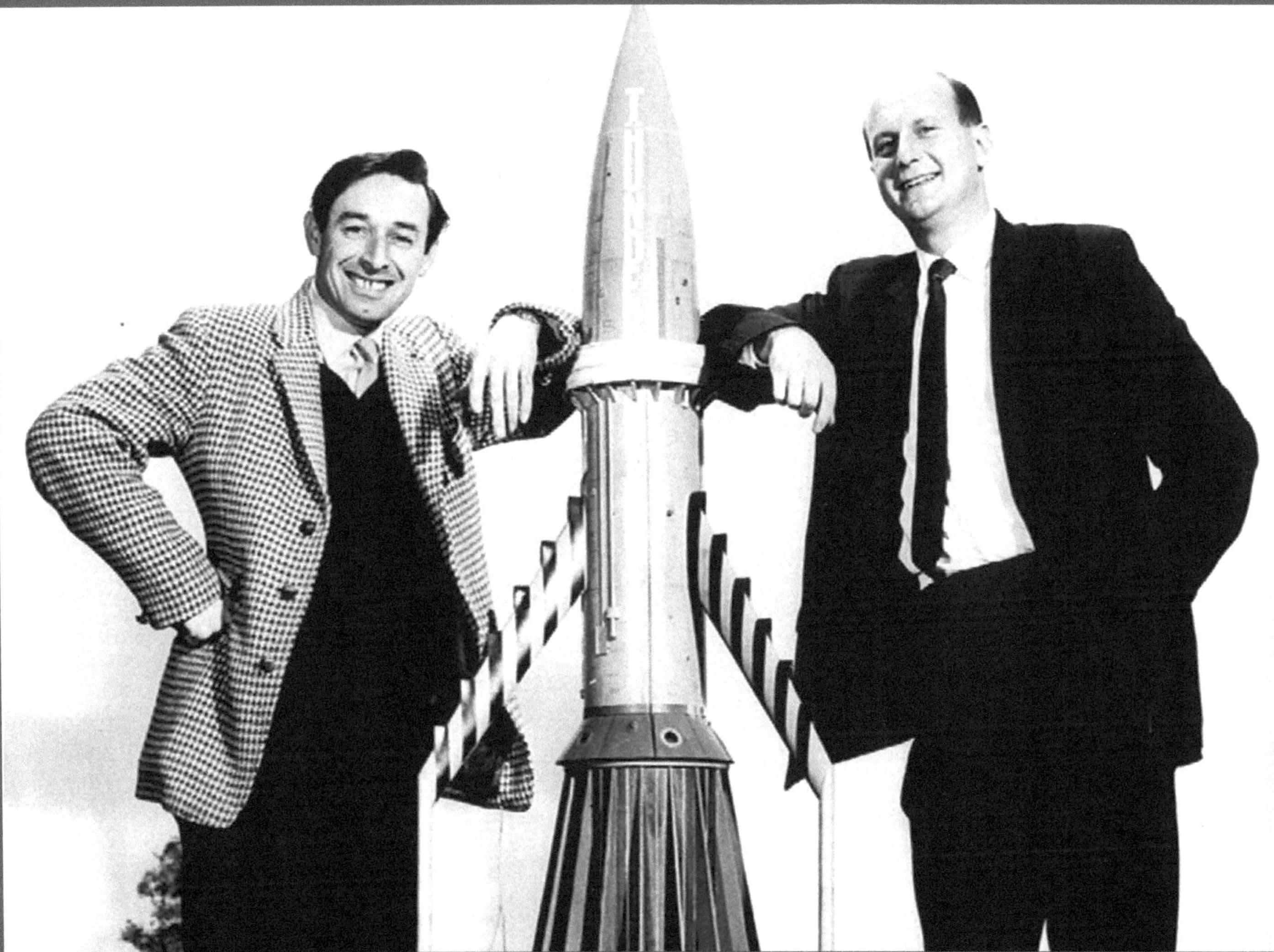

A.P. Films' production photographer Doug Luke and Gerry pose with the 6ft model of Thunderbird 3.

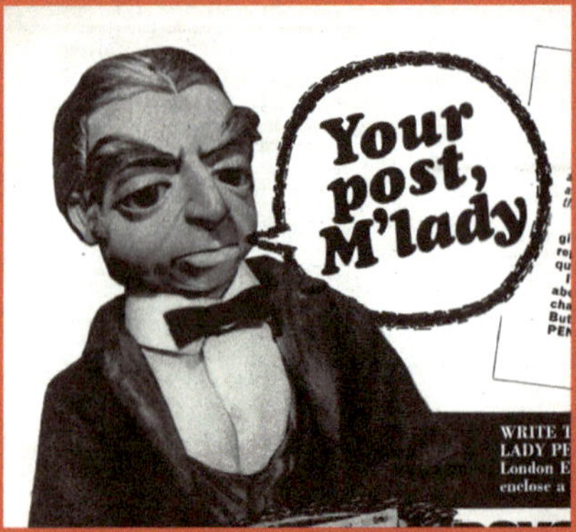

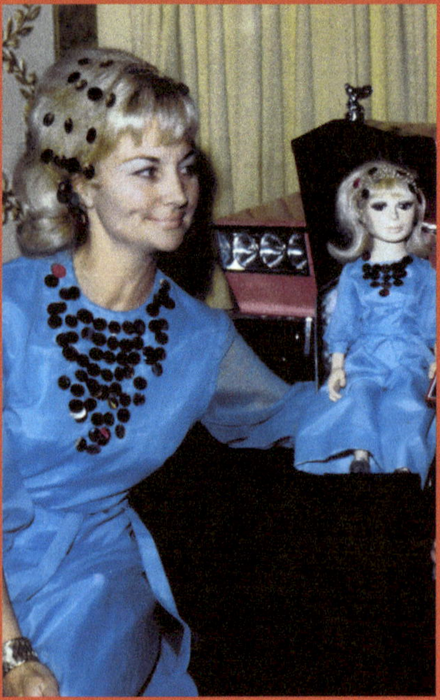

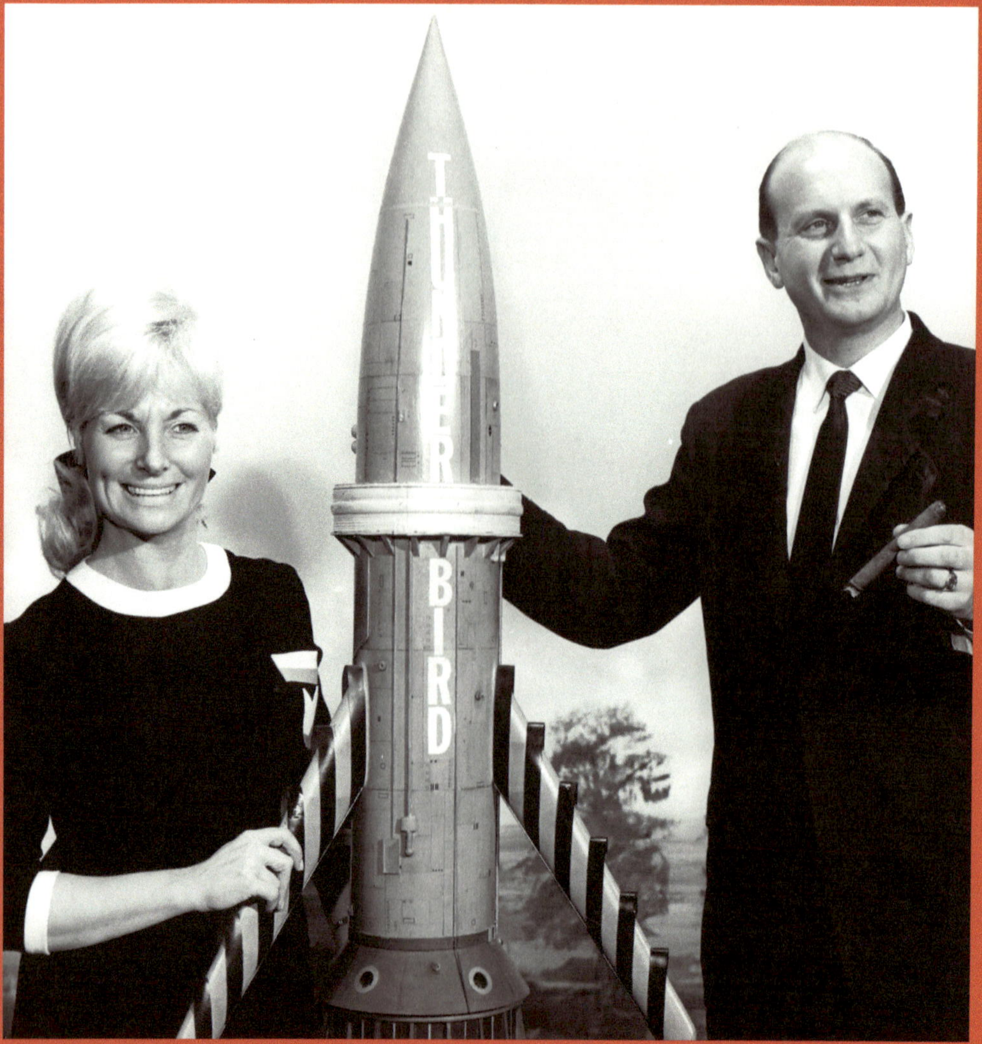

Above left: Such was the success of *Thunderbirds* and the other APF shows that the studio was inundated with sack loads of post. Where possible, they always attempted to reply – sometimes in character. **Below left:** Sylvia poses with her puppet counterpart, Lady Penelope, at the Royal Television Society Awards. **Right:** Sylvia and Gerry with Thunderbird 3.

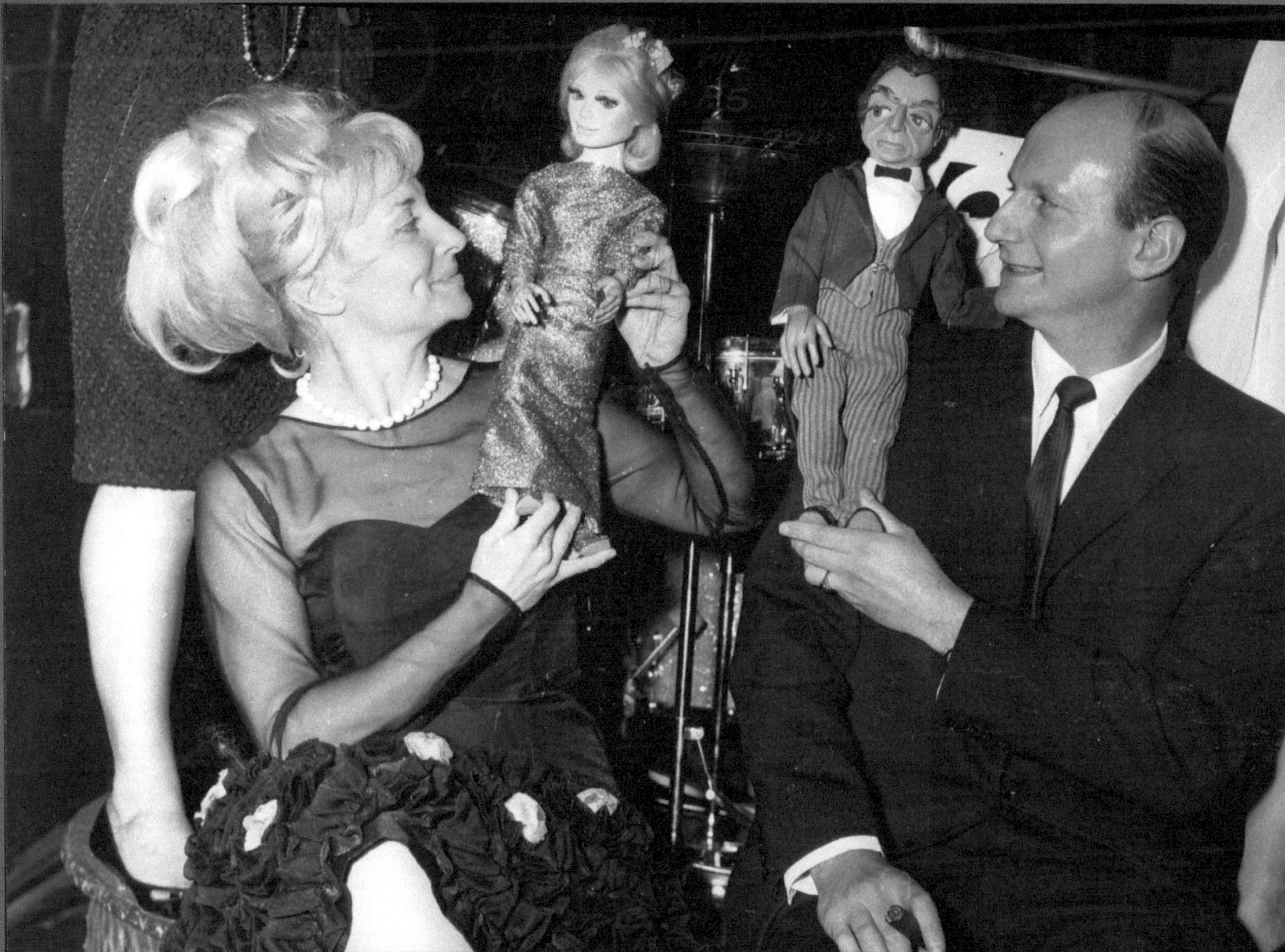

Gerry and Sylvia pictured with two of their most successful creations, Penelope and Parker. Originally envisaged as supporting characters, the 'cockney butler' and 'posh lady with the twin set and pearls' soon became a hit with television audiences. Lady Penelope even had her own comic.

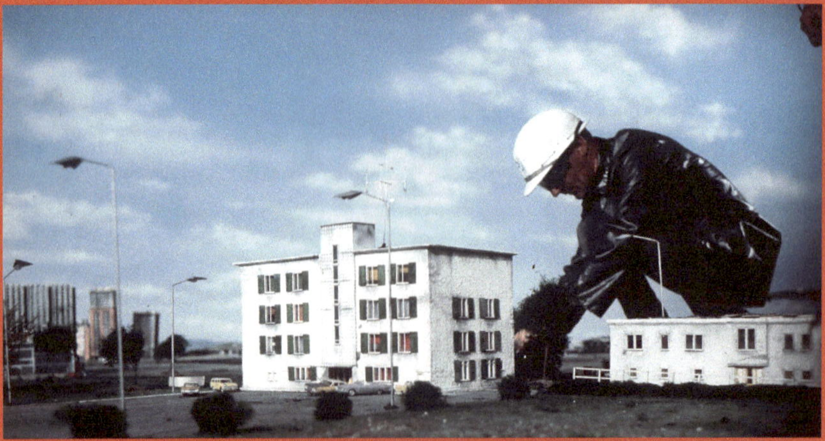

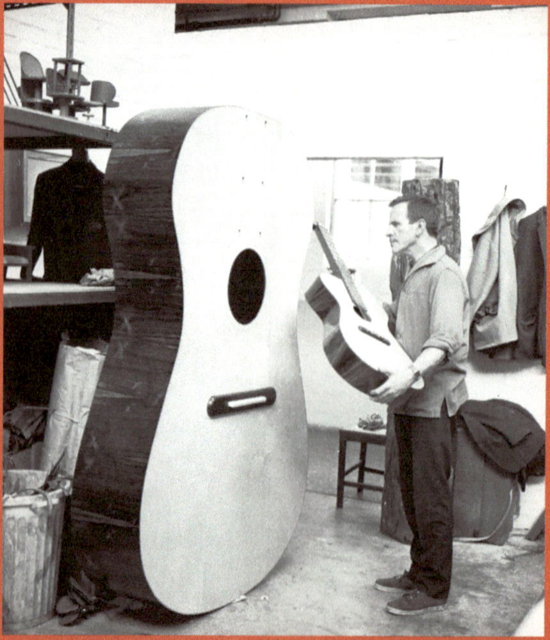

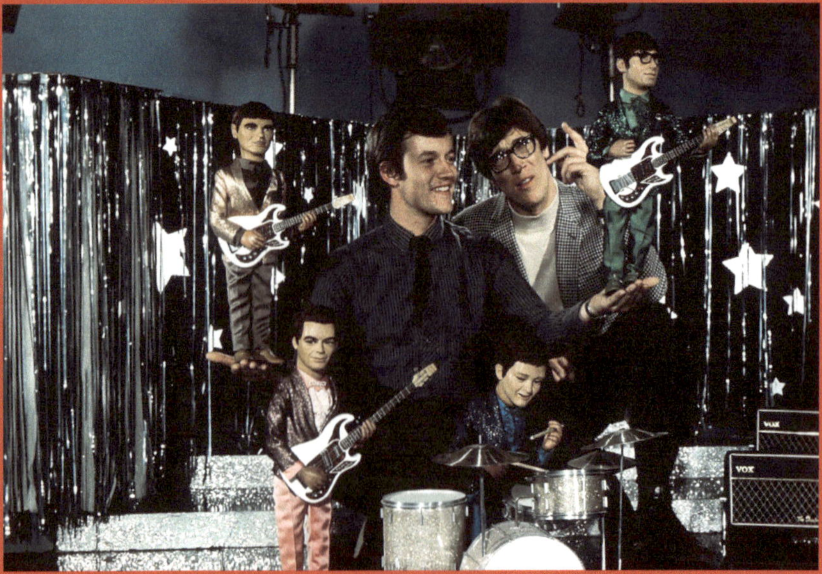

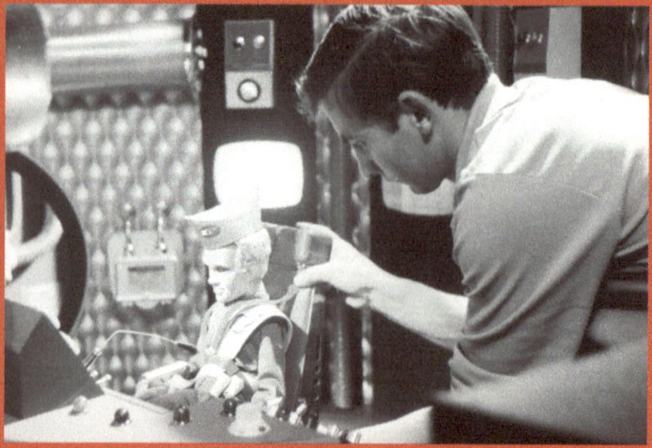

Lew Grade loved *Thunderbirds* so much that, before the first episode had even aired, he committed to making a feature film. **Above left:** Derek Meddings prepares to incinerate another model town. **Below left:** Hank Marvin and Brian Bennett pose on the Swinging Star set with their puppet doppelgängers. Cliff Richard and the Shadows appear in the film's dream sequence. **Above right:** Art Director Bob Bell ponders issues of scale. **Below right:** David Lane on set. Only in his early 20s, David was one of the youngest feature film directors in the country.

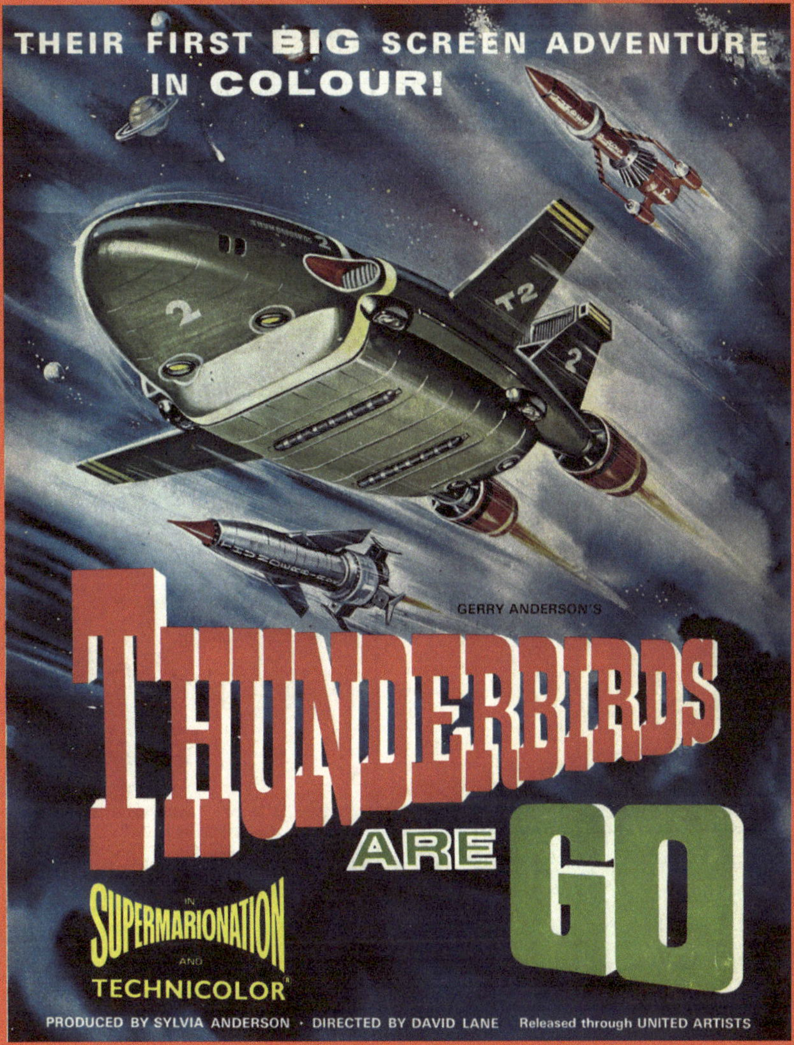

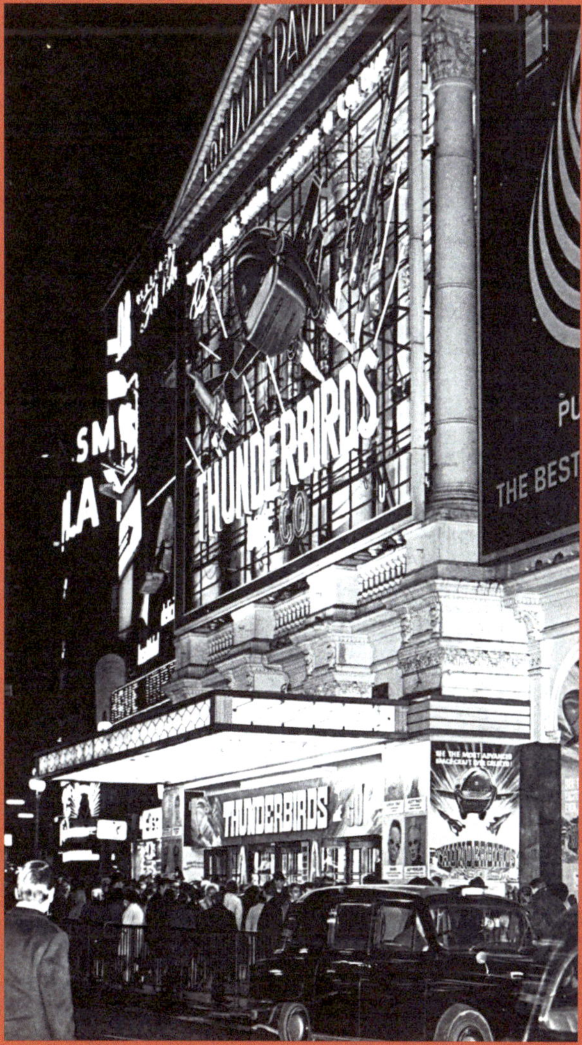

Left: One of the movie posters for *Thunderbirds Are Go*. **Right:** 12th December 1966. *Thunderbirds Are Go* is unveiled at a glittering premiere at the London Pavilion.

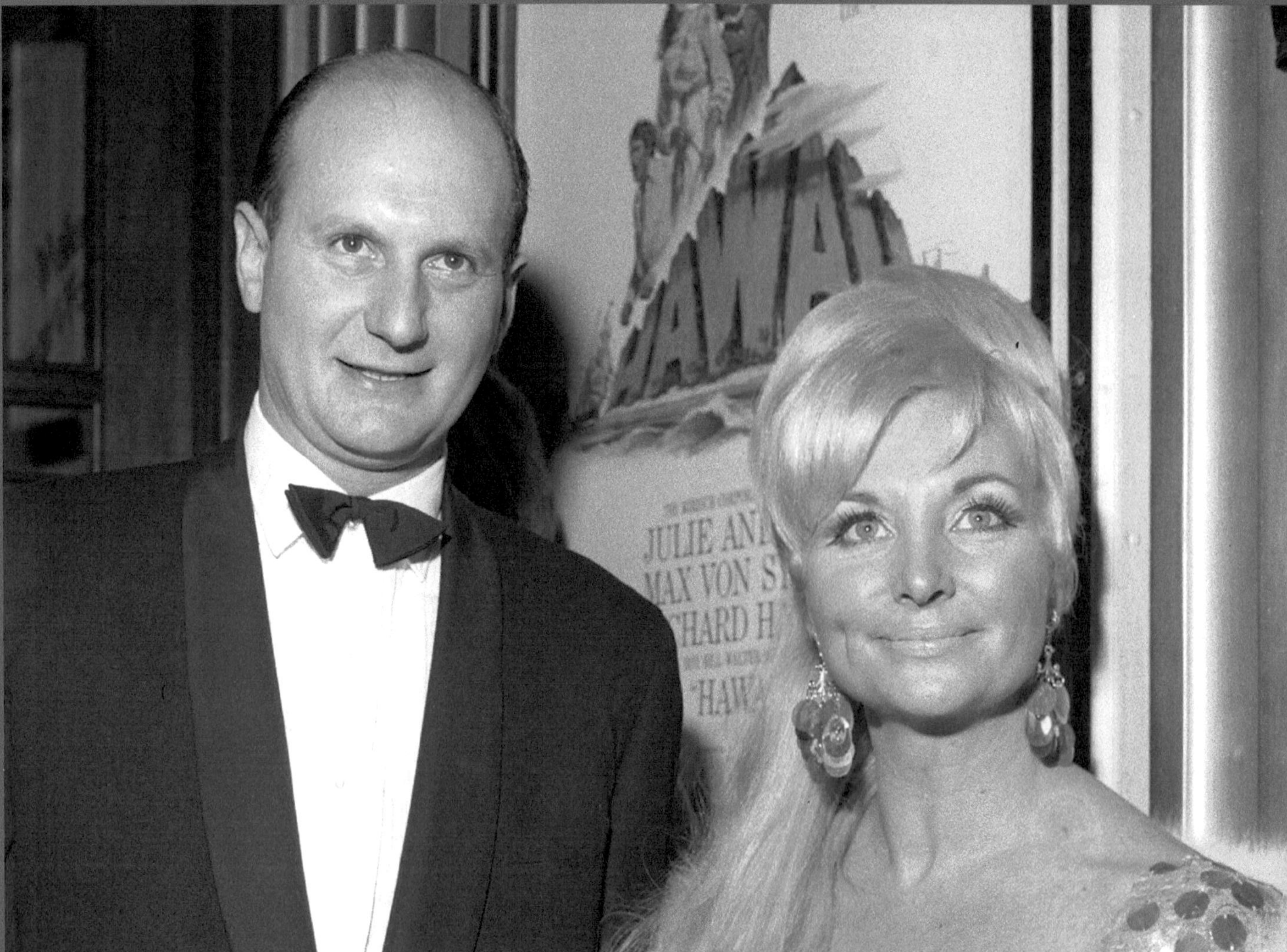

The premiere was perhaps the pinnacle of the Andersons' careers. Sadly though, despite arousing expectations of being 'bigger than Bond', the film failed to attract a big audience. The TV series, which was a massive success around the world, didn't get the American sale it needed either, and so *Thunderbirds'* life was prematurely curtailed.

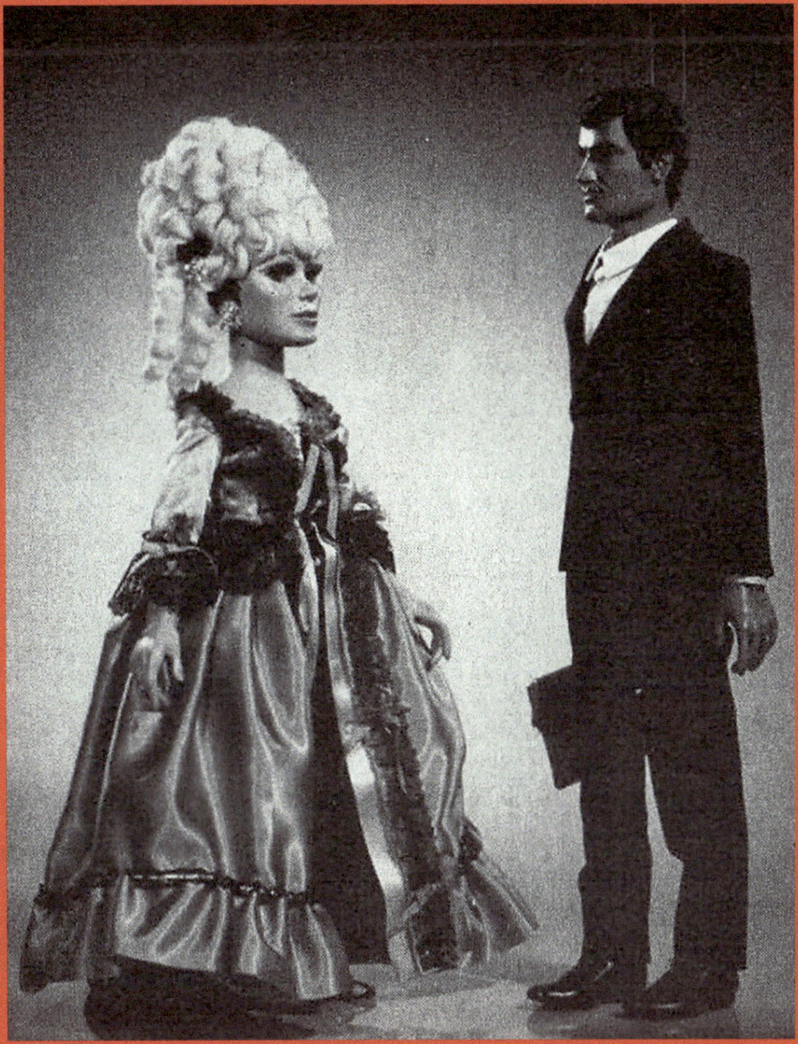

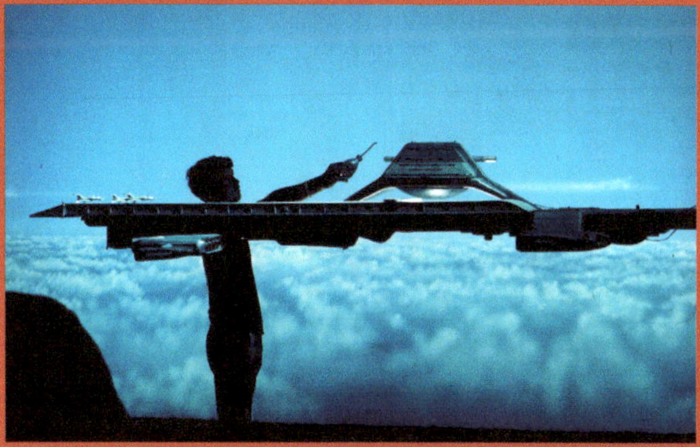

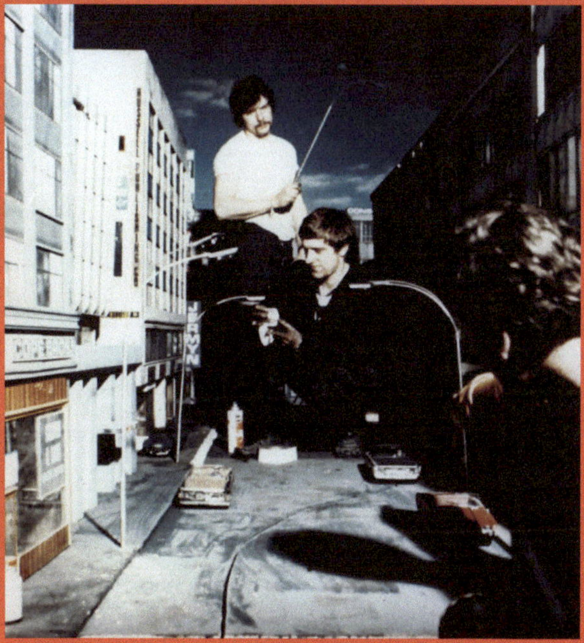

Left: As *Thunderbirds* came to an end, the boffins in the puppet studio finally solved the issue of scale. Gerry had always wanted the puppets to look human. By relocating the lip-sync solenoids from the head to the chest, this was made possible, and the new generation of puppets was put to work on *Captain Scarlet and the Mysterons*. **Above right:** A technician paints out the wires holding the enormous Cloudbase model. **Below right:** By this time, the effects technicians were building large scale miniature worlds.

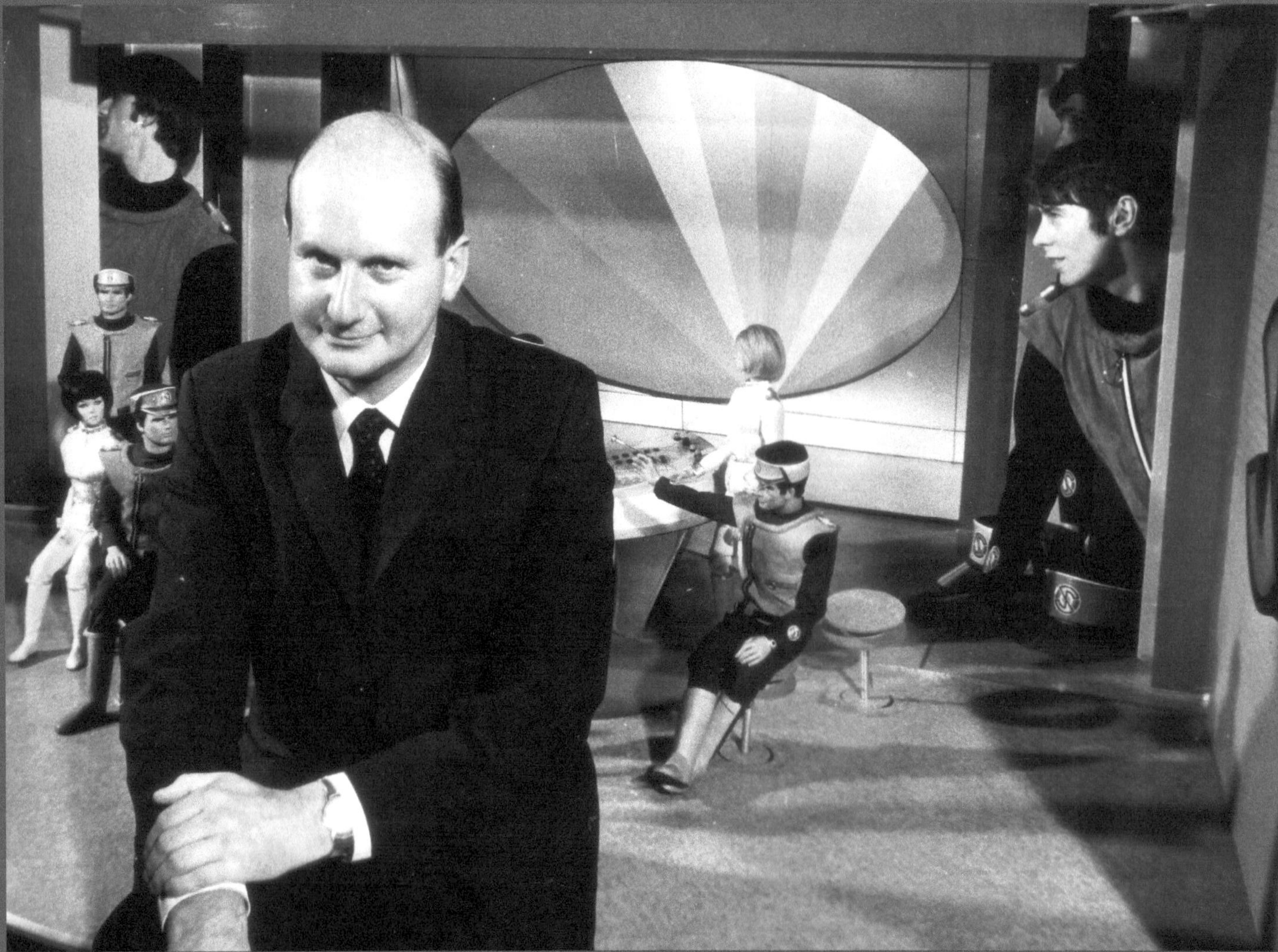

Gerry poses on set, with members of the pop group The Spectrum in the background. By 1967, new projects away from the Slough studios were occupying Gerry, so he increasingly left important roles to his trusted team.

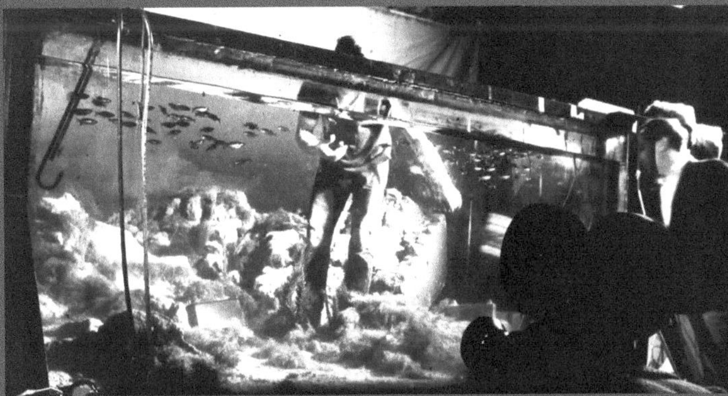

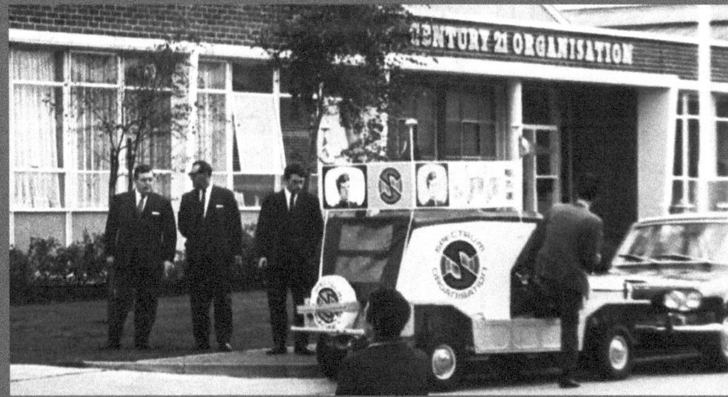

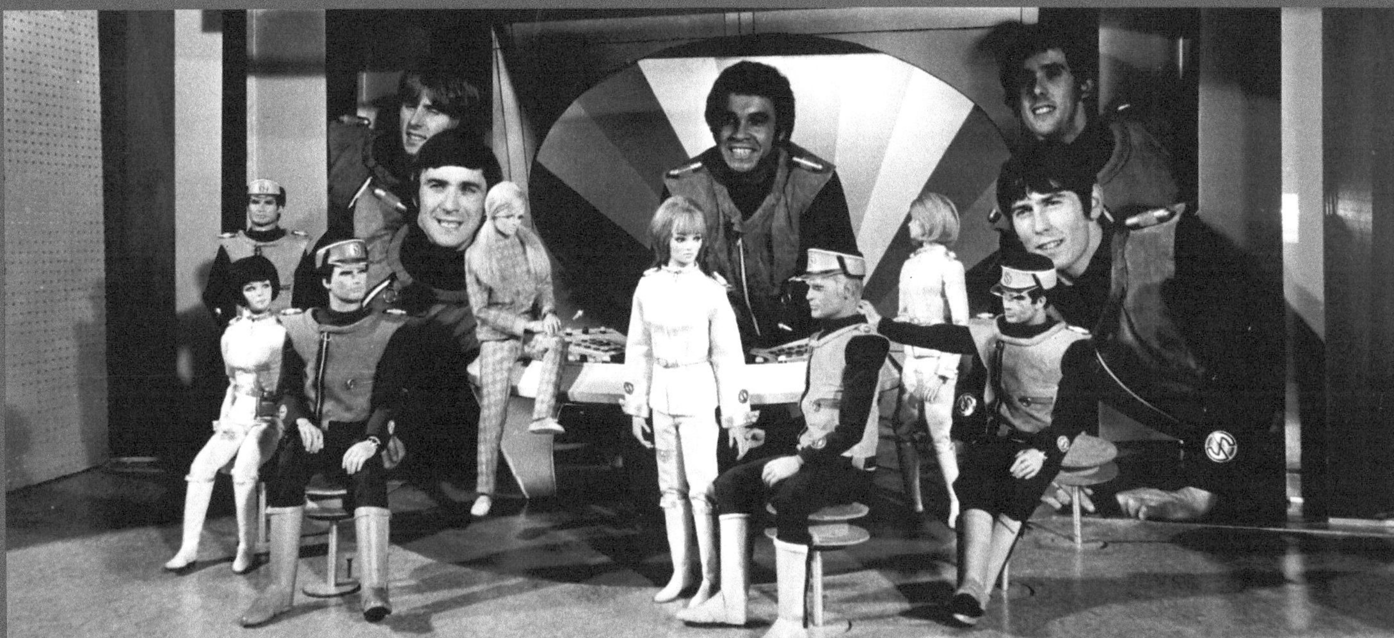

Above left: To film underwater scenes during production of *Supercar*, Reg Hill came up with the ingenious solution of shooting through an ultra-thin fish tank. This rare photo of a tank shoot was taken during filming of the *Captain Scarlet* episode 'Renegade Rocket'. **Above right:** By this time, the company (now renamed Century 21) was a well-oiled machine. This shot comes from a publicity campaign for the series. **Below:** To sing the end titles, the appropriately named pop group The Spectrum was signed up.

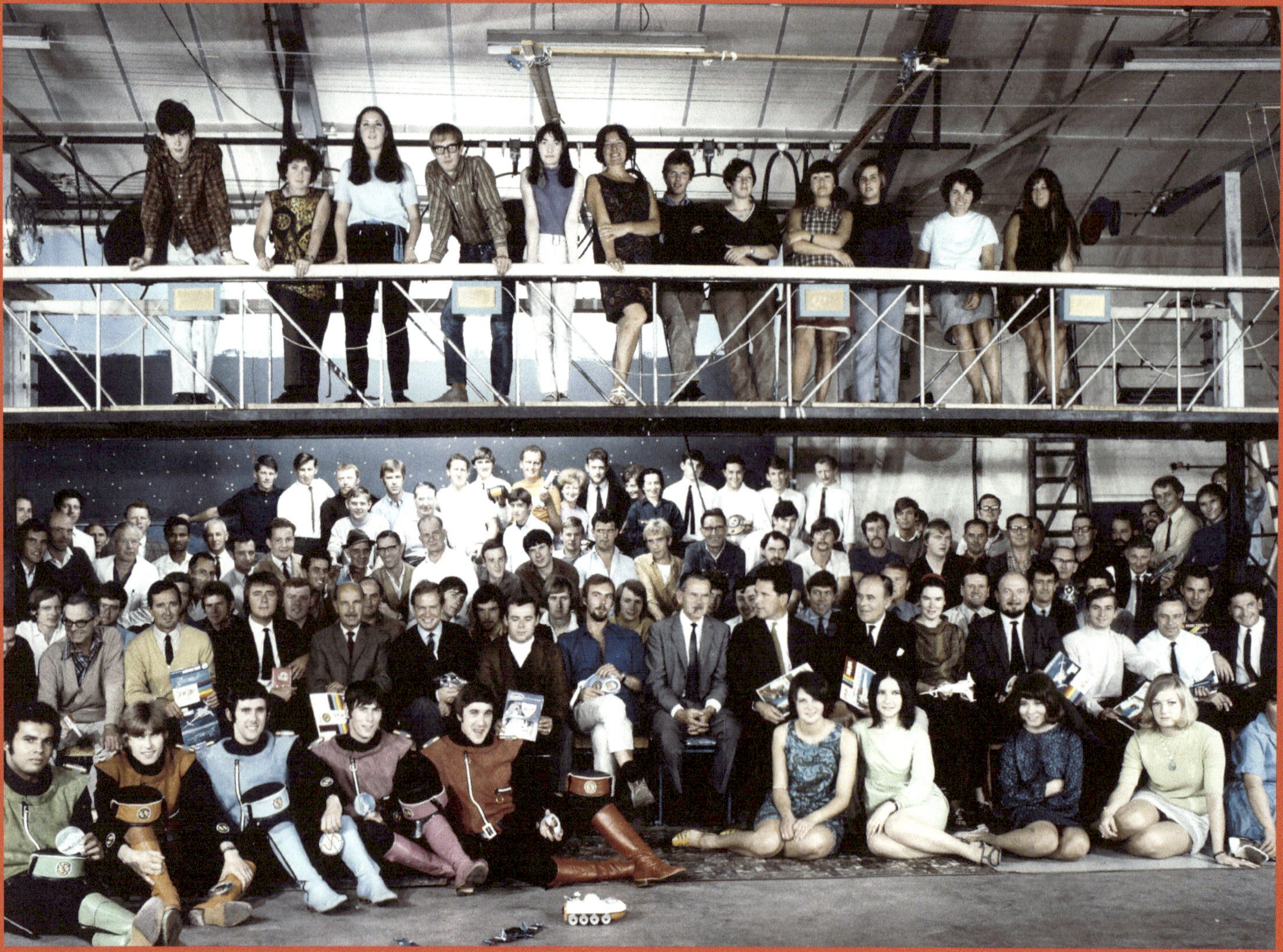

By 1967, studio life was really swinging. Whereas once crew turned up in suits (even for dirty jobs like special effects), smart casual was now the order of the day. As older members of the team moved up to management, a second generation of young technicians and artists joined the company.

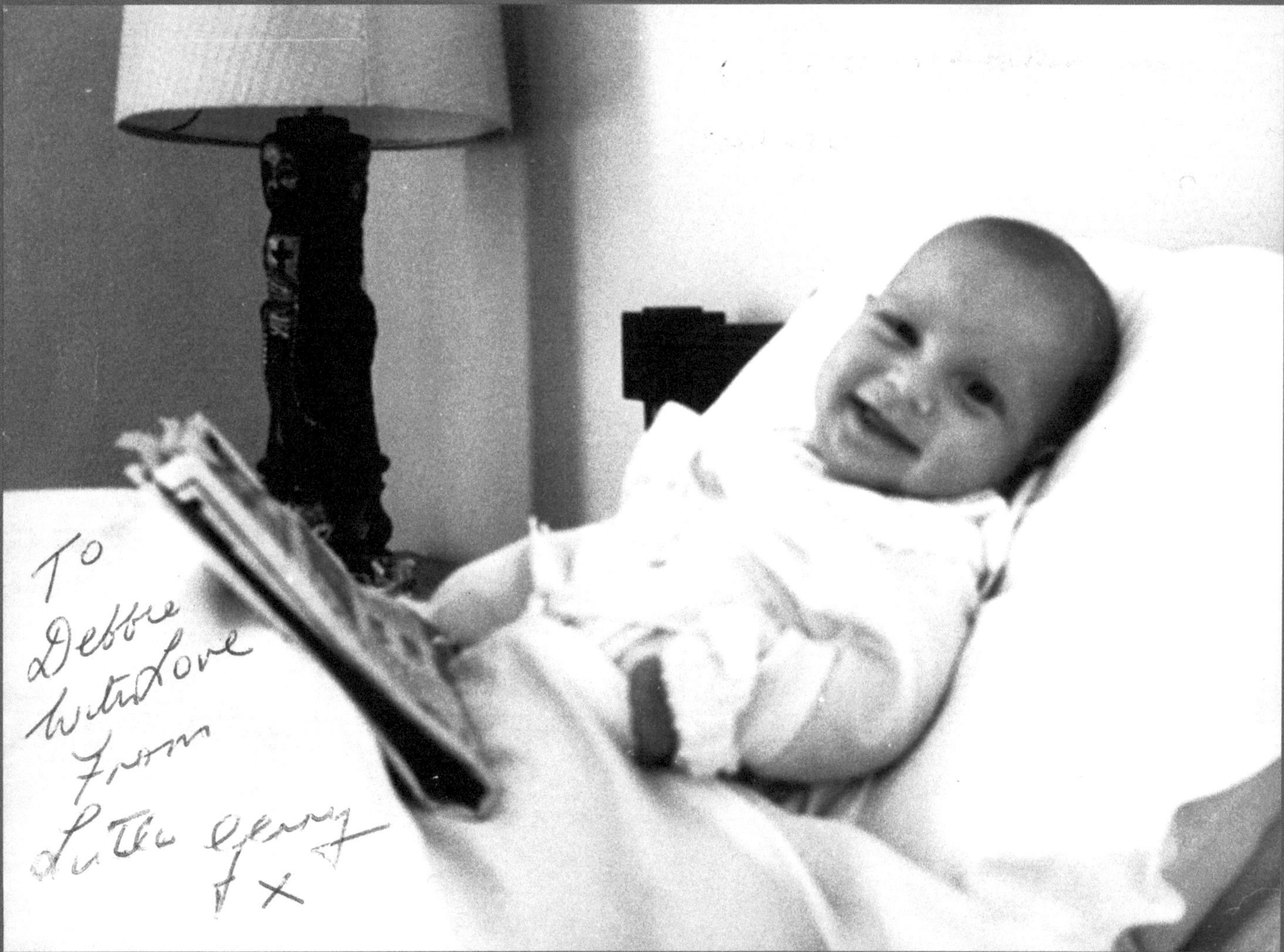

While *Captain Scarlet* finished its final weeks of production, Gerry and Sylvia had a baby. Gerry Anderson Jnr was born at the end of July 1967.

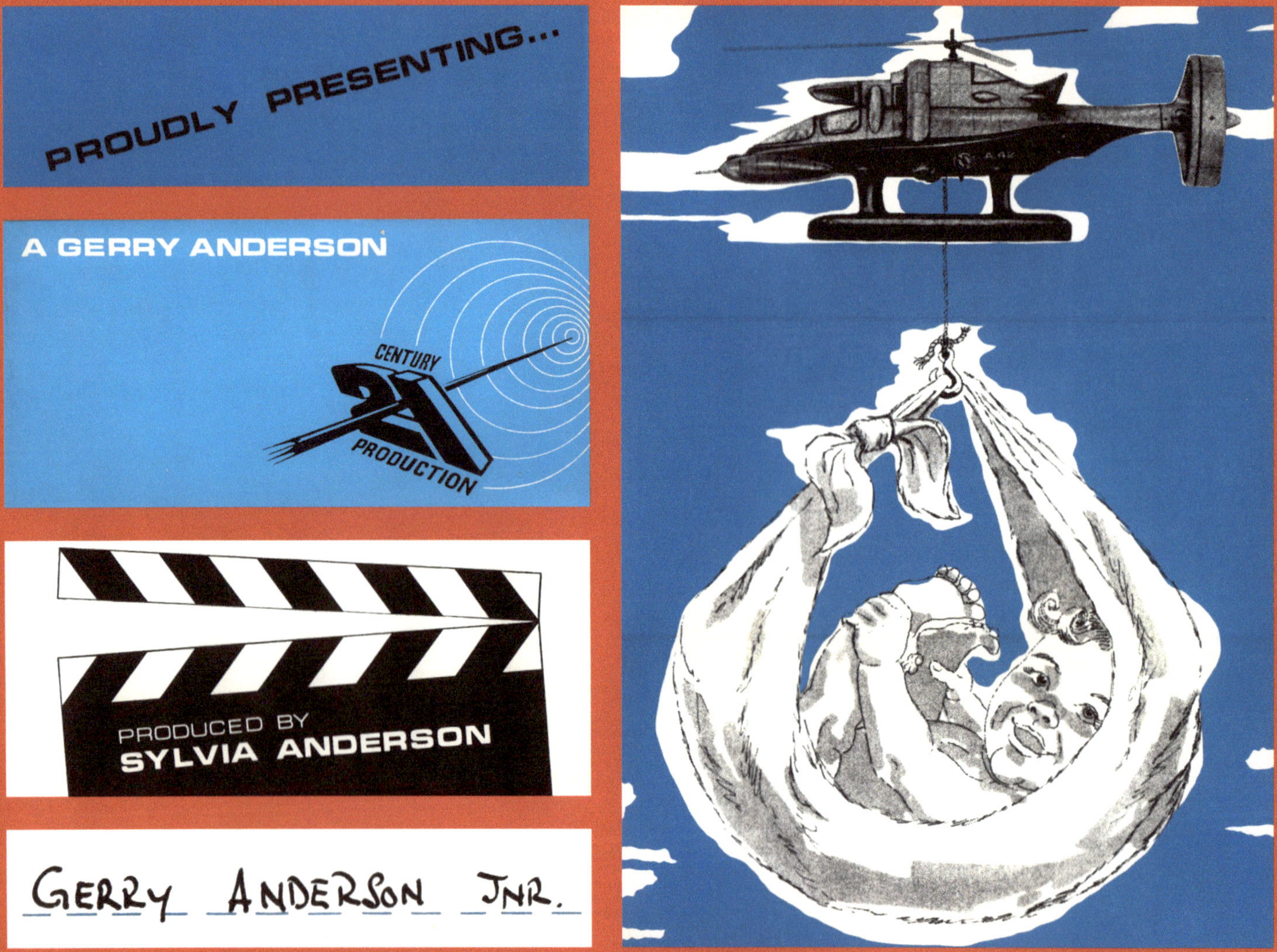

Above and opposite: This amusing, specially produced announcement card was distributed to friends and colleagues.

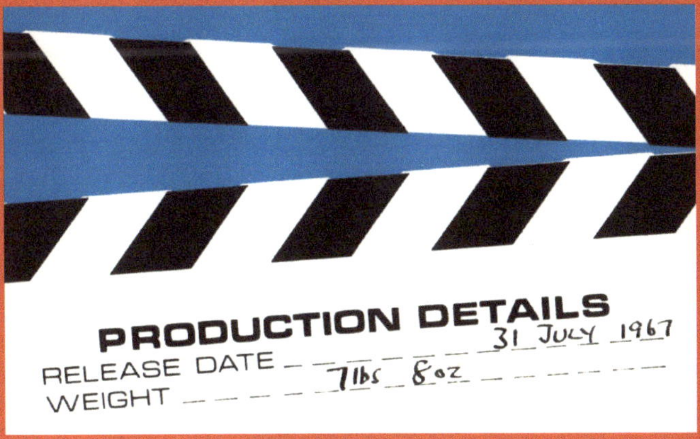

OPINIONS

- "A brand new & fantastically successful production by the well known team of Gerry & Sylvia Anderson" DAILY EXPRESS
- "Let's have more like this!" DAILY TELEGRAPH
- "No superlatives can do justice to this..." DAILY MAIL
- "Obviously a truly co-operative effort!" DAILY MIRROR

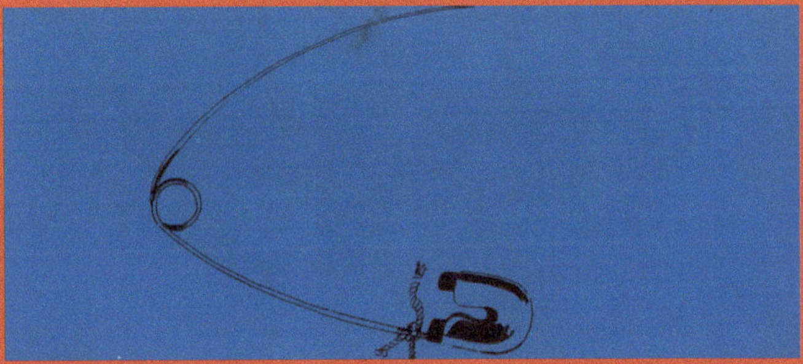

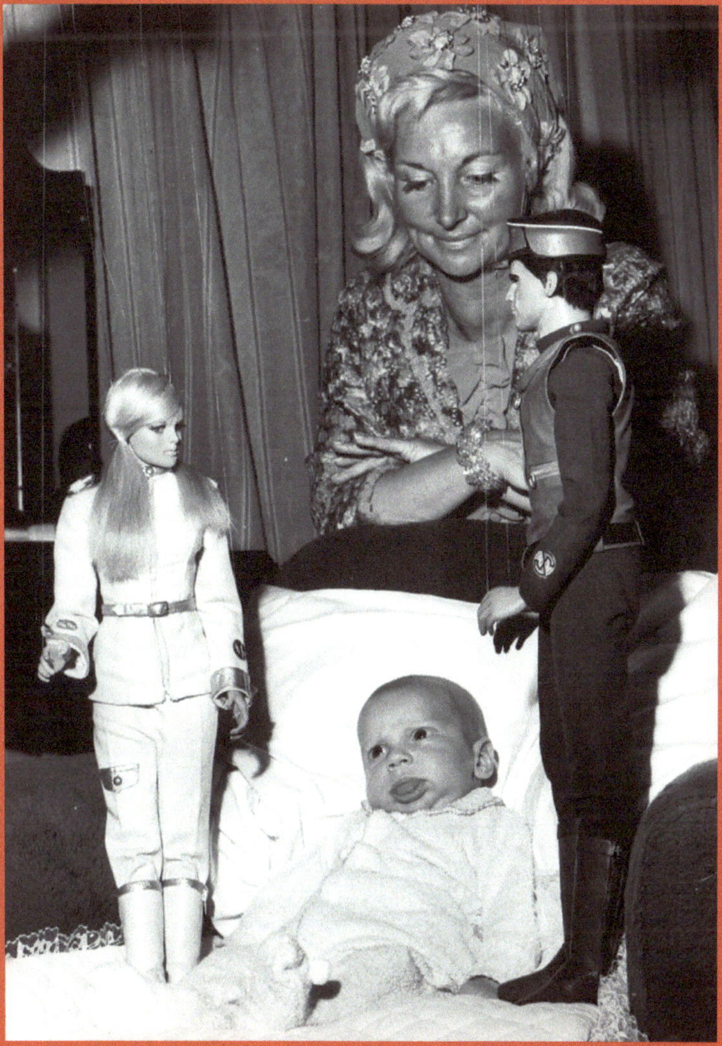

Right: While off duty, Captain Scarlet and Destiny Angel visit Gerry Jnr.

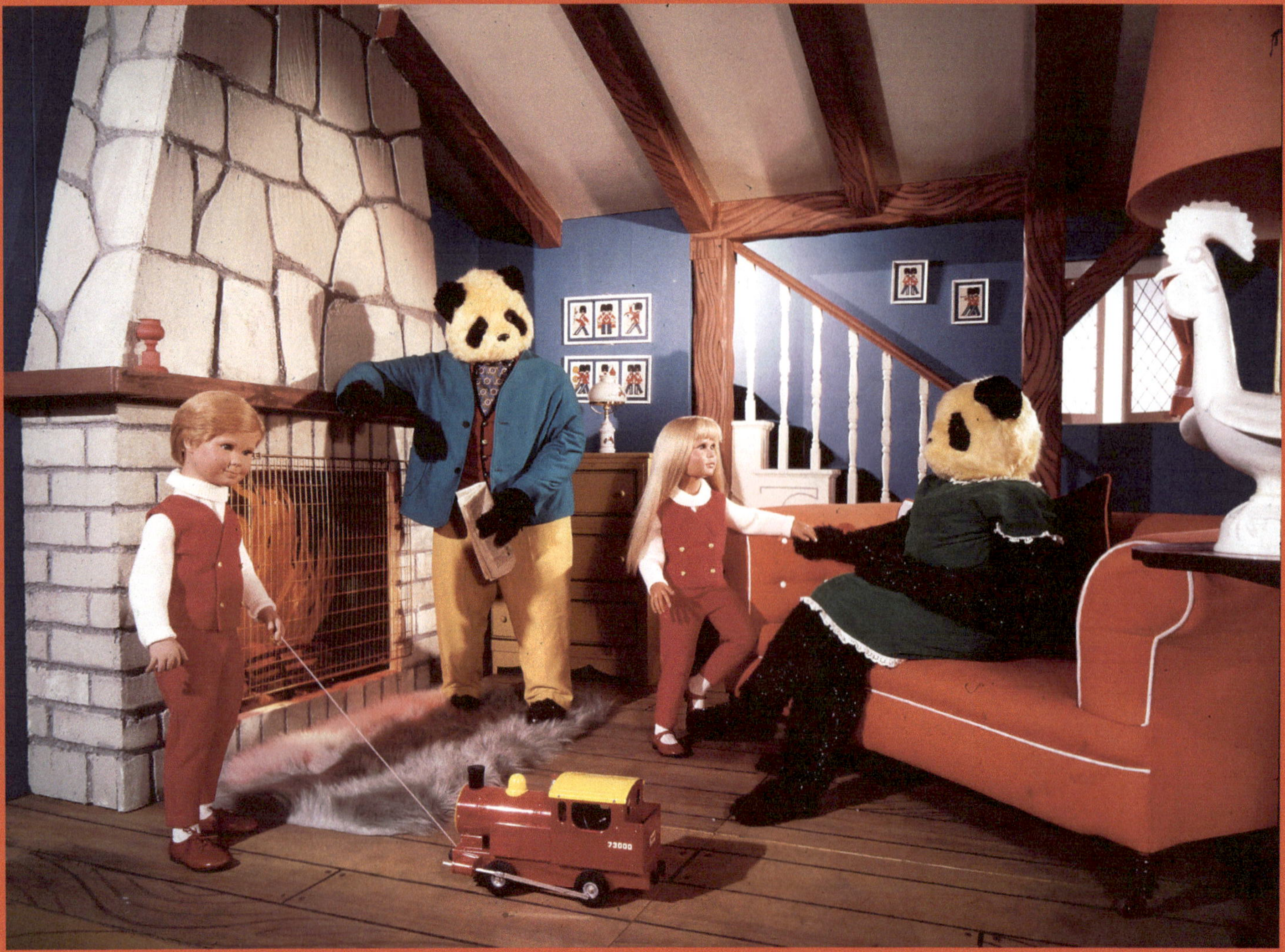

By the middle of the 1960s, Gerry was at the top of a puppet empire. APF's successful puppet shows spawned a huge amount of merchandise, all of which was overseen by APF's own marketing company, A.P. Films (Merchandising) Limited. TV Century 21, a comic based around the Supermarionation shows, was hugely successful. However, not all of the company's merchandising was based around their television shows...

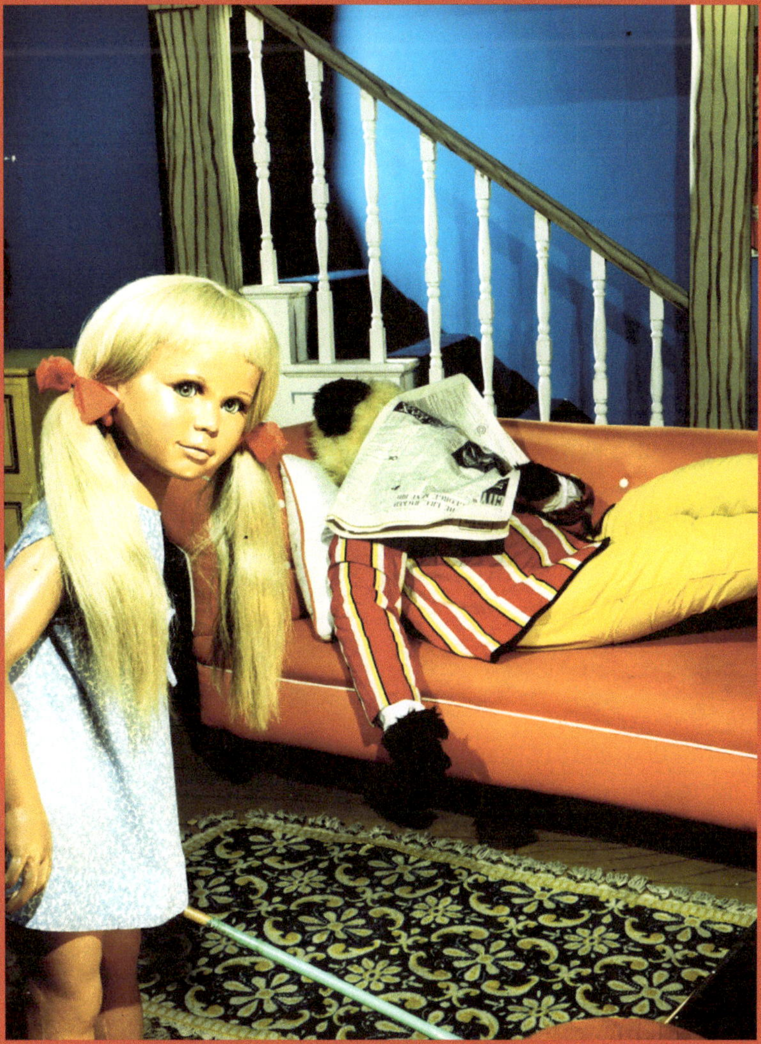

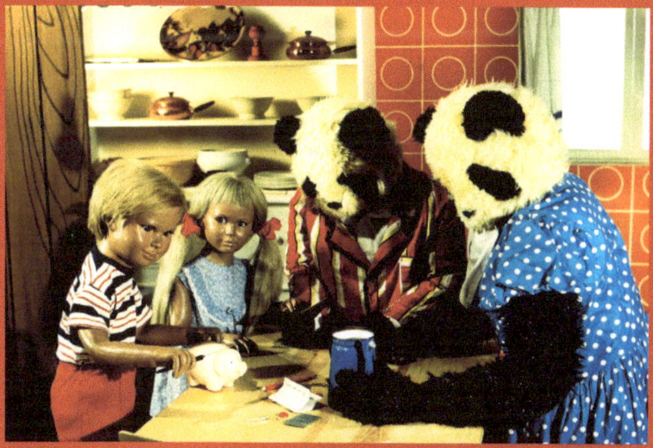

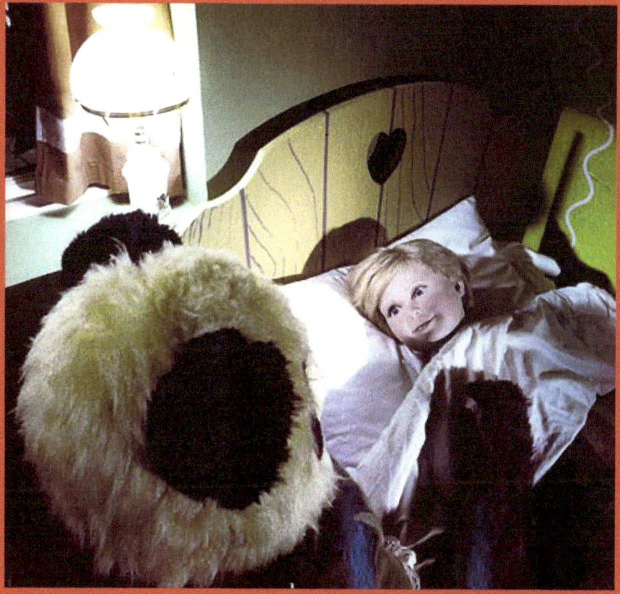

One of the odder ideas dreamt up by Gerry was *Candy and Andy*, which featured two plastic children living with married pandas called Mr and Mrs Bearanda. Astonishingly, this psychedelic trip lasted for more than 150 issues and several books!

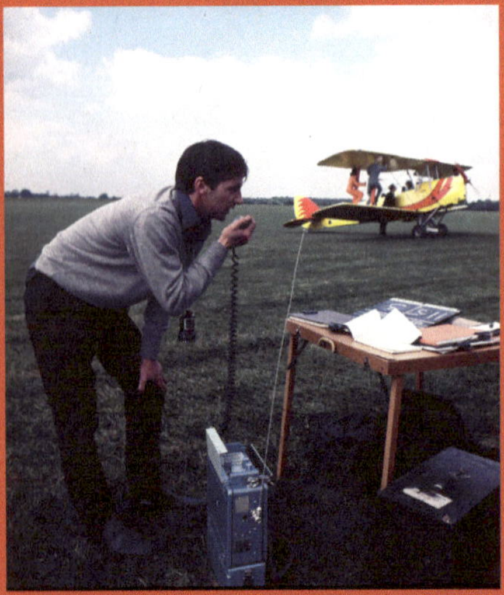

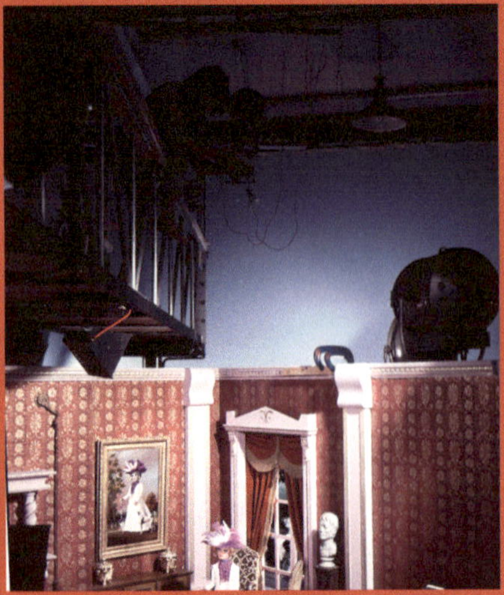

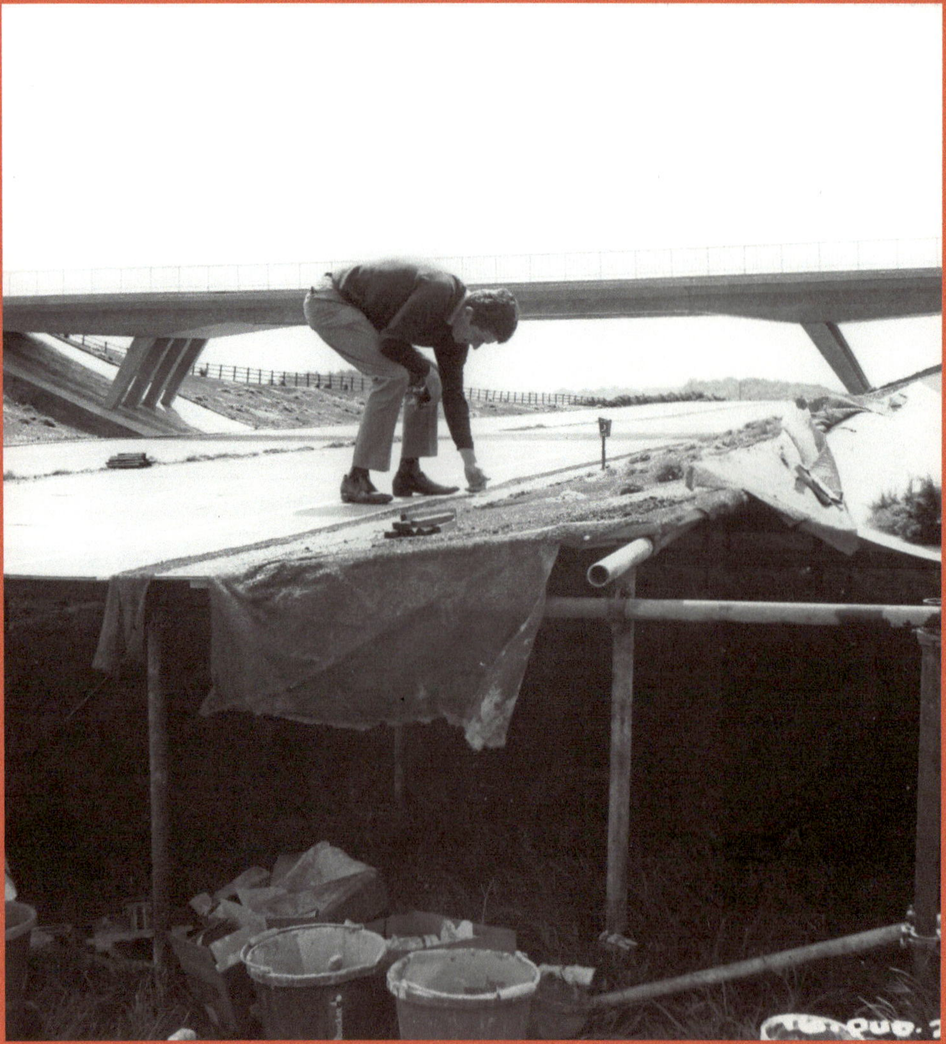

Bewildered by the failure of the first *Thunderbirds* feature film, executives were keen to have a second stab and commissioned *Thunderbird 6*. **Above left:** David Lane issues instructions to pilot Joan Hughes. **Below left:** Filming a scene at Lady Penelope's mansion. **Right:** After police halted filming with the full-sized Tiger Moth on the M40, the effects team set to work building an amazing scale replica to complete the shots.

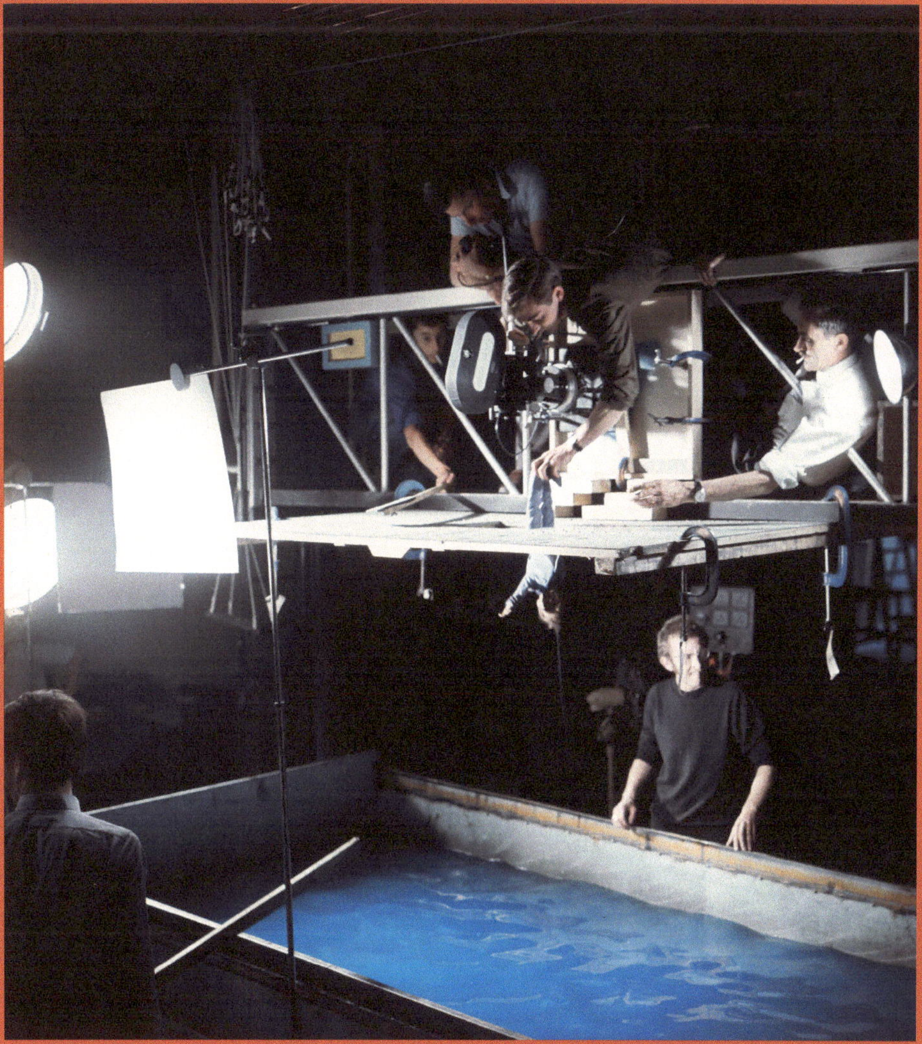

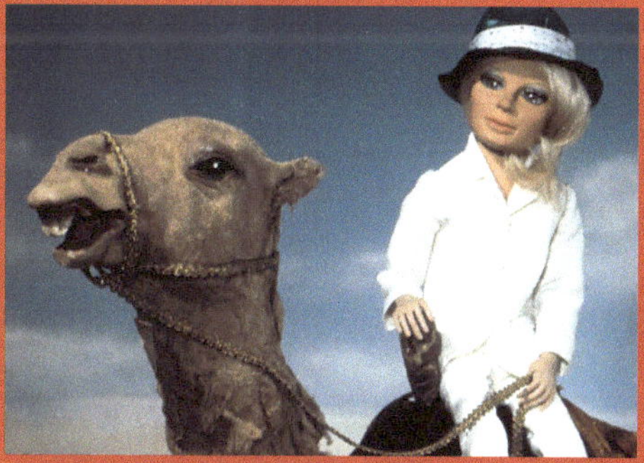

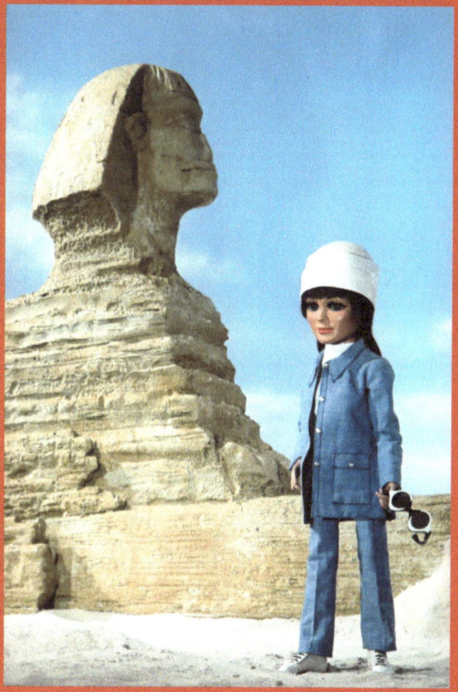

Left: David Lane oversees the grizzly job of disposing puppet corpses into the sea. **Above and below right:** Lady Penelope and Tin-Tin stop off in Egypt on their round-the-world trip. The beautiful recreations of famous landmarks are a highlight of the film.

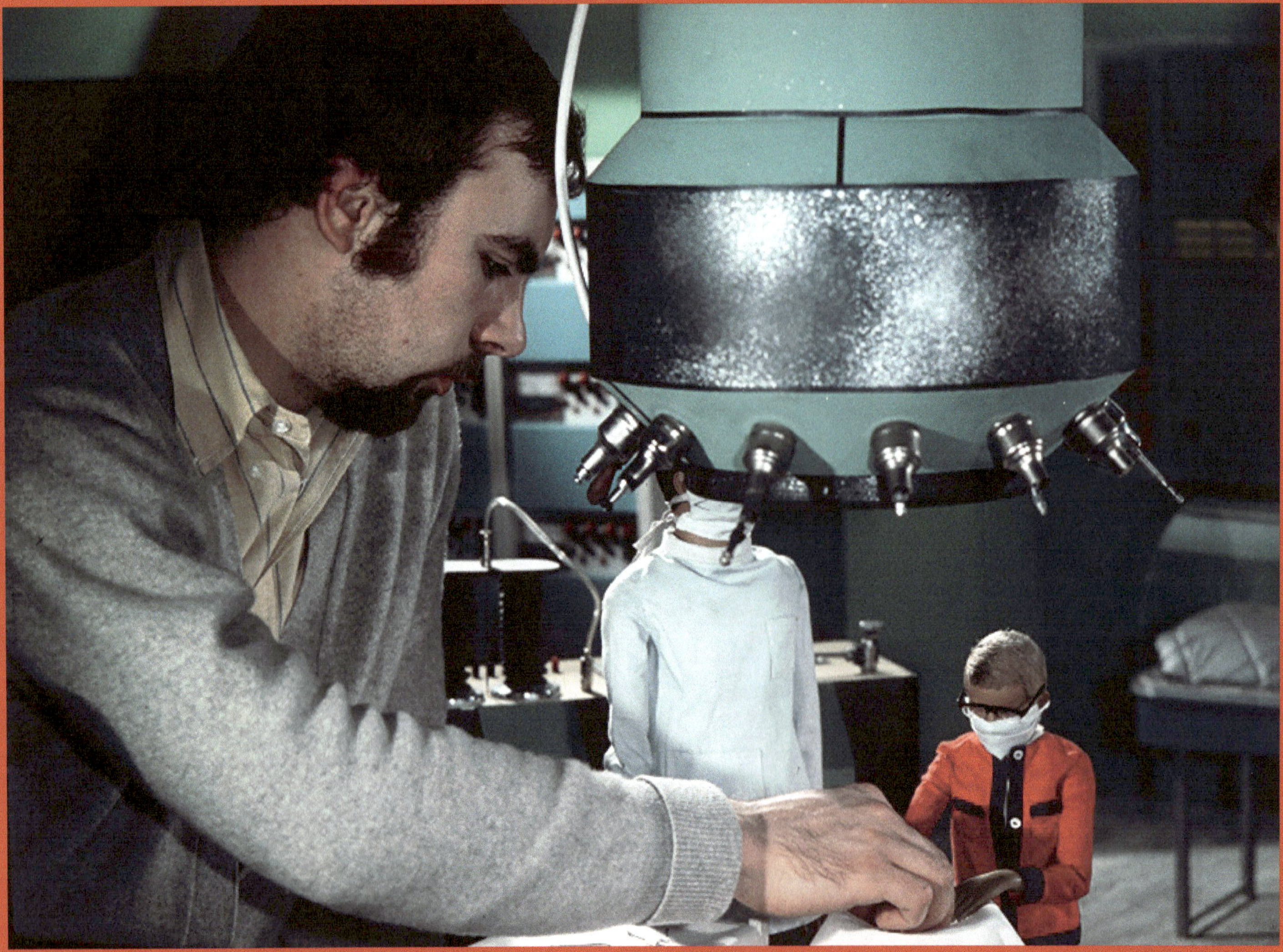

For the next series, Gerry thought back to the arrival of magnetic tape during his days in the cutting room. Struck by the ingenuity of being able to record and erase information that one couldn't see, he pondered if it would be possible to do the same with brain patterns; *Joe 90* was born. In this shot, Ken Turner sets up young Joe for a scene in 'Operation McClaine'.

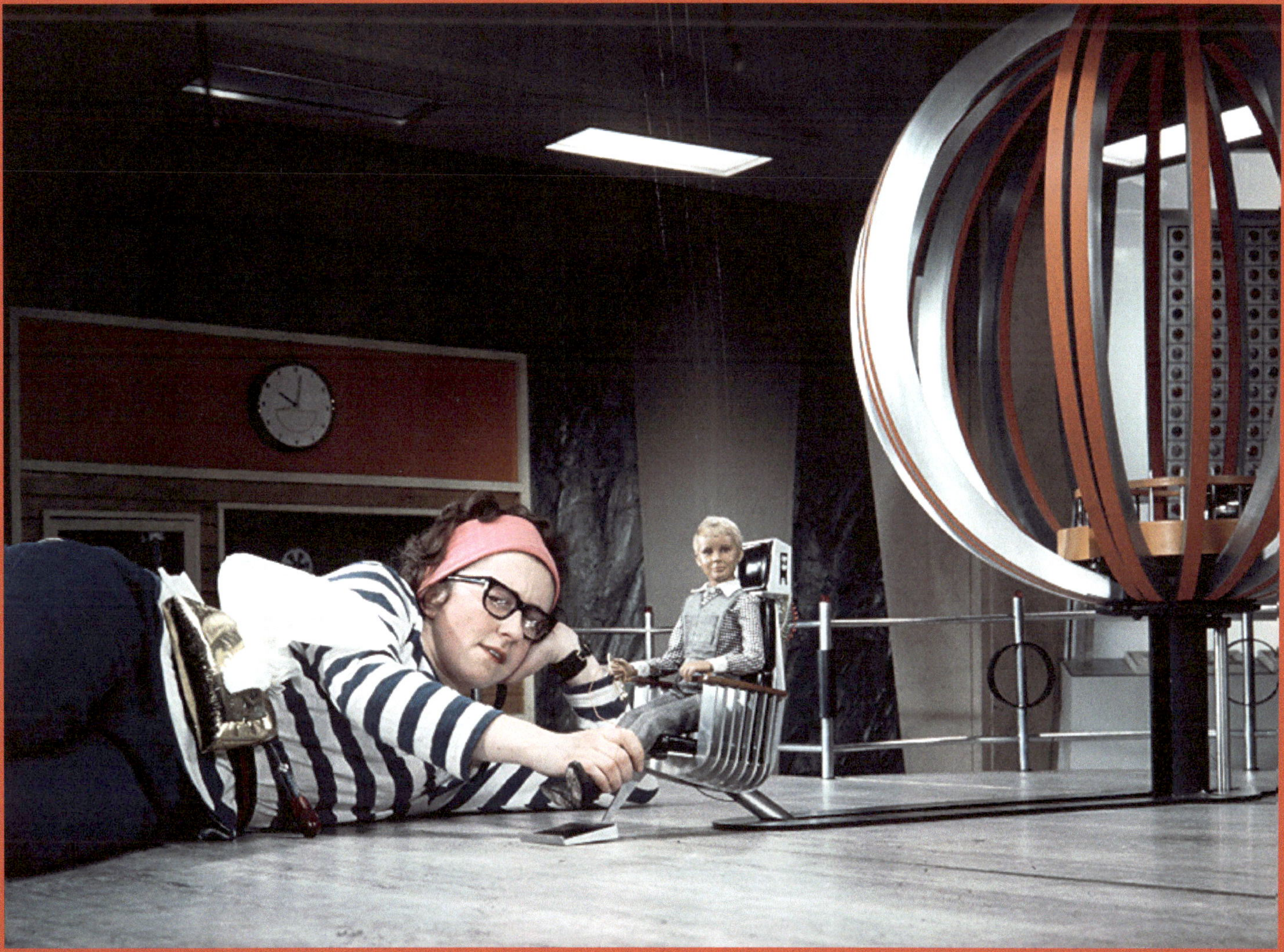

A puppeteer poses with Joe on the BIG RAT set. By this time, the art department had really honed their skills and were producing stunning miniature environments for the puppets to inhabit.

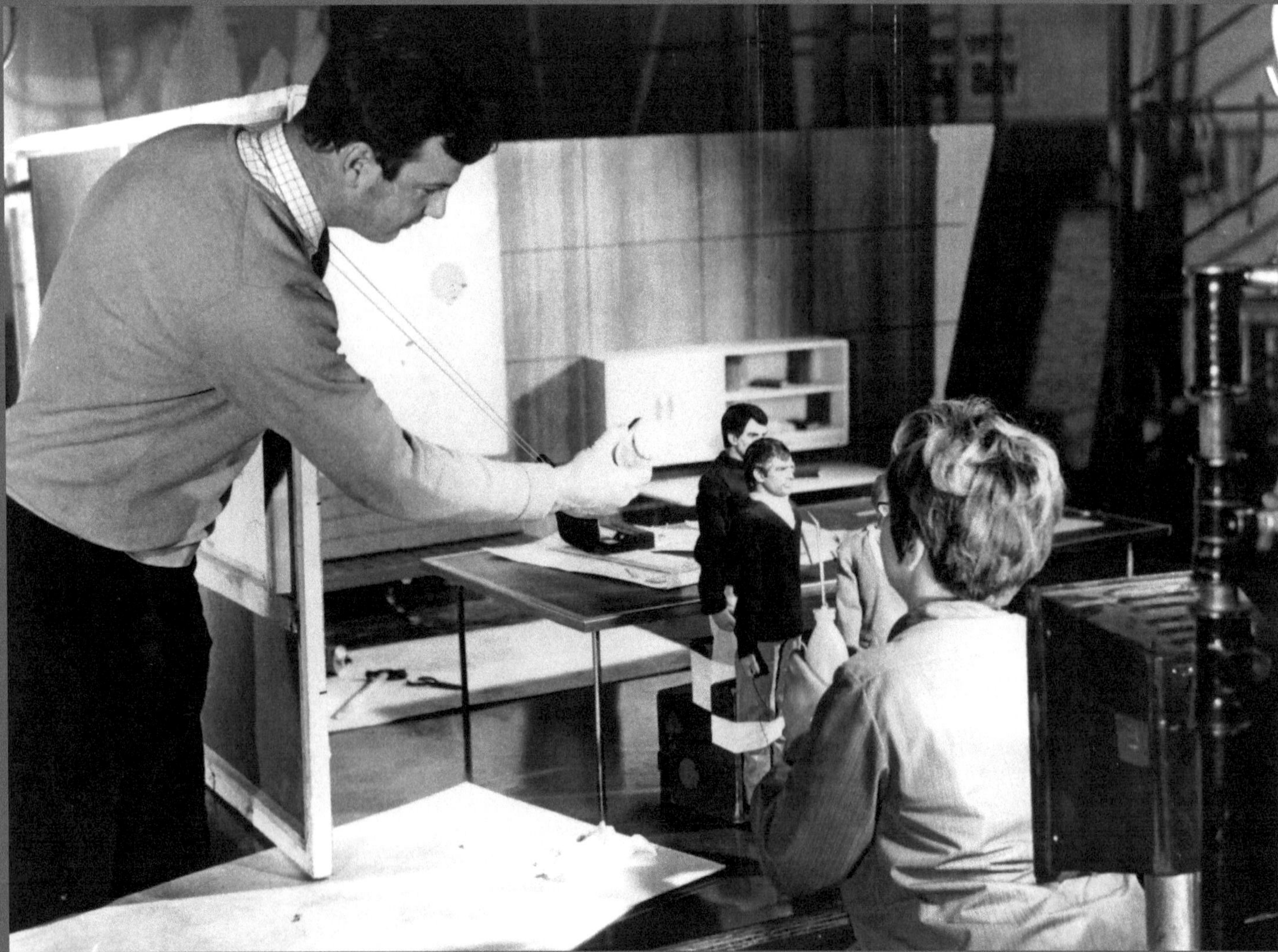

Paddy Seale lights Sam Loover and Shane Weston. The new puppets looked more realistic, but were incredibly difficult to operate in a suitably 'non-puppety' manner. Note that in order to prevent unwanted movements, the puppets are taped to blocks.

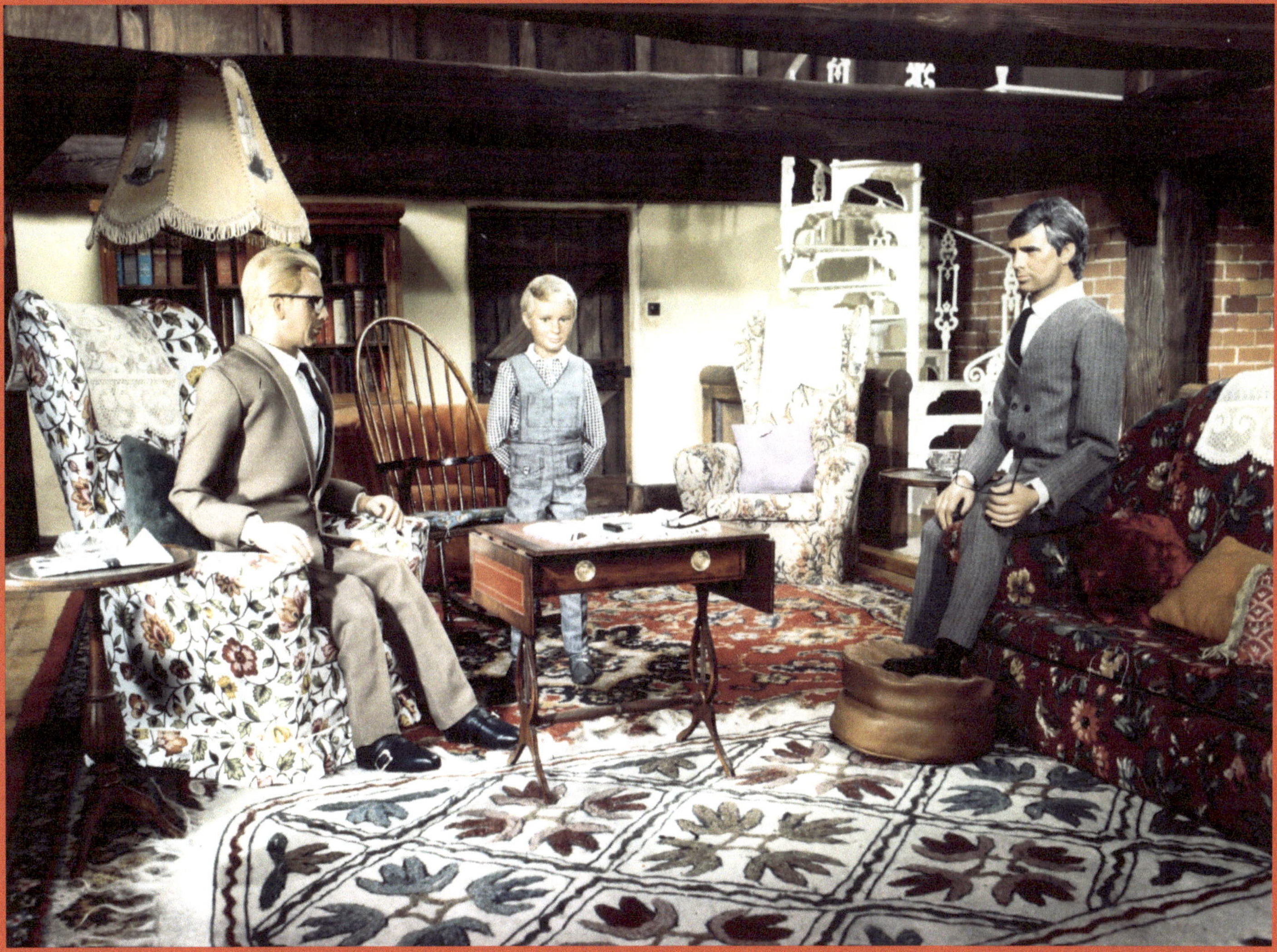

Professor McClaine, Joe 90 and Sam Loover on the beautiful set for Mac's cottage. So specialised was the work Century 21 were doing that almost every item seen on screen had to be either made or adapted.

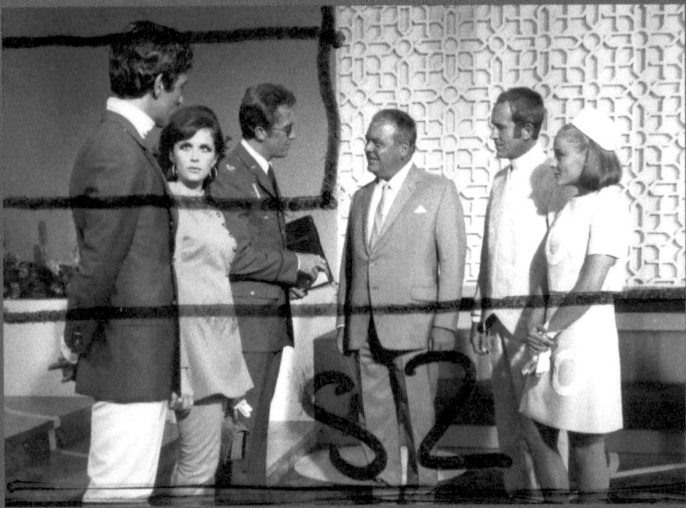

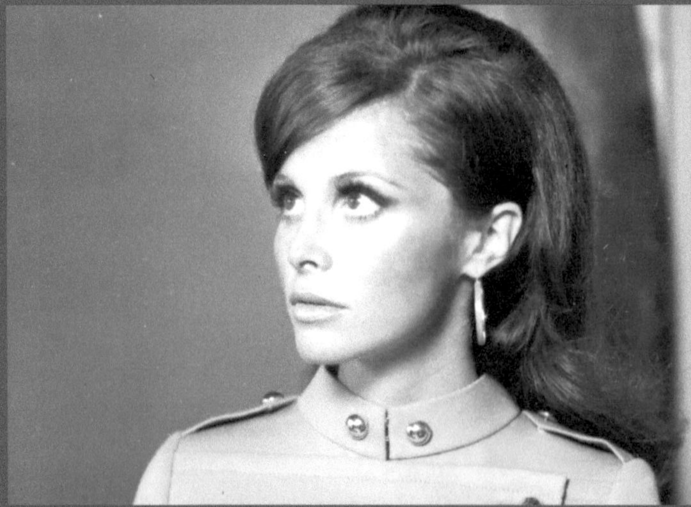

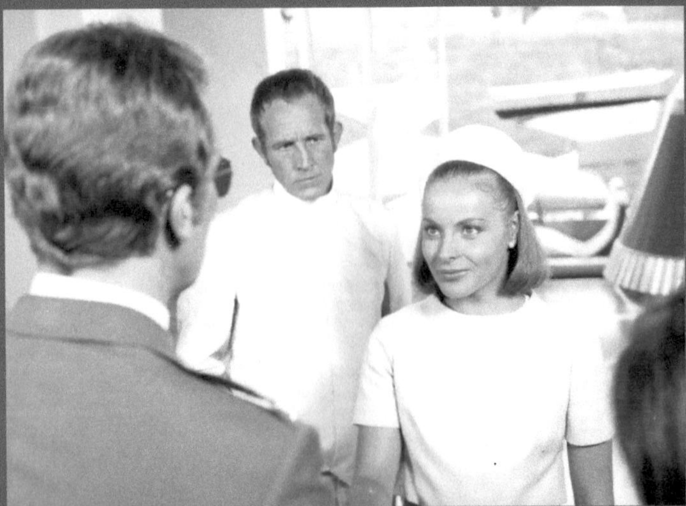

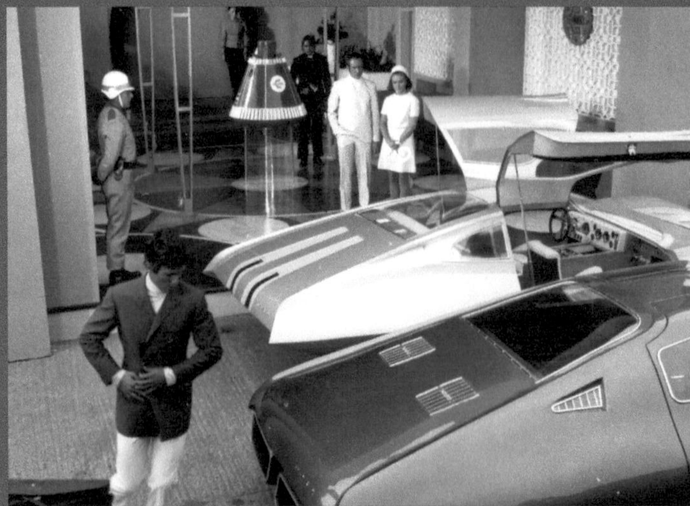

As successful as the puppets were, Gerry and Sylvia still longed to escape them and make proper grown-up films with humans. In 1968, their wish was finally granted when Universal and Lew Grade put up the money for *Doppelgänger*, a tale about a planet that is the mirror image of Earth on the opposite side of the sun.

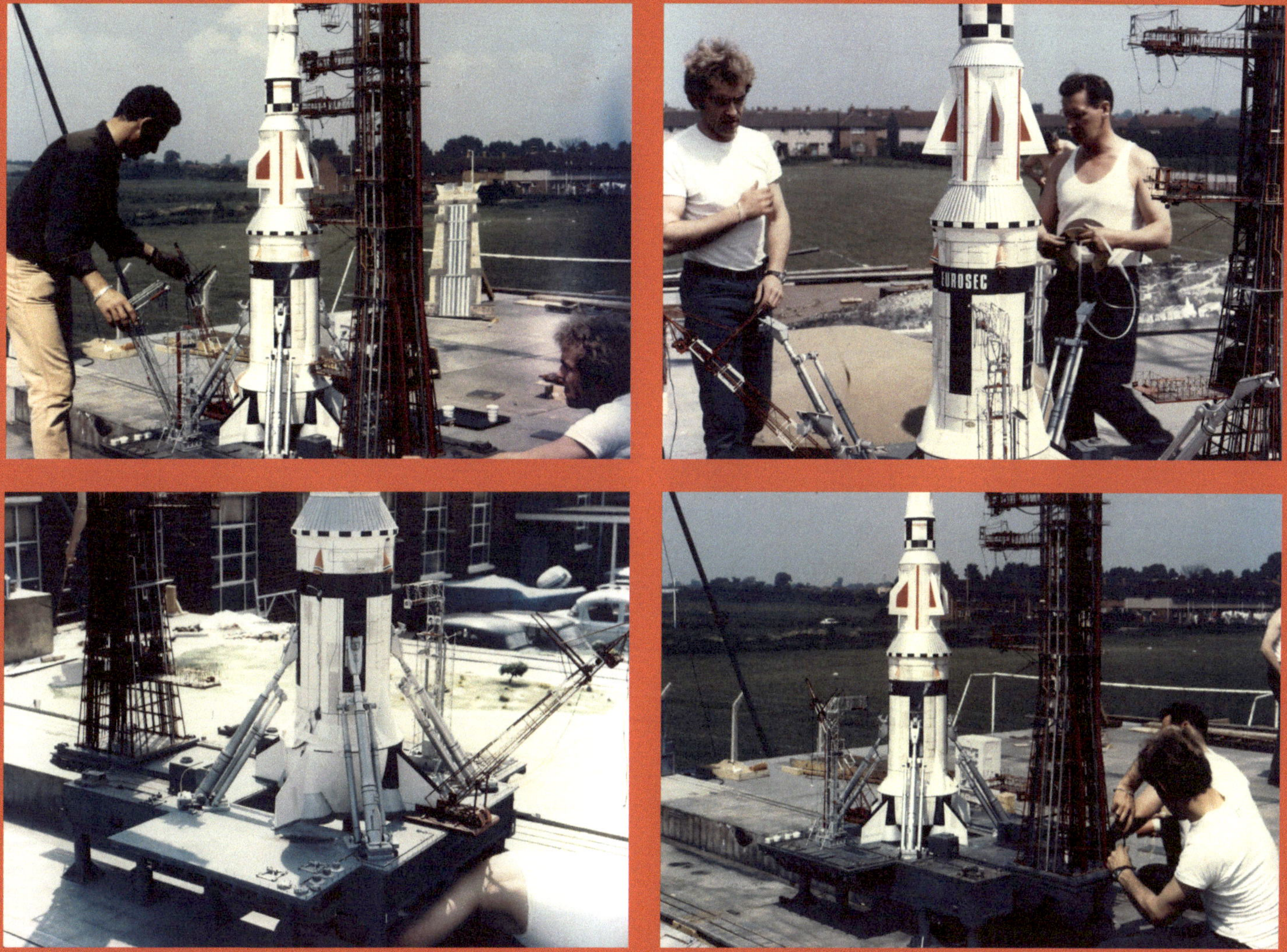

The special effects team magnificently rose to the challenge of producing effects that would blend with actors instead of marionettes. Here, we see them preparing the Eurosec rocket for lift-off at the Slough studios. The launch is often regarded as the special effects team's finest shot.

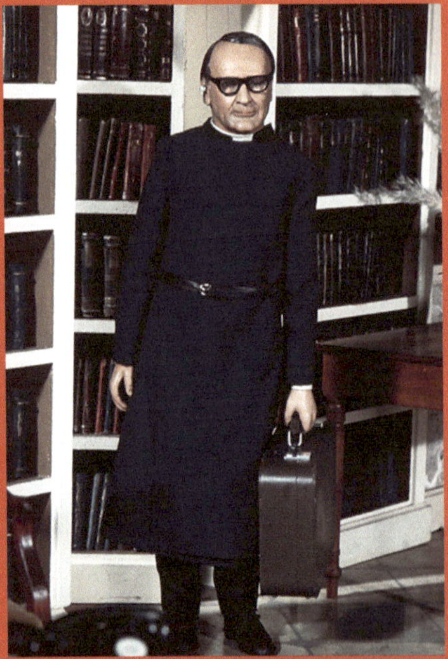

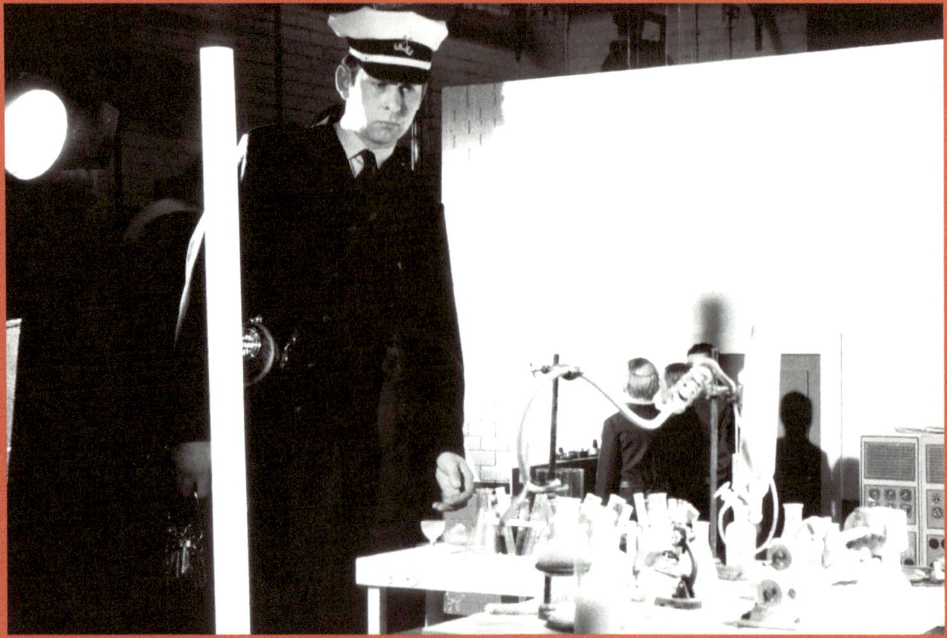

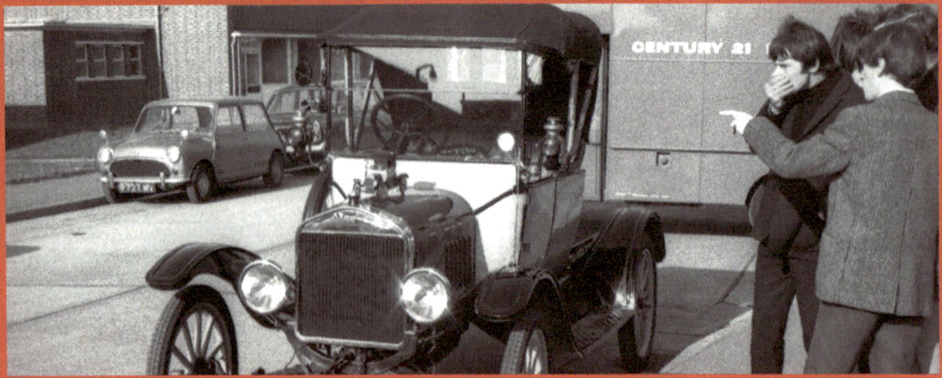

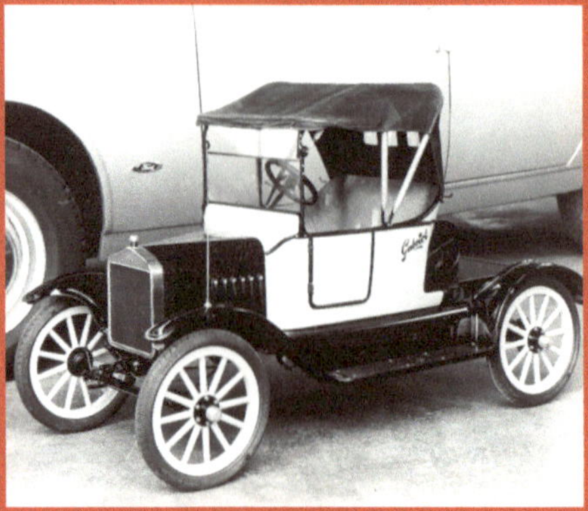

The company was rapidly becoming a victim of its own success, with their unique shows flooding the airwaves. *The Secret Service* was to be the final Supermarionation production. **Above left:** Mary Turner created a beautifully accurate puppet version of entertainer Stanley Unwin. **Above right:** A security guard patrols the studio. **Below left:** A mini Gabriel sits on the bonnet of the real thing. **Below right:** The fully working miniature version of Father Unwin's car, Gabriel.

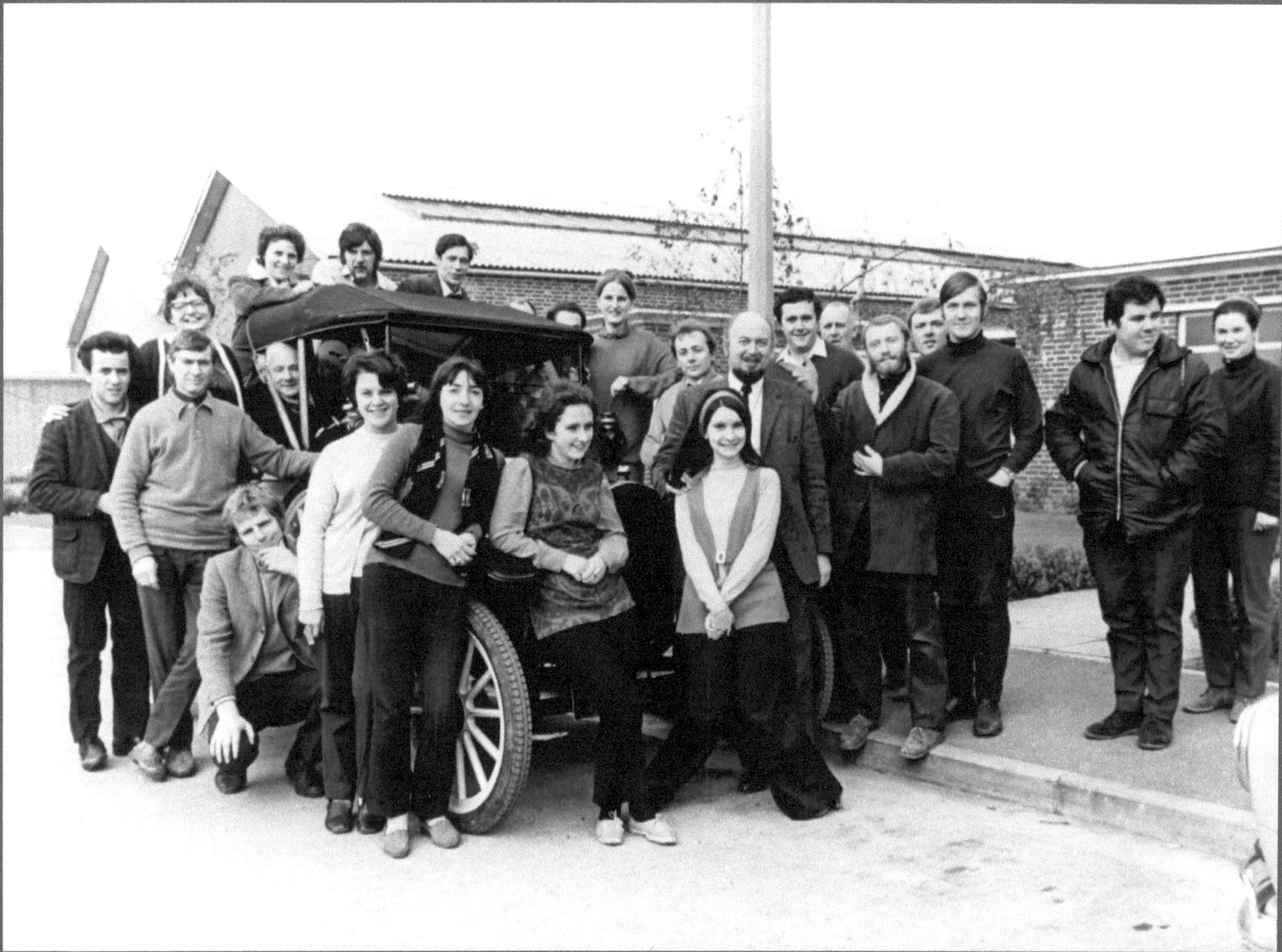

Lew Grade didn't care for *The Secret Service* and the series was canned after just 13 episodes, bringing the Supermarionation era to an end. *Doppelgänger* had proved that the Andersons could translate their unique style of filmmaking to the real world without puppet stars. Some of the team would move onto *UFO*, but for many, their services were no longer required. This picture, alleged to have been taken on the final day, shows the team together for the last time. A new era awaited.

1970s

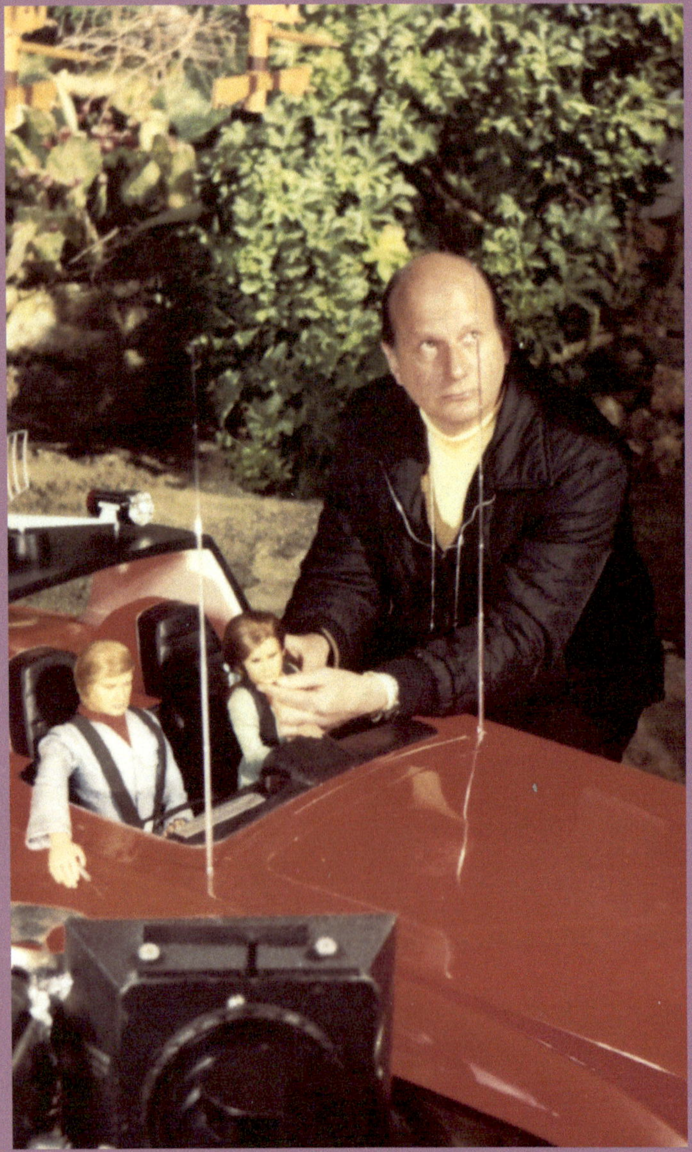

'They speak. And their mouth is in sync with the words. And they can walk. And they can pick up things. Boy this is going to be absolutely fabulous. That was my first impression.'

The puppets had brought Gerry incredible success, but he shed no tears at their demise. The failure of *Thunderbirds Are Go* had been a watershed moment for the marionette superstars and as the '60s drew to a close, the Andersons felt increasingly that there was little more that they could do with Supermarionation. Finally, the long-held dream of making a live-action series was coming to fruition, and Gerry was able to consign the puppets to the skip.

However, despite an initially promising start, it soon became apparent that humans could be just as difficult to deal with as puppets. In direct contrast to the halcyon days of the 1960s when Gerry and Sylvia were masters of their miniature world, the '70s were a turbulent time. Ongoing political issues at ATV meant that Lew Grade's support slowly dwindled, whilst increasing American interference affected Gerry's personal creative ambitions. At home there were troubles too, with Gerry and Sylvia's marriage slowly disintegrating.

The '70s produced two of Gerry's most successful television series, but the dramas involved came at a personal cost.

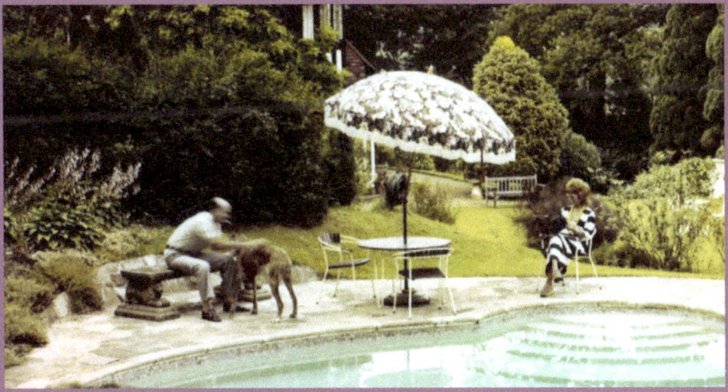

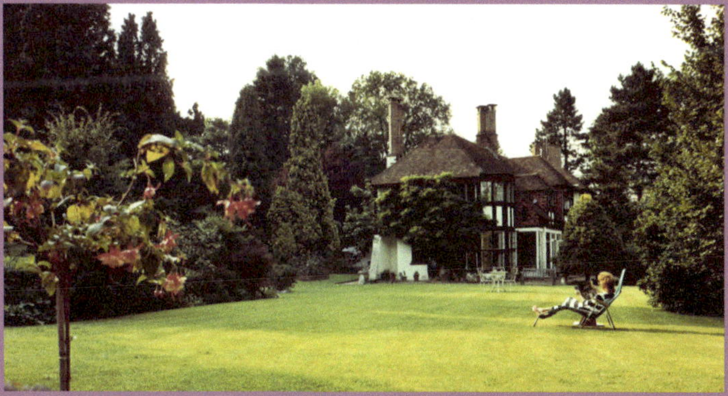

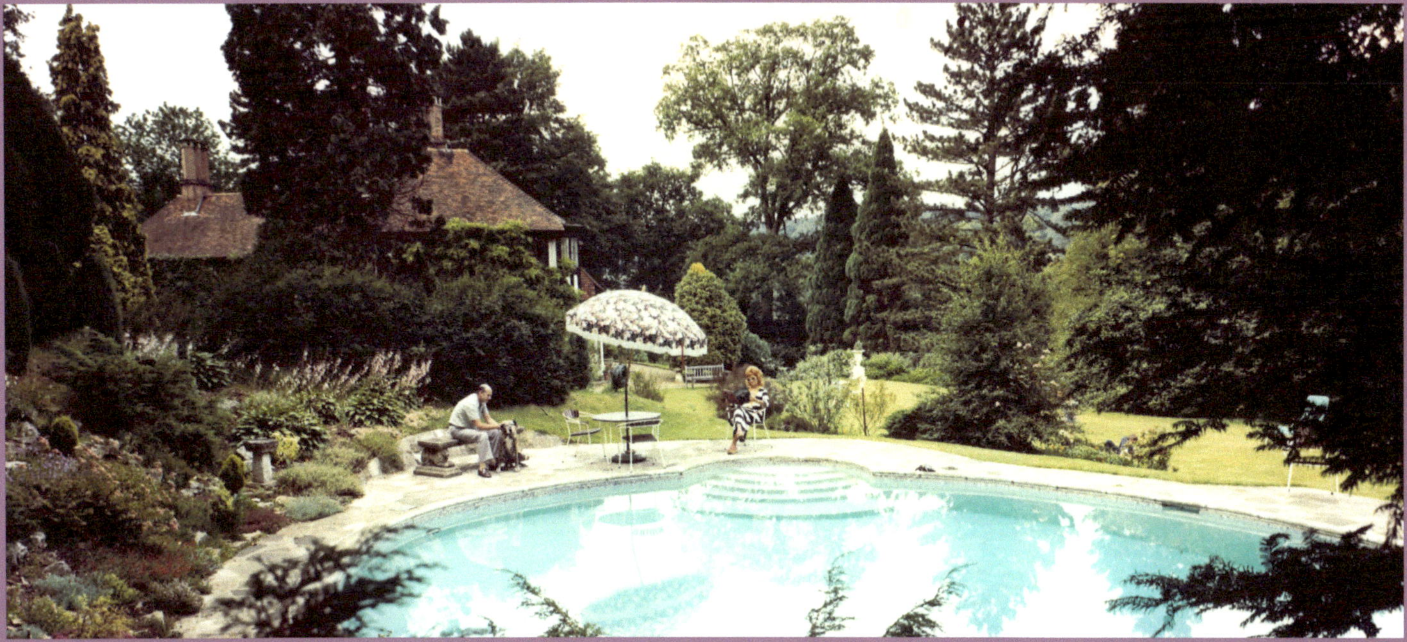

Previous: Gerry, on location in Malta, helps set up the next shot for a pilot called *The Investigator* in 1973. **Above:** The 1960s were an amazing time for Gerry. The sale of A.P. Films in 1962, combined with the continued success of the puppet shows, meant that the boy who had been raised in near poverty now found himself enjoying a life of financial comfort that must have once seemed unimaginable. Here, the Andersons relax at their home, White Plains in Gerrards Cross, at the end of an extraordinary decade, and the beginning of a turbulent one.

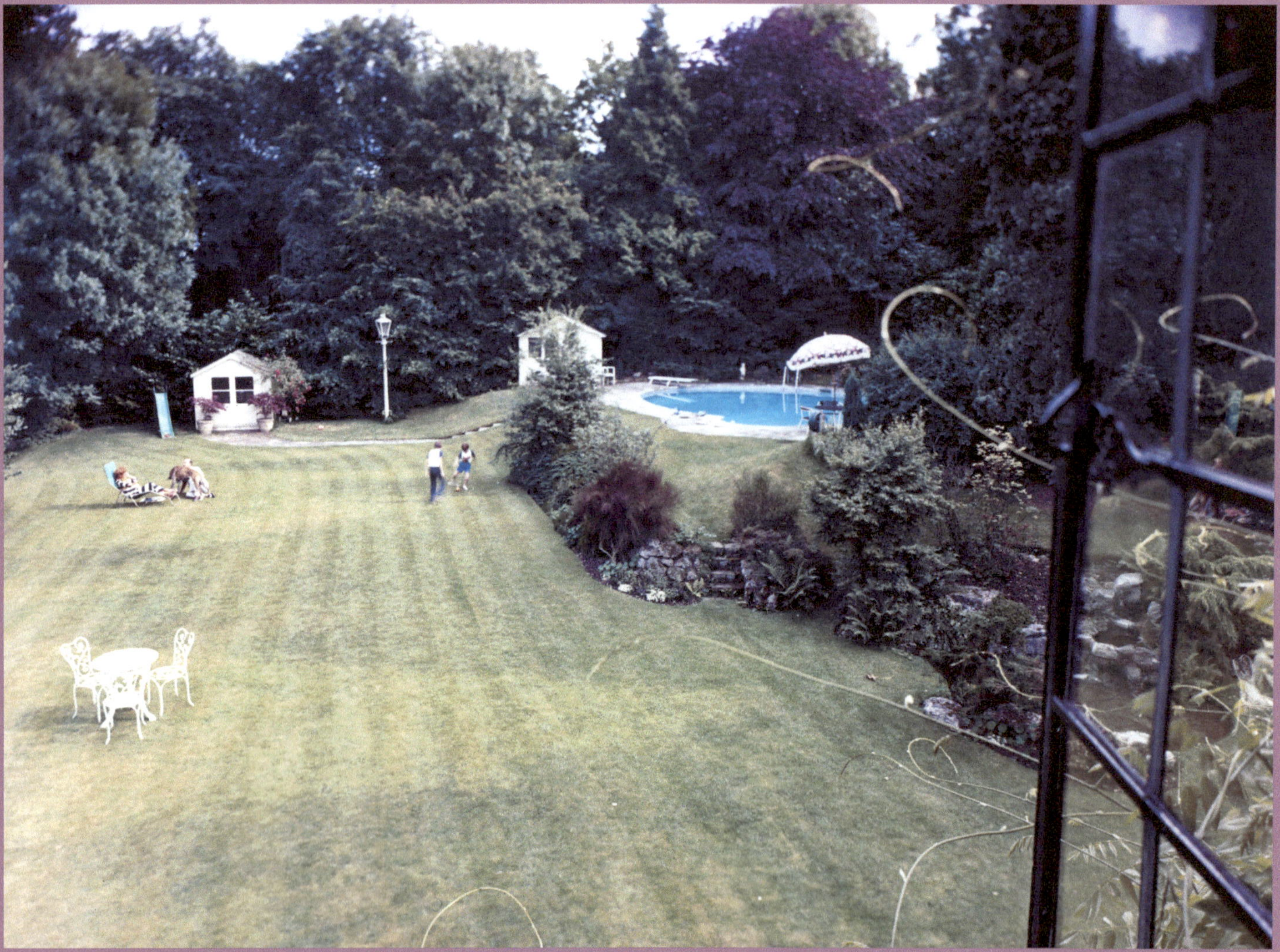

The enormous garden at White Plains, which was host to many memorable parties throughout the various productions.

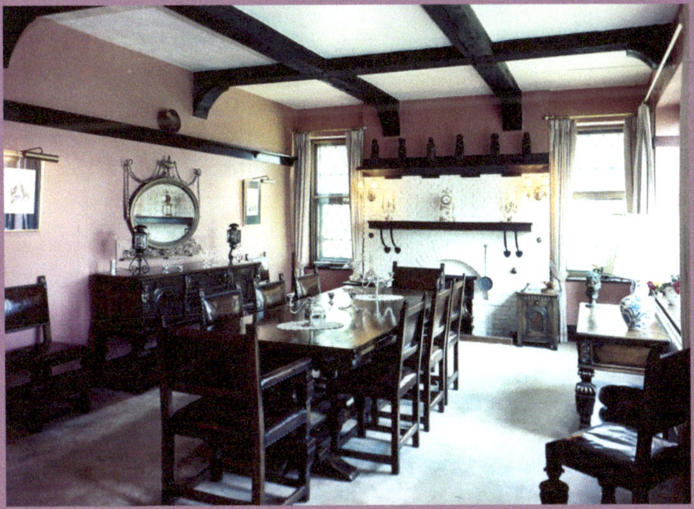

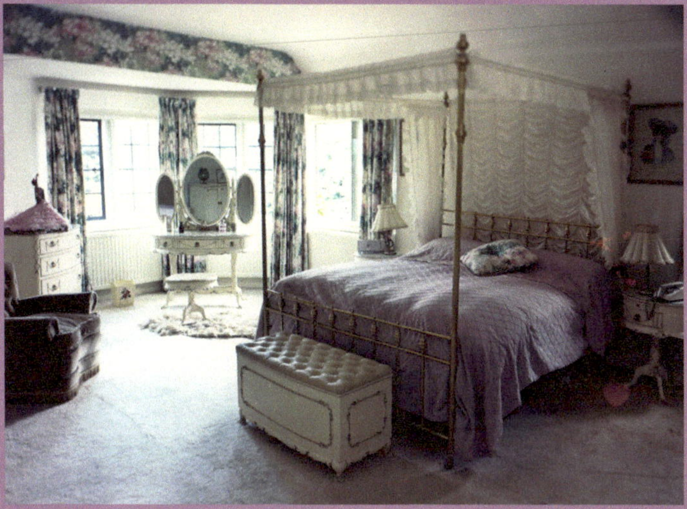

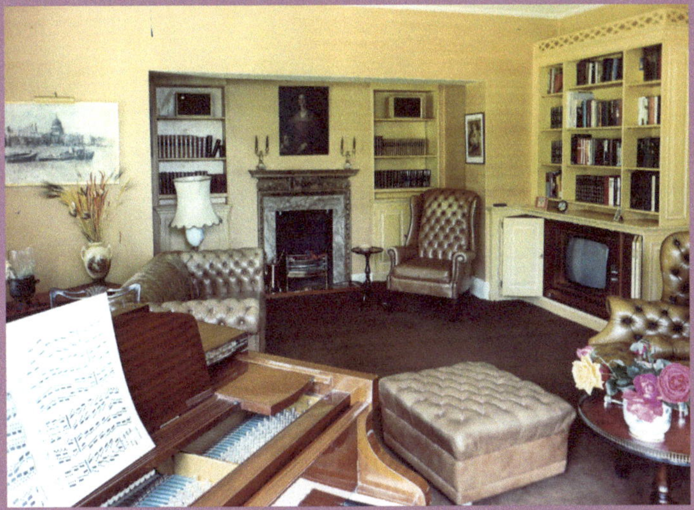

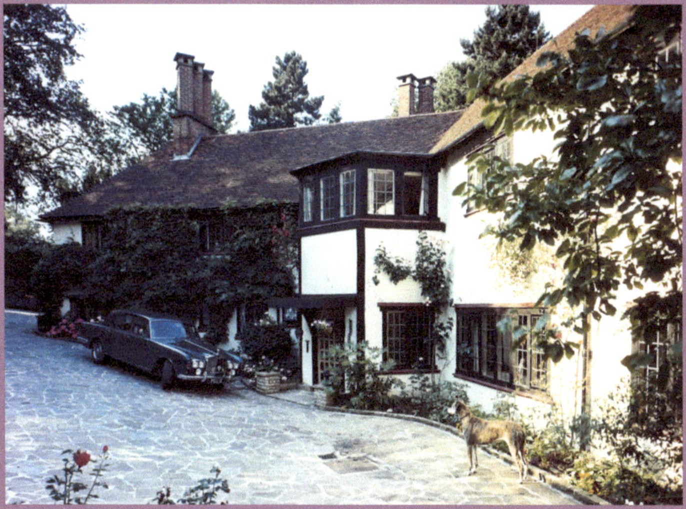

Views of the interior and exterior – a reflection of a successful decade.

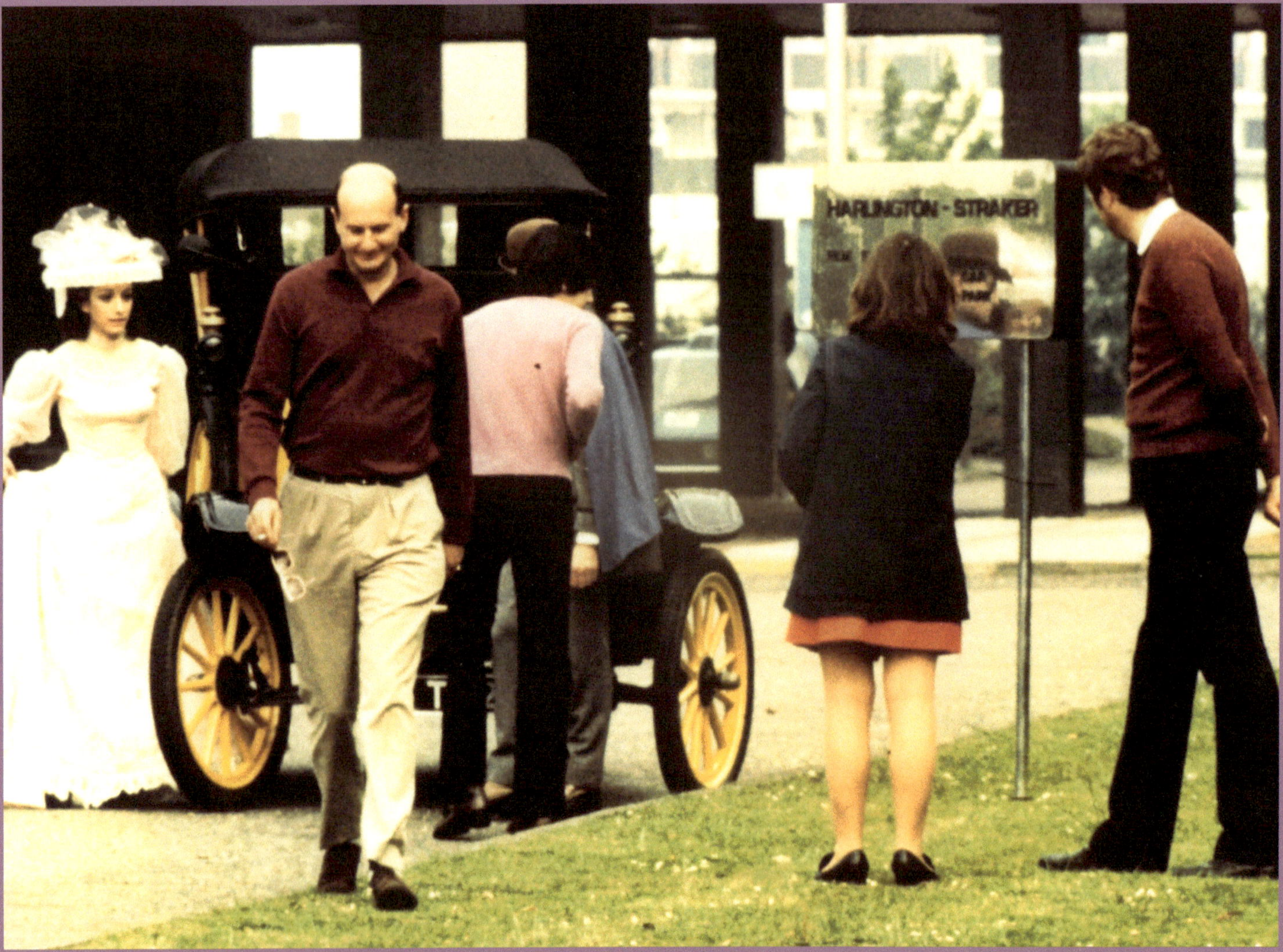

The world's first heart transplant in December 1967 by Doctor Christiaan Barnard fascinated Gerry. Along with partners Reg Hill and Sylvia Anderson, he was inspired to create his first live-action series, *UFO*. **Above:** Gerry at Elstree Studios, where many of the exteriors were filmed. In order to save on location costs, it was decided to set SHADO's headquarters under a fictional film studio.

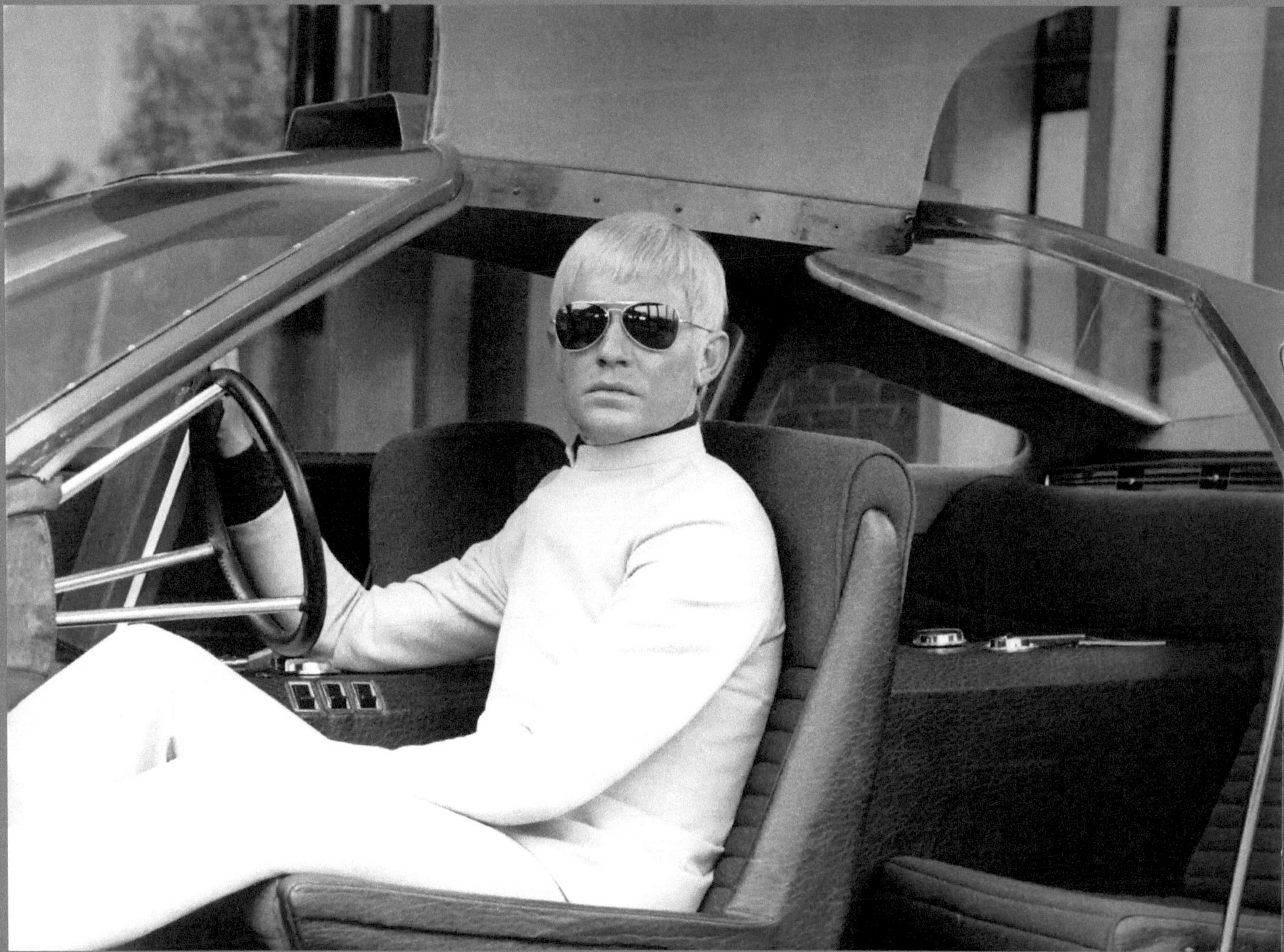

While preparing *Captain Scarlet,* the Andersons auditioned young American actor Ed Bishop for the role of Captain Blue. Both Gerry and Sylvia rated Ed highly, casting him again in *Doppelgänger* before giving him the leading role in *UFO*.

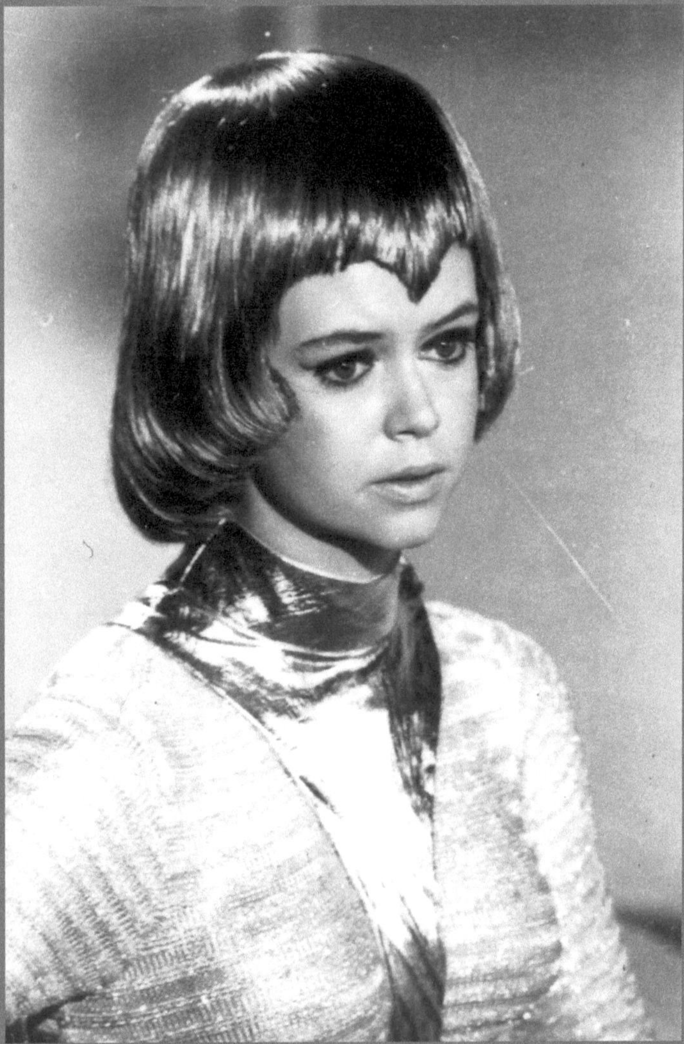

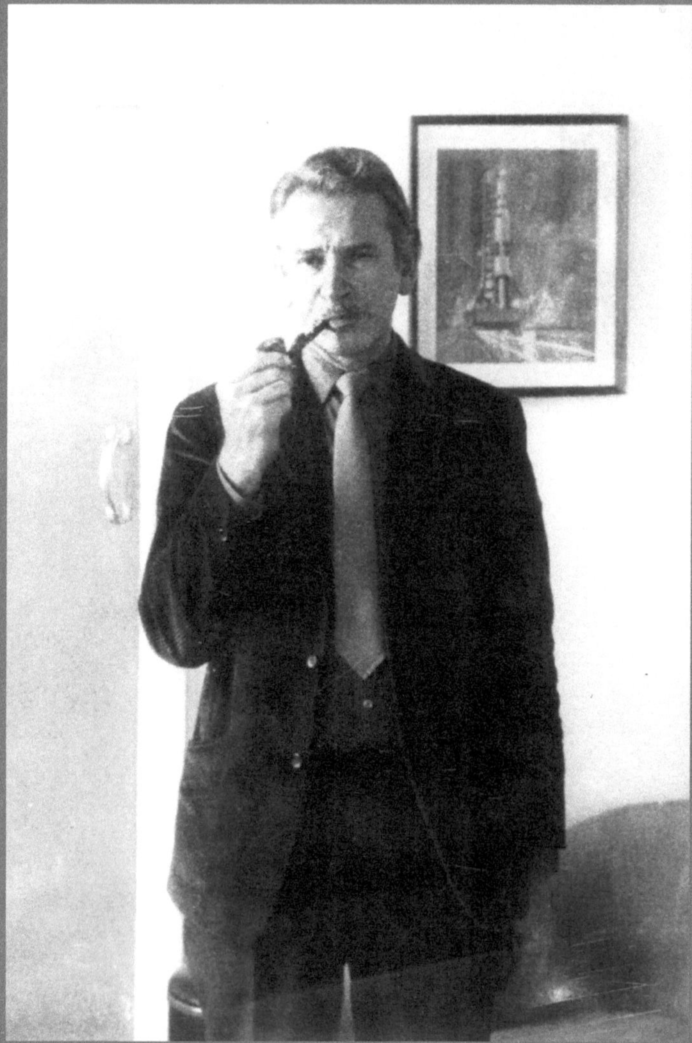

Left: A number of actors were auditioned and tested in full costume for the various characters. Gabrielle Drake, seen here during one of the tests, was cast as Lt Gay Ellis. **Right:** One of the unsung heroes of many Anderson productions was Gerry's business partner Reg Hill. A brilliant designer and methodically minded individual, Reg earned the nickname of 'The Car Park Attendant' for his strict adherence to the rules and concerns about health and safety. He worked with Gerry until the late 1970s.

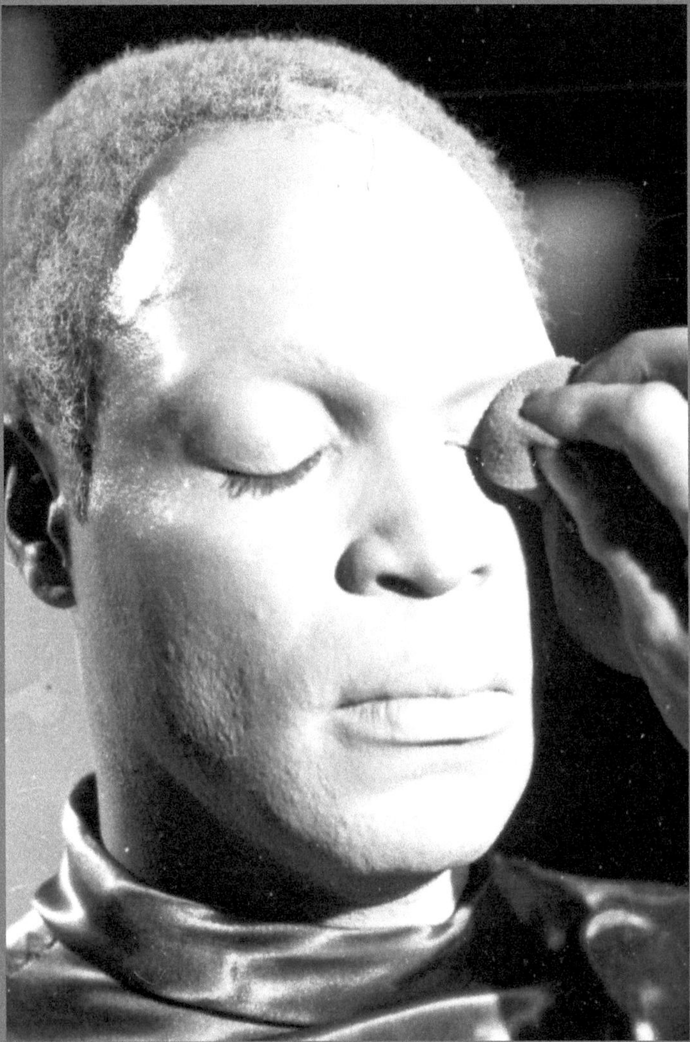

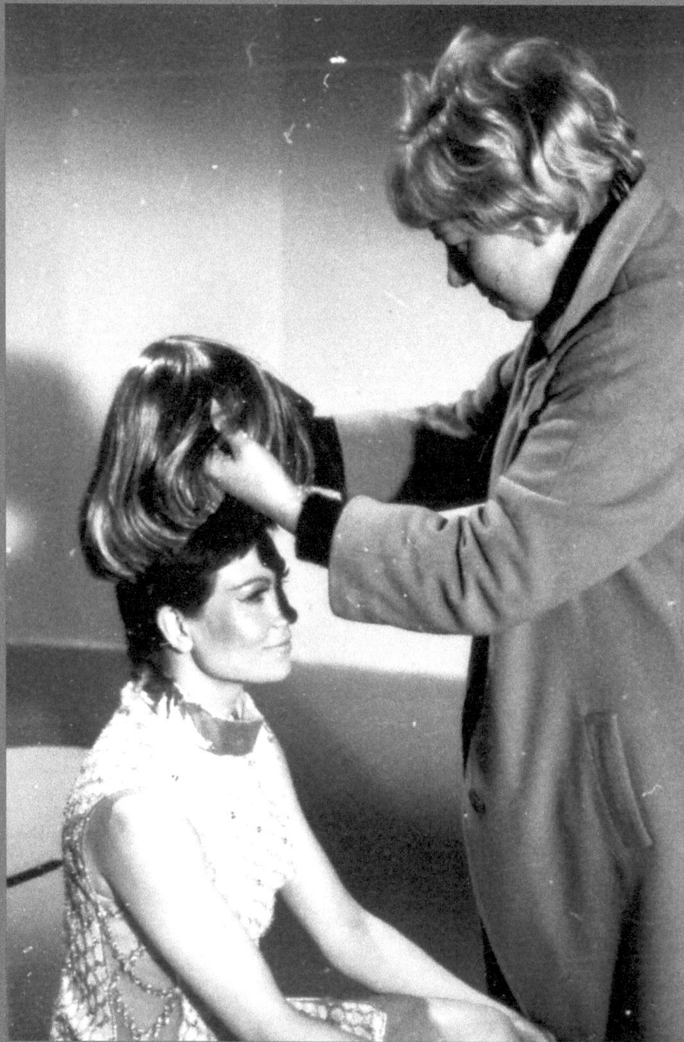

Further screen testing. Harry Baird (**left**) has make-up applied, whilst Antonia Ellis (**right**) is fitted with her purple wig.

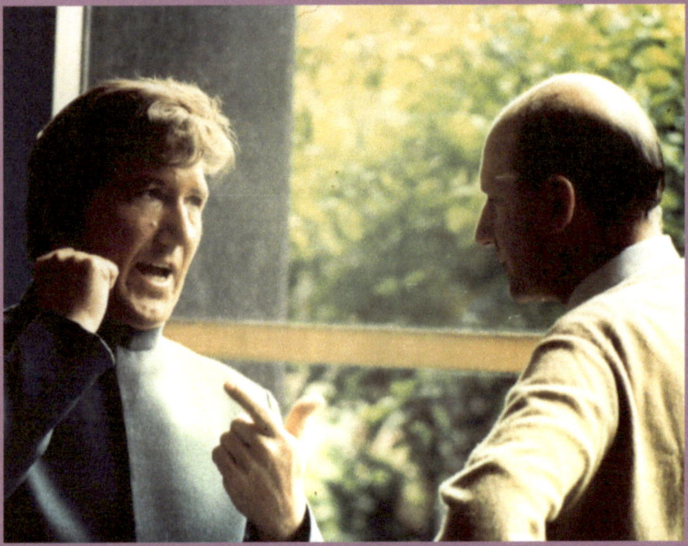

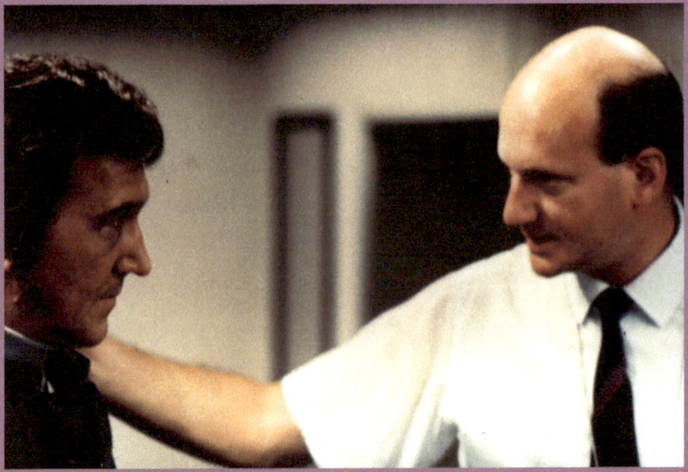

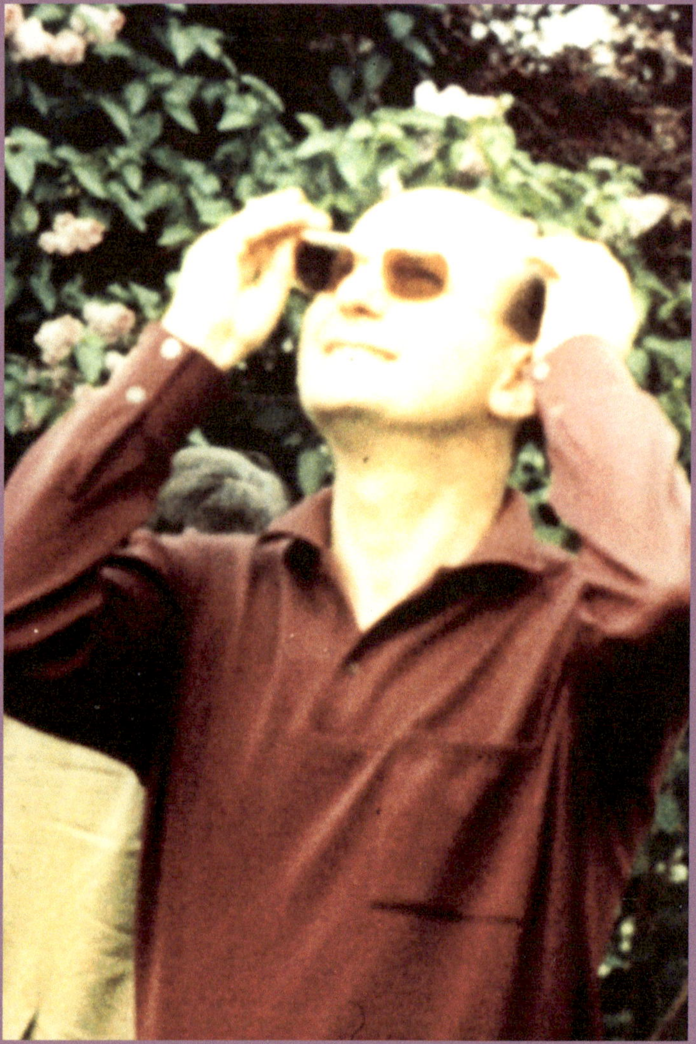

Gerry on set with George Sewell during filming of the first episode, 'Identified'. Always keen to set the style of any new series they did, the Andersons often undertook to write the first episode. For *UFO* though, Gerry decided to direct the first instalment too. It had always been his wish to be a director, and in the early days of A.P. Films he directed their entire output. However, the demands of the company soon meant he had to focus on his duties as producer. *UFO* was one of the last times he would direct an episode of one of his shows.

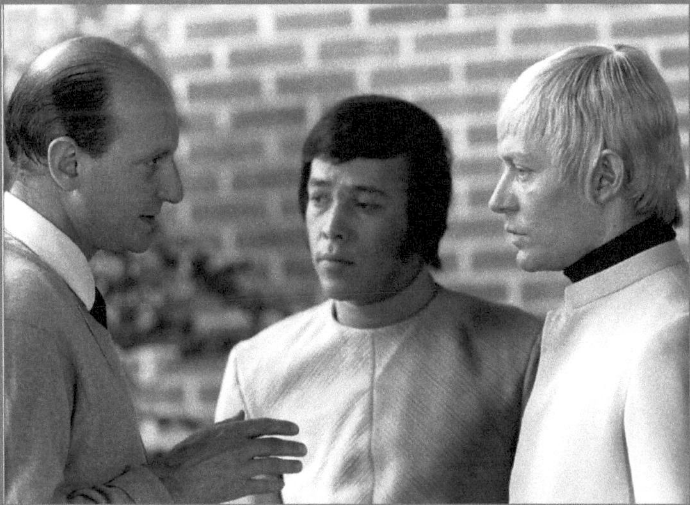

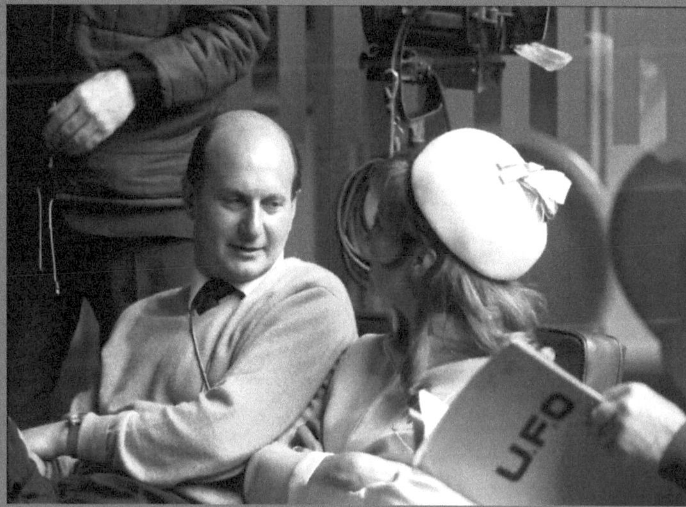

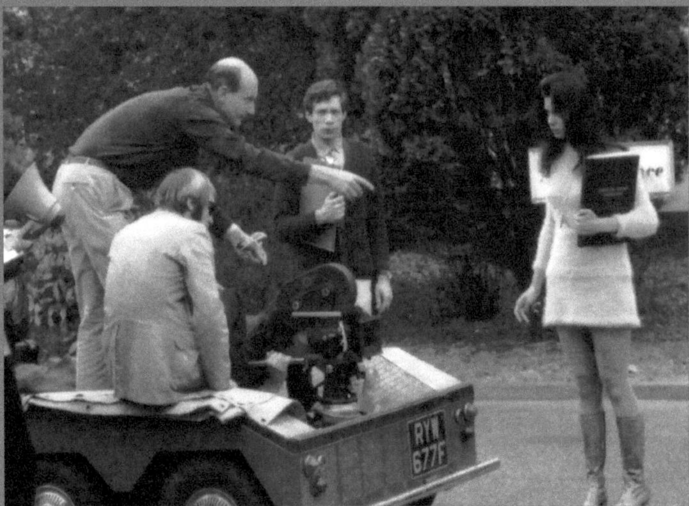

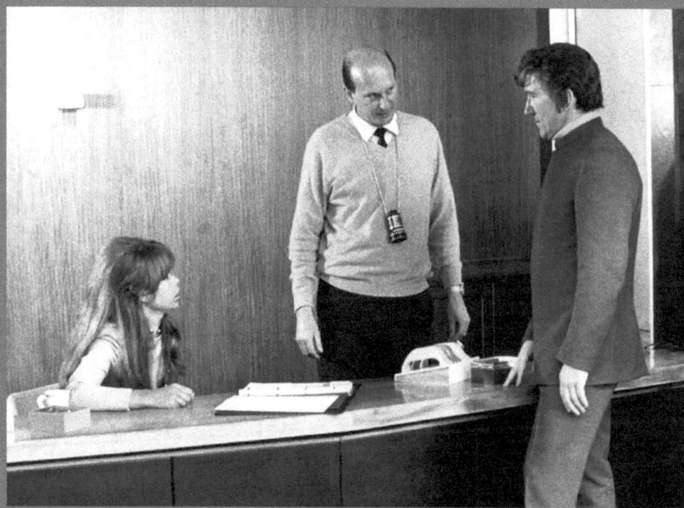

Gerry directs the action on 'Identified'. He later expressed disappointment with his direction of the episode, as he felt he was too distracted with concerns about other aspects of the series. In spite of a shaky start, the series soon found its stride.

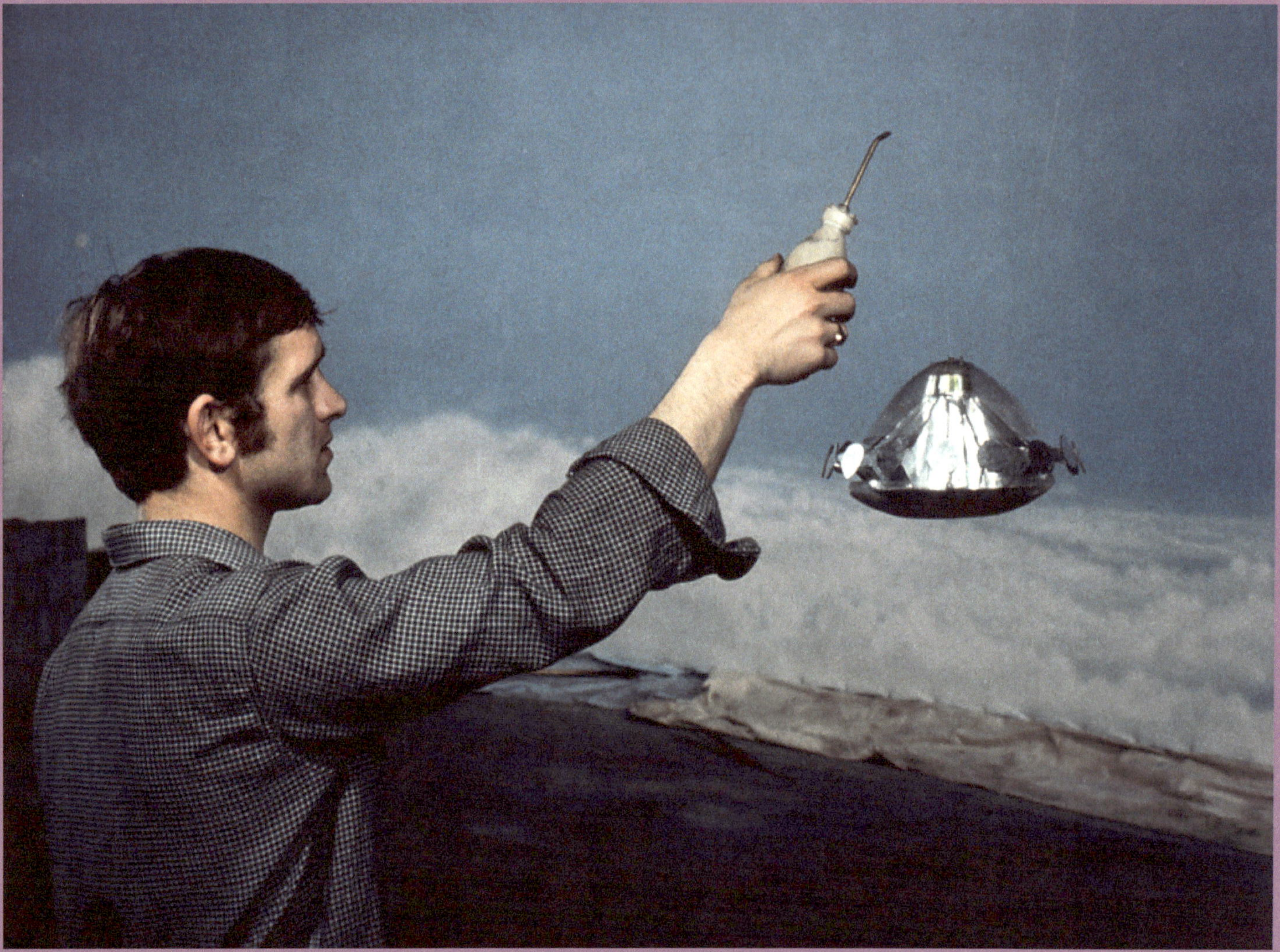

"If you ask me which were the difficult shots to do, I would say, on reflection, those damn flying saucers!' said Derek Meddings in later years. Here, an effects technician puffs powder paint to conceal the model's tungsten wires.

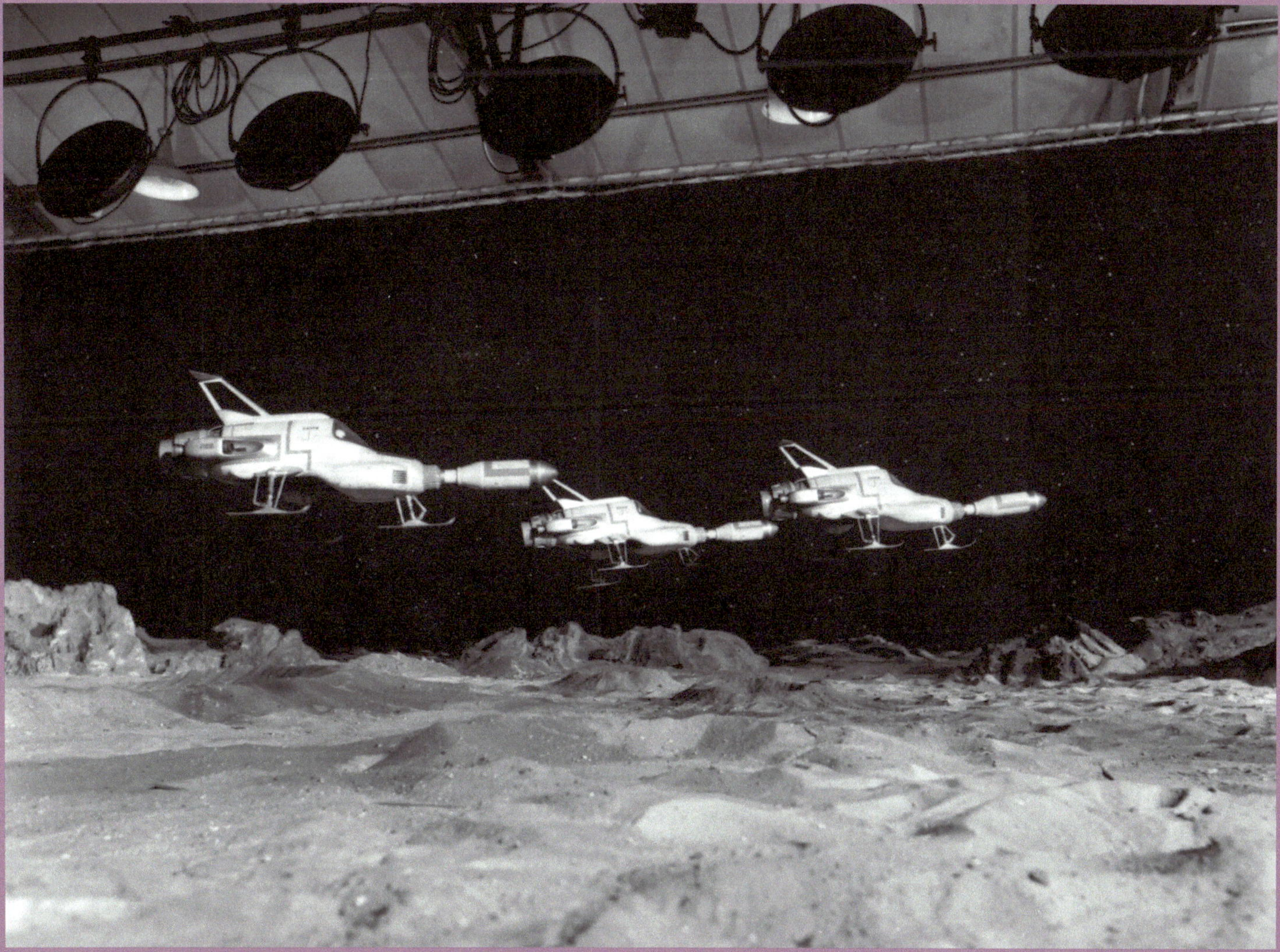

Immediate launch! The interceptors head out to greet another UFO. After the puppet stages closed in 1969, the special effects crew expanded into the space, giving them the opportunity to make their miniature effects work more impressive than ever. However, their time was soon to come to an end and, at the completion of *UFO* in 1970, the Slough studios were finally closed. The last vestiges of the team disbanded, and the models followed the puppets into the skip. Century 21 was no more.

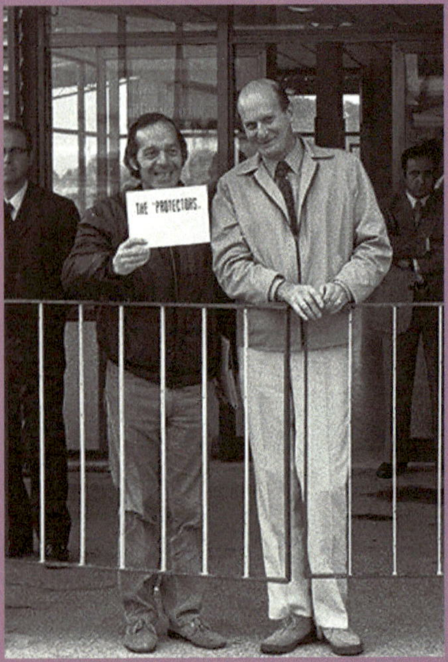

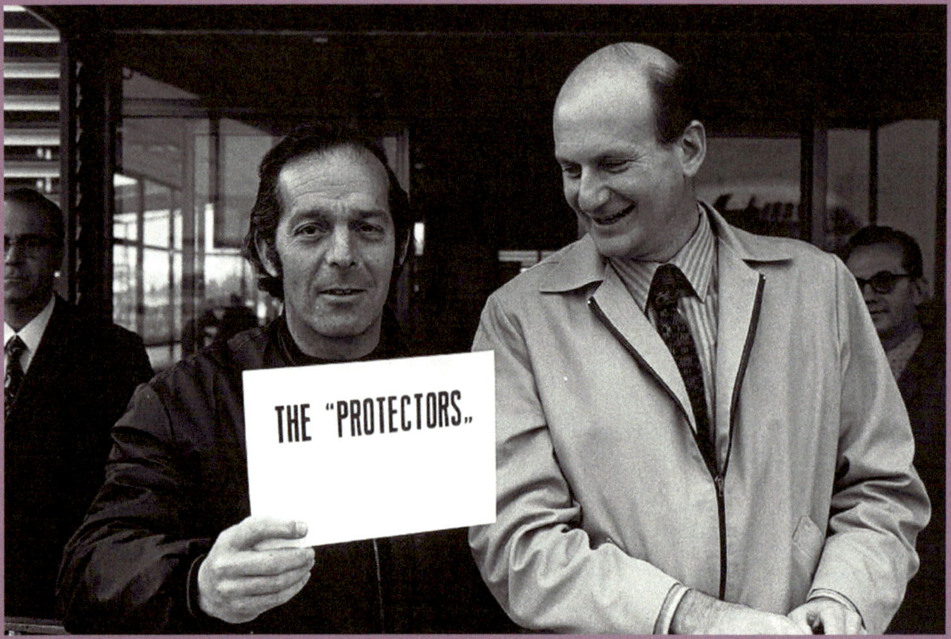

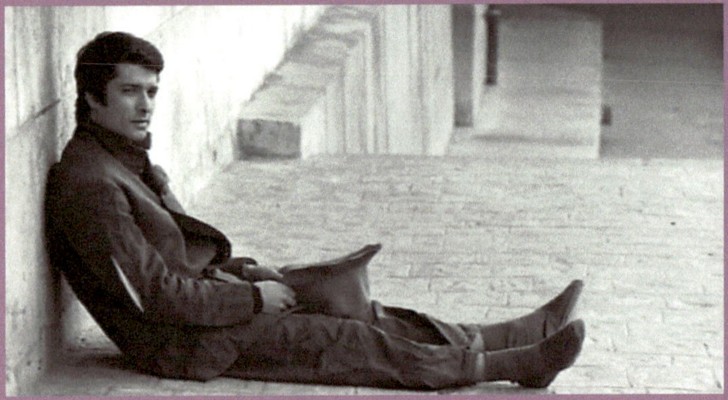

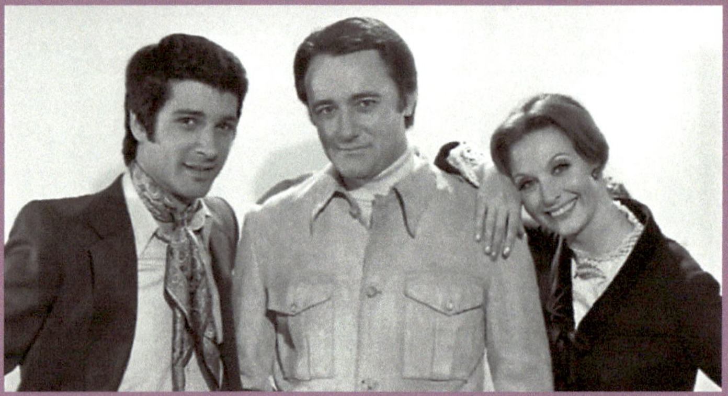

The genesis of the next series illustrated how the wheels were starting to come off the golden partnership with Lew Grade. Following the demise of Century 21, Gerry, Sylvia and Reg formed Group Three Productions. At one of their customary 7am meetings, an unusually terse Lew thrust the outline of a new spy series into Gerry's hands. *The Protectors* marked the first time since 1960 that Gerry was producing someone else's idea. **Above:** *The Protectors* featured a lot of overseas location filming to give it a genuinely international feel that earlier ITC series lacked. **Below left:** Good-looking Tony Anholt was the only one of the three leads cast by Gerry himself. **Below right:** The Protectors: Tony Anholt, Robert Vaughn and Nyree Dawn Porter.

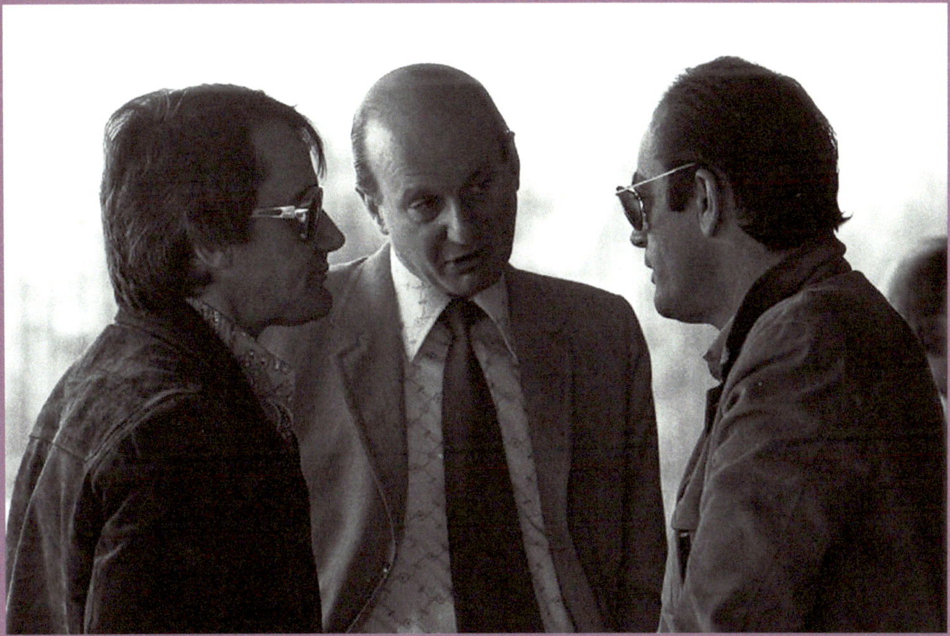

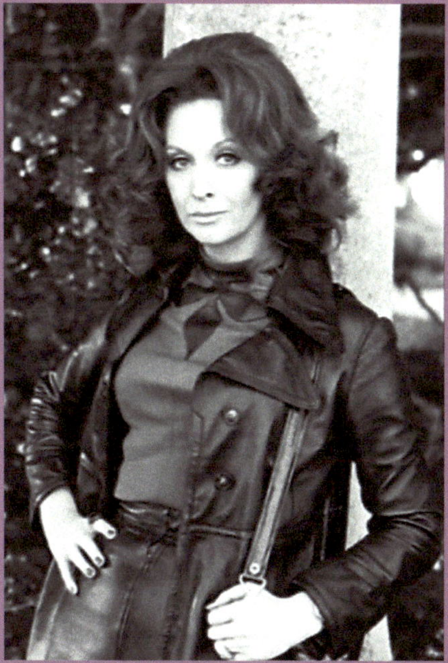

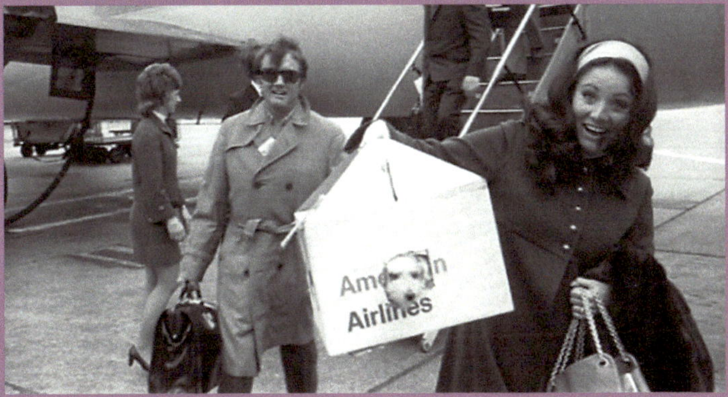

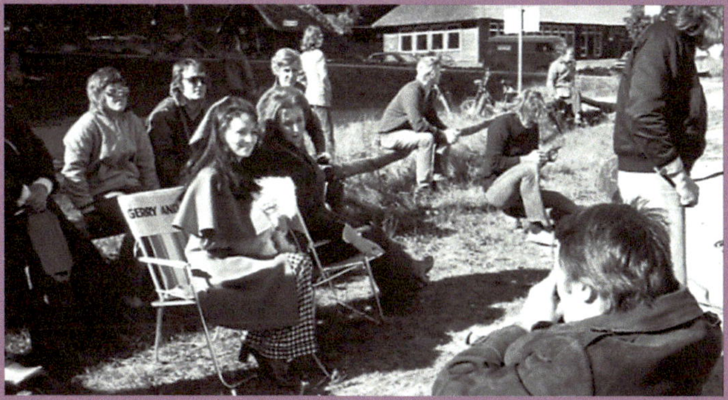

Above left: Gerry confers with Robert Vaughn (left) and Vaughn's business partner Sherwood Price. **Above right:** Nyree Dawn Porter was approached by Lew following a speech she'd given for the Writers' Guild. She signed up to the series knowing almost nothing about it. **Below left:** Robert Vaughn disembarks from a plane with his girlfriend and canine friend. Vaughn's relationship with Gerry and Lew was fraught, even reaching the point of threats to walk off the series and return to America. **Below right:** It was not an entirely unhappy experience though, and the difficulties produced a camaraderie. Here, the crew relax between takes. Since the boss is absent, Vaughn's girlfriend Linda Staab has borrowed his chair!

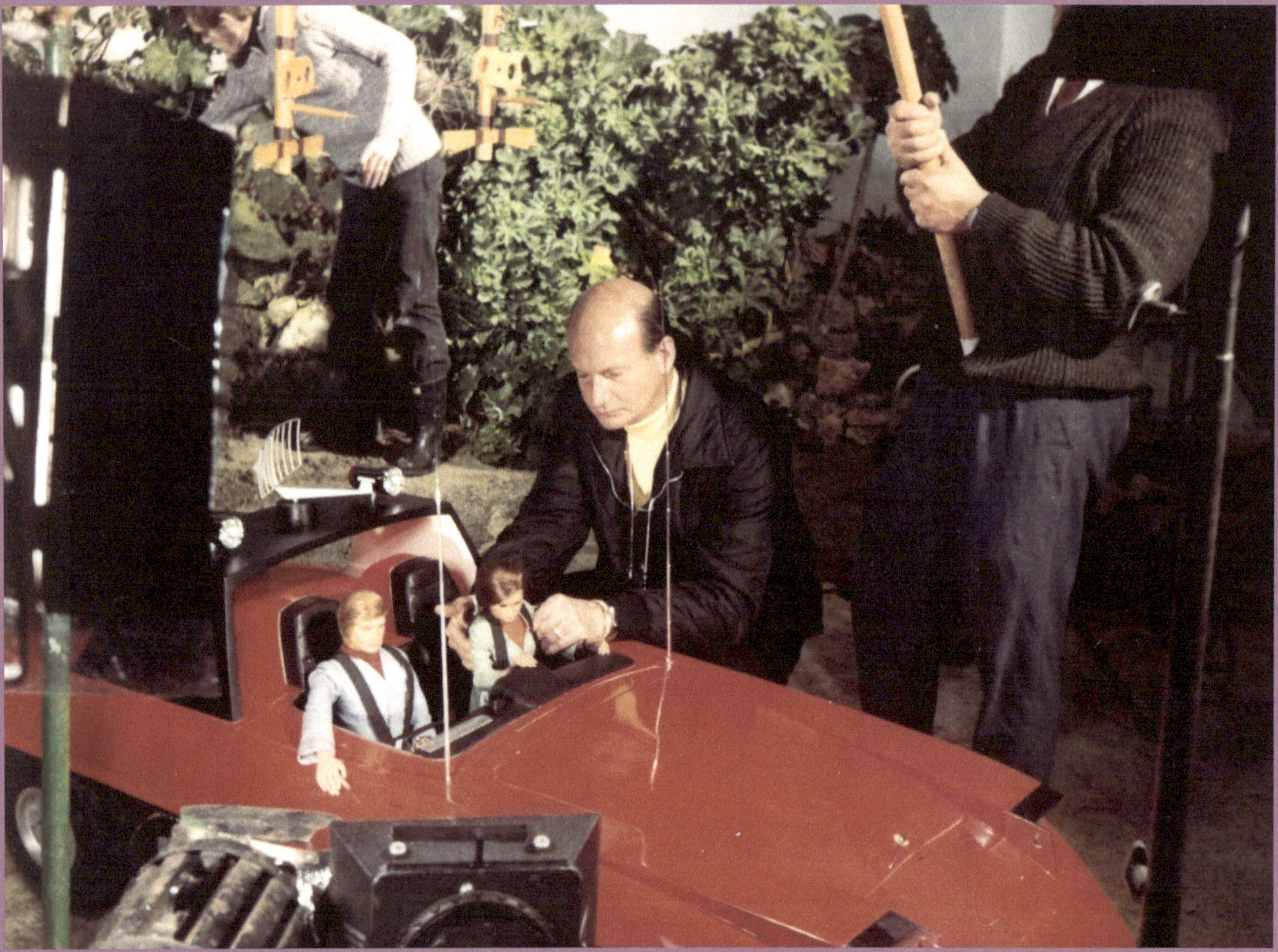

In 1973, Gerry decided to produce a pilot for NBC in America to demonstrate the potential for a new Supermarionation series. Having recently been in Malta to film *The Protectors*, he believed the island would present an excellent opportunity to showcase puppets against stunning location scenery. The finance was raised privately, with the script being written by Sylvia and *Thunderbirds* voice artist Shane Rimmer.

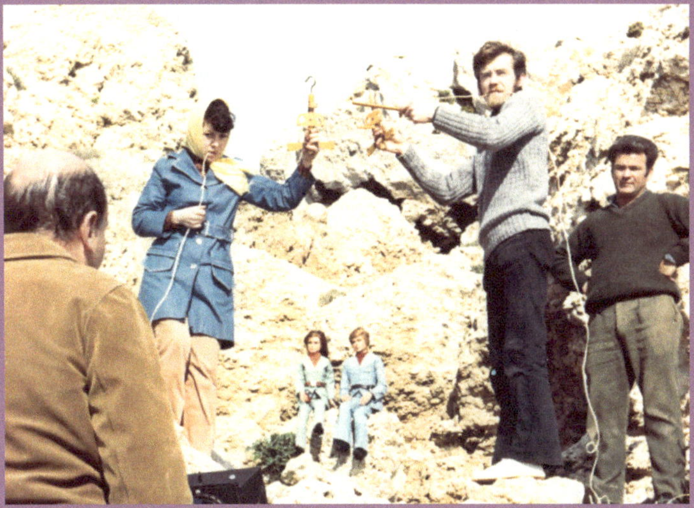

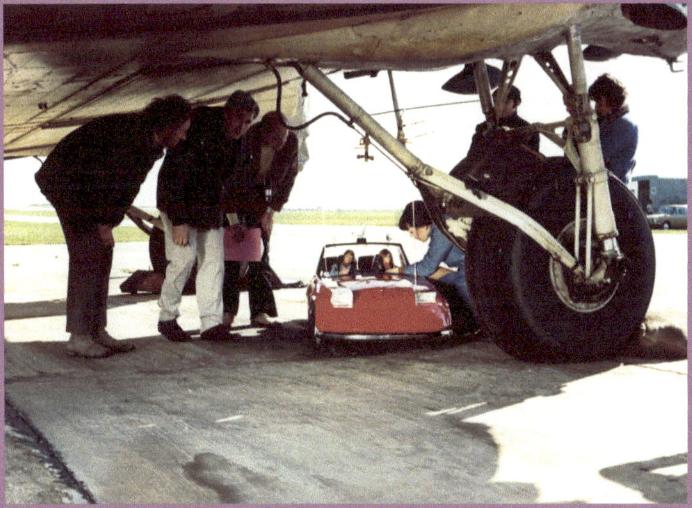

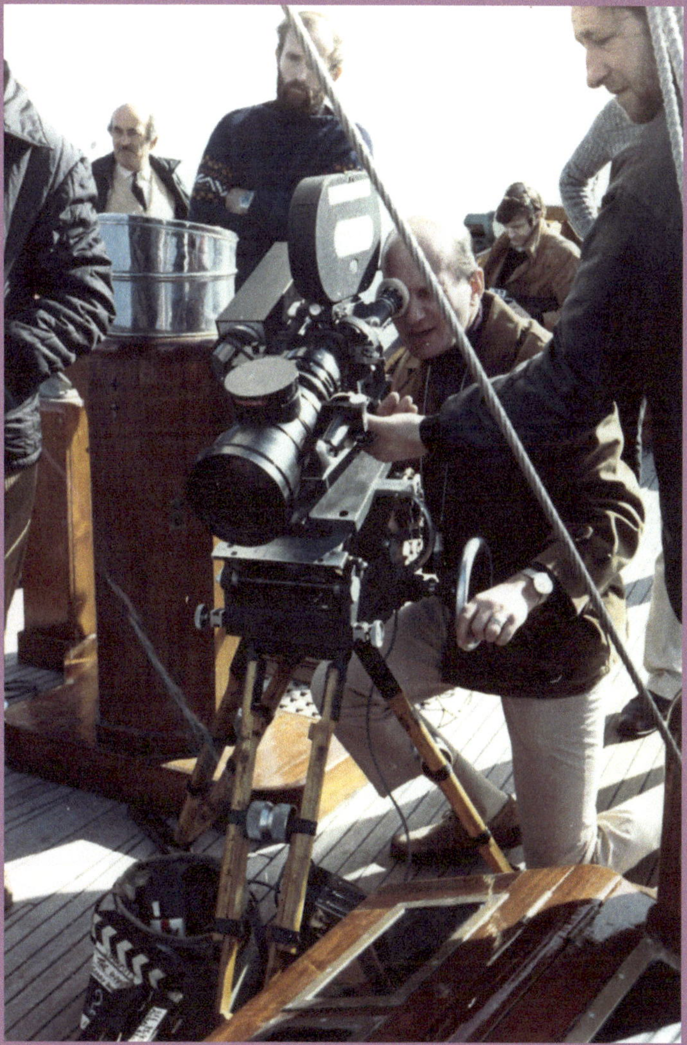

Above left: Puppeteers John and Wanda Brown operate John and Julie. Note that they are perilously carrying the electrical wires that operate the lips in their mouths! **Below left:** One of the many problems faced during production was that the puppet-sized car that had been specially built by Space Models had endless technical issues, often resulting in it taking on a life of its own and driving in random directions. **Right:** Gerry sets up the next shot. Issues with depth of field meant that showing off the puppets in the settings as intended was almost impossible. Upon viewing the results, it was decided that the project was a failure and it was consequently scrapped.

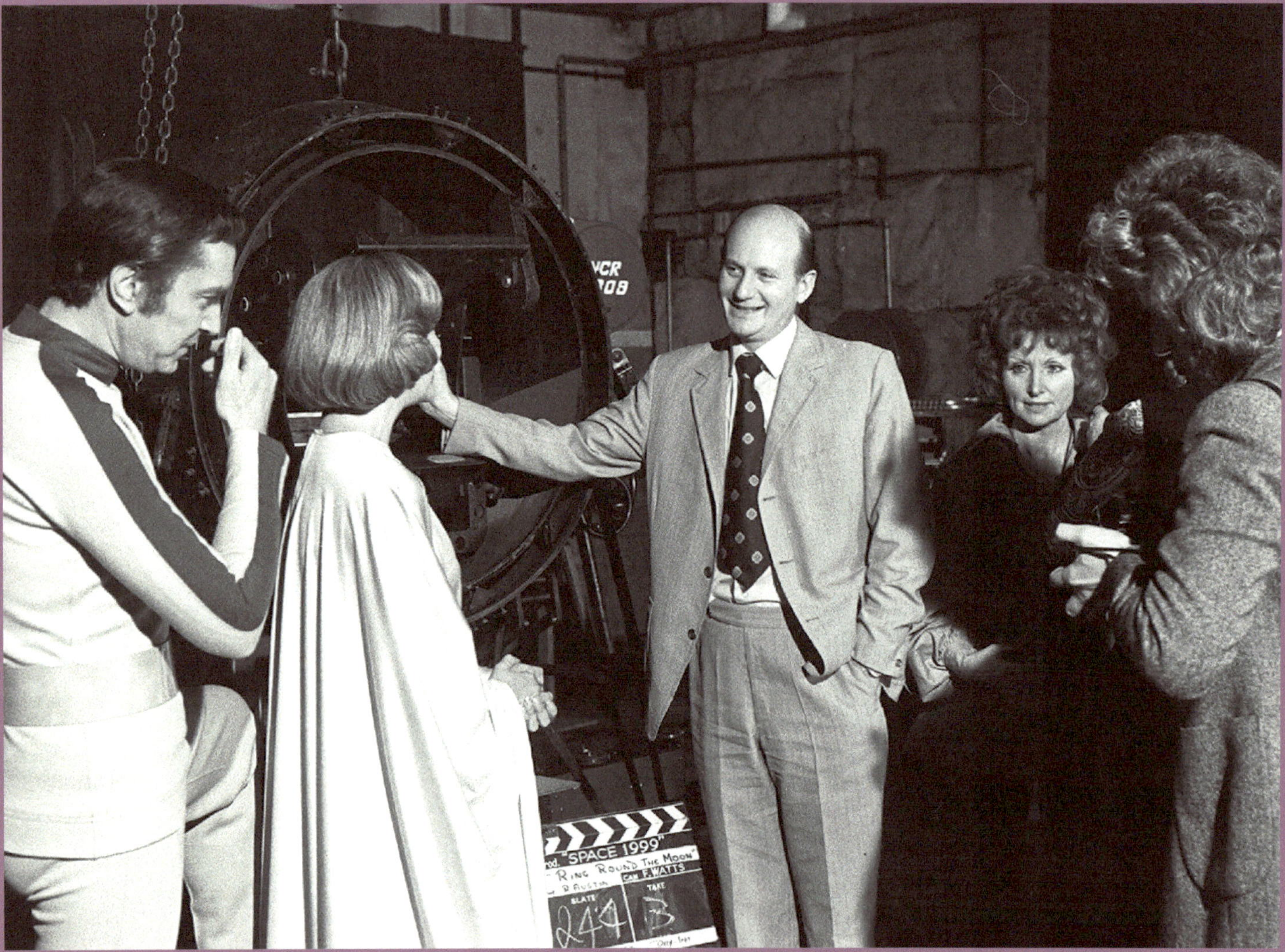

It had been intended that *UFO* would carry on for another run of episodes. However, despite initially promising results in the States, ratings suddenly took a dip and caused ITC America to panic. The show was canned whilst series two pre-production was underway. Determined to salvage some of the work that had been done, Gerry proposed reworking the concept into a new series. It was accepted, though with one stipulation: the Americans didn't want a single episode set on Earth. **Above:** Lead actors Martin Landau and Barbara Bain are seen with the Andersons on the set of *Space: 1999*, the last series Gerry and Sylvia would produce together.

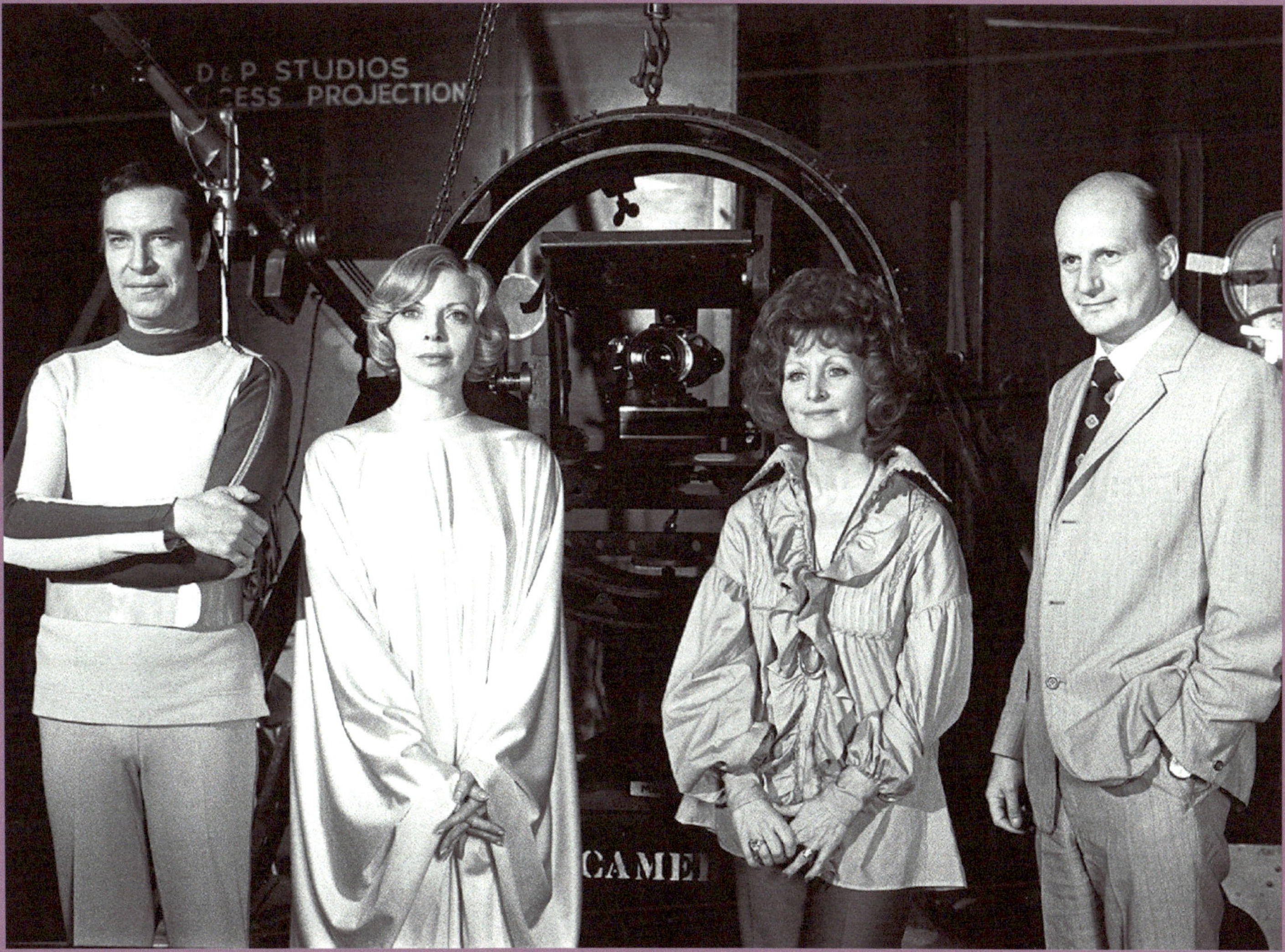

Husband and wife Martin Landau and Barbara Bain were well-known following their roles in *Mission Impossible*, and ITC America insisted that casting them was essential to the success of the series stateside. Negotiations were protracted, with ever increasing demands for money, but eventually their services were secured. The first series comprised of 26 episodes and was promoted as being the most expensive series ever made.

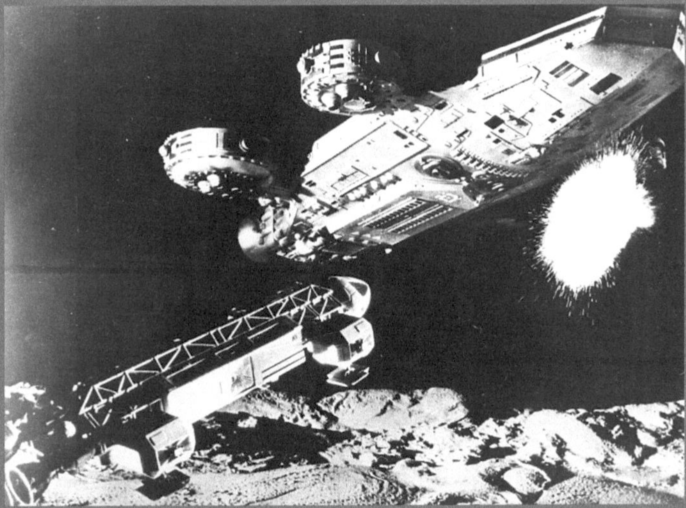

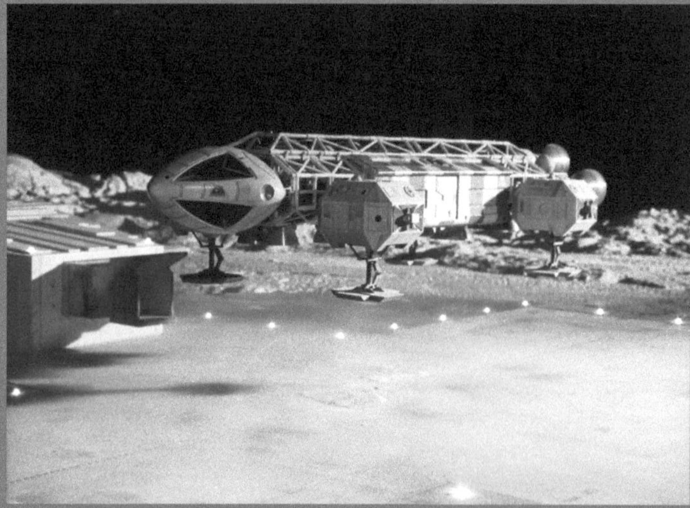

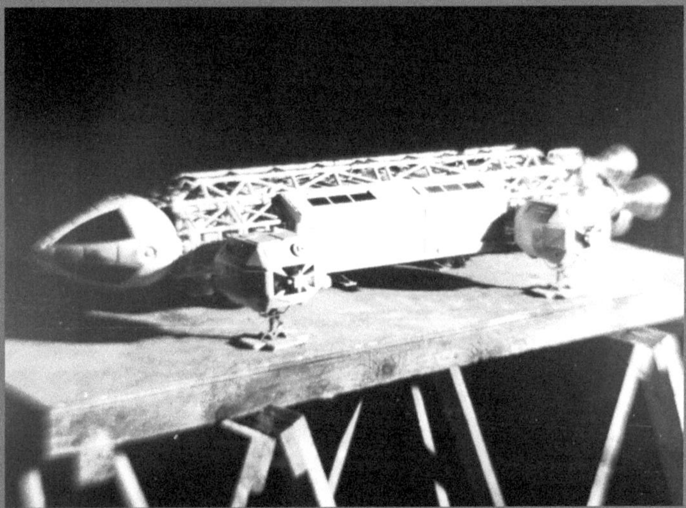

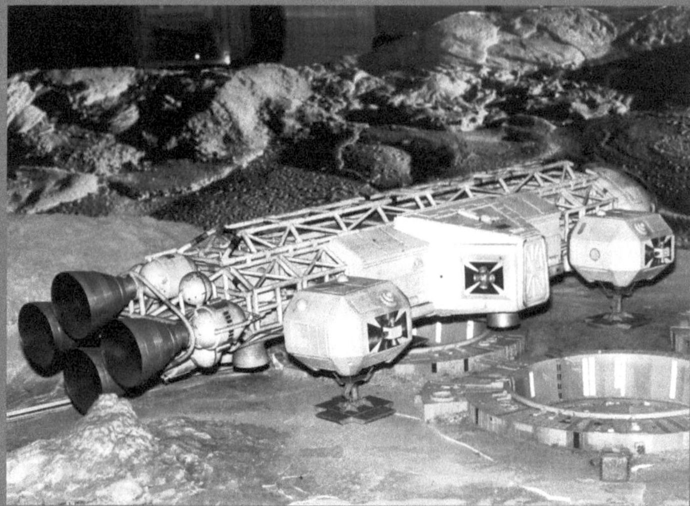

A series of views of the Eagle, designed by Brian Johnson. Brian had worked with A.P. Films from *Supercar* to *Thunderbirds*, but decided to leave the company to join Stanley Kubrick's crew on *2001: A Space Odyssey* in 1965. The decision lead to a confrontation between the two men, since Gerry wanted to keep the company's specially developed effects techniques a secret from the wider industry. Fortunately, they patched up their differences for *Space: 1999*, and Brian went on to create some of the most stunning model effects ever seen on television.

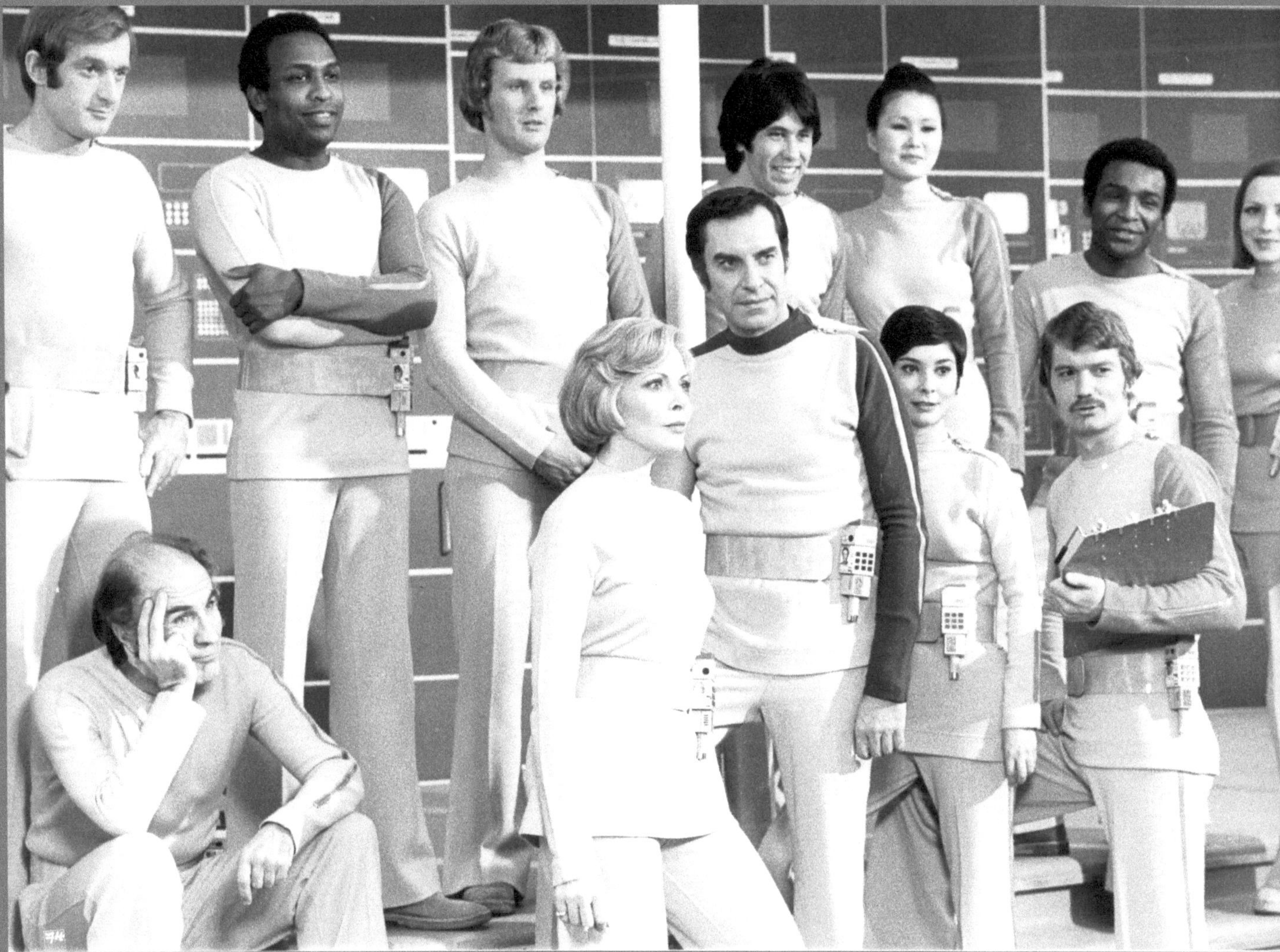

The main cast (and background extras) from the first series (left to right): Nick Tate, Barry Morse, Clifton Jones, Barbara Bain, Martin Landau, Andy Dempsey, Chai Lee, Zienia Merton, Prentis Hancock, Loftus Burton and Suzanne Roquette.

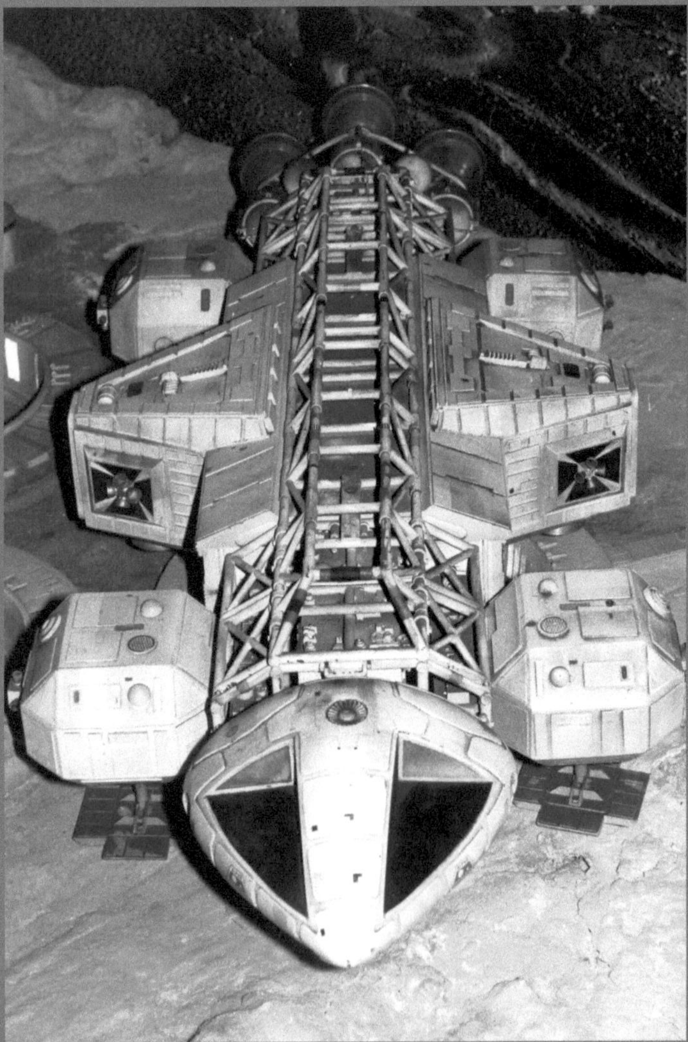

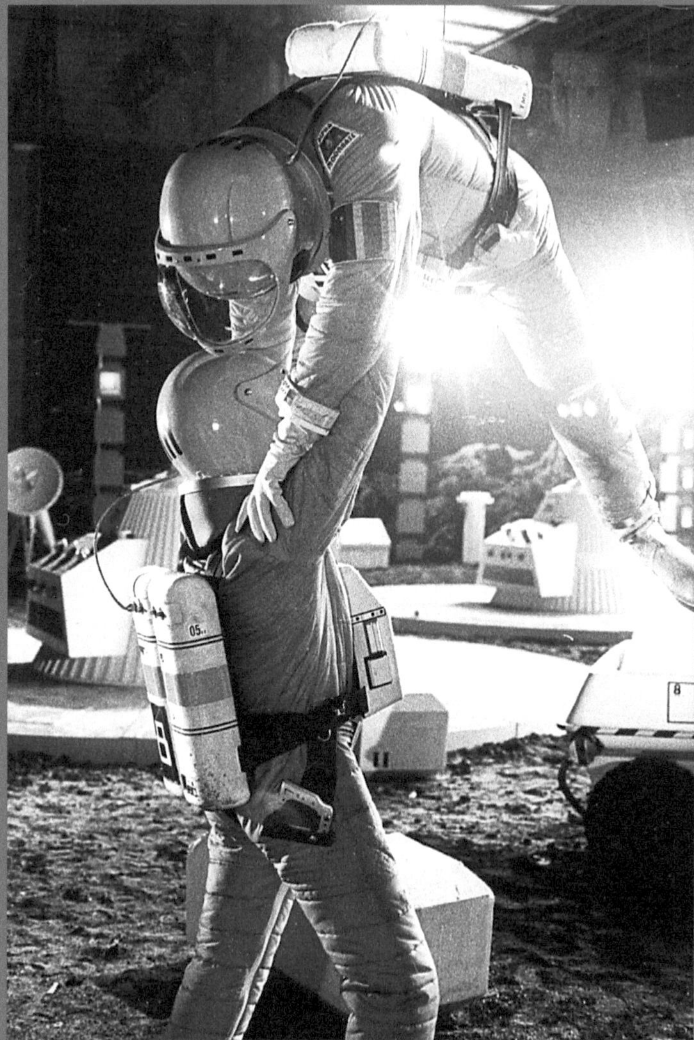

Left: A laboratory Eagle. **Right:** Stuntmen Roy Scammell and Alf Joint during filming of the pre-credits fight sequence from the first episode, 'Breakaway'.

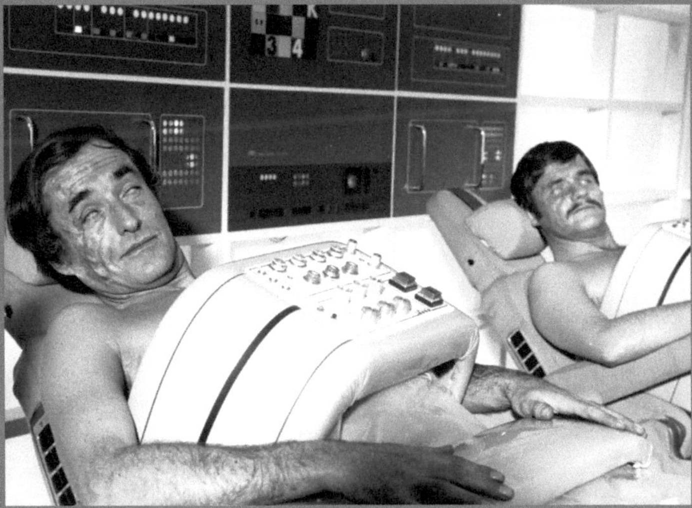

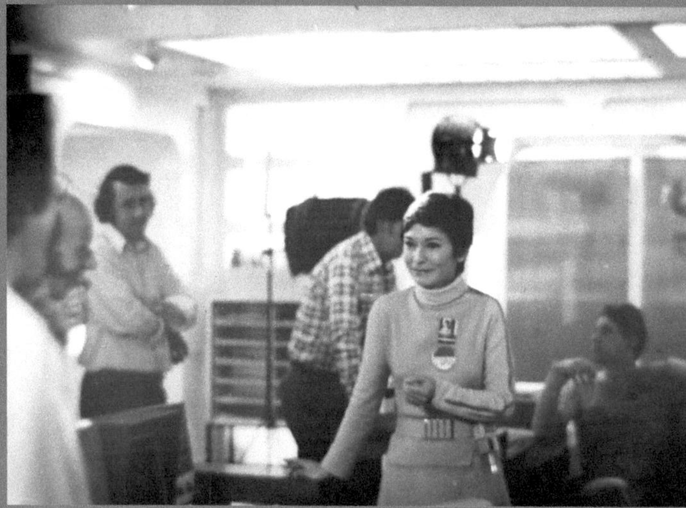

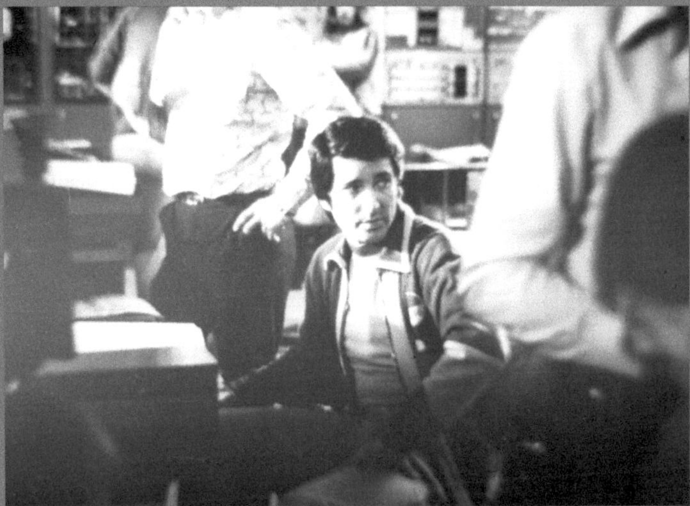

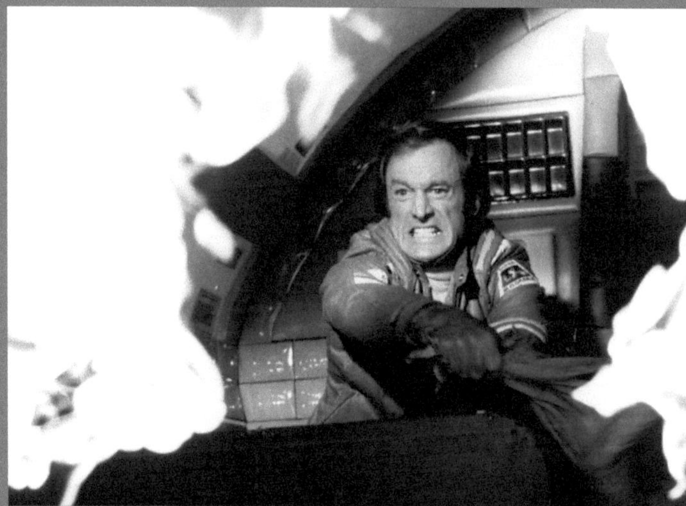

Above left: A shot of Sparkman and Warren, the two Meta probe astronauts from 'Breakaway'. **Above right:** Zienia Merton shares a joke on set. **Below left:** Tony Anholt between takes. **Below right:** Nick Tate as Alan Carter. Nick's father, John, had worked for Gerry a decade earlier as a voice artist on *Thunderbirds*.

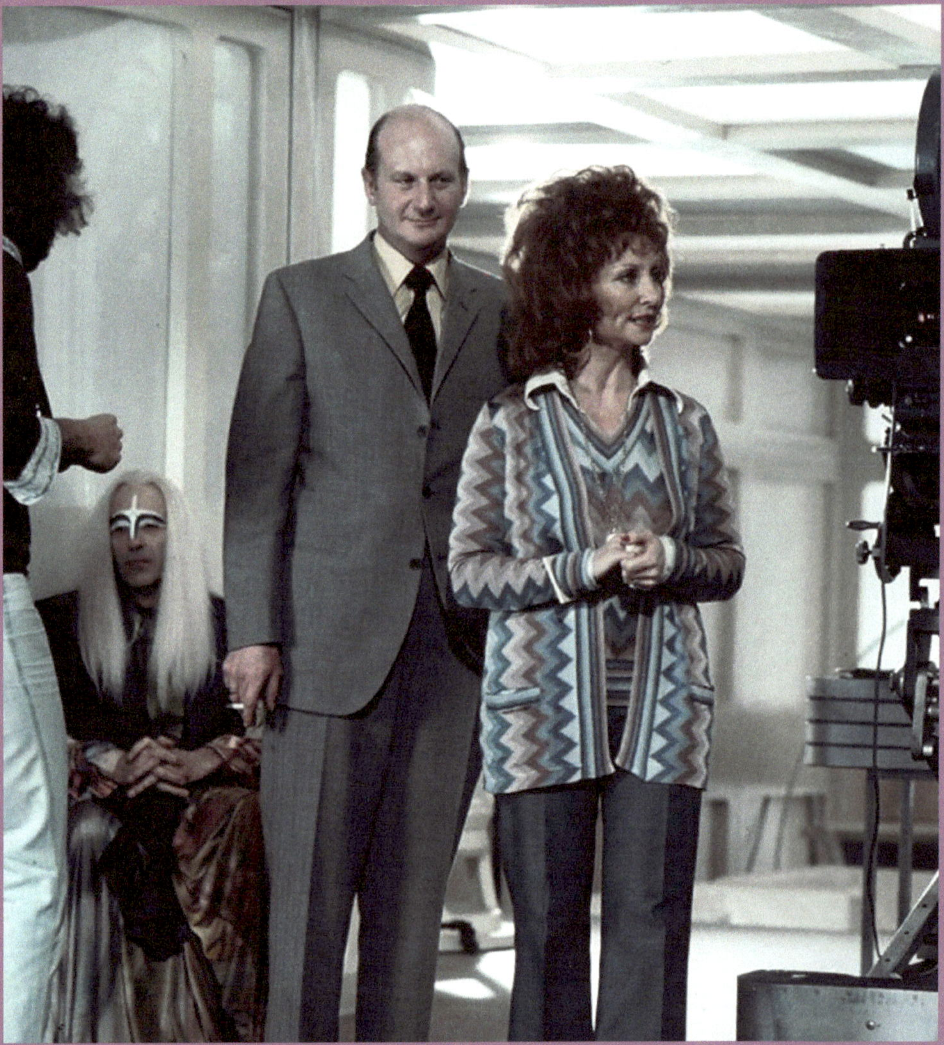

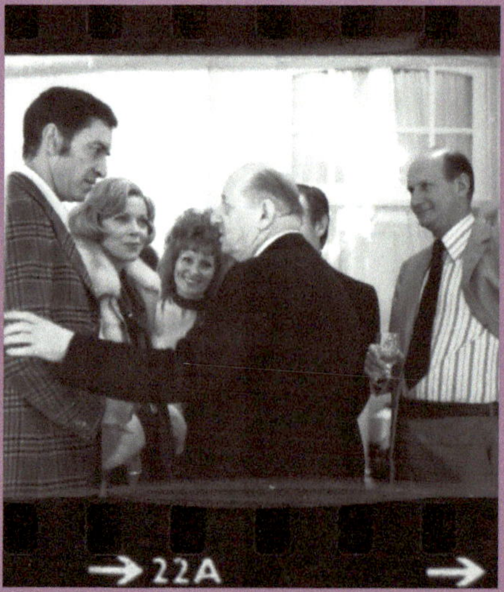

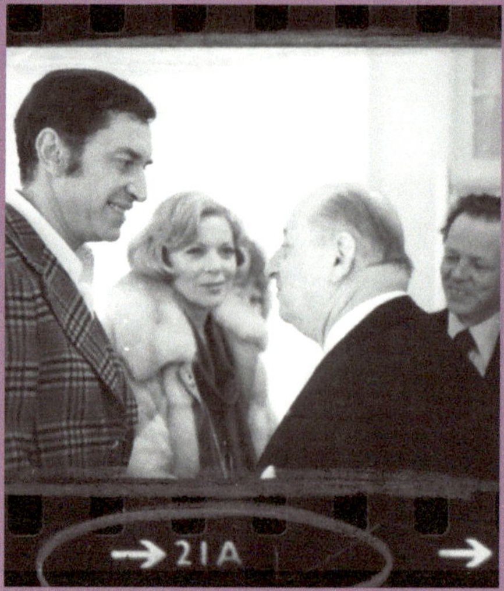

Left: Gerry and Sylvia's relationship was falling apart. At the wrap party for the first series, things finally came to a head. Sylvia relinquished her role on the show, and an acrimonious divorce that was to last five years began. For the second series, Sylvia was replaced by Fred Freiberger, an American producer known as 'the man who killed *Star Trek*' and the 'Serial Killer' for the number of shows that had ended under his watch. **Right:** Lew Grade, Martin Landau, Gerry and Sylvia at a party. Times were tough for Lew Grade too, and in the late '70s he decided to shift his focus towards the movies. *Space: 1999* marked the end of his collaboration with Gerry. It really was the end of an era.

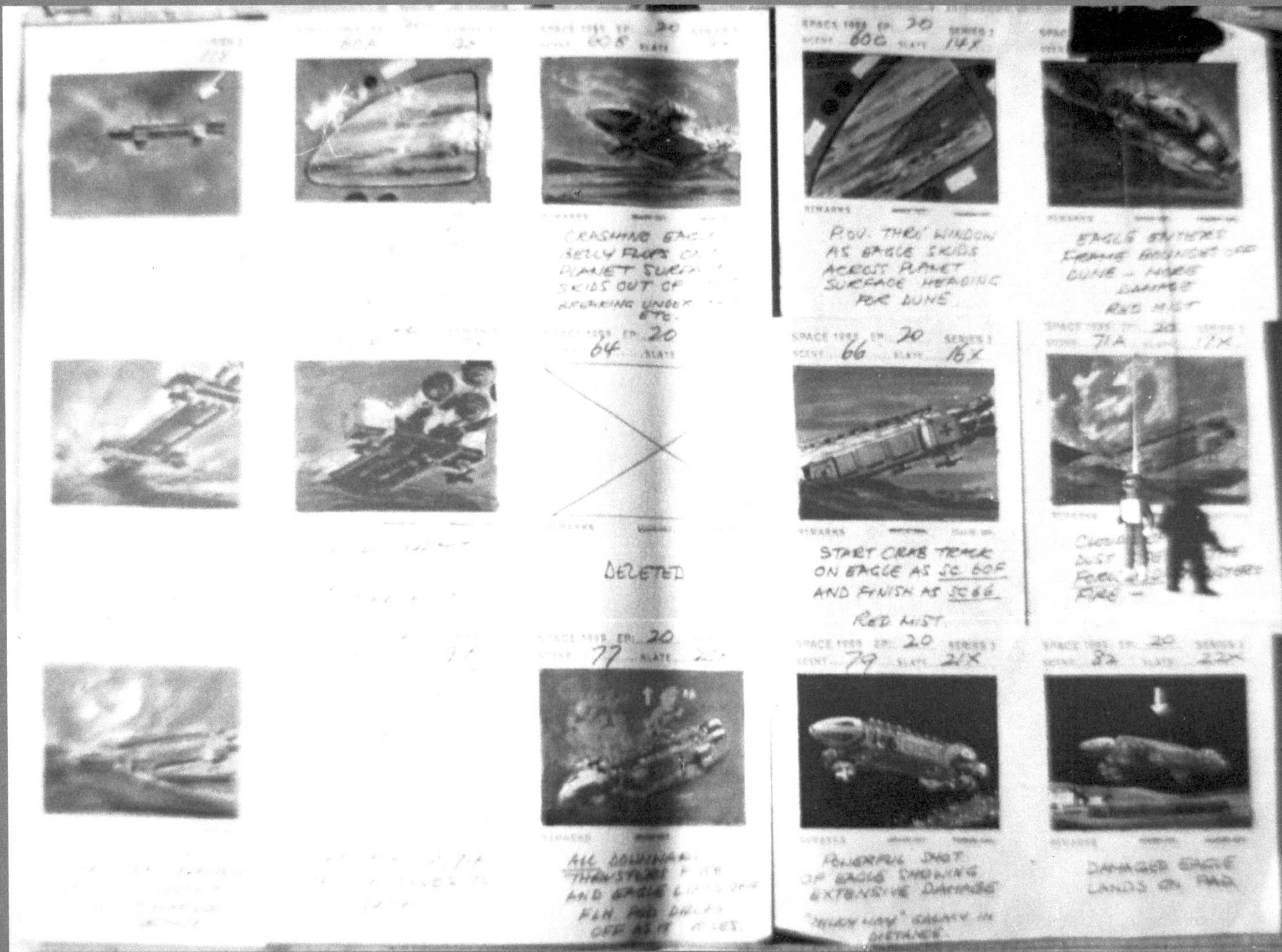

The carefully storyboarded Eagle crash sequence from the series two episode 'The Seance Spectre'.

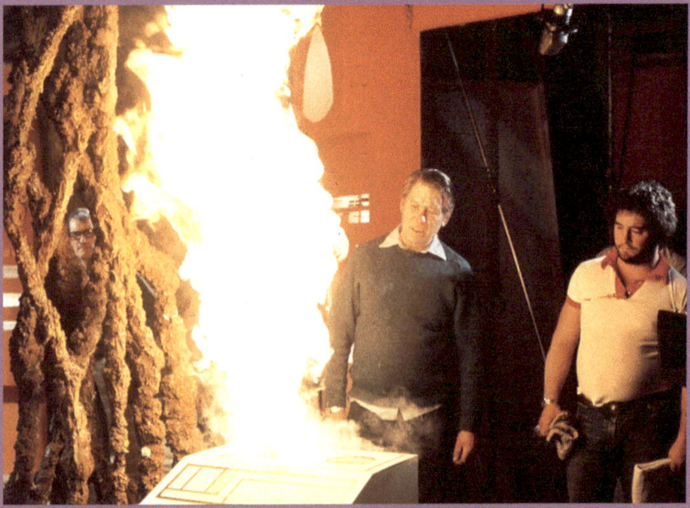

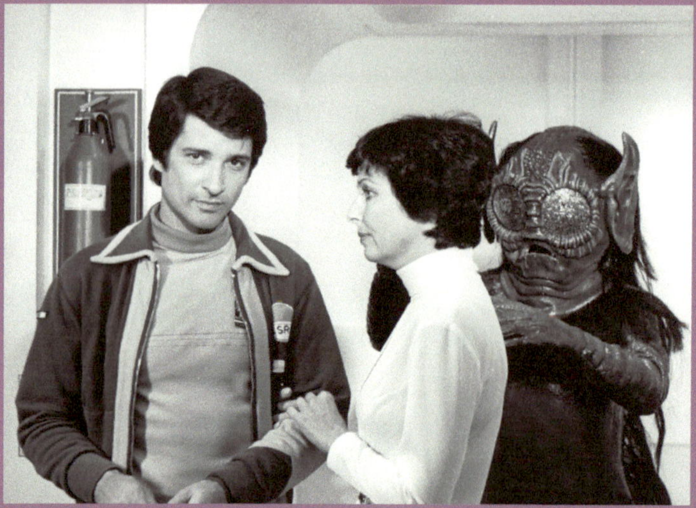

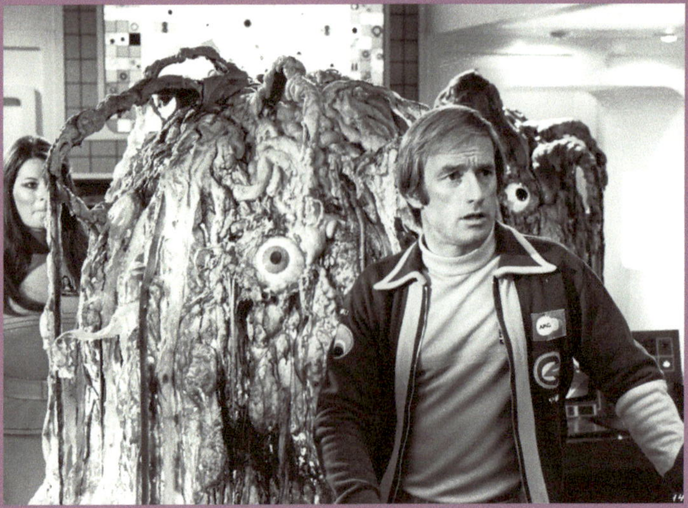

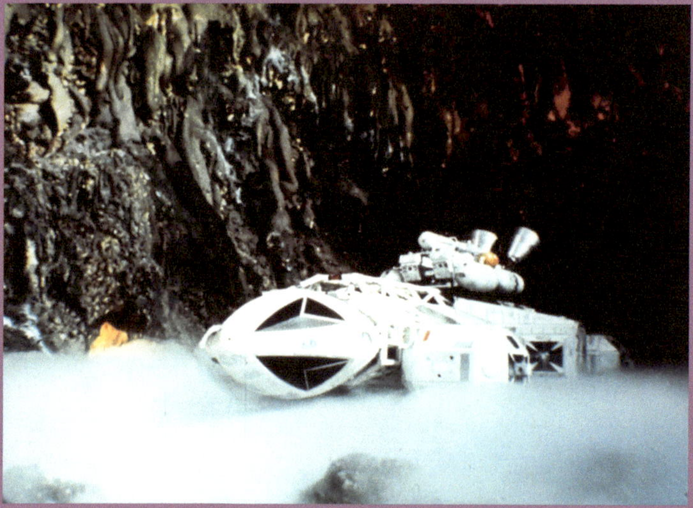

Above left: Setting fire to Mentor's lab at the end of the series two episode 'The Metamorph'. **Above right:** Tony Anholt, Toby Robins and Albin Pahernik (in costume) during filming of 'The Bringers of Wonder'. **Below left:** Jenny Cresswell and Nick Tate on set with a friend in 'The Bringers of Wonder'. **Below right:** An Eagle on the surface of Psychon in 'The Metamorph'.

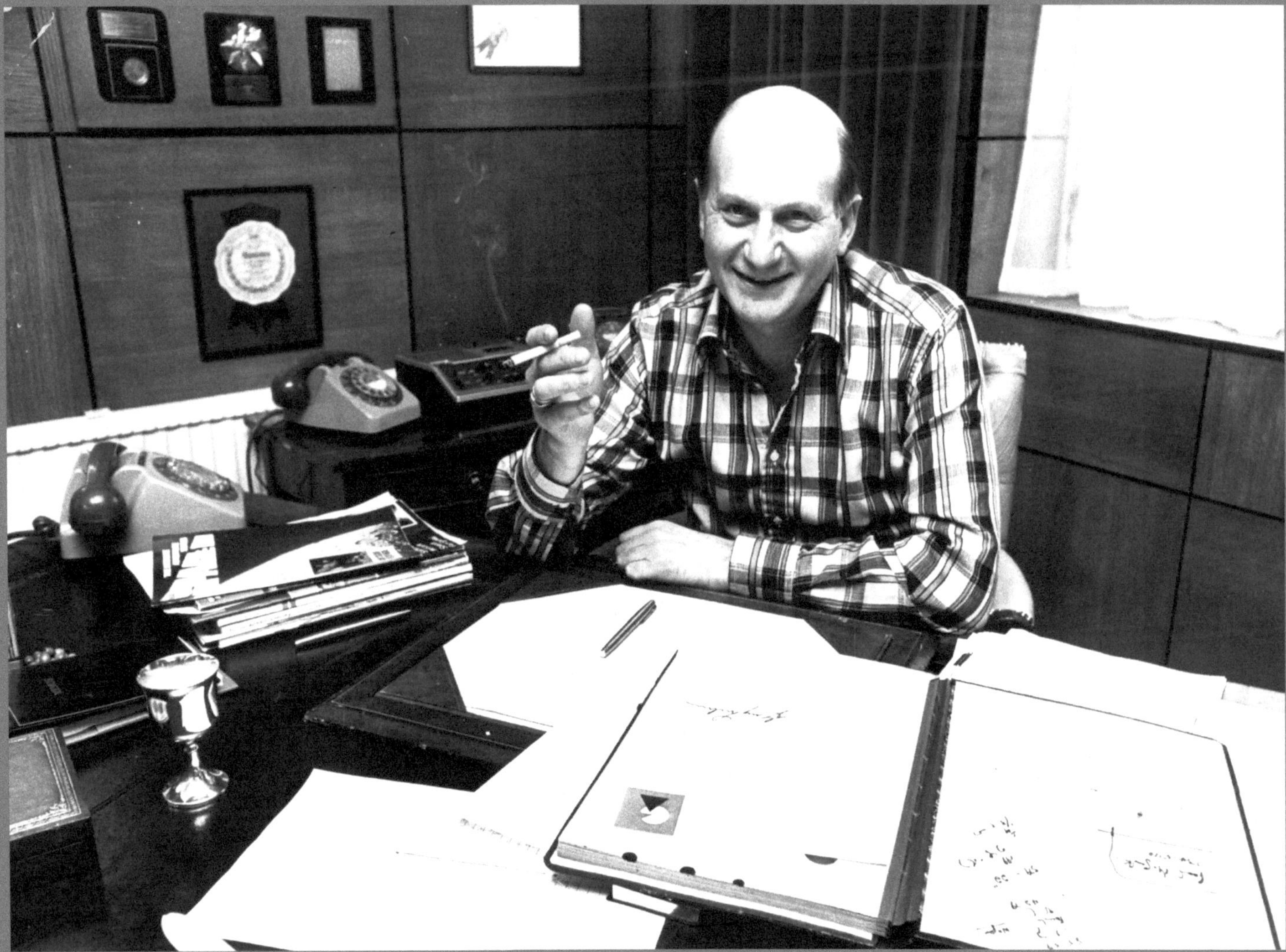

Gerry in his office during *Space: 1999*. By the second series, despite the 'Executive Producer' credit, his influence on the production was minimal; the American branch of ITC called the shots with regards to the style of the series.

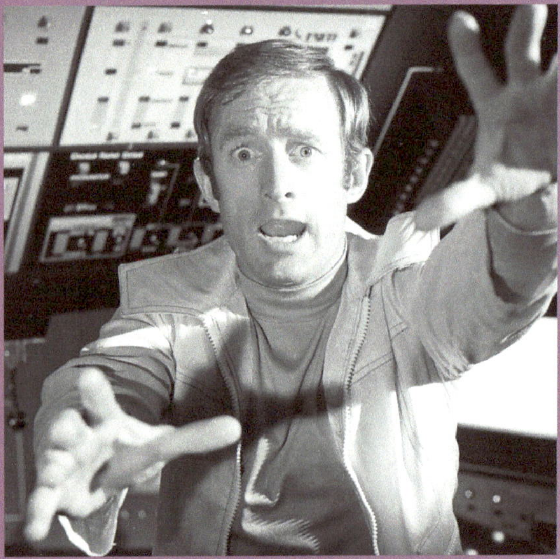

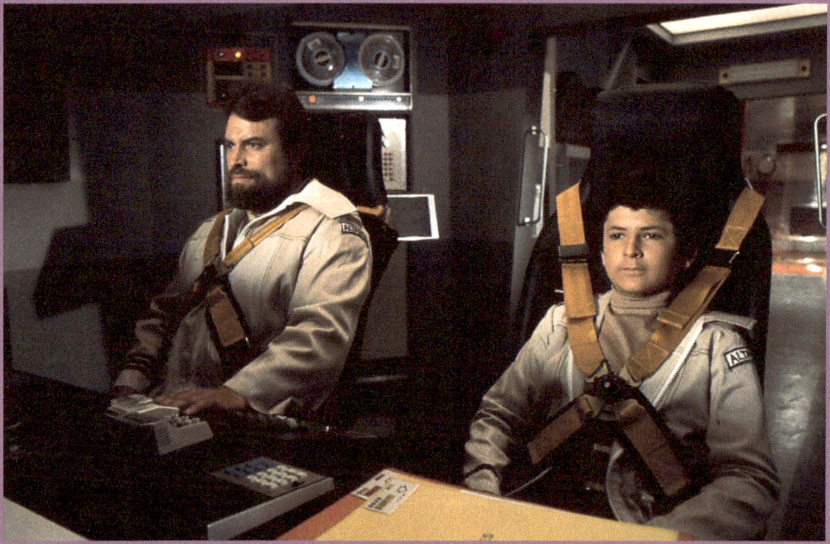

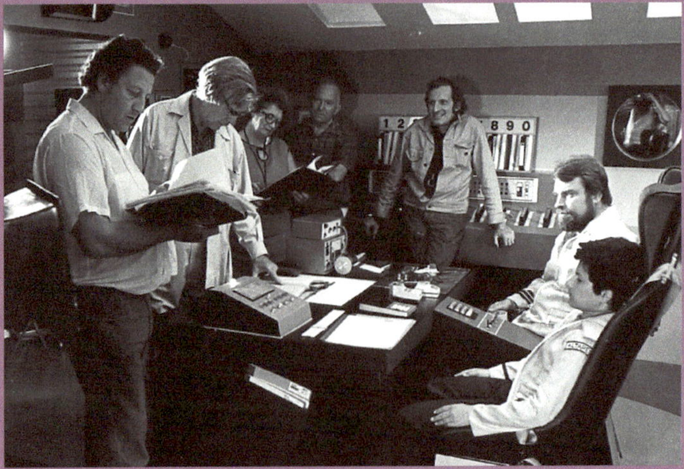

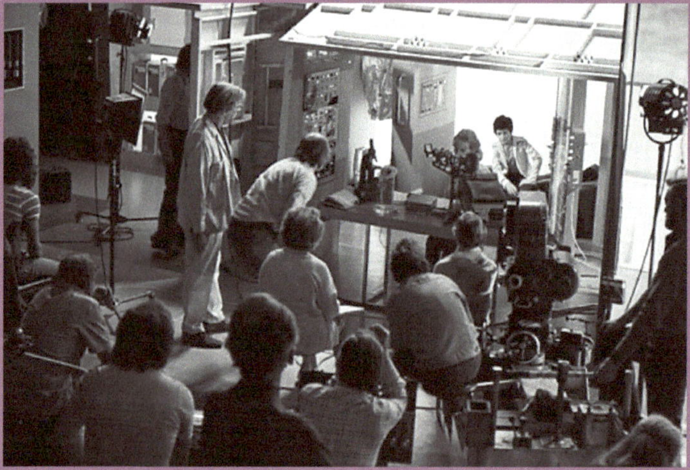

Between the two series of *Space: 1999*, Gerry received a commission from a friend of his at NBC, George Heinemann. Heinemann had devised an educational series called *Special Treats*, designed to teach concepts that children might find boring through drama. Using cast and crew from *Space: 1999*, Gerry produced *The Day After Tomorrow*, which dealt with Einstein's theory of relativity. **Above left and right:** Stars Nick Tate, Brian Blessed and Martin Lev. **Below left and right:** Behind the scenes at Pinewood Studios on the set of the Lightship Altares.

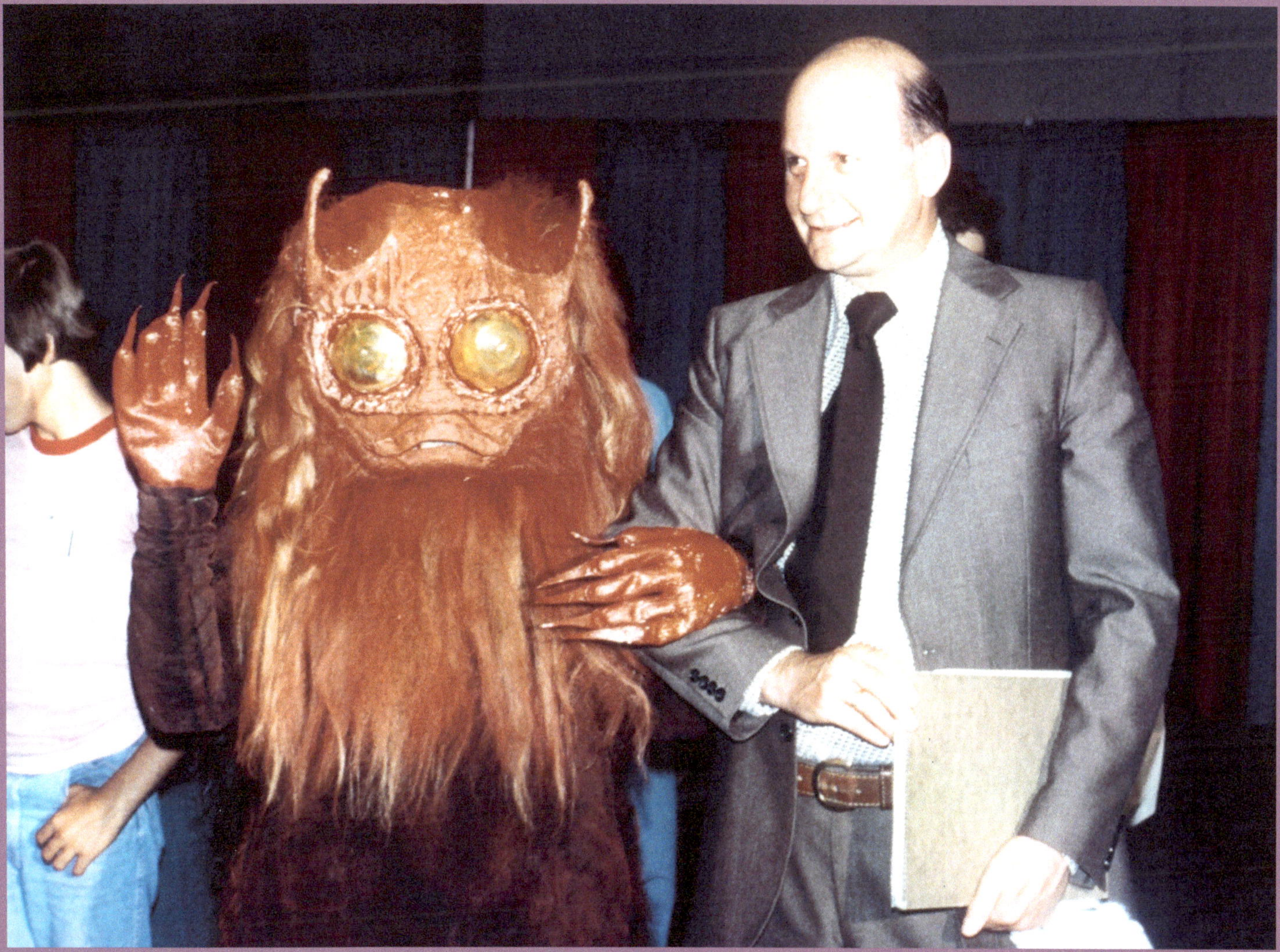

Towards the end of the 1970s, the fans of Gerry's original shows were now grown up and fandom for his work was born. In this shot, Gerry is seen at a *Space: 1999* convention. In the early '80s, ITC brought various fan factions together and created Fanderson, a fan club for Gerry's work.

1980s

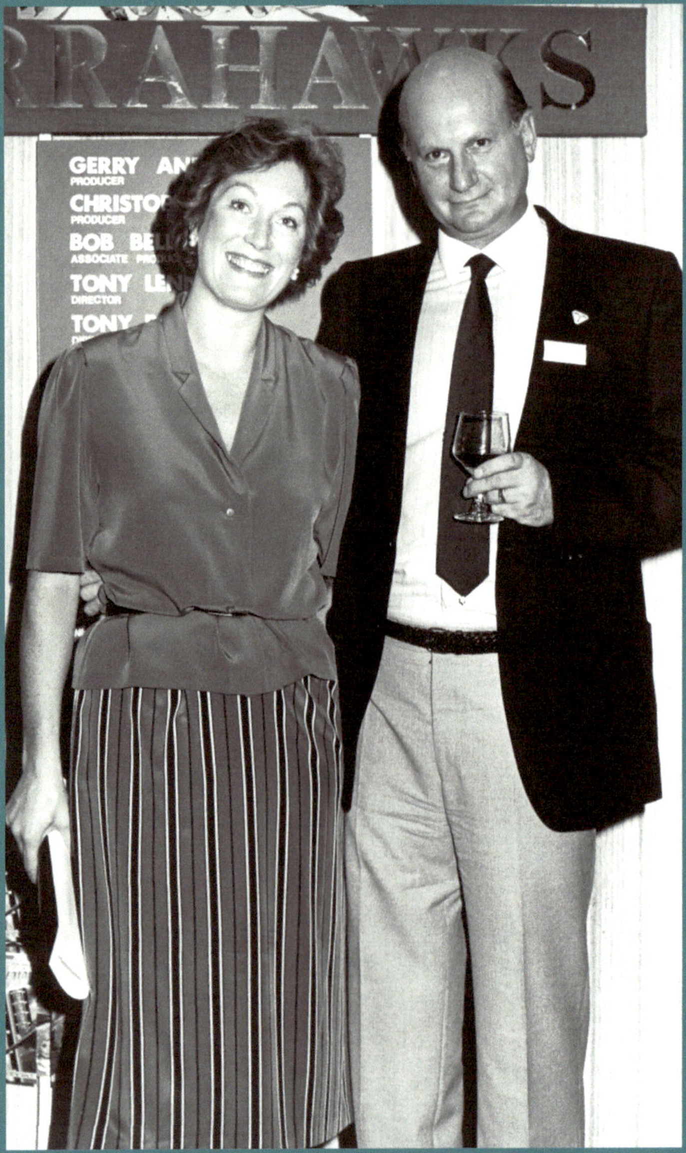

Life following *Space: 1999* was difficult for Gerry. He continued to devise concepts for new productions, but without Lew's backing it proved impossible to bring any of these to fruition. Soon, the man who once earned a reported £1000 a week found himself writing a history of telecommunications whilst wearing extra coats during the winter to avoid putting the heating on.

Family life was also something he struggled with. Work had always been the most important thing in his life, and as such he had limited contact with his now grown-up daughters, Linda and Joy. His divorce from Sylvia quickly turned into a bitter court battle over their son, Gerry Jnr – something that ensured Gerry and Sylvia would never speak again.

However, the early '80s saw a reversal in Gerry's fortunes. He started the decade with a new wife, Mary, and a new business partner, Christopher Burr.

When it came to raising finance, Gerry finally recognized that Japan, which had a huge following for his shows, was as important a market for a new series as America.

He revisited a concept he'd devised for the Japanese with Reg Hill in the '70s called *Thunderhawks* and reworked it into a new format entitled *Terrahawks*. By 1982, he was back in production, and a new generation of children awaited.

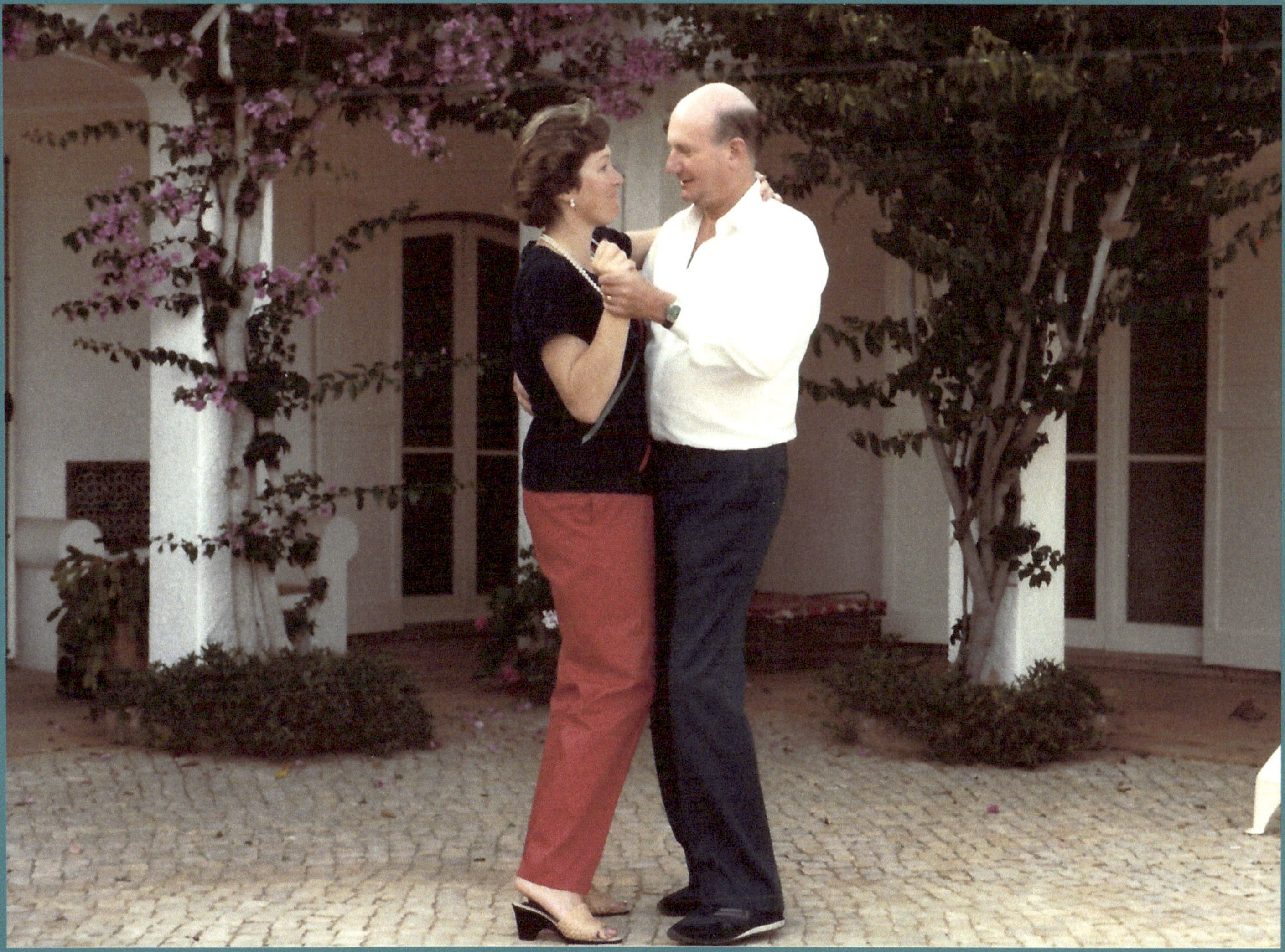

Gerry met his third wife, Mary Robins, while he was working on *The Day After Tomorrow*. She was Special Effects Supervisor Brian Johnson's secretary. In spite of his enormous success, Gerry remained an inherently shy individual, resorting to inventing a job as an excuse to call her rather than asking her out directly. They married in 1980.

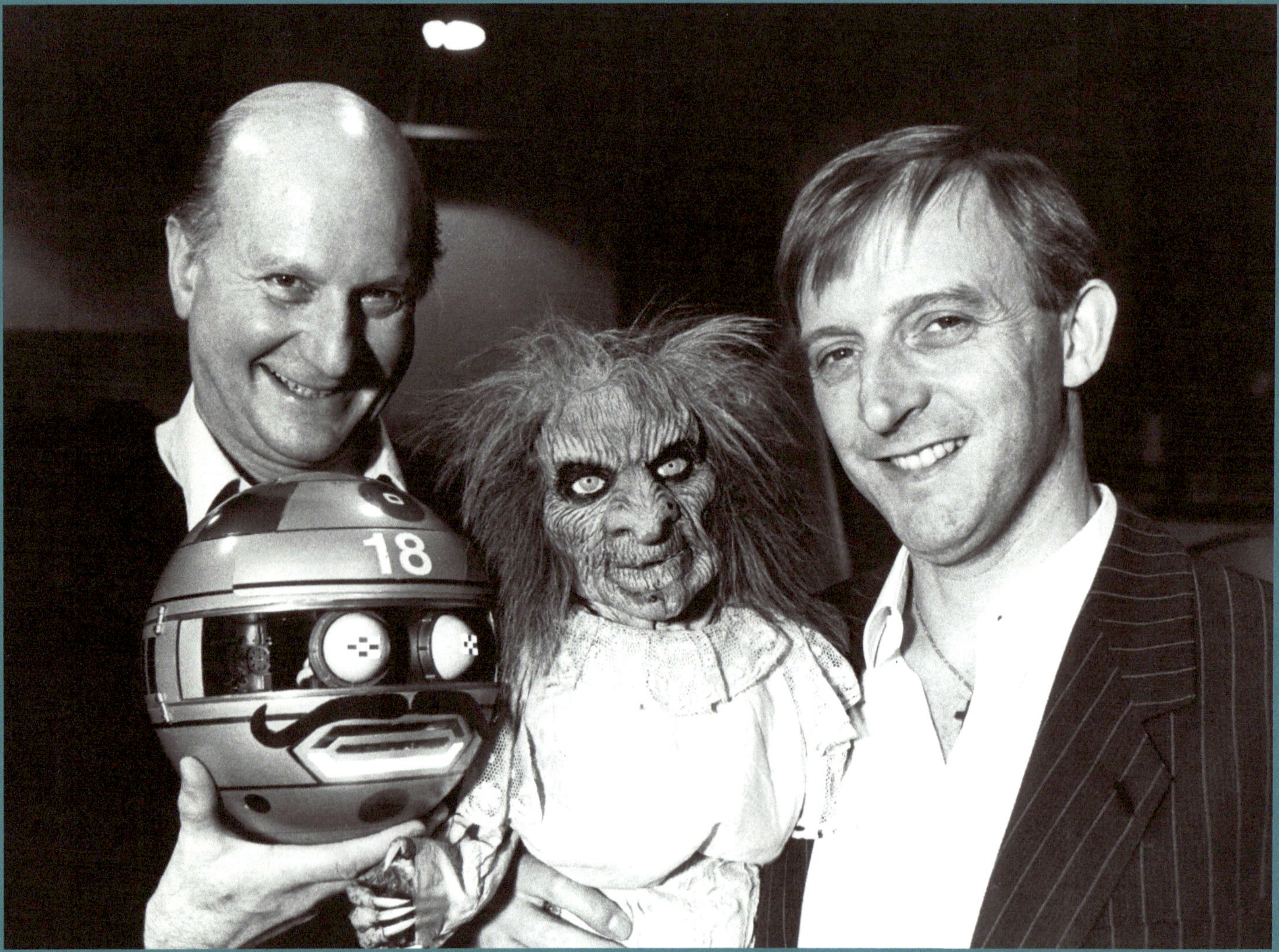

Gerry encountered young businessman Christopher Burr when he was invited to become the chairman of a consortium looking to win the franchise for Southern Television. The bid came to nothing, but the two men hit it off. Christopher had the business acumen that Gerry lacked, and together they formed a new production company, Anderson Burr Pictures Ltd. Here, Gerry and Christopher pose with Zelda and Dix-Huit, one of the Zeroids.

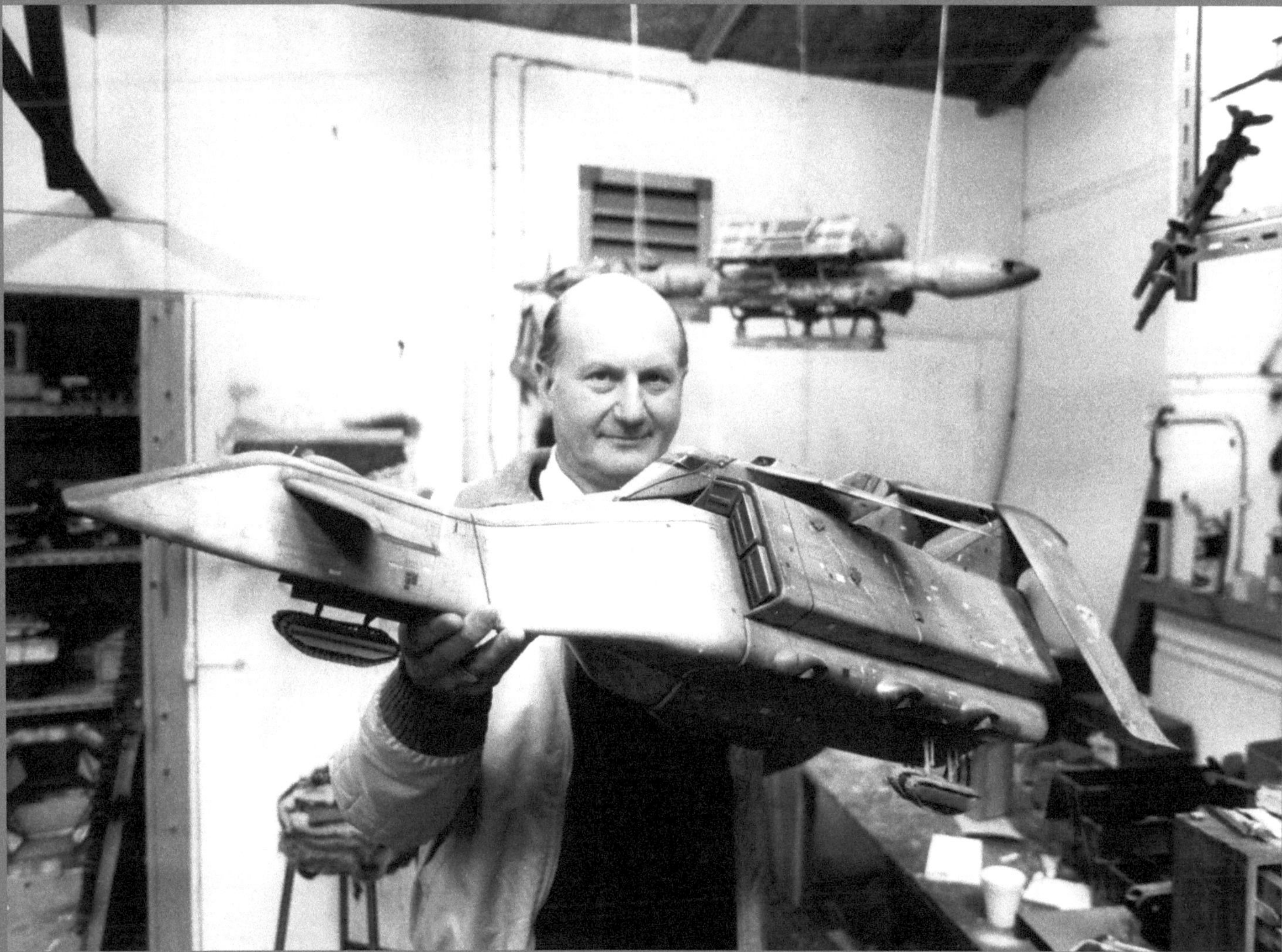

Terrahawks did not have the enormous budgets of the earlier puppet series. This meant concessions such as filming on 16mm, a format Gerry disliked, instead of the superior 35mm. However, the budget put no limit on his imagination, and *Terrahawks* featured as many craft and characters as his previous shows. Here, he is pictured in the workshop at Bray Studios holding the Battlehawk, with the Spacehawk (known by the crew as the Razorhawk for the number of Bic razors stuck to it!) suspended in the background.

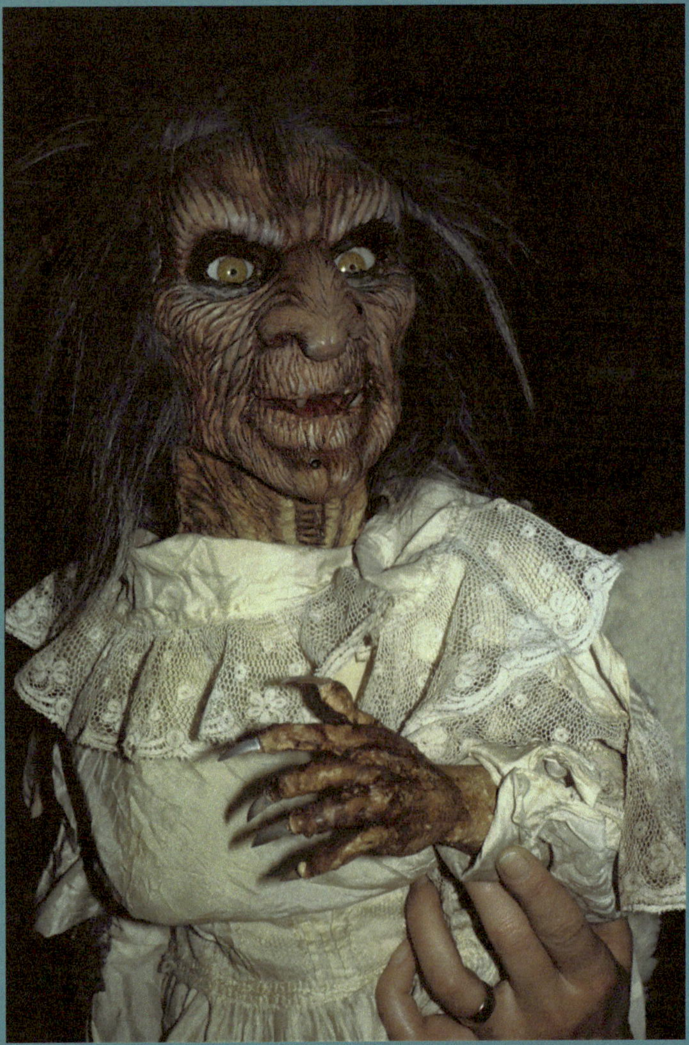

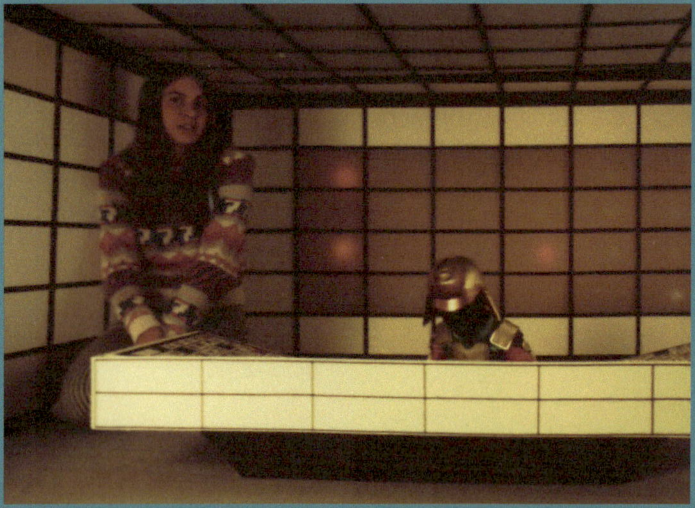

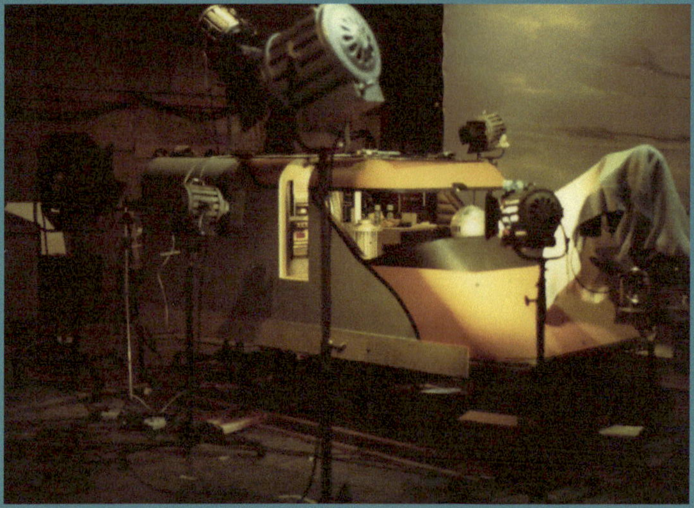

Left: The most successful character by far was Zelda, evil android Queen of the Planet Guk. Sculptor Susan Moore's original maquette for the character featured her deceased grandmother's dentures! **Above right:** Puppeteer Judy Preece crouches next to the Space Samurai. **Below right:** The Terrahawk cockpit puppet set between takes.

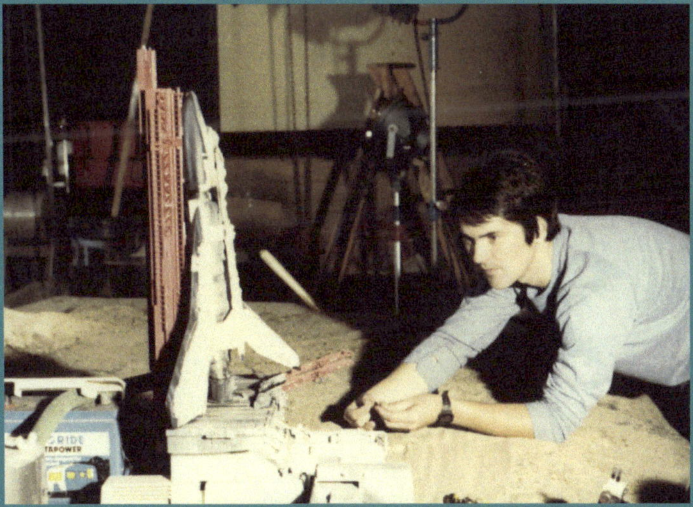

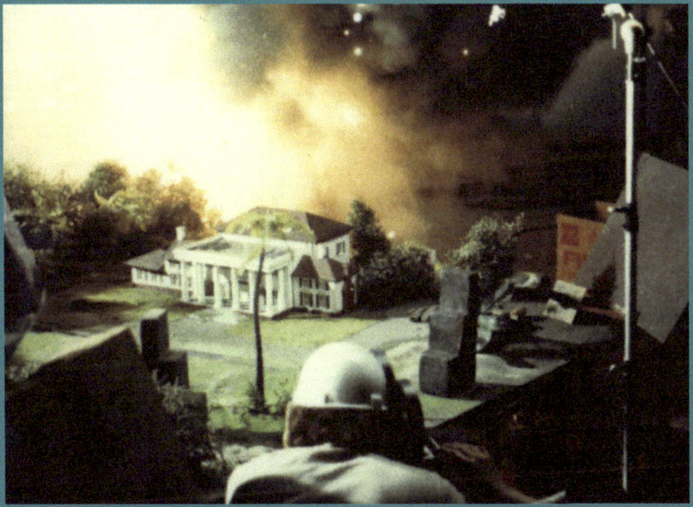

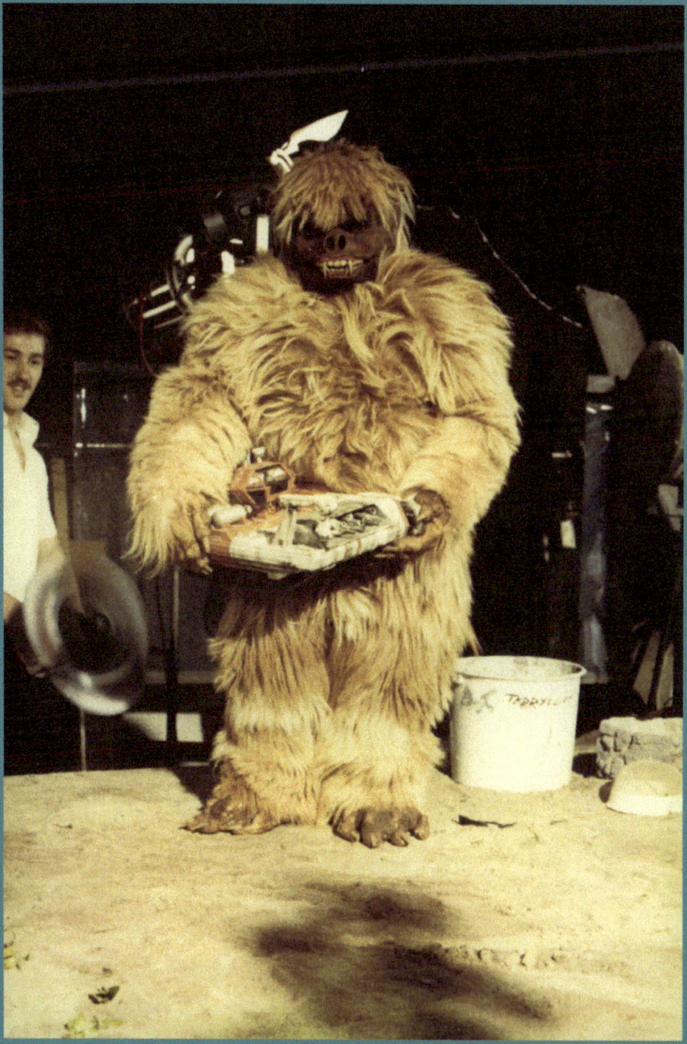

Setting up again for *Terrahawks* was difficult, as Gerry no longer had a regular team around him. Derek Meddings was now working on big feature films, and so Gerry initially turned to another former associate, Ian Scoones, to handle the special effects. When initial rushes proved to be unsatisfactory, Scoones was let go and newcomer Steven Begg was thrown in at the deep end. It was a baptism of fire that Begg rose to impressively. **Above left:** An effects technician prepares a rocket for launch. **Below left:** A 120 frames per second Derek Meddings-style explosion goes off behind the Terrahawks' secret base. **Right:** The Sporilla is fanned by a member of the crew.

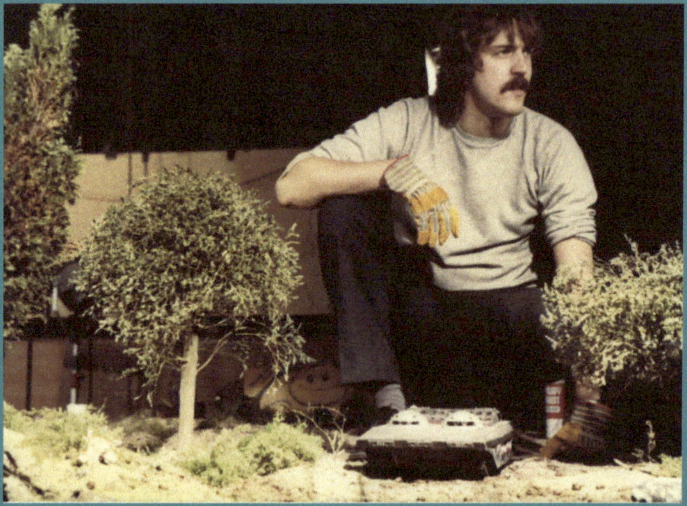

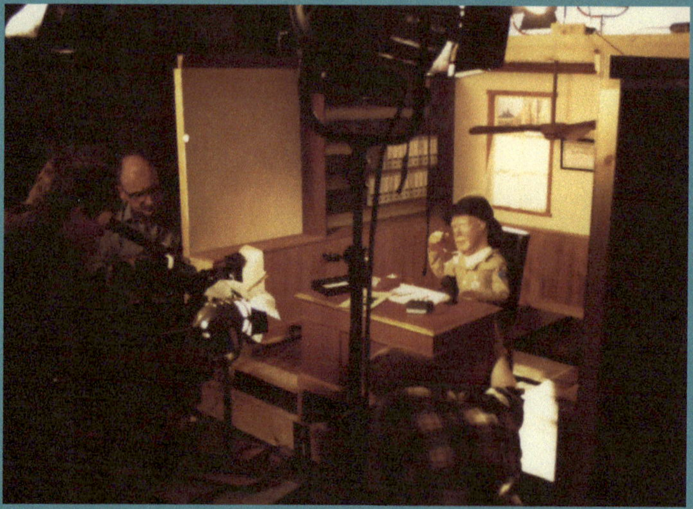

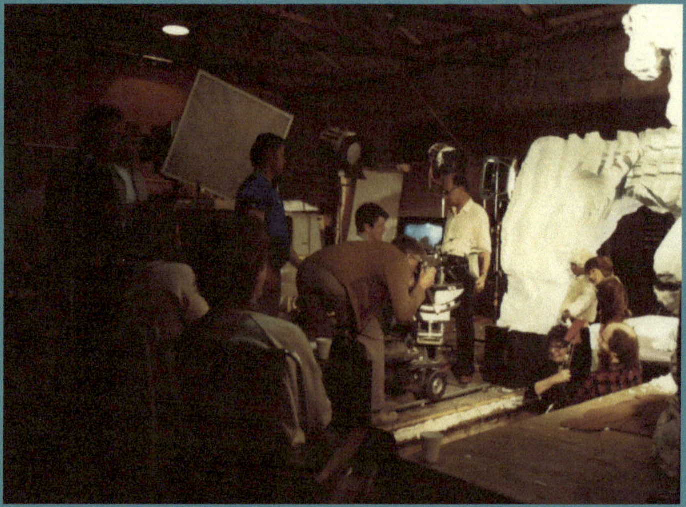

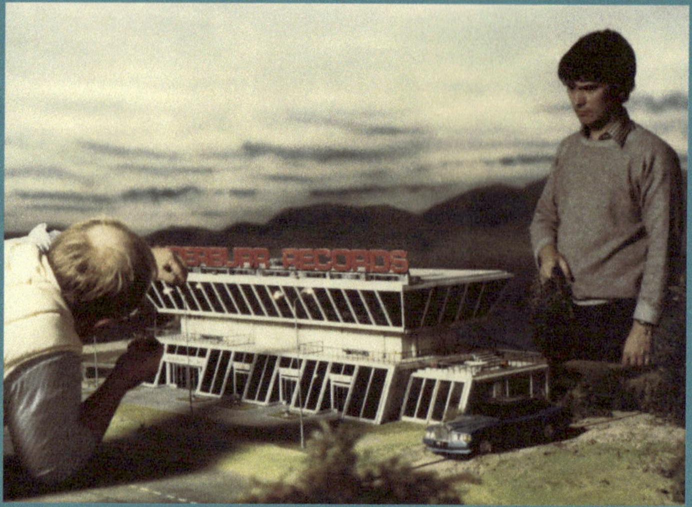

Above left: Steve Begg on set with the Battletank. **Above right:** Filming Sheriff Bull in his office. Moving on from Supermarionation, it was decided to use glove puppets for *Terrahawks*. Advances in technology allowed for the puppets to have rubber faces, enabling a greater range of expression. The puppets were operated from pits (**below left**). **Below Right:** The Anderburr Records miniature.

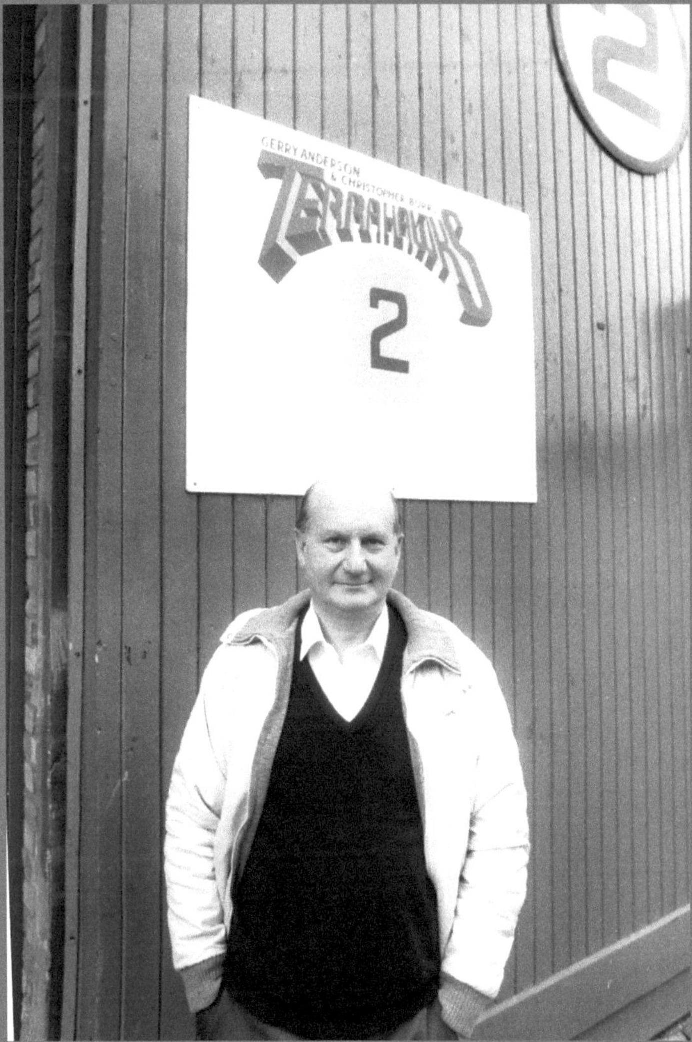

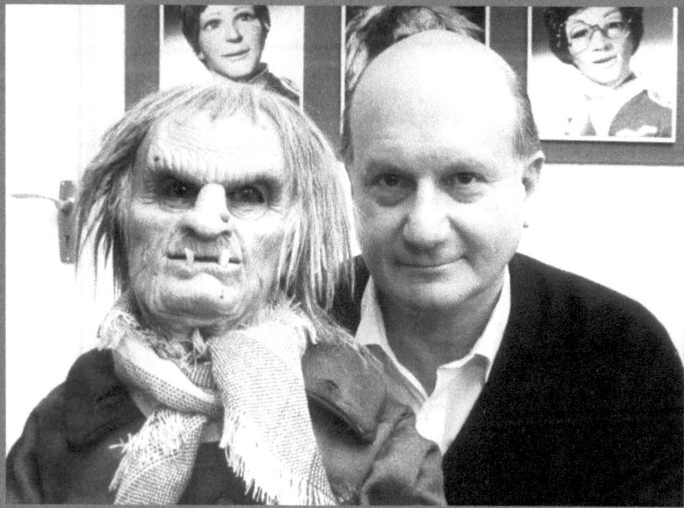

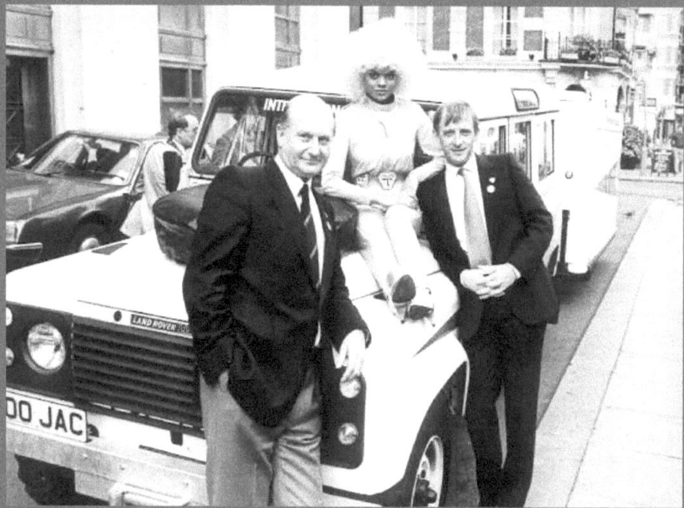

Left: Gerry standing outside the *Terrahawks* shed at Bray Studios. **Above right:** Gerry in his office with Zelda's foolish son, Yung-star. Note the hero portraits of the lead characters on his wall. **Below right:** One of the many gimmicks for the series was to have a 'real life' Kate Kestrel. Gerry and Christopher pose with 19-year-old singer Moya Griffiths.

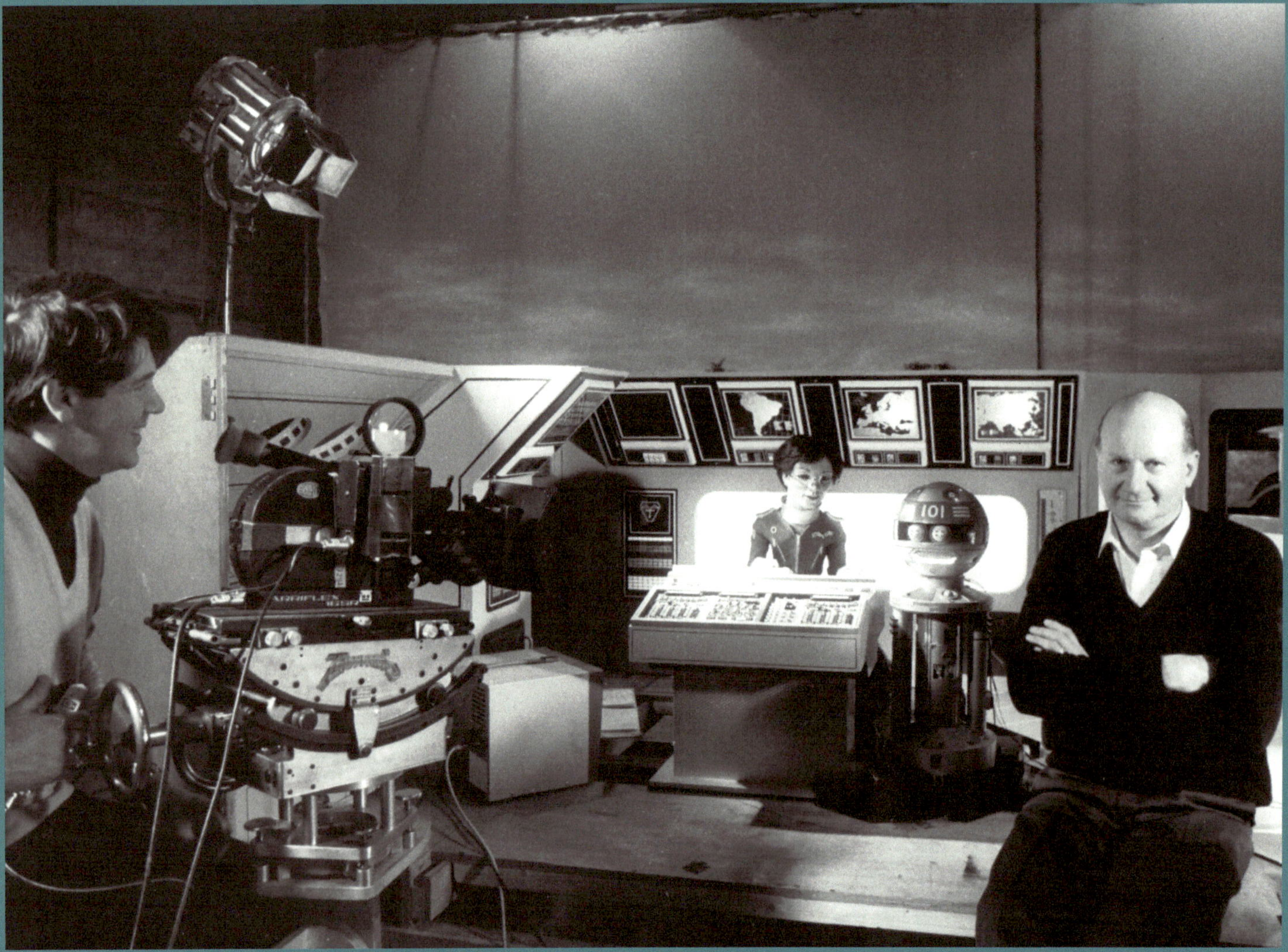

Gerry on the Spacehawk puppet set with Lt Hiro and Space Sergeant 101. *Terrahawks* was a ratings and merchandising success, running to two series. Scripts were prepared for a third series, but it fell through. It was time to develop a new concept.

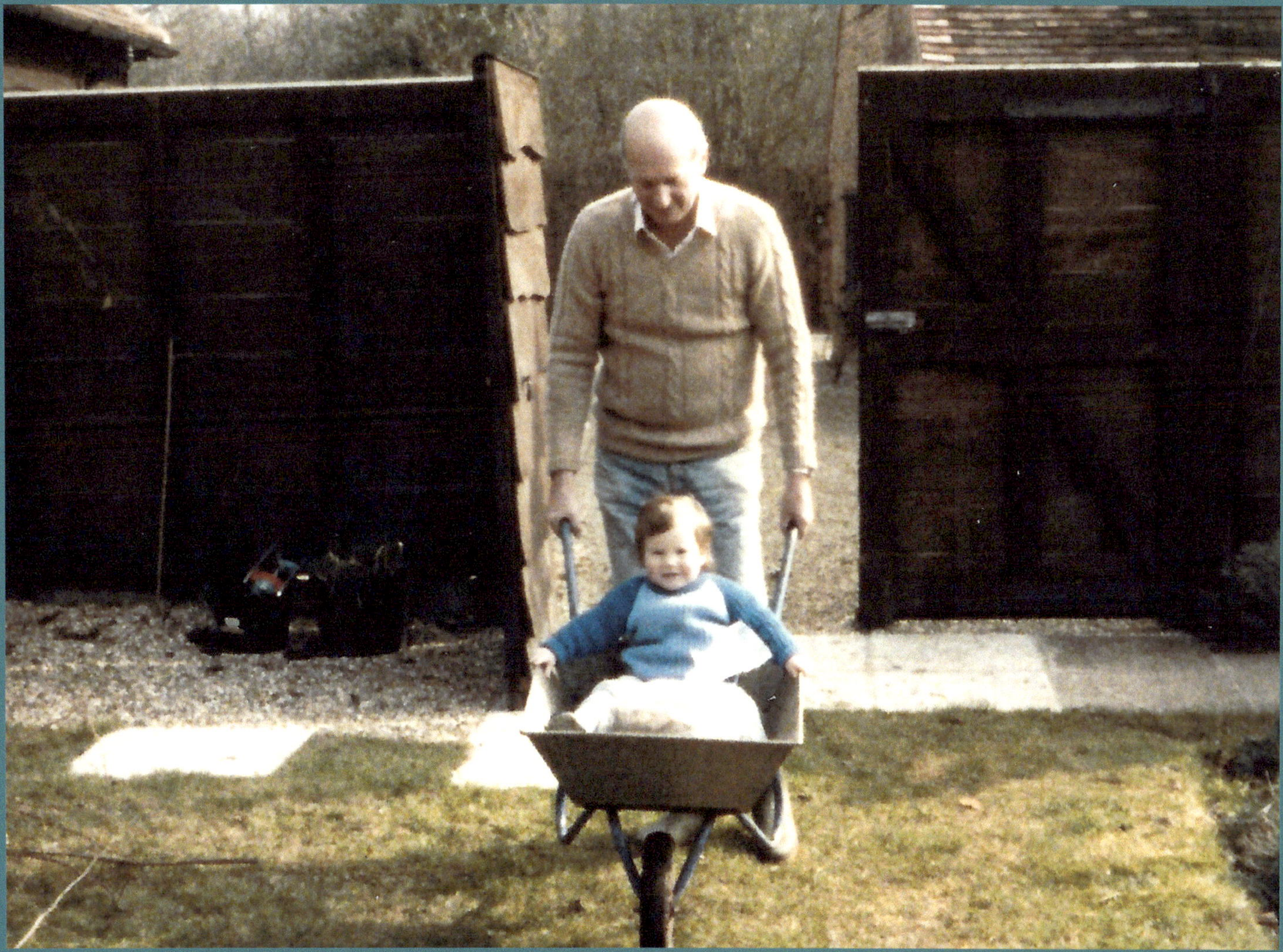

In 1985, Gerry, now aged 55, became a father once again. His new son was named James Lionel Anderson.

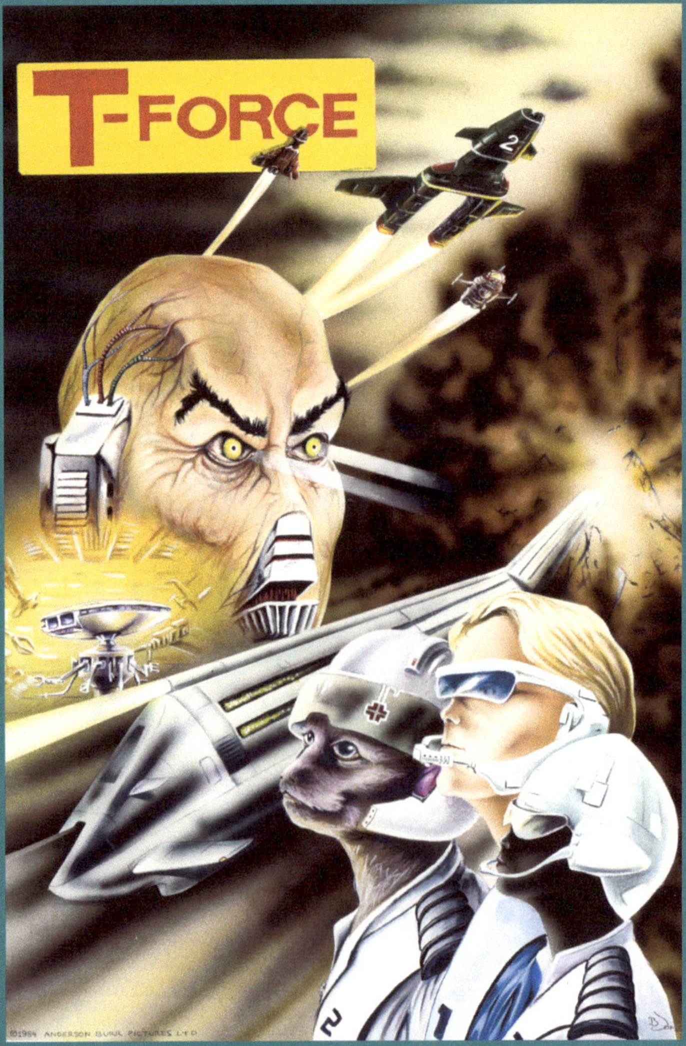

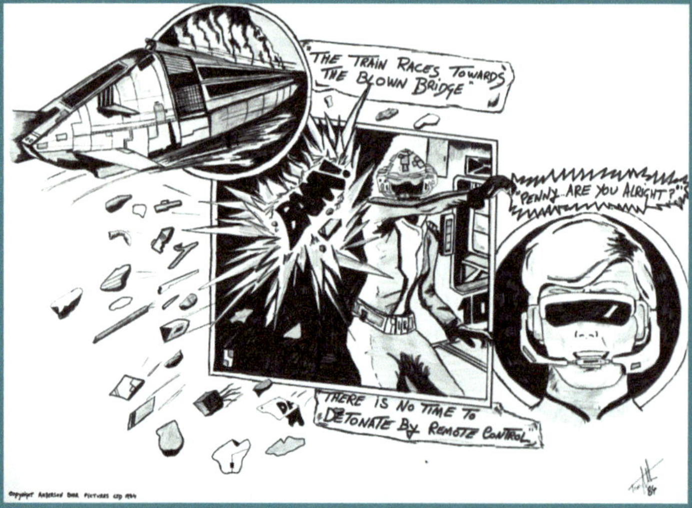

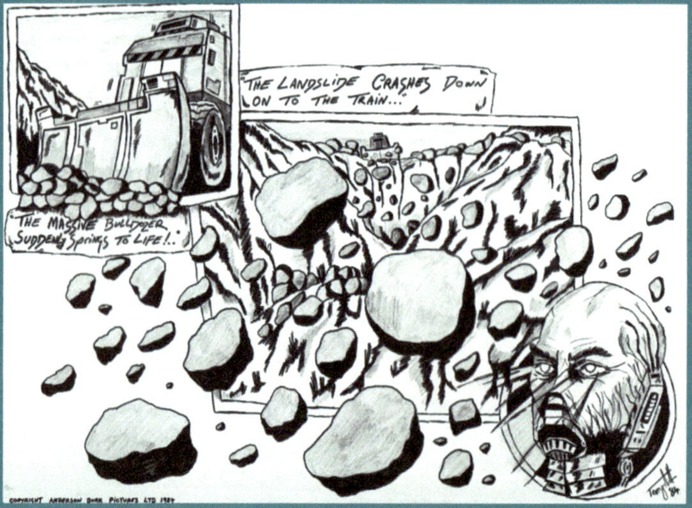

Gerry was a prolific creative force, and in the middle of one series he was always seemingly looking forward to the next. In the 1980s, he hoped to revive *Thunderbirds* in a redeveloped form. This concept took various guises.

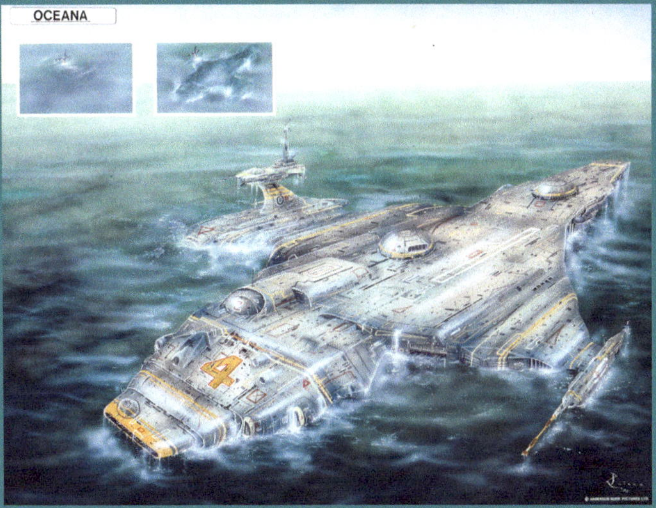

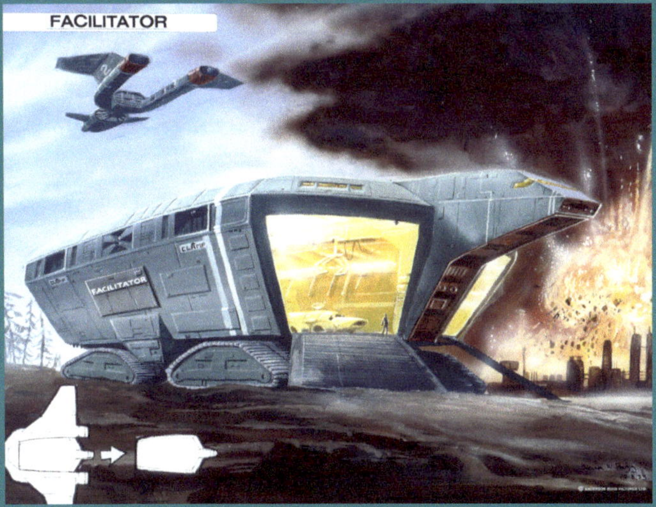

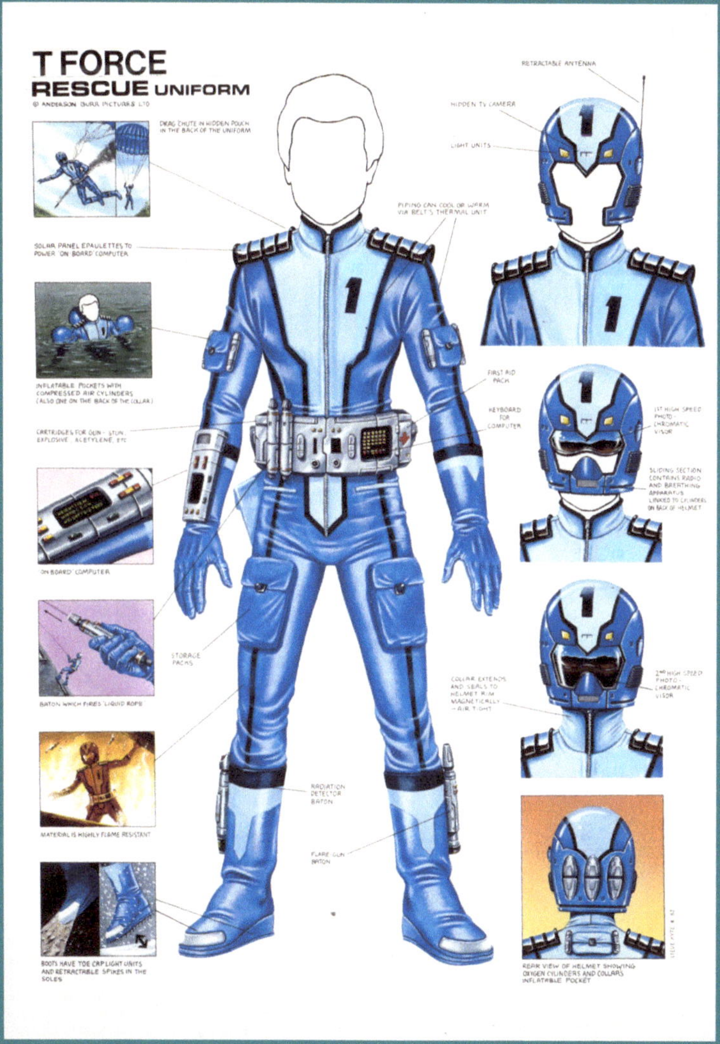

Here are concept pages from one of those formats for a series called *T-Force*. Despite expectations that it would go into production, the series never materialised.

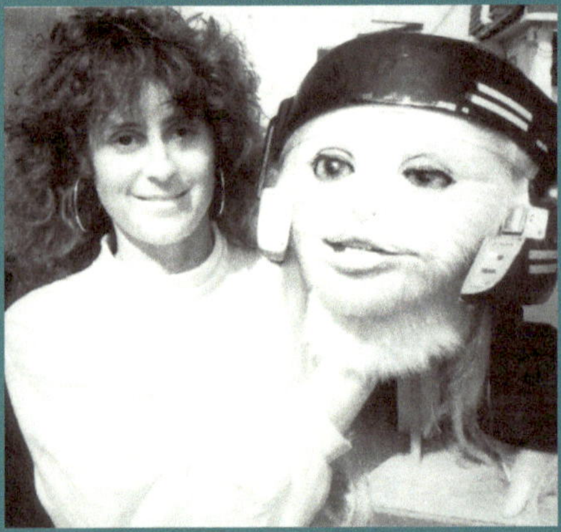

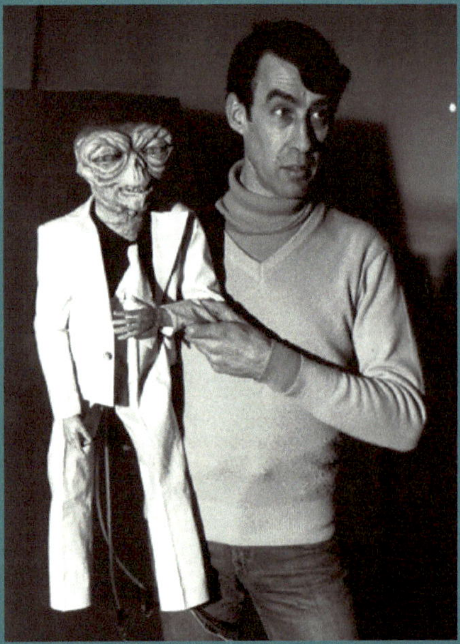

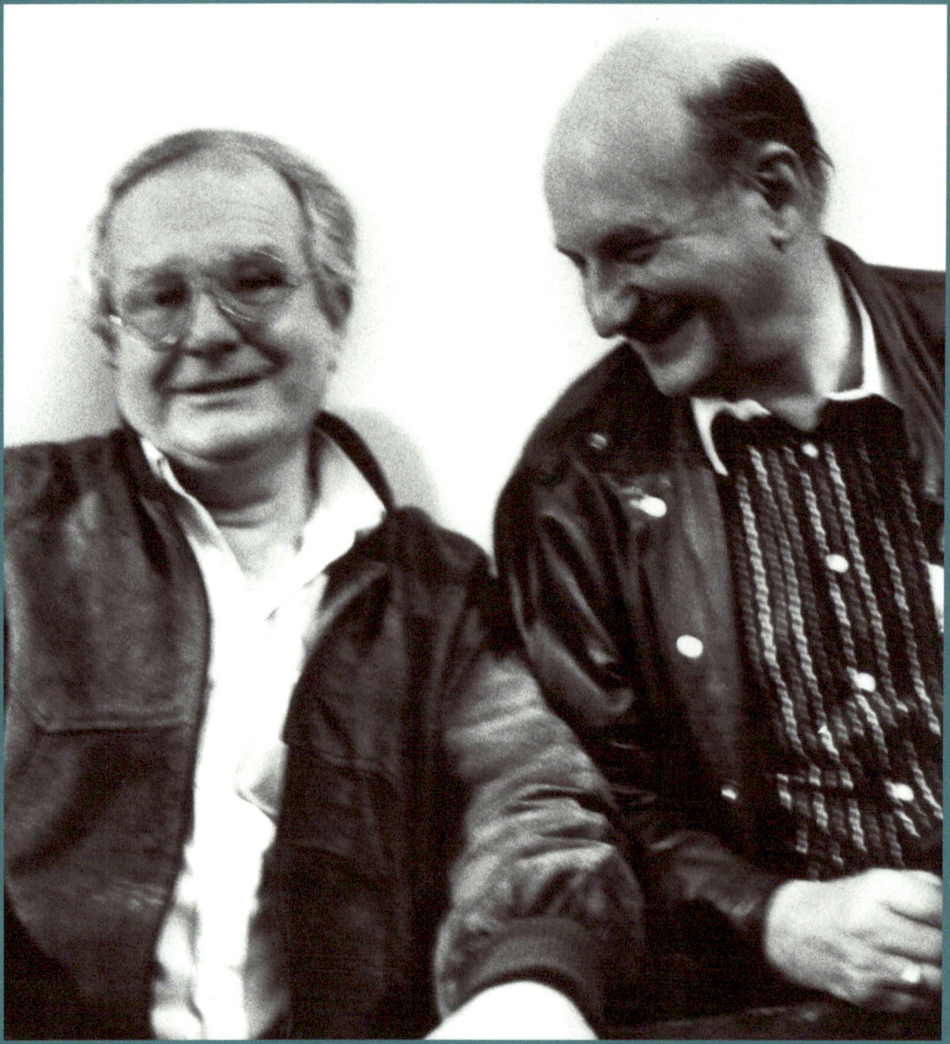

In 1986, Anderson Burr Productions put up finance for a new pilot called *Space Police*, a concept that was supposed to be *Hill Street Blues* in space. The pilot built upon the 'Supermacromation' puppet technology used for *Terrahawks* and also included sophisticated animatronic masks. Despite being well produced, it would be eight years before the series appeared in a reworked guise. **Above left:** One of the animatronic heads. **Below left:** A puppeteer with the villainous E-Vil. **Right:** Gerry Anderson and long-term collaborator Shane Rimmer.

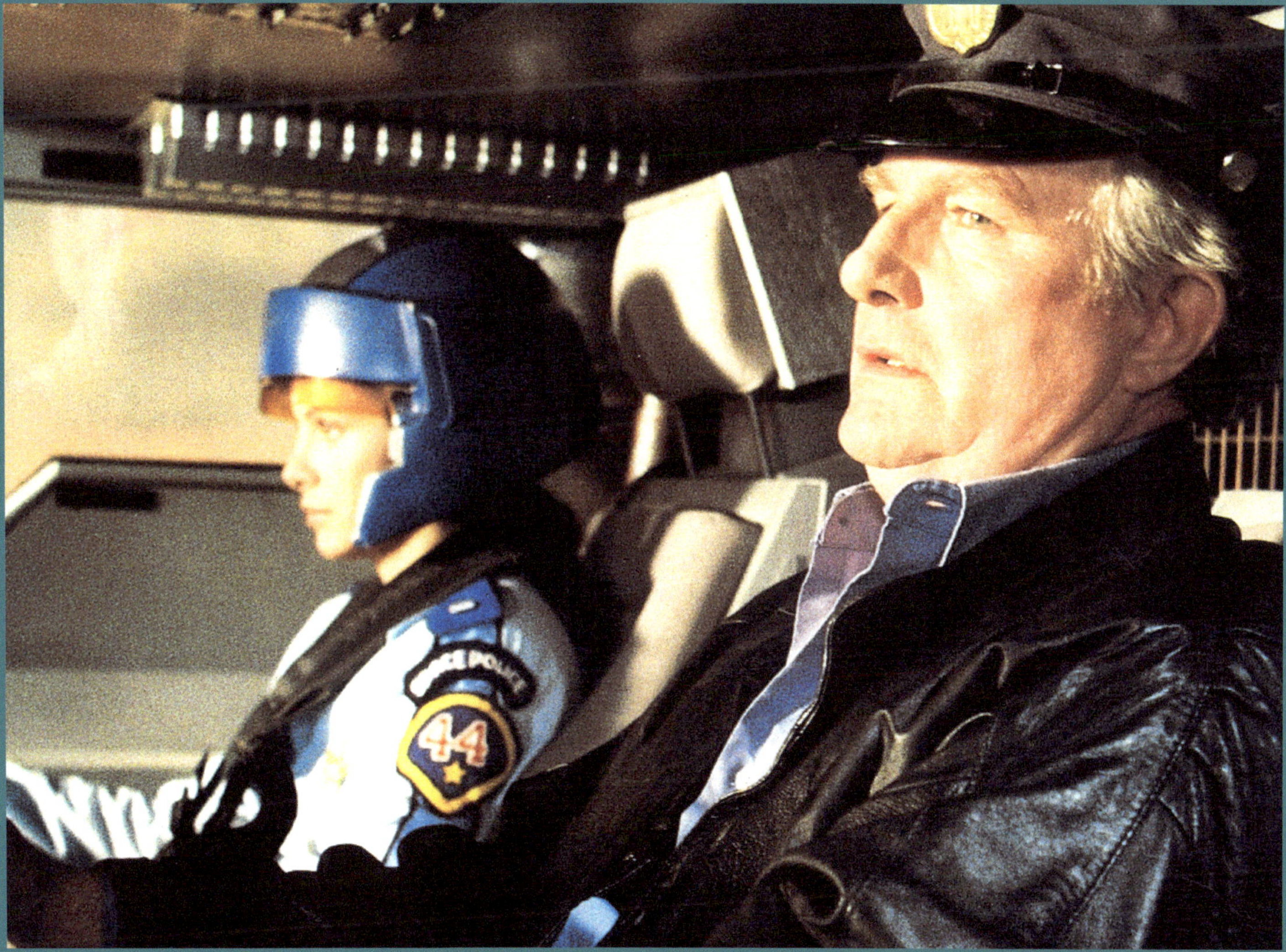

For the pilot, Shane Rimmer played Lt Brogan. He would later be replaced by Ted Shackleford when the series was launched as *Space Precinct*.

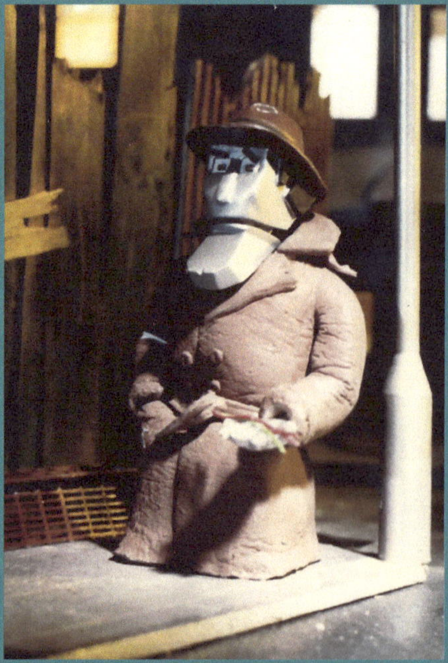

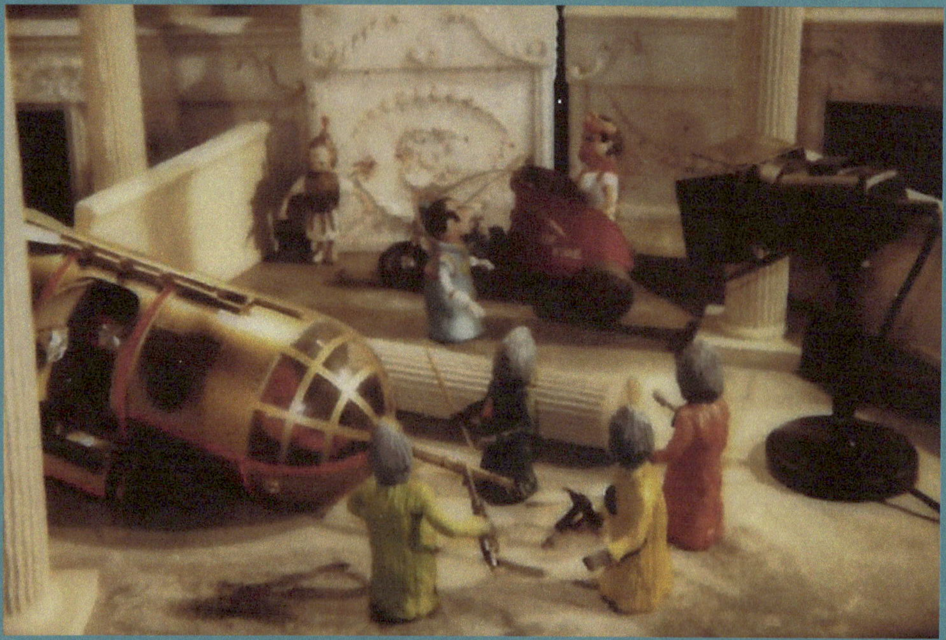

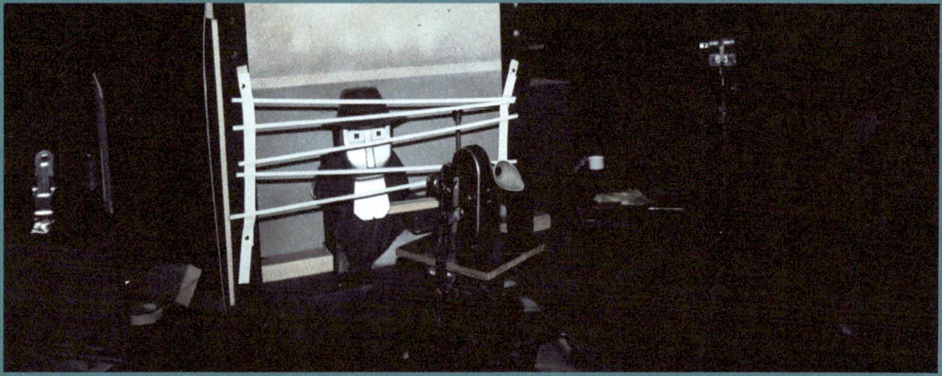

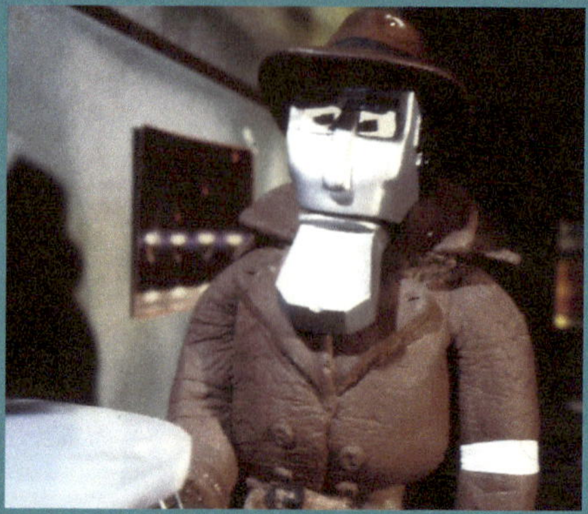

In the late '80s, Gerry was approached by broadcaster and journalist Janet Street-Porter, who was looking for a humorous animated series to put on her Sunday morning show on Channel 4, *Network 7*. The result, conceived by model maker Terry Adlam, was *Dick Spanner*, a stop motion series about a wisecracking private eye robot.

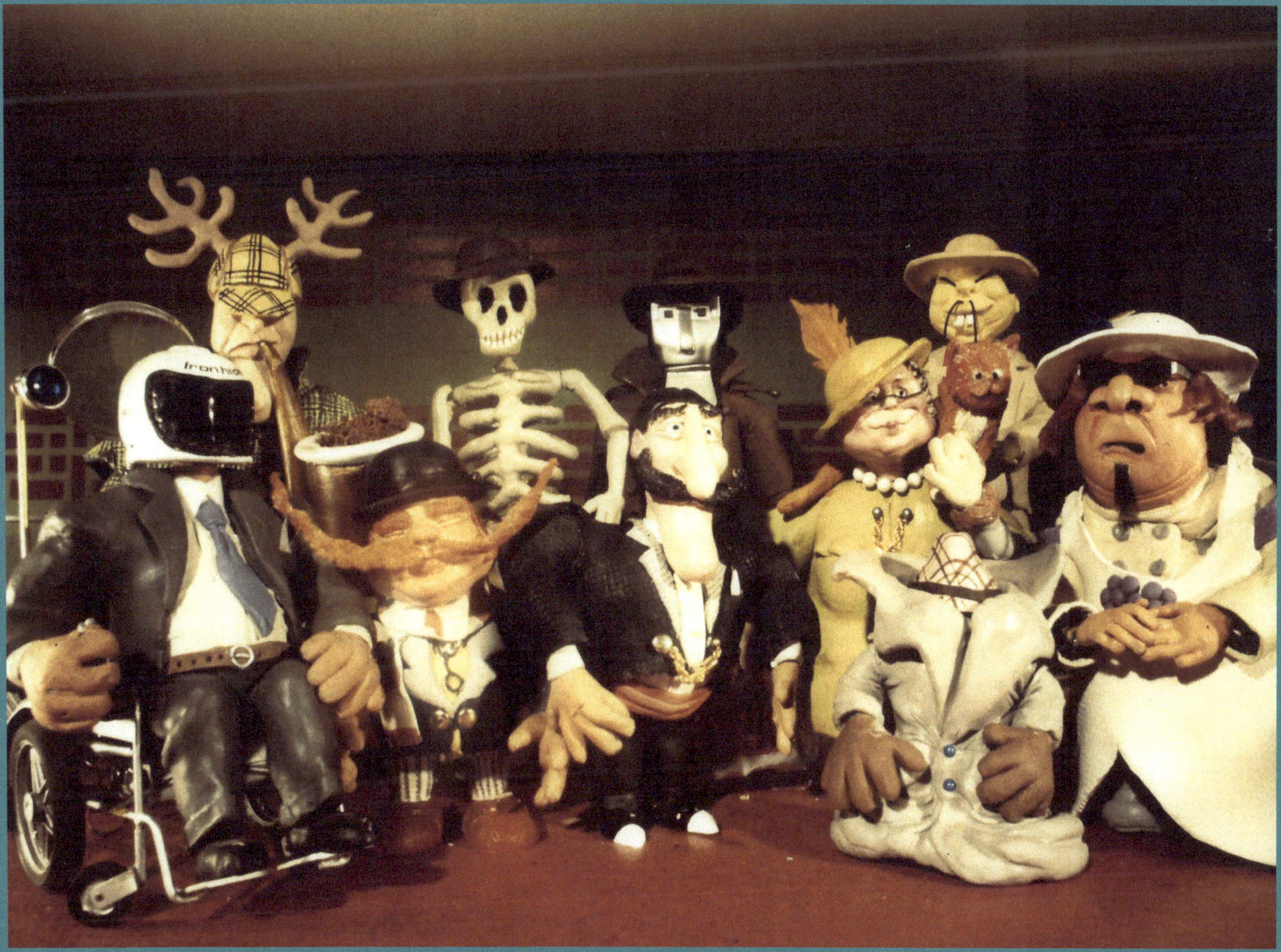

Two stories consisting of 22 episodes were made and screened on *Network 7*. The shot above comes from a 23rd episode, the start of an abandoned third adventure for Spanner. This forgotten episode was found amongst Gerry's possessions in 2013.

1990s

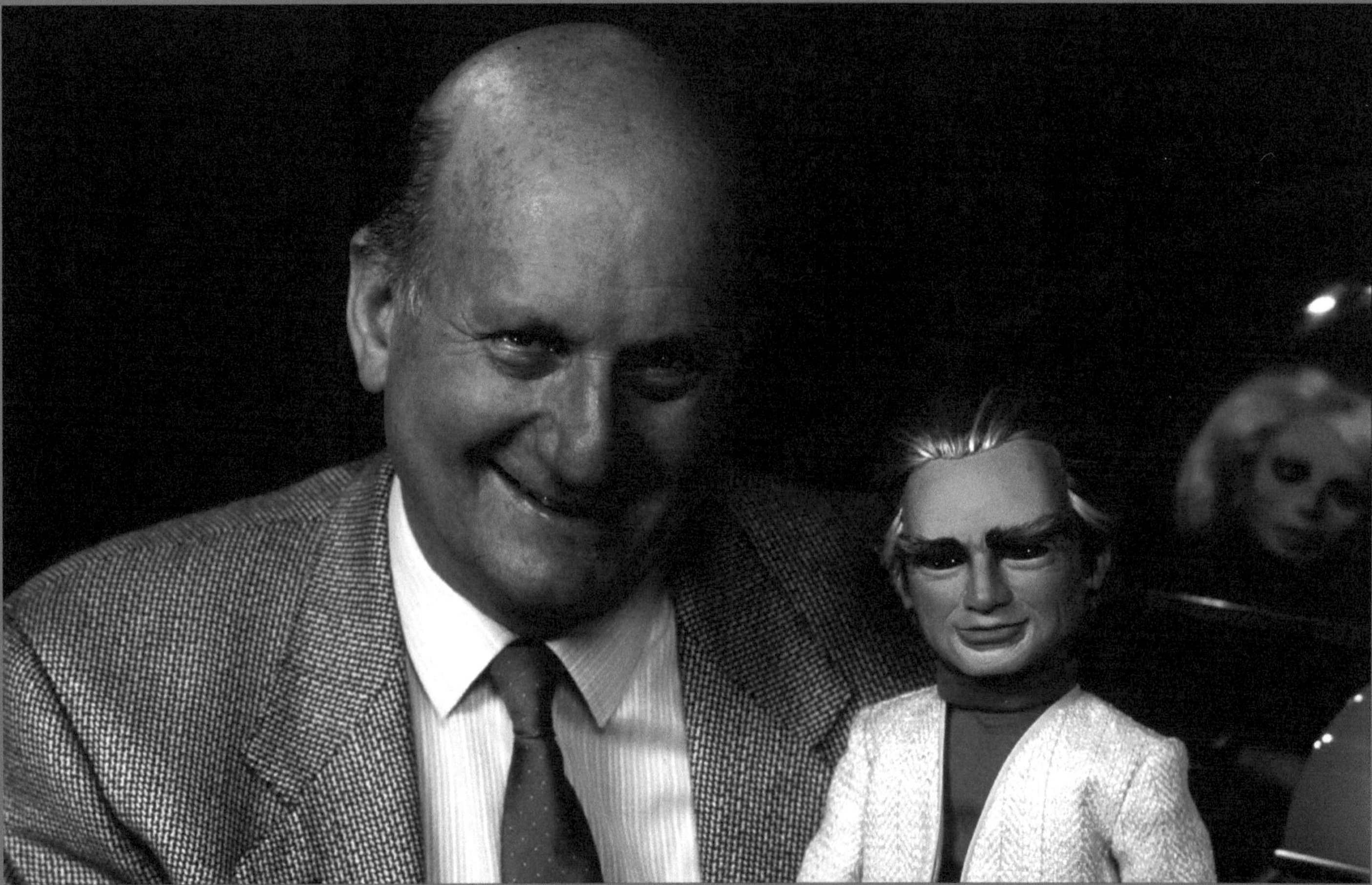

The '90s were an unexpected renaissance for Gerry. In 1991, the BBC acquired the rights to screen *Thunderbirds* on BBC2, which proved to be a surprise smash hit. A new generation of children was introduced to the daring adventures of International Rescue, and soon a Tracy Island playset was Christmas toy of the year. *Stingray, Captain Scarlet* and *Joe 90* were revived too, and Anderson-mania reached a peak comparable with the '60s. This revived interest helped Gerry to launch a new, ambitious series, *Space Precinct*. Now in his 60s, Gerry had no intention of retiring.

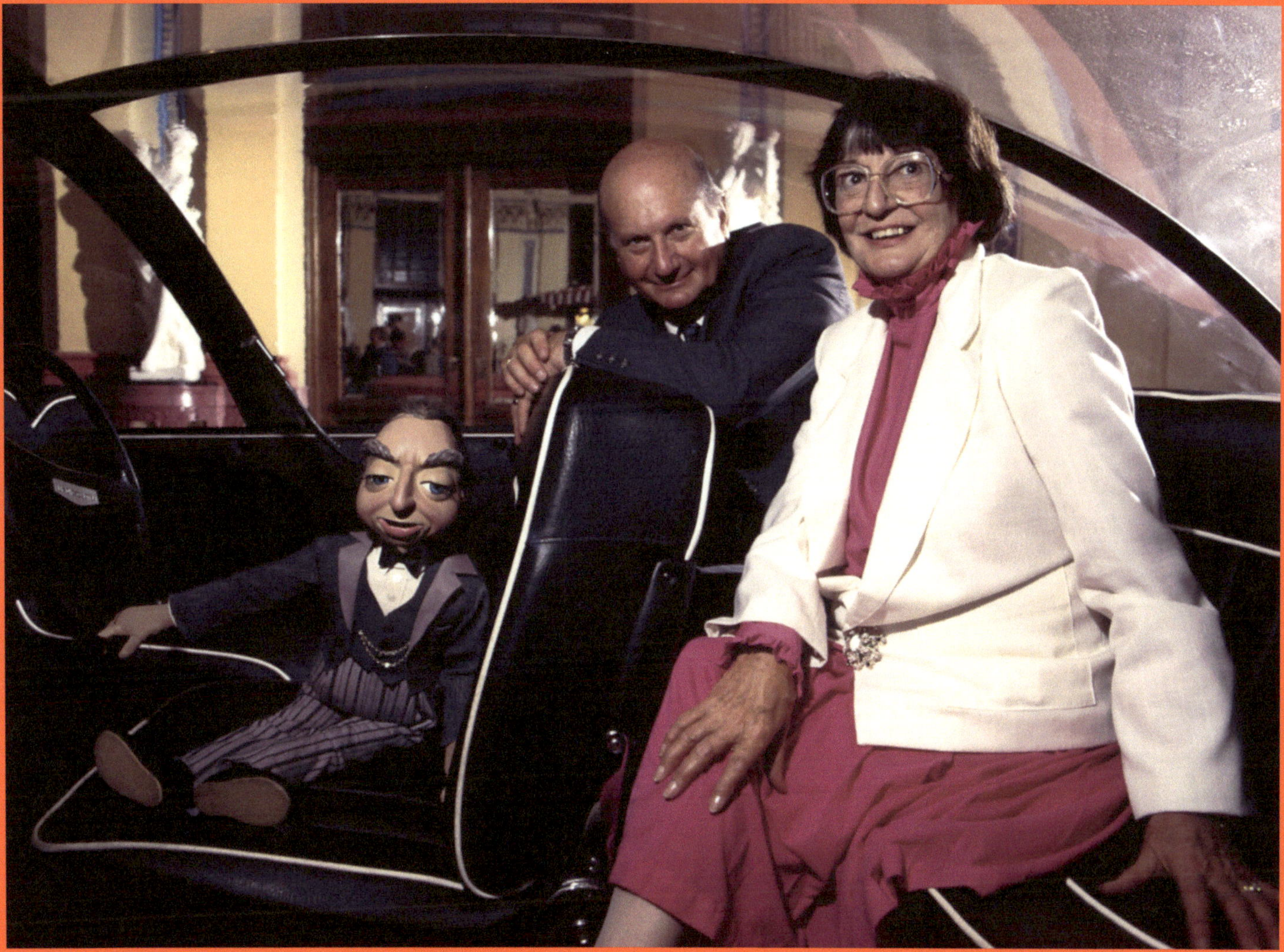

Gerry with long-term collaborator Christine Glanville. Christine had joined Gerry at the beginning of *Twizzle*, and continued working with him right up until her untimely death in 1999. Here, they're sitting in the full-sized replica of FAB 1, built in the 1960s, posing with a puppet of Parker created for a short-lived 1970s stage show version of *Thunderbirds*.

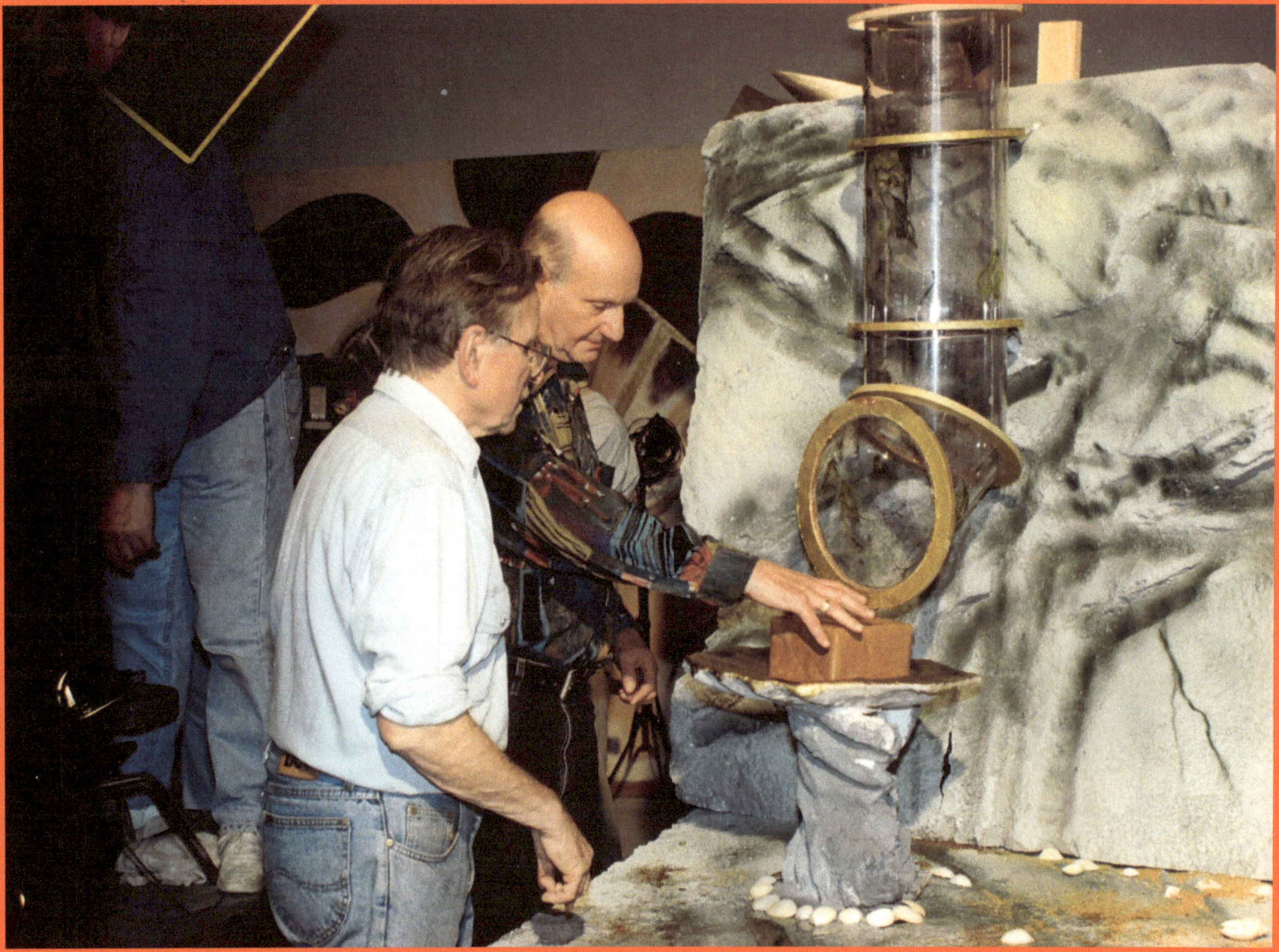

During the late '80s and early '90s, Gerry found himself working in advertising again, which he used to his advantage when the sudden Supermarionation revival meant that advertisers were lining up to be associated with the puppets. Twenty-five years after leaving the puppets behind, old APF colleagues reunited to bring them back to life.

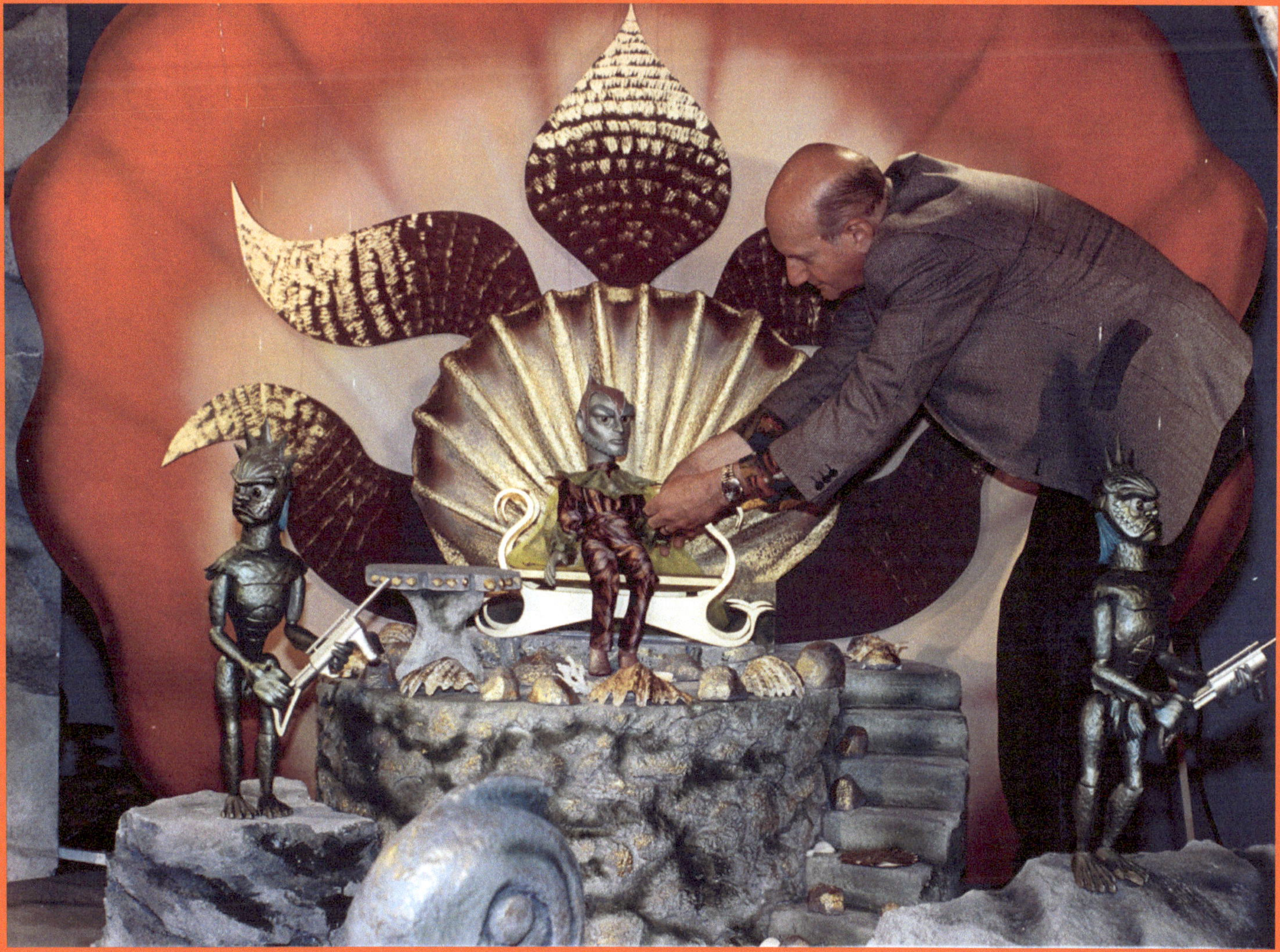

Gerry on a recreation of Titan's throne room set. The evil King of Titanica was back – and this time his plan involved Weetabix!

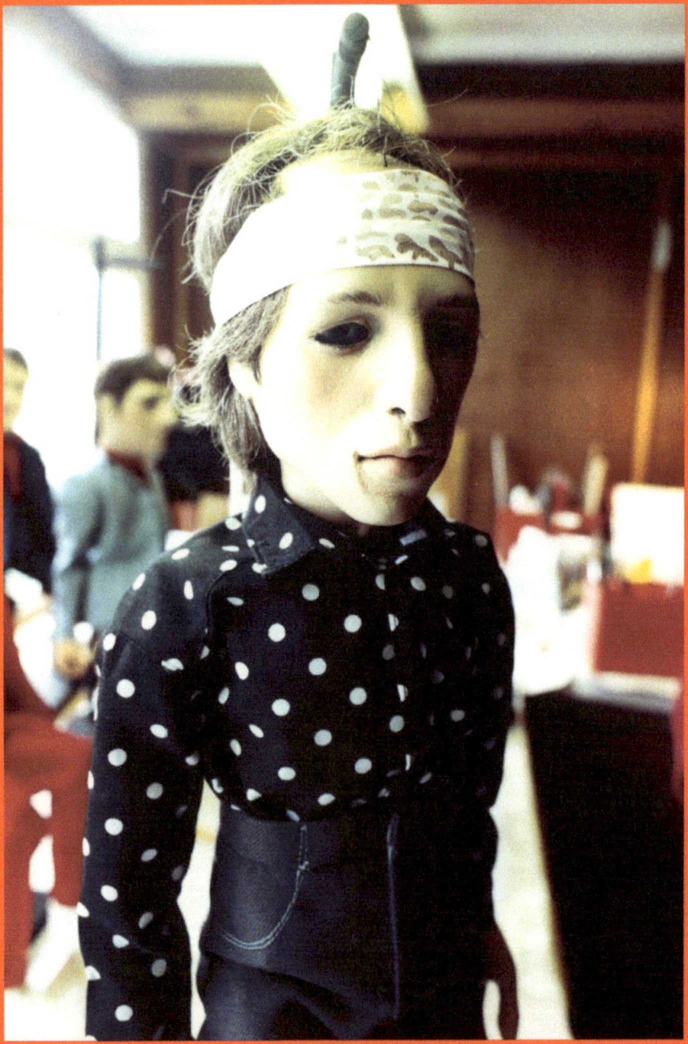

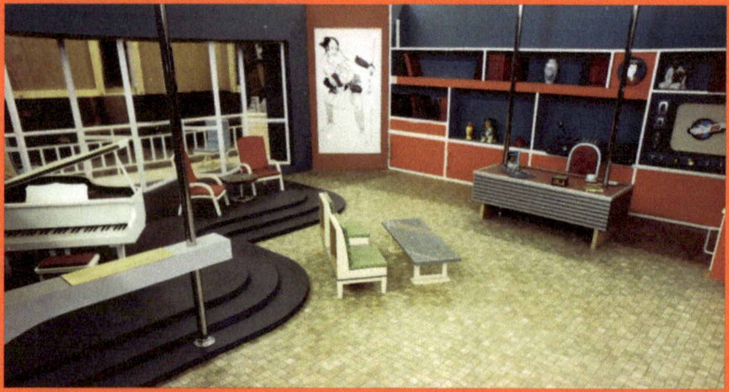

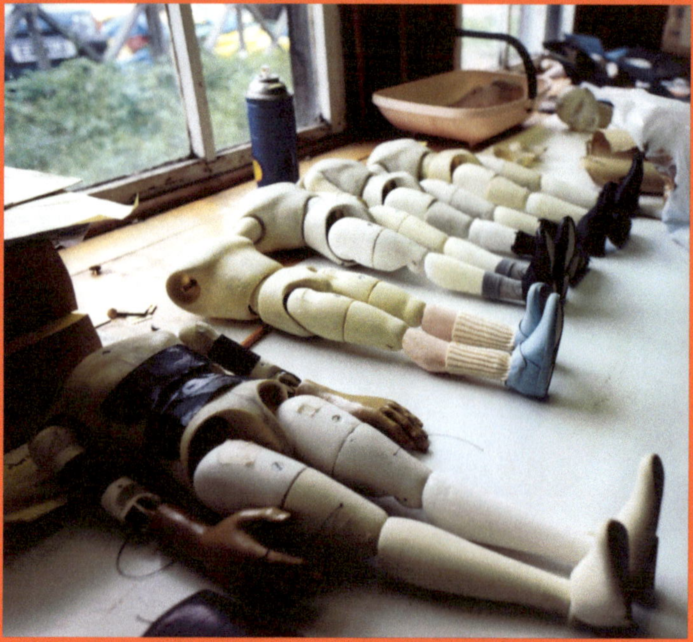

Another unusual commission during this time came from rock band Dire Straits, who wanted to feature *Thunderbirds* and Supermarionation in their music video for 'Calling Elvis'.

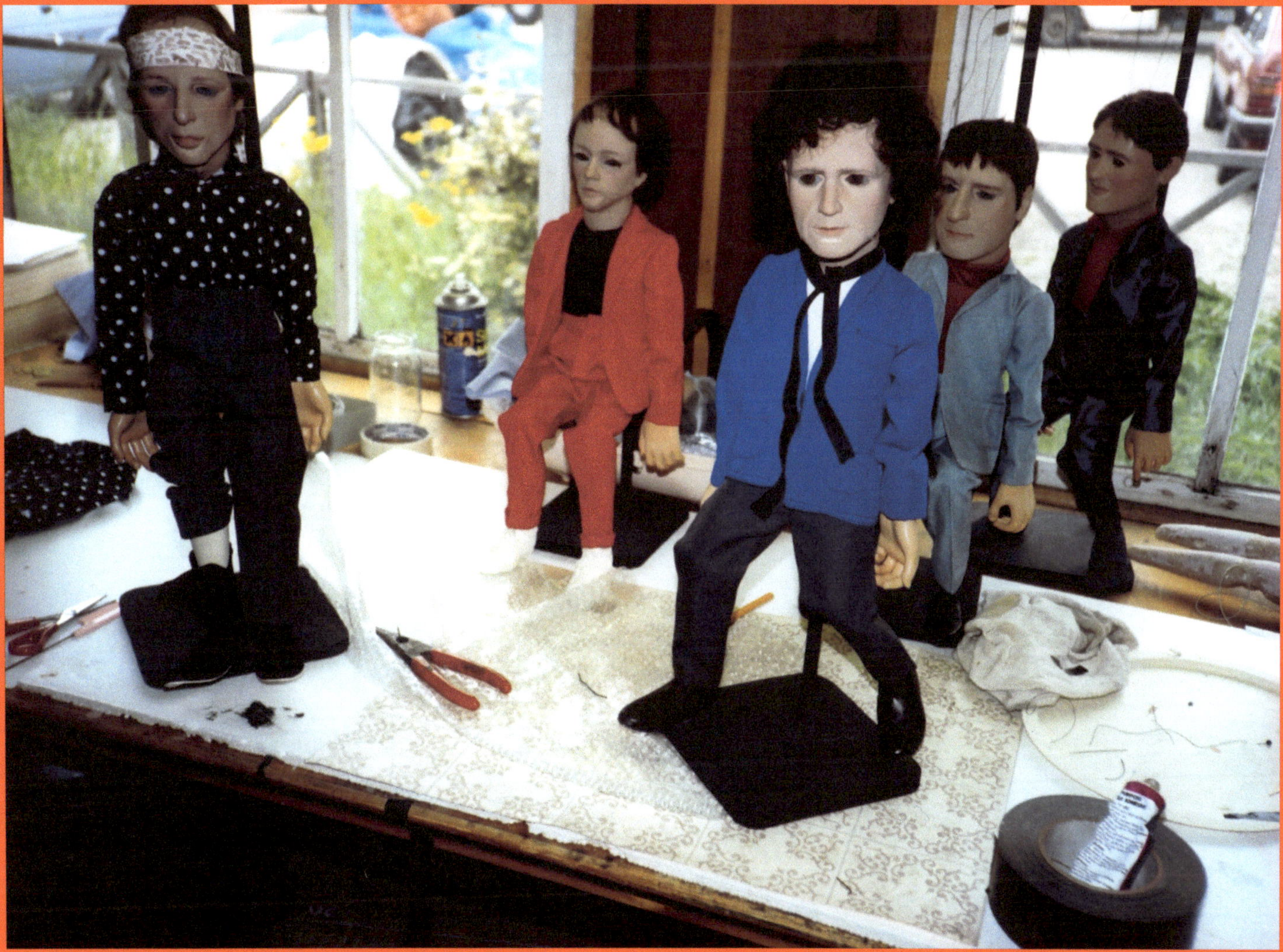

Echoing the appearance of Cliff Richard and the Shadows in *Thunderbirds Are Go*, the band appeared in the video as puppets.

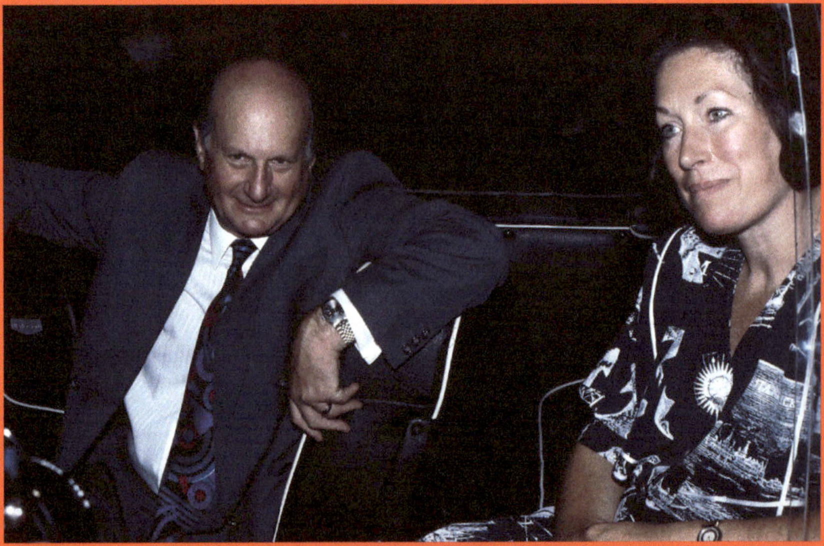

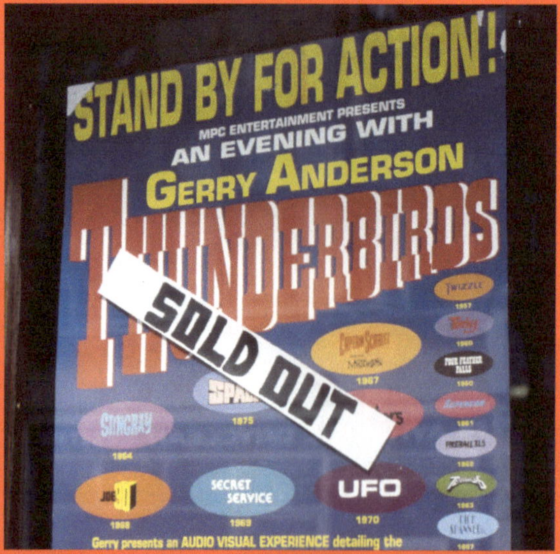

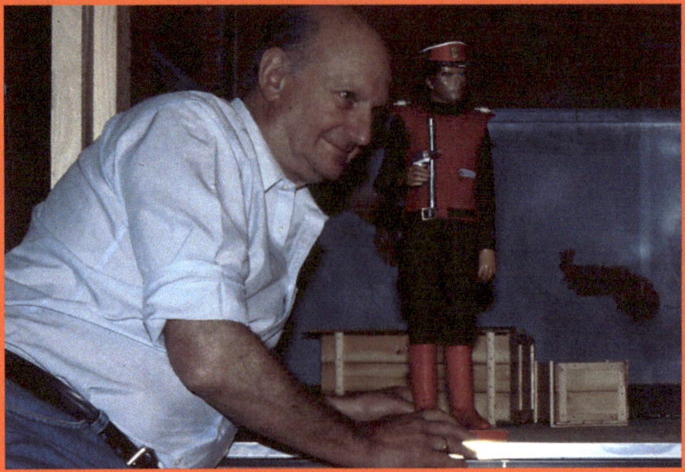

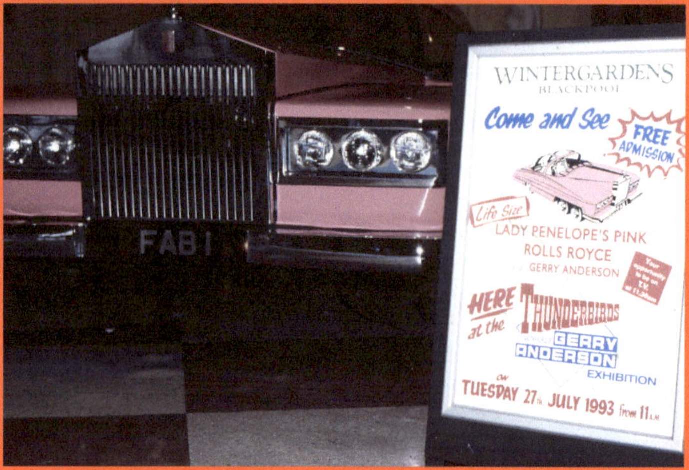

The sudden interest in their work caught many of the old A.P. Films team by surprise. After all, the shows were now nearly three decades old. However, many children didn't seem to notice. **Above left:** Gerry and Mary in FAB 1. **Below left:** Gerry poses with his indestructible creation, Captain Scarlet. **Above right:** An evening with Gerry Anderson sold out promptly. **Bottom right:** Visitors flocked to an exhibition in Blackpool.

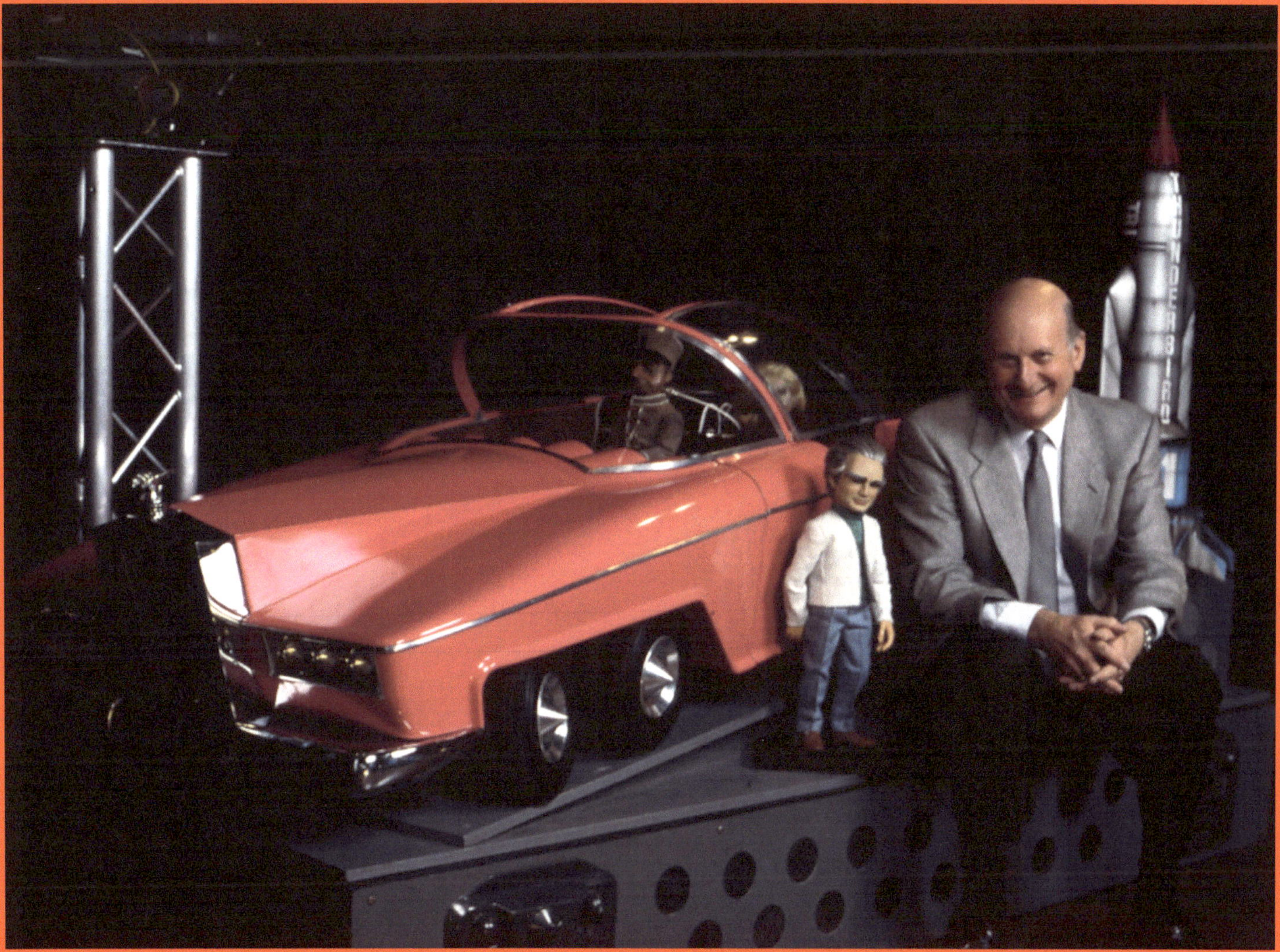

Gerry, who always claimed he hated the puppets, now became (perhaps happily) resigned to the fact that he was always going to be associated with them. The extraordinary works he and his team created in the 1960s had captured the imaginations of a new generation of children, and charmed parents who remembered the shows from their original broadcasts.

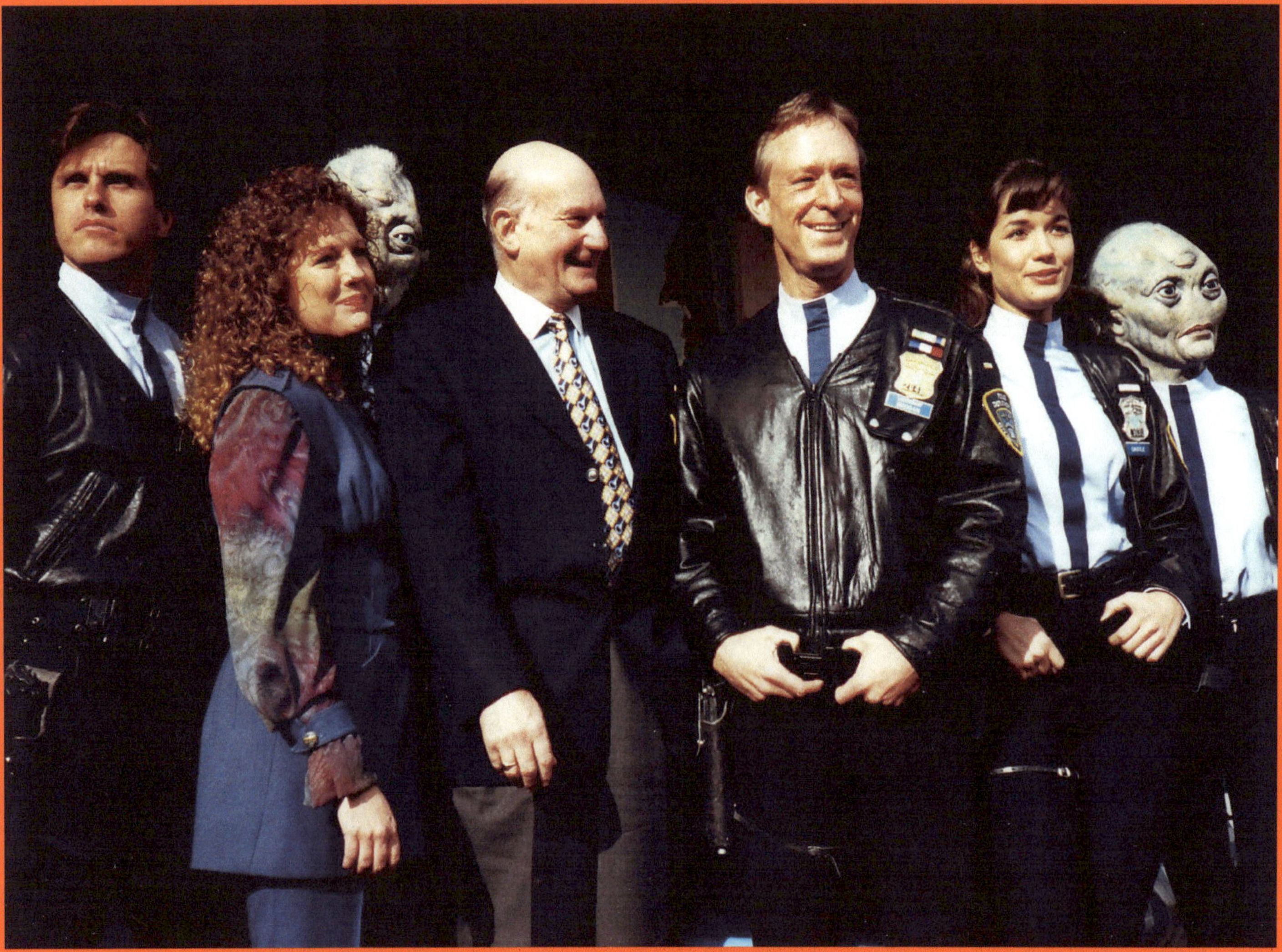

Eight years after *Space Police* had been made, Gerry joined forces with John Needham at Mentorn Films, and the multimillion-pound project entered production at Pinewood as a reworked concept called *Space Precinct*. Here, Gerry poses with his new cast (left to right): Rob Youngblood, Nancy Paul, David Quilter, Ted Shackleford, Simone Bendix and Mary Woodvine.

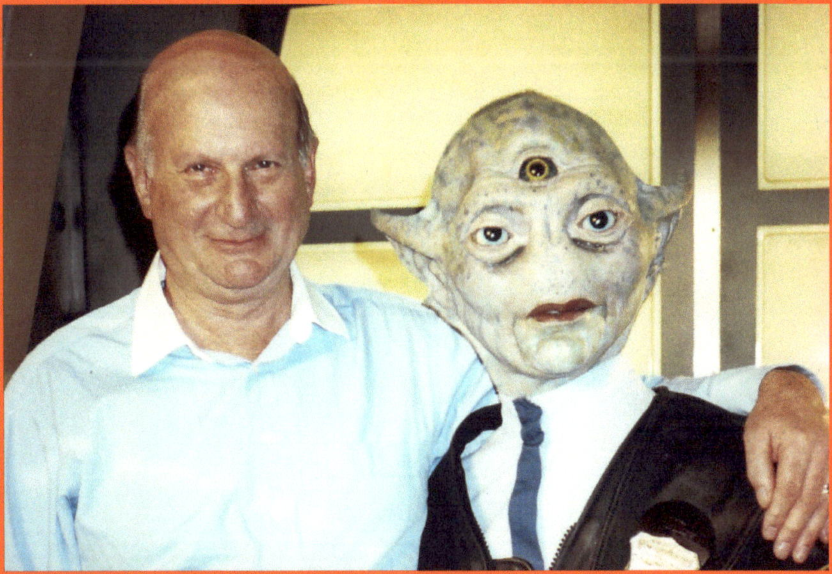

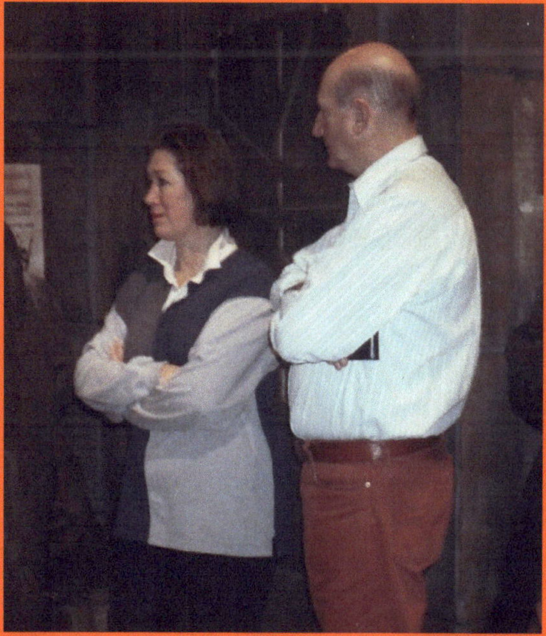

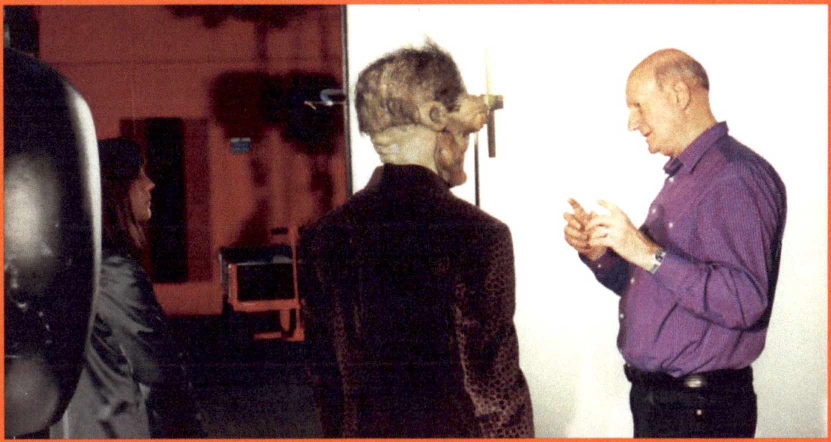

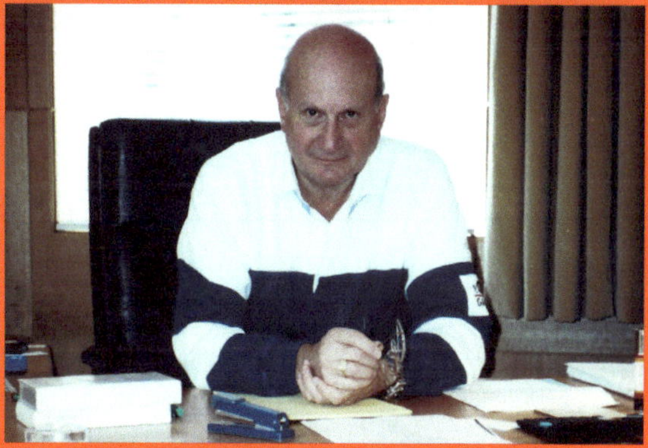

It was an extraordinarily difficult production, with finance nearly falling through during filming. Though the show was successfully completed, it failed to find the audience that Gerry's previous shows did. In spite of this, many elements of the production remain impressive, notably the prosthetic animatronic masks used for the alien characters. **Above left:** Gerry poses with Officer Aurelia Took (Mary Woodvine). **Above right:** Gerry and Mary on set. **Below left:** Conferring between takes. **Below right:** Gerry at his desk at Pinewood Studios.

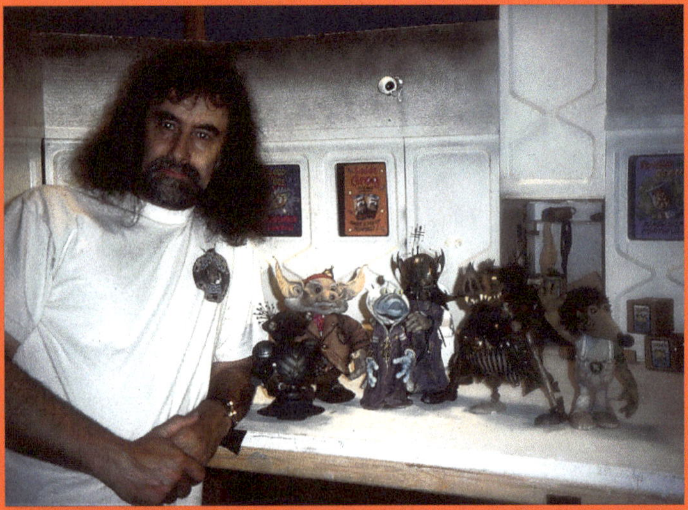

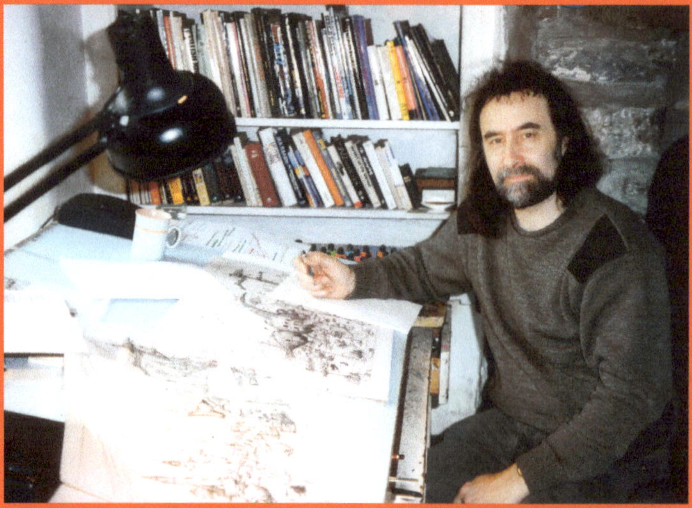

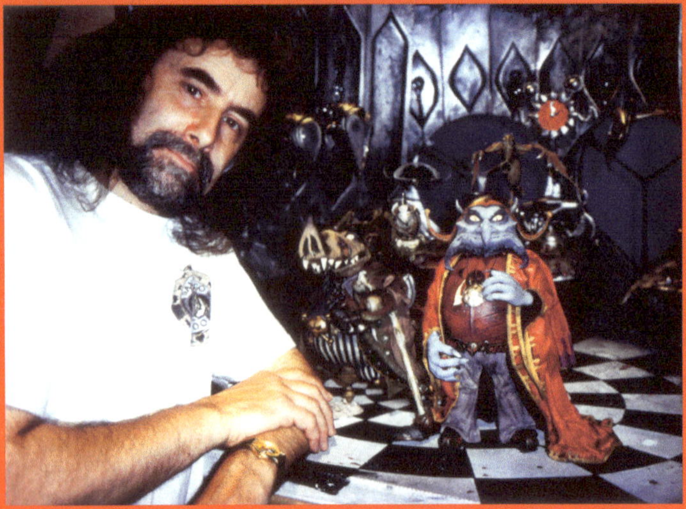

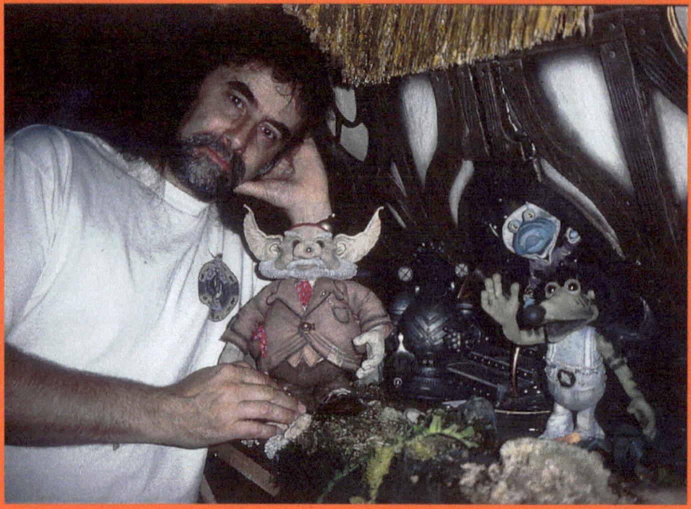

In the late '90s, Gerry found himself working in animation once again. He teamed up with artist Rodney Matthews, who had devised a series called *Lavender Castle*. The series, which followed Captain Thrice and his crew on a quest to find Lavender Castle, ran for one series. Despite proving to be a success, the hoped-for second series wasn't to be.

FINAL YEARS

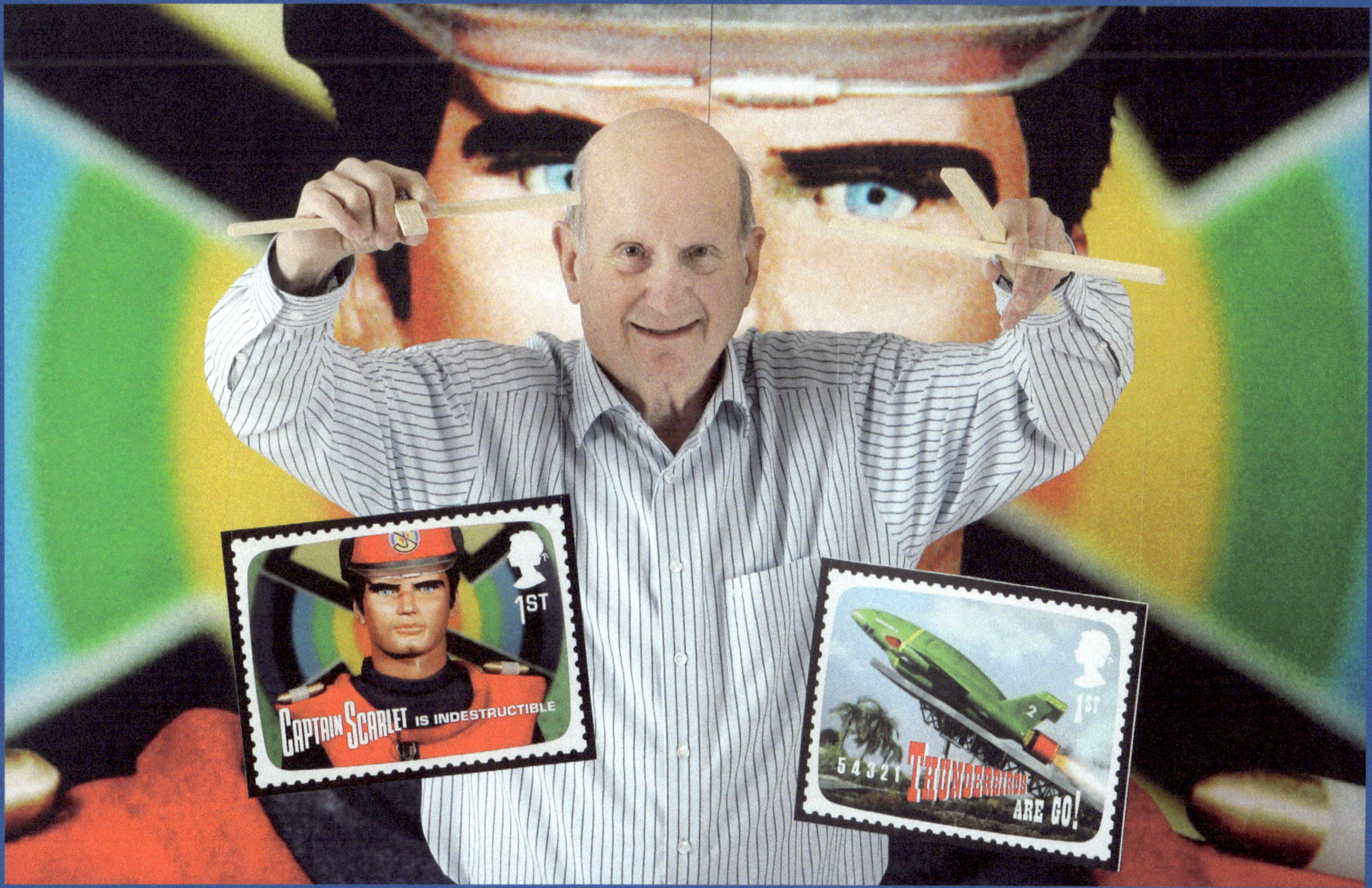

The real 21st century began with a second surprise revival of *Thunderbirds*. New transfers of the series were broadcast throughout the world, and *Thunderbirds*-mania hit again. DVDs and videos sold in astonishing numbers, and for the second time in eight years a Tracy Island playset was the must-have toy.

Now in his 70s, Gerry continued to try and raise finance for a new production. His reimagining of *Captain Scarlet* was, for him, his proudest achievement yet. It was to be his final production, though. Unknown to Gerry, he had developed Alzheimer's Disease. His final years were amongst his most creative, but his illness ensured he wouldn't live to see his last ideas realised.

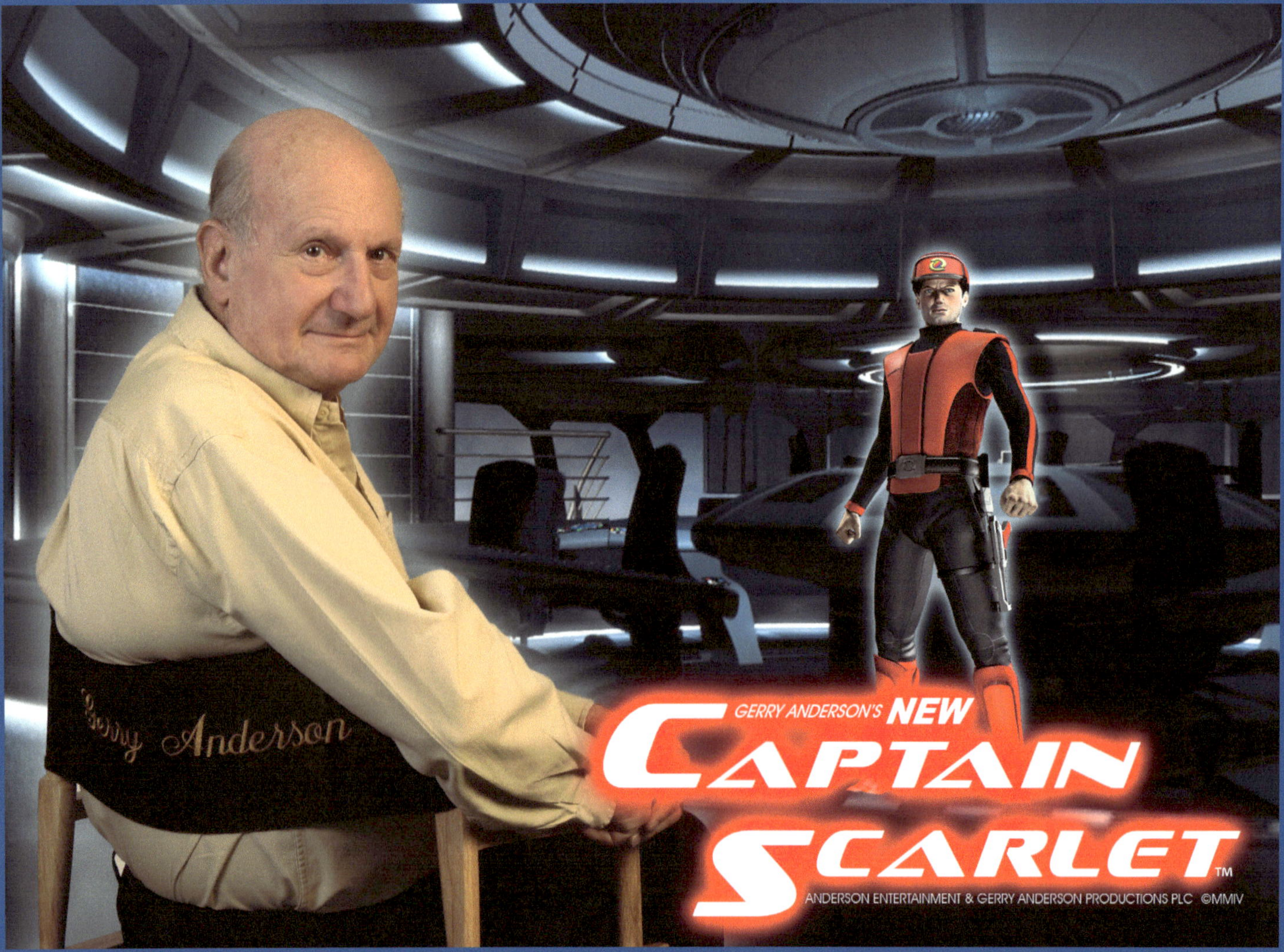

In 2003, production commenced on *New Captain Scarlet*, Gerry's multimillion-pound reworking of his cult 1967 series. Even at this point in his life, he continued to embrace new technology and turned to CGI to free him from the limitations of the marionettes. 26 episodes were produced at Pinewood Studios.

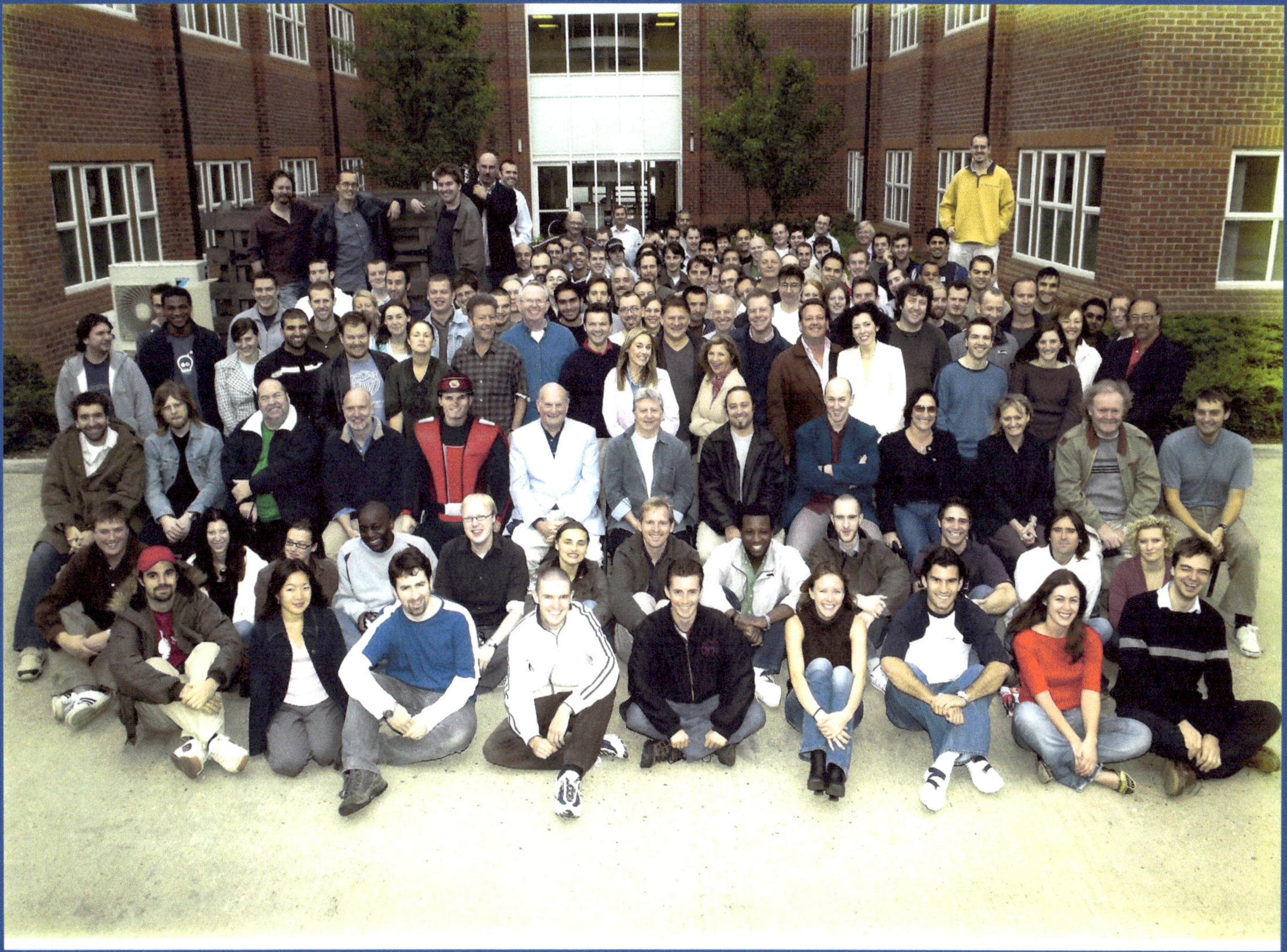

Gerry and the *New Captain Scarlet* team. When the series debuted in 2005, blinkered politics led to it being poorly scheduled as part of the Saturday morning kids' show *Ministry of Mayhem* and killed its chances of success. 'I won't mince my words,' said Gerry ruefully. 'They destroyed it.'

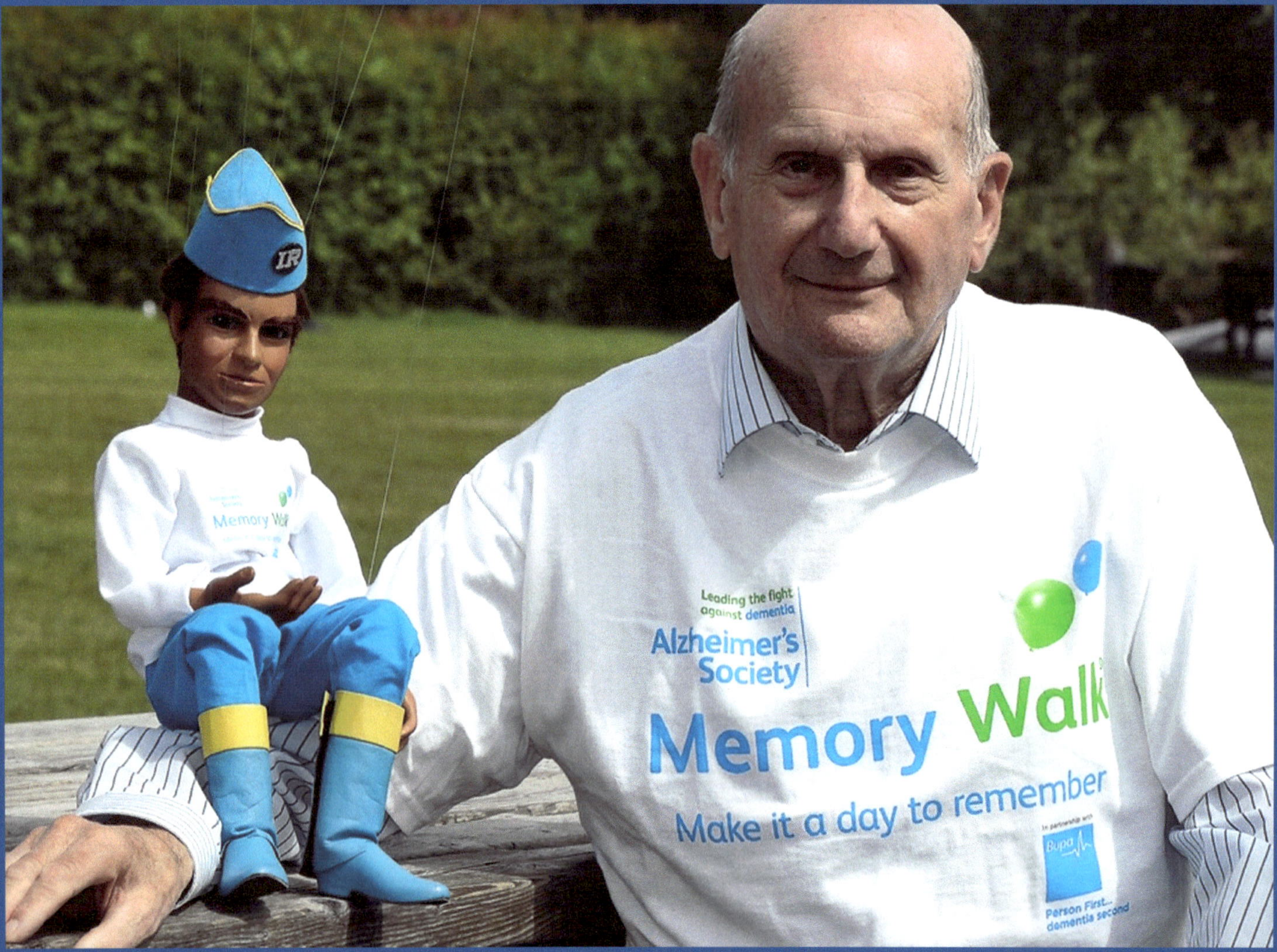

Gerry's life was his work, and following the failure of *New Captain Scarlet* he tried hard to raise finance for a new series of *Thunderbirds*. However, he had unknowingly been suffering from Alzheimer's since 2002. The disease had initially progressed slowly but, in his last years, began to accelerate. Finally a diagnosis was made in 2010.

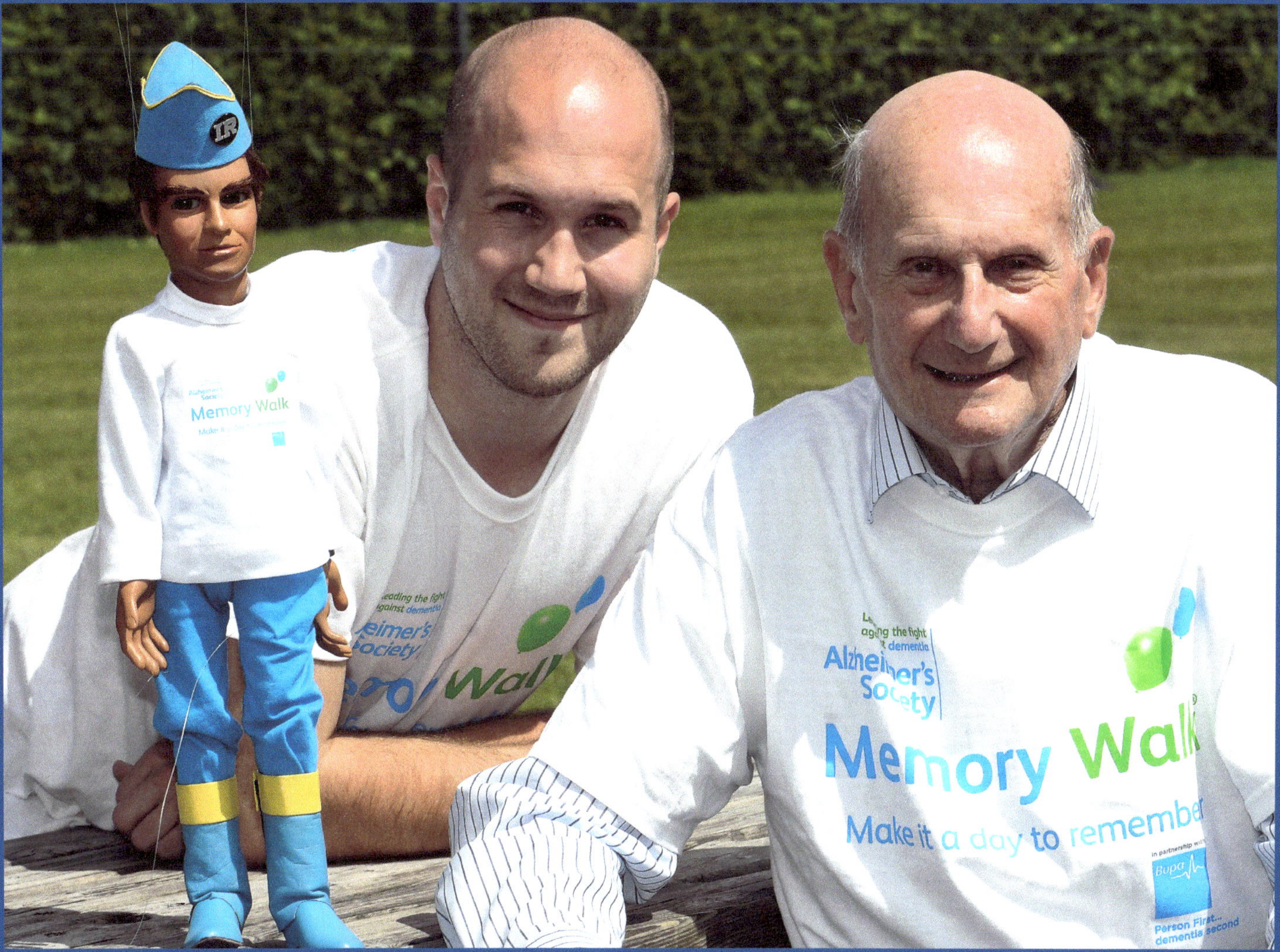

He continued to try and work following the diagnosis, but that soon became impossible and he was forced to abandon his current projects. Realising that he didn't have long to go, he became a celebrity patron for the Alzheimer's Society, helping to raise a million pounds in a year. The disease progressively destroyed the memories of his life. Soon, even *Thunderbirds*, his greatest creation, had been erased.

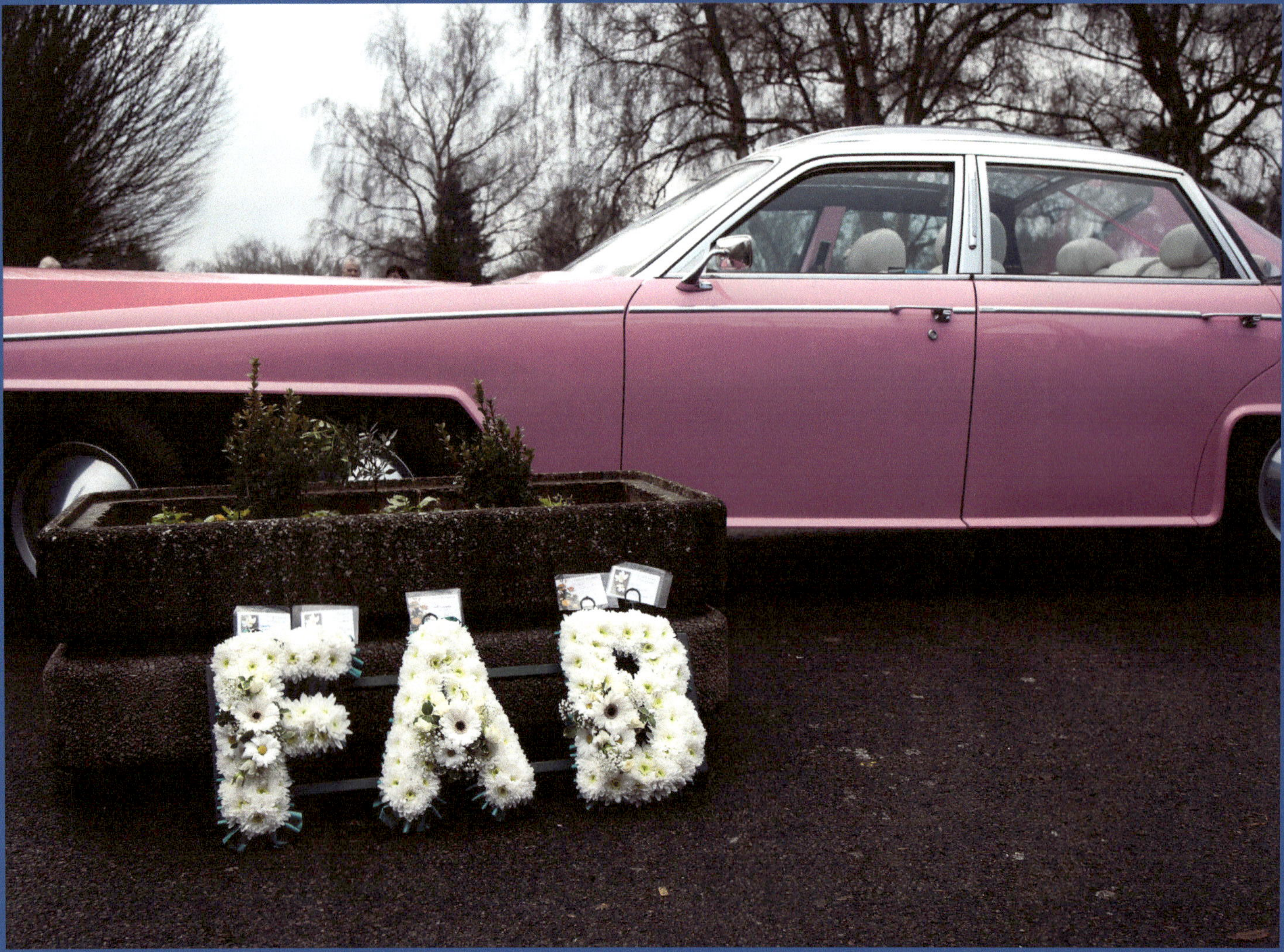

Gerry died on Boxing Day 2012. In a final amazing act, he donated his brain to medical science to aid the search for a cure for Alzheimer's. His funeral on 11th January 2013 was attended by family, friends, colleagues and fans from across the world.

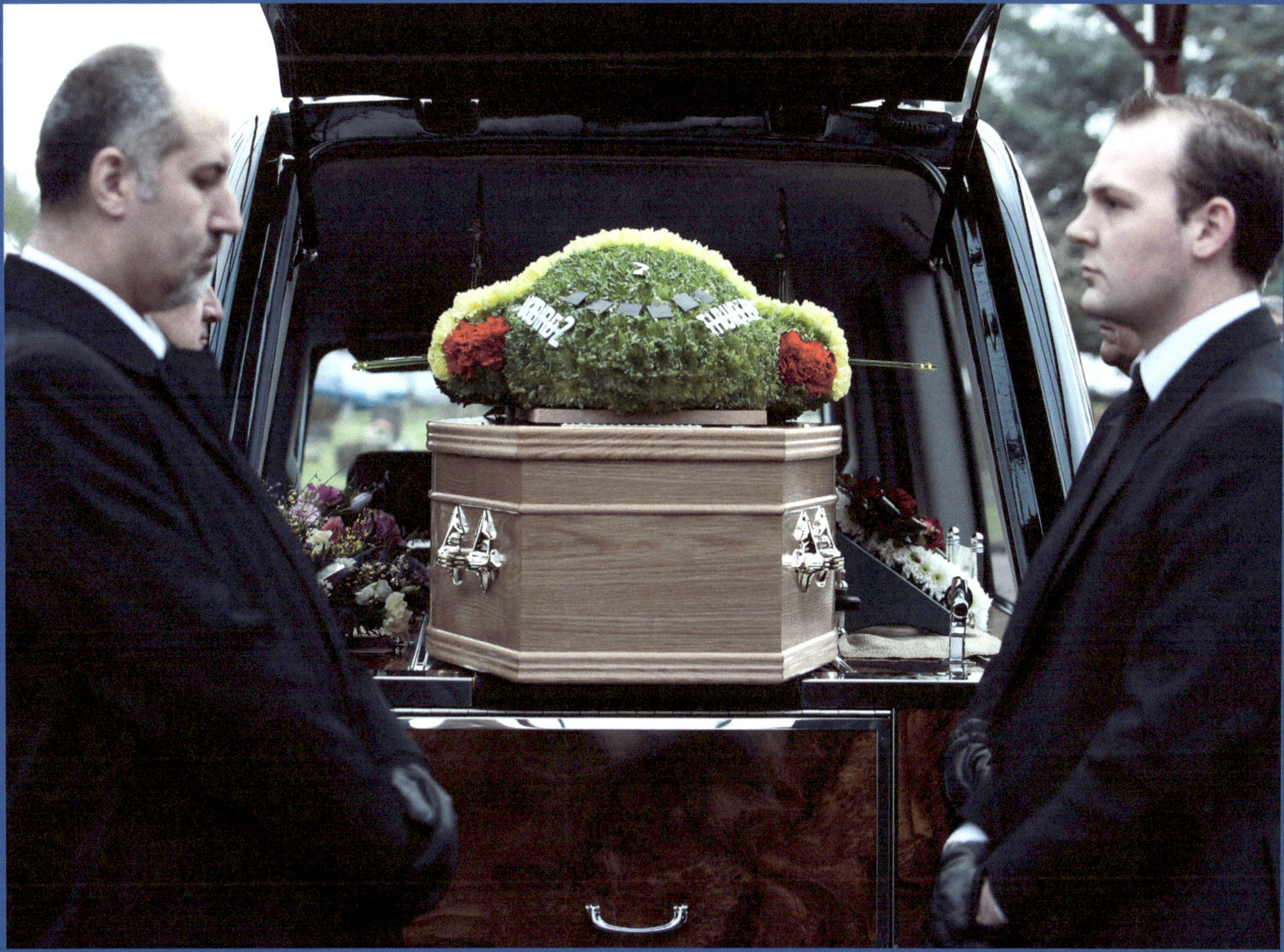

Gerry Anderson's final journey, his coffin adorned with a beautiful floral Thunderbird 2.

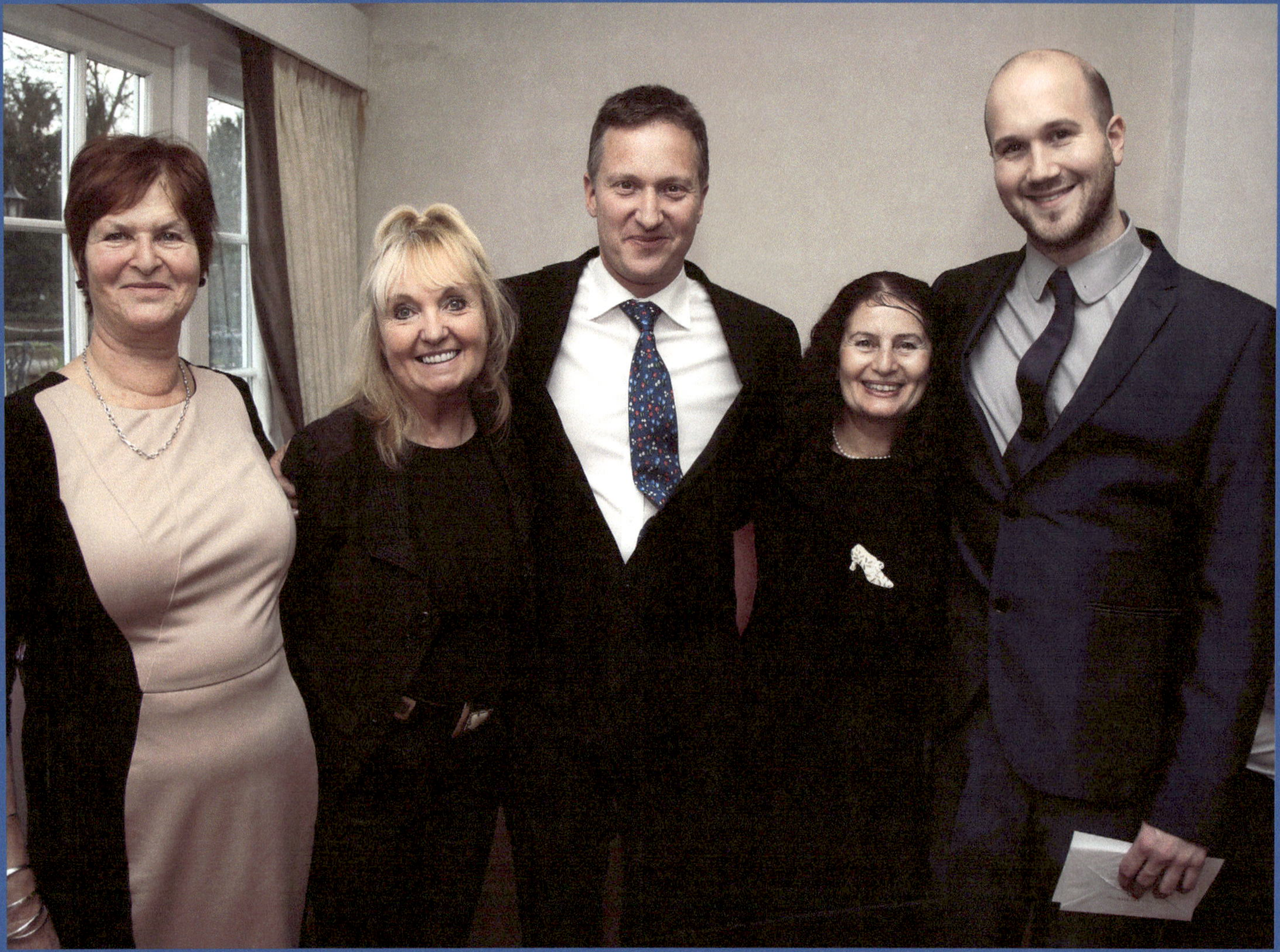

A turbulent personal life marked by two divorces had divided the Anderson family. Finally, all of Gerry's children gathered together for the very first time (left to right): Linda, step daughter Dee, Gerry Jnr, Joy and Jamie.

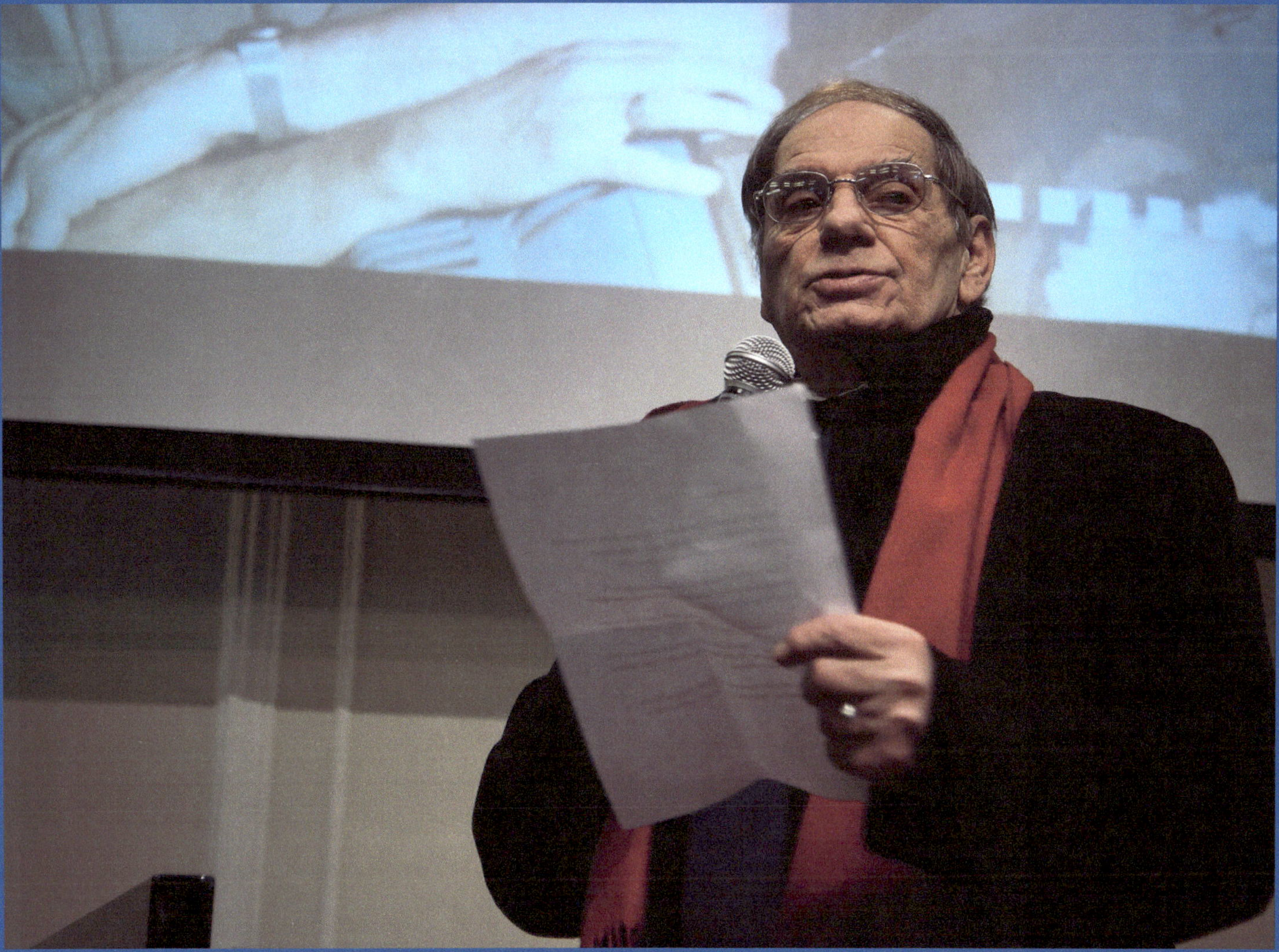

Following the service, many attended the wake to recall a man that had given so much joy to so many through his work. Here, *Thunderbirds* voice artist Matt Zimmerman pays tribute.

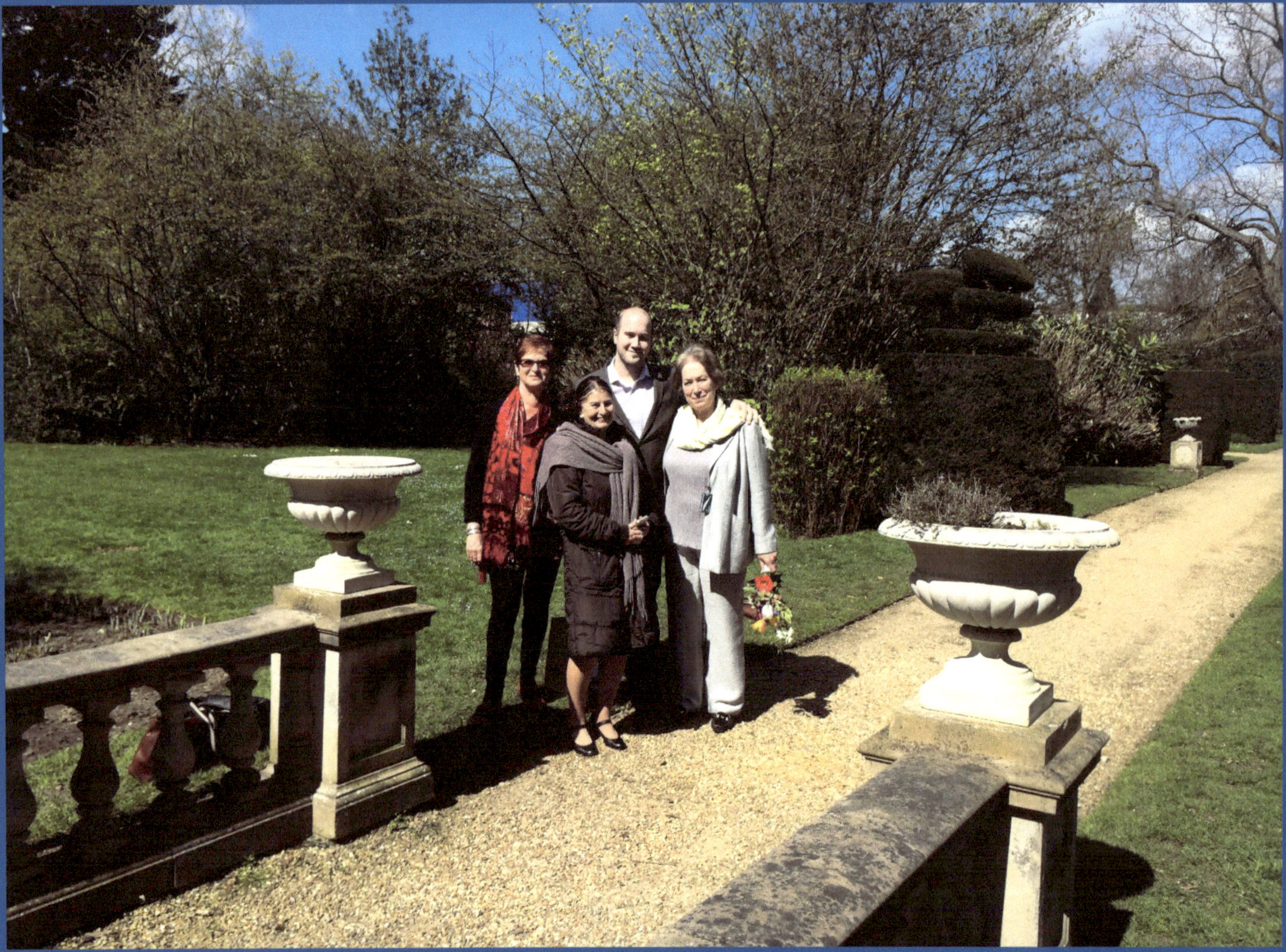

14th April 2014: On what would have been Gerry's 85th birthday, Mary, Linda, Joy and Jamie gathered to scatter his ashes at Pinewood Studios, the site of many of his biggest productions.

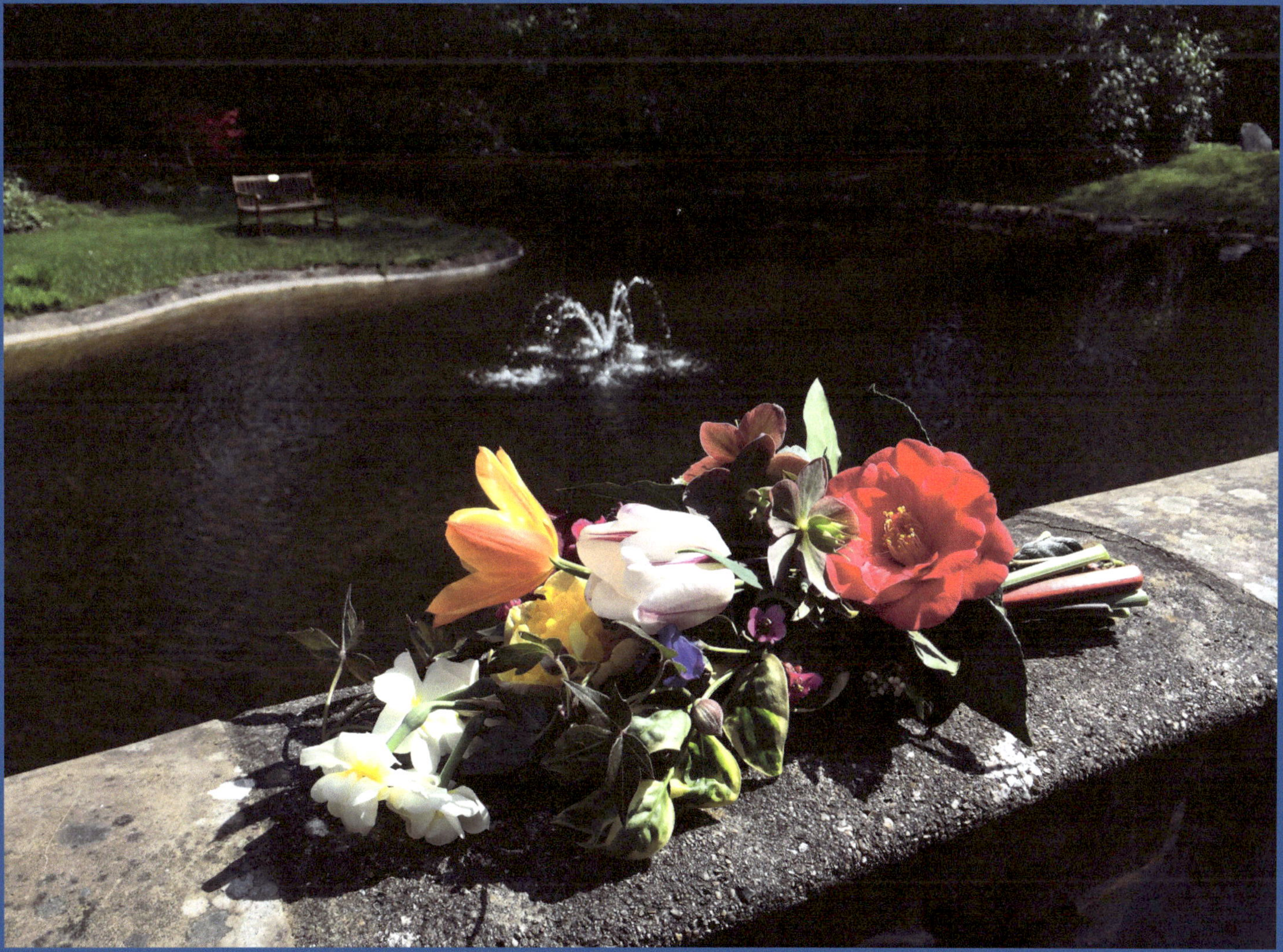

It was the end of an extraordinary life.

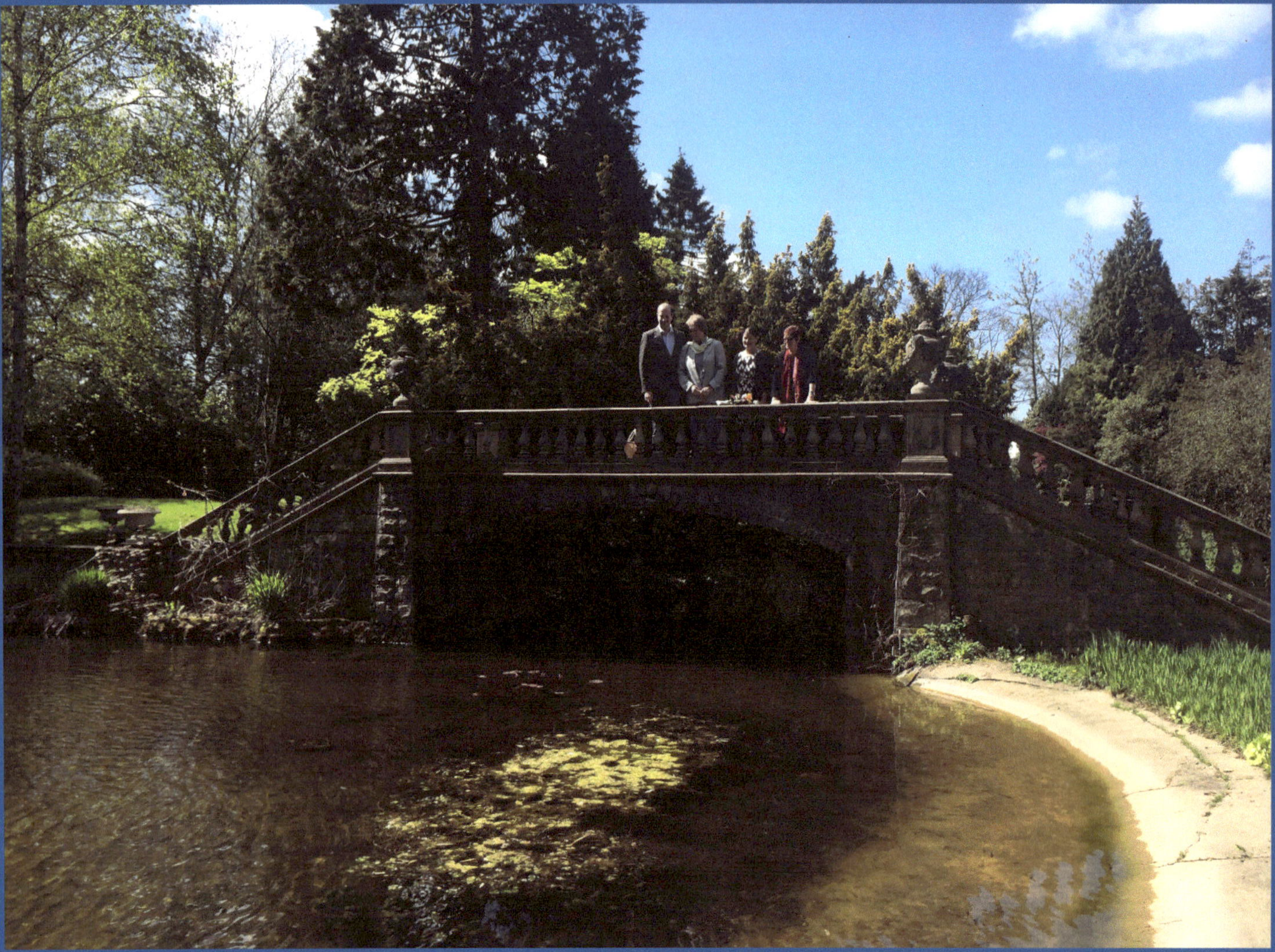

CPSIA information can be obtained
at www.ICGtesting.com
Printed in the USA
BVHW021019200919
559002BV00010B/89/P

* 9 7 8 0 9 9 2 8 6 9 5 0 2 *